Sufism

Sufism

A Global History

Nile Green

WILEY-BLACKWELL

A John Wiley & Sons, Ltd., Publication

This edition first published 2012
© 2012 Nile Green

Blackwell Publishing was acquired by John Wiley & Sons in February 2007. Blackwell's publishing program has been merged with Wiley's global Scientific, Technical, and Medical business to form Wiley-Blackwell.

Registered Office
John Wiley & Sons Ltd, The Atrium, Southern Gate, Chichester, West Sussex, PO19 8SQ, UK

Editorial Offices
350 Main Street, Malden, MA 02148-5020, USA
9600 Garsington Road, Oxford, OX4 2DQ, UK
The Atrium, Southern Gate, Chichester, West Sussex, PO19 8SQ, UK

For details of our global editorial offices, for customer services, and for information about how to apply for permission to reuse the copyright material in this book please see our website at www.wiley.com/wiley-blackwell.

The right of Nile Green to be identified as the author of this work has been asserted in accordance with the UK Copyright, Designs and Patents Act 1988.

Wiley also publishes its books in a variety of electronic formats. Some content that appears in print may not be available in electronic books.

Designations used by companies to distinguish their products are often claimed as trademarks. All brand names and product names used in this book are trade names, service marks, trademarks or registered trademarks of their respective owners. The publisher is not associated with any product or vendor mentioned in this book. This publication is designed to provide accurate and authoritative information in regard to the subject matter covered. It is sold on the understanding that the publisher is not engaged in rendering professional services. If professional advice or other expert assistance is required, the services of a competent professional should be sought.

Library of Congress Cataloging-in-Publication Data

Green, Nile.
  Sufism : a global history / Nile Green.
    p. cm.
  Includes bibliographical references and index.
  ISBN 978-1-4051-5761-2 (hardcover : alk. paper) – ISBN 978-1-4051-5765-0 (pbk. : alk. paper)
  1. Sufism–History. I. Title.
  BP188.5.G74 2012
  297.409–dc23   2011032984

A catalogue record for this book is available from the British Library.

This book is published in the following electronic formats: ePDFs 9781444399066; ePub 9781444399073; Mobi 9781444399080

Set in 10/12pt Sabon by Thomson Digital, Noida, India
Printed in Singapore by Ho Printing Singapore Pte Ltd

1 2012

For Karen
my sister and first friend

And now at last, arrived in Persia,
Within the confines of the great Sophy

– The Travels of the Three English Brothers (1607)

Contents

Maps and Illustrations

Preface and Acknowledgments

While many introductory books on Sufism already exist, among them several excellent accounts of either specific periods or beliefs and practices which have moved beyond the flaws of the old mysticism model critiqued in the Introduction to this book, there exists no overall survey of Sufism that devotes equal value and emphasis to each period of its history. Aimed at students of history and religious studies, as well as the general reader, this book is just such a general and interpretive narrative tracing Sufism from its period of origins until recent times. In large part, the incrementally global ambit of the narrative presented here reflects the abundance of scholarship that is now available. Since this wealth of scholarship is increasingly difficult to navigate, ample references are provided in the endnotes to allow more committed readers to follow up whichever aspects of Sufi history concern them. More importantly, the attempt to redistribute attention through each period and region articulates a rejection of the idea that Sufism more truly resided in one "homeland" or "classical" era than in another. In the Introduction, I argue that Sufism is better understood through the rubric of "tradition" rather than "mysticism." Since tradition is by definition that which is transmitted through time and space, any genuine attempt to pursue the history of a tradition must accept the temporally diachronic and spatially distributive nature of the exercise. While synchronic or decontextualized accounts of the "essence" of Sufism have often presented themselves as more true to the spirit of Sufism, I have come to the view, in two decades of studying the writings of the Sufis, that the struggle with the passing of time and the changing of location is not only central to the concerns of the Sufis, but is fundamentally constitutive of their construction of a tradition from that which was *traditus* or "handed down" to them. Sufis have not sought communion with God and his Prophet by stepping out of time, but by connecting themselves to chains of knowledge and blessing that shuttle them through the centuries to the moment of Muhammad's revelation and Adam's departure from God's presence. In their many grapplings with the existential dilemmas of human life, Sufis have turned again and again to the lessons of the living masters and the books of the dead saints whose teachings-in-time have shown them the road to eternity.

Despite promising to be a "history", this book has often been obliged to rely on scholarship that is non-historicist (if nonetheless erudite). While I am aware that this may lend a certain methodological unevenness to certain sections of the book, there is, in an introductory survey, little opportunity to address the historiographical issues involved and so my evaluations are ultimately implicit in the usage made of particular data or arguments. In a relatively concise volume, my emphases on conceiving Sufism through the lenses of tradition, society and power has also meant that less attention has been paid than in other introductory volumes to the private realms of rapture, love and experience. However, this shift of emphasis from private to public is based on a belief in the explanatory value of these emphases for making sense of the place of Sufism in the surrounding contexts of Muslim and global history. In this regard, the aim of this volume is to normalize the history of Sufism by placing it into the mainstream of the social, political and intellectual history of the Muslim peoples and in so doing to clear the vaguely suspicious air that has surrounded the study of Sufism since the emergence of a secularized historiography of the Muslim world in the early twentieth century. As such, rather than produce an introspectively discrete history of Sufism, the narrative as a whole aims to link Sufi history to broader contours of world history by pointing to the embeddedness of Sufism in the wider Muslim historical experience.

*

In writing this survey, I am indebted to a huge number of scholars and I would like to acknowledge here the work of those who have directly or indirectly influenced the writing of what is by its nature an exercise in synthesis. The very possibility of writing this book is born from the work of what now comprises a vast international network of scholars of Sufism that could rival in scale even the grandest of Sufi brotherhoods. While it is impossible for me to thank every historian, textual specialist and anthropologist from whom I have learned, the truest acknowledgements, as ever, lie in the notes and citations. However, I would like to specifically thank the several scholars who have most influenced my understanding of Sufism over my years of study, as well as several colleagues who were generous enough to read through and comment on the manuscript. Thanks go in the first order to Julian Baldick, Carl W. Ernst and Ahmet T. Karamustafa for vicariously shaping the development of my ideas on Sufism at different points in my career and to Christopher Melchert for his exemplary intellectual generosity. For detailed comments and suggestions on the manuscript, I would like to offer my special thanks to: Ali Anooshahr (University of California, Davis);

Devin DeWeese (University of Indiana, Bloomington); Michael Cooperson (University of California, Los Angeles); Ahmet T. Karamustafa (Washington University in St. Louis); Christopher Melchert (Oxford University); Azfar Moin (Southern Methodist University); and my two anonymous readers. The overstatements, misinterpretations and mistakes are all my own. Thanks to Gillian Andrews for copyediting the script and to Hazel Harris for handling the production process. For permission to reproduce images, I am grateful to: the Smithsonian Freer Gallery of Art and Arthur M. Sackler Gallery (Fig. 1.1 & Fig. 3.3); the Universiteitsbibliotheek of Leiden University Library (Fig. 2.1); the British Library (Fig. 3.2); the Staatliches Museum für Völkerkunde München (Fig. 3.2); the Bridgeman Art Gallery (Fig. 4.1); and to Allen F. Roberts & Mary Nooter Roberts (Fig. 4.2). All other images are my own photographs or items from my own collection.

If I have learned much from my academic masters and fellow travelers, then my overall conception of Sufism and its place in the social lives of its participants is no less a product of my encounters with the living legacy of Sufi tradition in the various forms it has acquired in many different regions. Over the twenty years in which I chose to study their tradition, I met with Sufis and looked on their legacies in places as distant as Morocco, Spain, Egypt, Syria, Yemen, Turkey, Iran, Afghanistan, India, Pakistan, Singapore, Malaysia, South Africa and Europe. The conception of Sufism as a "tradition" that is presented here is ultimately drawn from what I saw in action among these self-proclaimed Sufi heirs of the Prophet.

Final thanks to my parents, Geoffrey and Olivia Green, for encouragement over a lifetime and for driving me to the *ribat* at Guardamar on the last station of this book's journeys.

Nile Green
Los Angeles, July 2011

Toledo

Cordoba

AL-ANDALUS • Guardamar

Silves

• Fes

NORTH AFRICA

Palermo

Tunis

Tripoli

Constantinople
(Istanbul)

AN

Alexar

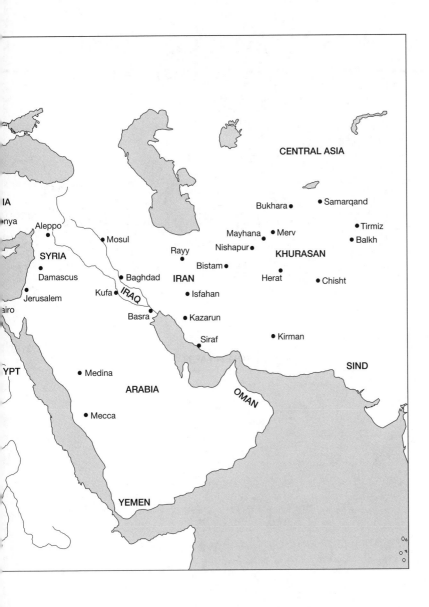

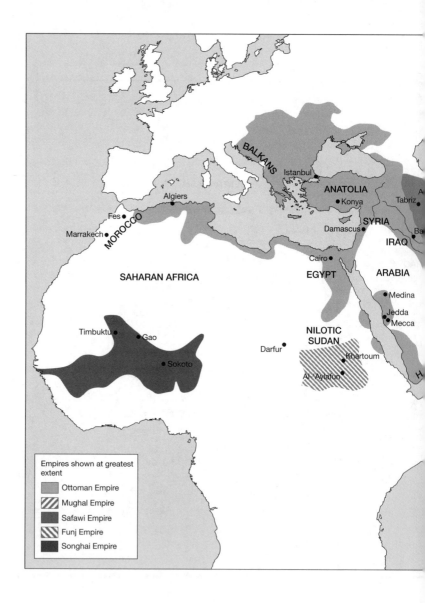

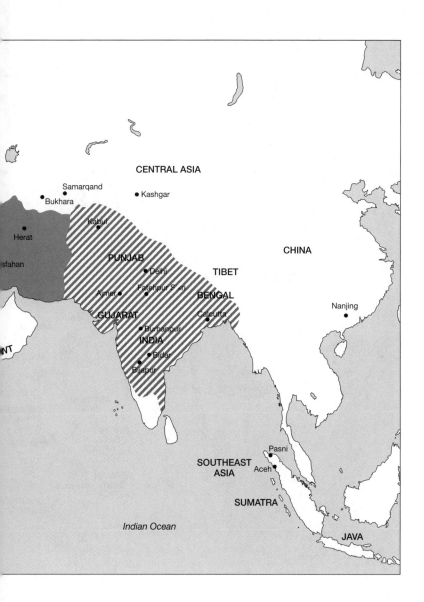

Ottoman Empire c.1900

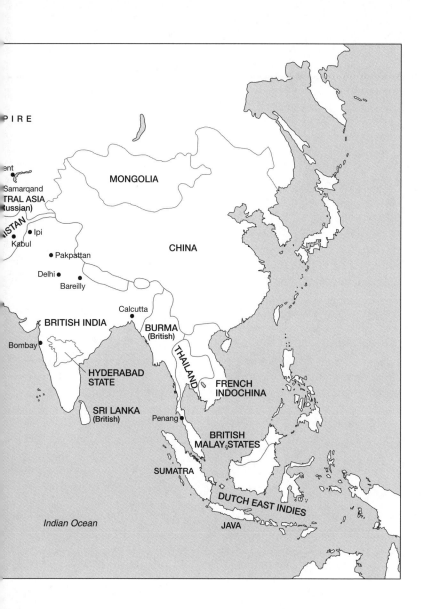

PIRE

ent

Samarqand

TRAL ASIA
Russian)

STAN

Ipi

Kabul

Pakpattan

Delhi

Bareilly

Calcutta

MONGOLIA

CHINA

BRITISH INDIA

BURMA
(British)

Bombay

THAILAND

HYDERABAD
STATE

FRENCH
INDOCHINA

SRI LANKA
(British)

Penang

BRITISH
MALAY STATES

SUMATRA

DUTCH EAST INDIES

Indian Ocean

JAVA

Introduction

From Mysticism to Tradition: Conceptualizing Sufism

Sufism has often been defined as Islamic "mysticism," comprising a set of techniques by which Muslims have sought a direct personal encounter with the divine. While it is true that Sufism encompasses many mystical elements, the broad social reach that it acquired over centuries of expansion rendered it much more than the path of an esoteric elite. In recognition of this problem, in his highly influential introduction to Sufism the Cambridge orientalist A.J. Arberry recognized that Sufism comprised the religious way of both the popular Muslim masses and the smaller number of elevated mystics.[1] For Arberry and for many later commentators, the tension in the model of a "mystical" and a "popular" Sufism was resolved through a narrative of decline: what had begun as a genuinely "mystical" movement of individuals seeking personal communion with God was corrupted in the medieval period into a cult of miracle-working saints which held nothing in common with "true" Sufi mysticism. "It was inevitable," wrote Arberry in scornful tones, "as soon as legends of miracles became attached to the names of the great mystics, that the credulous masses should applaud imposture more than true devotion."[2] For Arberry as for many others writing in his wake, the consequence of this decline model was that from the later medieval period onwards Sufism was unworthy of study. This was if nothing else ironic, in that the medieval and early modern periods that saw Sufism reach its greatest influence and success were precisely those which were to be overlooked as the ages of post-classical decline.

Over the past thirty years, this model of classicism and decline has been thoroughly rejected, and more recent scholarship on Sufism has done much to overturn the grand narrative of Arberry and such later decline theorists as J.S. Trimingham.[3] Even so, in many discussions of Sufism key aspects of the

Sufism: A Global History, First Edition. Nile Green.
© 2012 Nile Green. Published 2012 by Blackwell Publishing Ltd.

older tendencies remain, not least the central problem with the earlier school of interpretation that was the model of "mysticism" itself. As conceived by European and American scholars in the early twentieth century, the notion of mysticism relied on a culturally Protestant, temporally modernist and intellectually cosmopolitan construction of religion in which the authority of the solitary individual's direct, unmediated experience was seen to be the fountainhead of authentic religiosity across all cultures and all periods.[4] In similarly Protestant mode, "religion" was itself regarded as a category properly (or at least preferably) distinct from the corruptive sphere of "politics." When these models were applied to the study of Islam, for many scholars the archetypal Sufi was the antithesis to the legalistic Muslim establishment, whether living in quietist seclusion from the affairs of the world or leading rebellions that ended in passionate martyrdoms.[5] Prescriptive rather than descriptive, at times this model of mysticism served as a dogma in its own right. When applied to more distant cultural or temporal contexts from that where it developed, the model tended to castigate or exclude much of what it was meant to explain. In the case of Sufism, such exclusion or castigation concerned many important dimensions of Sufi history that did not fit the model of the individual God-seeker, from hierarchical Sufi brotherhoods and elaborate rituals of saintly intercession to influence over the decisions of sultans.

Yet in contrast to the Western notion of the mystic, many aspects of Sufism were collective and public rather than individualistic and private. The centrality of the master-disciple relationship that emerged as the keystone of Sufi practice shows that even such "mystical" procedures as the destruction of the ego were not the result of private experiences of direct contact with God but were social processes based on disciplinary relationships with human third parties. As Sufi fellowships grew larger, these relationships (and the joint socio-psychological transformations they fostered) became more and more commonplace, such that their effects became even more widespread and collective. In many regions of the world, this saw Sufism shape configurations of social authority into the authoritarian models explored by the North African anthropologist Abdellah Hammoudi.[6] Along with its neglect of the social, the concept of mysticism also downplayed the physical, placing Sufism firmly within the realms of spirituality when, from their embodied rituals and veneration of relics to their shrine buildings and the blessing powers they were believed to contain in their flesh and blood, Sufis were equally invested in the tangible realms of physicality. Not so much a universally-accessible "mysticism" based on religious experiences which were democratically available to all, Sufism was in many settings an embodied Islam of authority based on blessing powers inherited through prestigious blood lineages. One anthropologist has thus defined Sufi shaykhs as "those in whose blood (recorded in personal genealogies) the Prophet's grace (*baraka*) flows."[7] The concept of mysticism also tends to be associated with the spontaneous and unrehearsed rather than the programmatic and political. Yet even the earliest handbooks on Sufi practice showed deep concerns with questions of etiquette and ceremony. Far from being a disinterested spiritual *avant garde*, in many regions Sufis were major political players who enjoyed the comforts drawn from vast landholdings and the support of armies of devoted followers. Through the series of developments traced in this book, Sufism became sufficiently authoritarian and anti-individualistic that in the modern period the rise of democratizing and individualizing tendencies among Muslims led millions to desert the teachings of the Sufis in droves.

Besides its narrowing and prescriptive tendencies, the model of mysticism also presents particular challenges to the writing of history. For if as "mysticism" the essence of Sufism lies in transcendental private experience, then historians are inevitably condemned to recording only its trivial outward shells by way of texts, institutions and actions. There are certainly different ways of tackling this dilemma. One way (most thoroughly pursued by the French scholar Henry Corbin) is to maintain the mystical model by using a phenomenological approach to historical documents in an attempt to interpretively "re-present" the inward character of past mystical experiences.[8] In various degrees and styles, this phenomenological approach has been adopted in a number of successful introductions to Sufism.[9] Another way is to move away from the model of mysticism and to conceive Sufism in terms that not only fit better with its complex array of characteristics, but also render it more amenable to historical description. Downplaying the notion of Sufism as the mysticism of a marginal party of God-seekers, the approach taken in this book is to conceive Sufism as primarily a *tradition* of powerful knowledge, practices and persons.[10] As the following chapters argue, from the very moment of its emergence, Sufism was rooted in a wider Muslim model of reliable knowledge in which the sanction and security of past authority (whether of the Prophet or of the saintly "friends" of God) was of overwhelming importance. This historical sensibility even shaped a large proportion of Sufi mystical experiences by way of the countless visionary encounters Sufis recorded with past saints and prophets, encounters which fulfilled their desire to connect themselves with the past luminaries of their tradition.[11] This link to the normative and beloved exemplars of tradition is extremely important, for it points not only to the strategy by which the Sufis were able to rhetorically present themselves as the living heirs of the Prophet. It also points to the axiomatically "backward-looking" nature of their teachings which emerged as a consequence of this need for the sanction of past authority and to the existential desire to return to the state of human being enjoyed by the primordial Adam and Muhammad at the beginning of time. As Steven T. Katz has perceptively explained, far from being instantaneous and inventive, mystical experiences are often acts of conservatism; and we might add, of conservation.[12]

This sense of the Sufis' deliberate rooting of their words and actions in the legacy of earlier Muslims also helps us recognize the pervasively Islamic character of Sufism that except in certain cosmopolitan cases has set Sufism apart from the universalist "mysticism" into which it has sometimes been categorized. As the French scholar Marijan Molé once explained, even if the Sufis un/knowingly adapted elements from other religious groups, "the Sufis have never wished to be anything other than Muslims; all the doctrines they profess, and all of their actions, customs and usages are based on an interpretation of the Quran and the Prophetic tradition."[13] This is a key point: Sufism developed as a set of teachings, practices and institutions that emerged as Muslims from the ninth century onwards ruminated on the legacy of the earlier exemplary life of the Prophet Muhammad and the revelatory moment of the Quran. In their attempts to channel the knowledge, comfort and authority of God (and his prophets and friends) into their private and public lives, Sufis built their tradition firstly by looking back to the time of the Prophet and revelation and secondly by looking back at the teachings and actions of those they identified as the saints who in turn connected them back to the Prophet's own communion with God. Whether in terms of texts they wrote, rituals they inaugurated or brotherhoods they founded, it was the many saintly "Friends of God" or *awliya allah* who appeared in every century who constituted the tradition that we call Sufism. With the exception of certain modernist reformulations, without the saints there is no Sufism.

Building on their early claim of inheriting the tradition of the Prophet, over time the Sufis gradually developed the wherewithal of their own tradition by way of lineages of saints and teachers whose sanction carried supplementary authority of its own. As we will see in Chapter 1, in the early centuries of Sufi history, this construction of a tradition in some cases involved the retrospective claiming as Sufis pious forebears who lived before the term *sufi* was even used. The emphasis placed here on tradition over mysticism is not to deny that many Sufis underwent mystical experiences which they subsequently held in high value. It is rather to make the point that these private experiences only acquired meaning and credibility through being absorbed into the collective and collaborative venture of different generations of Muslims who over the passage of time remained highly conscious of one another's exemplary actions and teachings. This sense of the historicity of mystical experience does not aim to reduce it, but rather to locate it in the temporal character of human existence. In this, I am in broad agreement with Steven T. Katz, who has written that "mystical reports do not merely indicate the post-experiential description of an unreportable experience in the language closest at hand. Rather, the experiences themselves are inescapably shaped by prior linguistic influences such that the lived experience conforms to a pre-existent pattern that has been learned, then intended, and then actualized in the experiential reality of the mystic."[14] As hundreds of Sufi writings make clear, for all of the emphasis on spontaneous individual experience in the twentieth century model of mysticism, Sufis were always acutely conscious of their discursive links to past precedent. It was this consciousness of tradition that rendered them Sufi *Muslims* rather than charismatic lone stars or prophetic founders of new religions. It is ultimately this self-consciousness of individual Sufis as being members of a larger community reproduced across time through the sanction of authoritative past masters that renders them members and perpetuators of a tradition. For as the sociologist Edward Shils has written, tradition is not only that "which is transmitted or handed down from the past," but also "that which has exemplars or custodians."[15] Correspondingly, as with the exemplary models of the remembered Sufi saints of yore, "there is an inherently normative element in any tradition of belief which is presented for acceptance."[16]

In contrast to the older model of a mysticism of lone marginal individuals, this model of a powerful collective tradition is helpful for making sense of Sufi history on several levels. Firstly, it recognizes the crucial roles of third-party external and past authorities in valorizing individual experiences, decisions, teachings and writings. Secondly, it recognizes the many non-spontaneous, authoritarian and at times anti-individualistic dimensions of Sufism. Thirdly, it suits the purposes of a historical survey since unlike the temporal collapsing that comes with the emphatic "now" emphasis of mysticism, the tradition model shows how the recipients of tradition possess their own historical self-consciousness as persons living in a perpetual (if interpretive and often creative) relationship with their past. Fourthly and finally, it allows for the accumulative character of Sufism through its gradual emergence as a multi-generational cultural product that emerges in time, so allowing room for development and diversification. Pointing to this dynamism that is often disguised by the apparent consistency of tradition, Shils describes how "tradition might undergo very great changes but its recipients might regard it as significantly unchanged."[17] It has been this backward-looking sense of the continuity of the teachings they regard as the legacy of the Prophet Muhammad to his saintly successors that allows us to define Sufism as a tradition in the terms defined by Edward Shils.

From Marginality to Power: Contextualizing Sufism

Having addressed this issue of tradition as both concept and content, we must now turn to this book's contextual emphasis by way of its presentation of Sufis as powerful and influential social actors rather than as conscientious objectors acting from the margins of society. As with the book's switch of emphasis from mysticism to tradition, in its stress on the power rather than the marginality of the Sufis we are dealing with a question of re-emphasis rather than rejection. While there certainly were many marginal (as well as outright antinomian) Sufis, the argument made here is that it was due to its powerful rather than marginal followers that Sufism was able to leave so great an imprint on the societies through which it spread. A result of the historical processes and collective strategies explored in the following chapters, this acquisition of power was certainly gradual. But by the medieval and early modern periods, it was sufficiently real to allow us to speak in many regions of the Muslim world in terms of a Sufi social and religious "establishment." While there were many marginal and deviant Sufis who lived in this period, the Sufi establishment achieved and maintained its status by its members' successful self-presentation as embodiments of the normative Islam of the Prophet Muhammad and indeed as being nothing less than his living heirs. Even where anti-normative and socially marginal Sufi groups flourished (as in the case of the medieval *qalandar* movement) it is probably fair to say that their ability to get away with breaching social norms was itself a reflection of the power and prestige which Sufism held by their time.

In speaking of the Sufis as powerful, we must delineate three main types of power which they will be seen acquiring in the following chapters: discursive power, miraculous power and economic power. Discursive power refers to the authority acquired by Sufism as a discourse comprising a legitimate vocabulary of words and concepts, influential models of society and cosmos, and exemplary paradigms of behavior and morals. This discourse of Sufism was in itself a configuration of tradition since it drew authority from connecting itself to the Quran and the Prophetic Example (or *Sunna*) of Muhammad. The discursive power which Sufism acquired through its association with the normative Prophetic Example points to the way in which Sufism was not merely a mode of experience or even belief, but a discourse with the power to shape other people's actions through their imitation of the exemplary models it provided. Moving us further beyond the emphasis on unmediated experience in the model of mysticism, this powerful ability to shape behavior and action was also a function of tradition in the ability of traditions to foster enduring "patterns or images of actions" and "the beliefs requiring, recommending, regulating, permitting or prohibiting the re-enactment of those patterns."[18]

The second type of power which we will see the Sufis acquire was miraculous power through their widely perceived ability to work miracles and wonders as a result of their especial closeness to God. For A.J. Arberry, no less than many twentieth century reformist Muslim commentators, this widespread traffic in the miraculous represented "the dark side of Sufism in its last phase" when "its influence at its most degraded period was wholly evil."[19] Yet in a historical survey such as this, the aim must be to describe and understand rather than to moralize. Even though the twentieth century's scientifically disenchanted and culturally Protestant model of mysticism drew a firm line of division between mystics and miracle-workers, the historical fact of the matter is that the Sufis' claim of working miracles was inseparable from their claim of mystical proximity to God. Once again, it is the saints whose words and deeds constituted Sufi tradition who must be positioned at center stage: the historical mystic was the saintly miracle worker. While there was always the occasional Muslim who challenged the Sufis' ability to wield such powers, as the following chapters show, from sultans and merchants to peasants and tribesmen, there were many more who sought to draw on these powers by entering relationships with the Sufis. And since, whether with regard to knaves or kings, these were typically relationships of discipleship, the power to wreak miracles was in turn transformed into the currency of social influence.

Drawing from and in turn cementing this social influence was the third of the forms of power which the Sufis acquired: economic power. For from the medieval period, prominent Sufis began to receive considerable (and in a few cases vast) endowments of landed property and real estate from disciples drawn from the ruling class as well as smaller offerings in cash or kind from their humbler followers. Despite their rhetoric of pious poverty, these forms of gift-exchange placed prominent Sufis among the tiny privileged elite of the pre-industrial societies in which they operated till modern times. In this respect too, we see the functioning of Sufism as a tradition, since the need to transfer property through family lineages saw the material heirs of economically powerful Sufis configured in parallel as the heirs of the Sufi tradition. Family Sufi lineages therefore typically passed down property alongside teachings and blessing power. Since no form of powerful knowledge can exist in isolation from material forms of power, the economic strength of Sufism was crucial to the overall profile it acquired and so ultimately the discursive, miraculous and economic power of the Sufis were each interdependent. If there was once a tendency to see the emergence of such power-holding as compromising the piety of the Sufi message, to see even religious history in such value-laden terms is sentimental and romantic. Here again it is helpful to think of Sufism as a tradition, for no tradition is ever able to perpetuate and reproduce itself through time without recourse to the material resources that provide homes and stipends for the texts, rituals and remembrancers that constitute *traditio* as "that which is handed down."

If in relation to many earlier presentations of Sufism, the shift in emphasis here towards power and tradition marks something of a Hobbesian turn, then this is perhaps a necessary corrective. For this sense of a powerful tradition not only renders more understandable the following the Sufis acquired, but also the opposition they increasingly provoked as their influence grew, whether from rival religious authorities in the medieval period, state-builders in the early modern period or Muslim reformers in the modern period. It is after all power, influence and privilege that typically garner the strategies of appropriation, incorporation and opposition that have so regularly punctuated the history of Sufism. If as a history of the Sufis rather than their rivals the following chapters inevitably place the Sufis into the spotlight, then the calls of their rivals from the shadows should be seen to echo the high status gained by Sufis proclaimed as the axis or *qutb* around which the whole cosmos turned.

From Contexts to Characteristics: Defining Sufism

In offering an outline of the basic characteristics of Sufism, it is essential in a historical survey such as this to note first that the defining profile we are about to read emerged only gradually through the series of developments traced in Chapter 1 and Chapter 2. This historicizing caveat accepted, we can now offer a basic definition of Sufism as a powerful tradition of Muslim knowledge and practice bringing proximity to or mediation with God and believed to have been handed down from the Prophet Muhammad through the saintly successors who followed him. From their earliest appearance, Sufis rarely perceived themselves to be anything other than Muslims and as Sufi tradition expanded its influence, for many millions of Muslims Islam appeared to be inseparable from Sufism. While convention prevents it, we might do better speaking of "Sufi Islam" than of "Sufism." For, with the exception of certain antinomian ("rule-breaking") groups, Sufis have generally followed the lifeways of Islamic custom, offering regular formal worship (*salah*), keeping the fast in the holy month of Ramadan, and abiding by whatever form of Shari'a was observed in their community. Crucially, Sufis have also followed a series of supererogatory ("above what is required") exercises, most importantly the chanted "remembrance" (*dhikr*) of God; meditation (*muraqaba*) on different aspects of the psyche and God; the cultivation of moral virtues (*ihsan*) through the observance of formal rules of etiquette (*adab*); and respectful interaction (*suhba*) with their master. Some (though by no means all) groups of Sufis used the ritualized listening (*sama'*) to music and poetry as a means to reach ecstatic states (*ahwal*) in which they were brought closer to God or the saints.

Sufis have long emphasized that all such practices must be pursued under the direction of a master (*murshid*) who has been a recipient of the tradition and so (in theory, at least) already trodden this path beforehand. Complete obedience to the master has widely been considered as fundamental to the Sufi life. Since the medieval period, such masters and disciples have conceived and grouped themselves in the form of "brotherhoods" (*tariqas*, literally

"Paths"). These brotherhoods formed the conceptual and eventually the institutional channels through time and space that served to constitute Sufism as a tradition regarded by its followers as the secret legacy of the Prophet. Rituals of initiation into such a "Path" or brotherhood and its accompanying pledge of allegiance (*bay'a*) to a master marked the formal entry to discipleship. While such initiations have often been undertaken by adult Muslims seeking spiritual enlightenment, in practice many Muslims received such initiations as children, assuring them of the social and supernatural protection of their masters on their own paths through life.

In theory, the purpose of entering a brotherhood has been to learn the practices of *adab* (etiquette), *dhikr* (chanting) and *muraqaba* (meditation) passed down by its masters, with the aim of experiencing the destruction (*fana*) of the lower-self (*nafs*) that leads to the survival (*baqa*) of the higher-self (*ruh*). Mapped out as formal "places" (*maqamat*) on the ascent towards God, such experiences have been seen as lending Sufis the authority to guide – to chastise and even punish – other Muslims. The claim to have passed through these "places" on the way to God has meant that both during and after their lifetimes the most celebrated masters have been regarded as the special intimates or "Friends" (*awliya*) of God. The most venerated and feared of these saints have been seen as living "interfaces" (*barzakh*) between the human and divine worlds, serving as intermediaries between the ordinary believer and the celestial hierarchy of the saints, prophets and God.

In varying degrees all of the saintly masters have been regarded as having access to God's divine qualities by way of their special knowledge (*ma'rifa*) and their ability to work miracles (*karama*). If claims to predict the future and make protective talismans have in modern times been seen as belonging more to the realm of "superstition" than "mysticism," then they have both been important services which disciples have asked of their Sufi masters. Since the miraculous powers of the saints ranged from curing sick children to shaping the outcome of battles, the disciples of such masters have included sultans no less than peasants. Even so, these disciples were no less important than their saintly masters for the continuation of Sufi tradition. For through their reception of teaching and miracles as much as their provision of patronage and commemoration, such followers allowed the actions and teachings of their masters to be celebrated and passed on. In reflection of these twin components of tradition, for the purposes of this book both masters and disciples are considered equal participants in the tradition of Sufism.

Given the centrality of these ties between disciples and masters, far from being the individualistic pursuit of personal liberation, Sufism can be regarded as the sum total of similar sets of relationships: between saints and their followers; between the readers and writers of Sufi texts; between the Prophet, the mediating master and the humble believer; between the subjects and objects of the devotion that has been the emotional heartbeat of Sufi tradition. Insofar as Sufis have pursued personal quests for salvation, they have usually done so by navigating these relationships between the living and the dead, the physical and the textual, the visible and invisible. It is this quintessentially relational profile of Sufism that has positioned its various expressions and exponents at the center of so many Muslim societies, which were themselves bound together by sets of relationships that became infused and intertwined with the blessed bonds of the Sufis. It is the consequences of these relationships that unfolded as Sufi tradition accrued in many places over many centuries that form the focus of this book.

The Narrative in Overview

What the following pages present is a narrative history of the emergence of Sufi tradition and the social and geographical expansion that attended its gradual acquisition of power and prestige. The need for a coherent and flowing narrative has meant that there is little explicit evaluation of different primary or secondary source materials, and so for critical evaluations of the historiography students should refer to the recent review articles written by such scholars as myself, Alexander Knysh and Dina Le Gall.[20] To help readers place the Sufis into larger conceptions of Islamic, comparative and ultimately global history, the narrative is divided into four fairly conventional periods, albeit periods which are argued as enclosing distinct developments within Sufi history itself. Covered over the course of four chapters, the periods in question are: the early medieval period (800–1100), the medieval period (1100–1400), the early modern period (1400–1800) and the modern period (1800–2000). The chapters are conceived in progressively different ways. While Chapter 1 focusses on the early thinkers and texts that provided the foundations and subsequent resources of Sufi tradition, Chapter 2 focusses on the processes by which this tradition was able to adapt and expand into different geographical and social contexts. Dealing with the period of "globalizing" Sufi expansion into Africa, Southeast Asia and even China, Chapter 3 is conceived in geographical terms, while Chapter 4 turns to political periodization to trace the fortunes of Sufi tradition in a modern era conceived in terms of two inter-related periods of colonization and postcolonial globalization.

Given the changing character of the source materials for these different periods, and the different kinds of scholarly expertise and approach that these materials have attracted, there is inevitably a shifting degree of focus as these chapters progress, from a focus on the writings of individual urban "great men" in the first chapter to the gradual incorporation of perspectives on other social groups and developments other than the doctrinal.

More astute readers will easily recognize this as part of the venture of both historical research and Sufi history itself: as more varied kinds of Sufis handed down different kinds of legacies – textual, material, ritual – to their successors, so have scholars been able to reconstruct fuller pictures of their worlds. Yet, unlike in previous surveys of Sufism, approximately equal space is devoted to each of the four periods, though given that the earlier periods have received much fuller synthetic coverage it is fair to say that specialists will find much that is already familiar in parts of the first two chapters. However, in pursuing the incrementally global expansion of the Sufis, Chapter 2 and particularly Chapter 3 and Chapter 4 provide coverage for regions in Africa, Central, South and Southeast Asia and ultimately Europe that have usually been seen as marginal to the Sufis' supposedly Middle Eastern "homelands." Even if individual readers do in places find themselves on familiar ground, it is hoped that the scope of coverage and the overall model of a tradition being gradually elaborated and distributed to so many different contexts lends originality to the narrative as a whole.

The risk of attempting to cover so much material within a single volume is a loss of clarity amid the overall mass of data, especially in the periods which saw Sufism increasingly expand in the early modern and modern eras. For this reason, it may be useful at this point to lay out in the simplest terms the overall interpretation of Sufi history that is embedded in the narrative. The argument in outline is that Sufi tradition was gradually constructed in the early medieval period among the same circles in which the normative Muslim notion of the Prophetic Example or *Sunna* was conceived. In the ninth and tenth centuries, a disparate group of thinkers based in Iraq and Iran wrote a series of Arabic works that became foundational in the sense of providing the lexical and conceptual resources that would be passed down to subsequent generations. Adopted as loanwords into various Muslim languages, this Sufi lexicon and the discursive models it elaborated would still lay the conceptual framework for Sufis in modern times.[21] From the early eleventh century, the third- and fourth-generation of Sufis built on the sometimes contradictory ideas of these early theorists by constructing lineages and pedigrees for their teachings that would link them back in time to the Prophet. From this moment forwards, this backward-looking tendency became crucial to the historical self-consciousness that constituted the teachings of individual Sufis as a tradition that they could present as the higher doctrine passed down unbroken from the Prophet Muhammad himself.

Fortified with what during the medieval period they transformed from a discursive rhetoric to a concrete institutionalization of tradition, the Sufis were able to maintain their respectable and normative position when the collapse of central Muslim authority rendered Sufis crucial middlemen for the weak tribal polities who patronized them in return. While then expanding into new frontier regions in Southeast Asia no less than Africa during the early modern period, the Sufis were able to maintain this establishment status even amid their increasing incorporation into more powerful imperial states and the crisis of conscience that followed the turn of the Muslim millennium in 1591. Amid the tumultuous collapse of Muslim commercial and political power in the modern era, Sufism was among the few premodern Muslim institutions to survive European colonization substantially intact. As the embodiments of Prophetic no less than Sufi tradition in the many societies in which they still possessed landholdings and controlled networks of teaching and initiation, the continued prominence of the Sufis in the nineteenth century saw them pulled in different directions by the demands of both local followers and colonial rulers.

Entering the twentieth century in many cases confirmed in their high status by recent alliances with colonial no less than Muslim states, the oppositional politics of Islamic reform rendered this Sufi establishment the natural target of competition and critique. Whether at the hands of upwardly-mobile reformists from such non-traditional backgrounds as government school-teaching or journalism, or at the hands of scientifically-educated modernists who rejected Sufism as the epitome of the degenerate traditionism that allowed the Muslims to be colonized, from the 1900s Sufism came under its most sustained and successful attack. While at the end of the twentieth century many millions of Muslims maintained their ties to the dead saints and living teachers of Sufi tradition, and globalization allowed entrepreneurial Sufi distributors of tradition to find new followers in America and Europe, for educated Muslims in particular Sufism had come to represent corruption, superstition and backwardness.

It is finally worth clarifying what is intended by the book's use of the term "global." What is "global" about the history presented here is not a direct engagement with the literature on globalization theory, but an attempt to provide coverage of each region of the planet to which Sufism expanded over the course of more than a thousand years. This incrementally global coverage is, moreover, pursued as a history of connectivity, showing Sufism to be a cultural technology of inter-regional connection and exchange. Ranging from the Eastern and Western Mediterranean to Central and South Asia in the medieval period to gradually reach into Southeast Asia, China and Africa in the early modern period and ultimately Western Europe, North America and even Australia by the early twentieth century, it is a reasonable claim that the scale of Sufi expansion was indeed global. More substantially, the narrative attempts to outline some of the processes by which a religious tradition formed in a particular spatial and temporal (no less than linguistic and discursive) context was transformed – adapted, vernacularized, institutionalized – through its introduction to new environments on an incrementally global scale. And on the other side of the coin, the narrative traces the problems that such global expansion presented to Sufism as a result of its adaptation to so many different milieux, particularly during its most rapid geographical expansion during the "globalizing" early modern and modern eras. Of particular importance here was the way in which from the seventeenth century the adaptive processes by which Sufism expanded into new areas resulted in a proliferation of locally variant forms of Sufi tradition. When this global strategy of adaptation combined with the economic and political upsets of the ages of globalizing capitalism and colonialism, it fed into a Muslim crisis of conscience that sought to reform and ultimately suppress the tradition that the Sufis had cherished and promoted over the past millennium. The cultural adaptation of tradition through incorporation of local vernaculars and customs was thence set in reverse by Sufis and ultimately anti-Sufis who sought to strip back the "accretional" momentum of tradition through a renewed emphasis on Arabic learning and the Prophetic Sunna. By the beginning of the twentieth century, when Muslims came into ever closer contact with European forms of knowledge, a Sufism that had ridden the wave of Islam's early modern global expansion increasingly became a casualty of its own earlier success. There was, then, an inherent push-pull dynamic that reveals itself through such a long-term and globally distributive survey.

While this outline presents only the briefest sketch of the main developments pursued in the following chapters, it should be clear that the overall aim of the narrative is to present the history of Sufism as shaped by a set of *longue durée* processes through which a tradition was gradually created, expanded, reconfigured and, for many, finally rejected in the twentieth century in the face of competition from the many alternative Islams offered in the global religious marketplace.

Notes

1. A.J. Arberry, *Sufism: An Account of the Mystics of Islam* (London: George Allen & Unwin, 1950).
2. Arberry (1950), p. 119.
3. J.S. Trimingham, *The Sufi Orders in Islam* (Oxford: Clarendon Press, 1971).
4. L.E. Schmidt, "The Making of Modern 'Mysticism'," *Journal of the American Academy of Religion* 71, 2 (2003), pp. 273–302.
5. See e.g. H. Dabashi, *Truth and Narrative: The Untimely Thoughts of 'Ayn al-Qudāt al-Hamadhānī* (London: Routledge, 1999) and L. Massignon, *The Passion of al-Hallāj: Mystic and Martyr of Islam*, 4 vols (Princeton: Princeton University Press, 1982 [1922]).
6. A. Hammoudi, *Master and Disciple: The Cultural Foundations of Moroccan Authoritarianism* (Chicago: University of Chicago Press, 1997).
7. I.M. Lewis, *Saints and Somalis: Popular Islam in a Clan-Based Society* (Lawrenceville: The Red Sea Press, 1998), p. 9.

8. N.S. Green, "Between Heidegger and the Hidden Imam: Reflections on Henry Corbin's Approaches to Mystical Islam," in M.R. Djalili, A. Monsutti & A. Neubauer (eds), *Le Monde turco-iranien en question* (Paris: Karthala, 2008).
9. W.C. Chittick, *Sufism: A Short Introduction* (Oxford: Oneworld Publications, 2000), C.W. Ernst, *The Shambhala Guide to Sufism* (Boston: Shambhala, 1997), and A. Schimmel, *Mystical Dimensions of Islam* (Chapel Hill: University of North Carolina Press, 1975).
10. For an excellent case study of the inner-workings of tradition in one Sufi brotherhood, see C.W. Ernst & B.B. Lawrence, *Sufi Martyrs of Love: The Chishti Order in South Asia and Beyond* (New York: Palgrave Macmillan, 2002).
11. N.S. Green, "The Religious and Cultural Roles of Dreams and Visions in Islam," *Journal of the Royal Asiatic Society* 13, 3 (2003), pp. 287–313.
12. S.T. Katz, "The 'Conservative' Character of Mystical Experience," in Katz (ed.), *Mysticism and Religious Traditions* (Oxford: Oxford University Press, 1983).
13. M. Molé, *Les Mystiques musulmans* (Paris: Presses Universitaires de France, 1965), p. 4, my translation.
14. S.T. Katz, "Mystical Speech and Mystical Meaning," in Katz, *Mysticism and Language* (New York: Oxford University Press, 1992), p. 5.
15. E. Shils, *Tradition* (Chicago: University of Chicago Press, 2006 [1981]), pp. 12, 13.
16. Shils (2006), p. 23.
17. Shils (2006), p. 14.
18. Shils (2006), p. 12
19. Arberry (1950), p. 122.
20. For critical evaluations of the historiography of Sufism, see N.S. Green, "Making Sense of 'Sufism' in the Indian Subcontinent: A Survey of Trends," *Religion Compass* (Wiley-Blackwell Online, 2008); A. Knysh, "Historiography of Sufi Studies in the West," in Y.M. Choueiri (ed.), *A Companion to the History of the Middle East* (Oxford: Wiley-Blackwell, 2005); and D. Le Gall, "Recent Thinking on Sufis and Saints in the Lives of Muslim Societies, Past and Present," *International Journal of Middle East Studies* 42, 4 (2010), pp. 673–687.
21. On this Sufi lexicon, see N.S. Green, "Idiom, Genre and the Politics of Self-Description on the Peripheries of Persian," in N.S. Green & M. Searle-Chatterjee (eds), *Religion, Language and Power* (New York: Routledge, 2008).

Chapter 1

Origins, Foundations and Rivalries (850–1100)

The Context

The place is Baghdad and the year is around 850. It is over eight hundred miles of desert from where the Prophet announced his revelation in Mecca and more than two hundred years since he died. Although the word *sufi* ("wool-wearer") has been around for many years as a nickname or even a reproach for the hermits of the surrounding wilderness, for the first time it is being used to refer to people in the city itself. And unlike the obscure and self-effacing renouncers in the mountains and desert, these men in the city not only wrote books telling others how to behave, but also achieved enough prominence in the eyes of their contemporaries and successors to have their books discussed and preserved. In one of the familiar paradoxes of religious history, the sheer fact that we know about these men tells us that they were not reclusive or anti-social figures who kept themselves apart from the world, but public men with public lives in perhaps the wealthiest and most cosmopolitan city in the world. By the mid-ninth century, eight generations of fathers and sons have lived since Muhammad established his community of Muslims and in its third capital the pious and the scholarly among the heirs of that foundational community were more conscious than ever of the responsibilities of preserving the Prophet's message in his absence. It is a time of unprecedented productivity, legal and moral, spiritual and intellectual; from the legacy of the Prophet and the first generations of Muslims, the many meanings of Islam are being created (and debated and sometimes suppressed). Over the past generation, the learned have found a new medium to publicize and exchange their ideas, for the city's great trade routes have brought paper from China to replace parchment and papyrus. Many books

Sufism: A Global History, First Edition. Nile Green.
© 2012 Nile Green. Published 2012 by Blackwell Publishing Ltd.

are being written (and copied and sold); new ideas are finding supporters and detractors; and Islam itself is acquiring the meanings, variations and institutions that later generations will inherit and push back into the lifetime of the Prophet or the words of the Quran he revealed. If the paper trail left by the early Sufis does not take the historian beyond this early ninth century period, then the same can be said for the codification of such other key Islamic institutions as the Law (*shari'a*) and the Prophetic Example (*sunna*). The small group of people being called Sufis in Baghdad by around 850 were not wholly separate in their concerns from the men who thought through the implications of legal principle or sought ways of distinguishing true from false reports of the Prophet's words and deeds. While in later times and other places, to be called a Sufi might mean many different things, here where the term first caught on, it signified individuals who were especially scrupulous in their behavior and piety. Such was their devotion to God, and their distaste for the pleasures of the world, that at first literally and over time metaphorically they donned the hot, coarse and stinking garments of wool that lent them their name: the Sufis or "wool-wearers."

In view of the fact that since the middle of the nineteenth century, academics have sought "origins" of Sufism in the period prior to that outlined above, it is worth reiterating just exactly what we do (and do not) have in Baghdad by the middle of the ninth century when the earliest reliable data on the Sufis emerged. What we have is primarily a nickname or designator (*sufi*) being applied to certain people in the Baghdad region (some of whom left written records) and, as we will see below, arguably also far beyond Baghdad (who left no written records). But what we do not have yet is a Sufi movement, a characteristic set of doctrines and still less a tradition, all of which would develop only later. For this reason, it makes little sense to speak of "Sufism" as though such an entity had any meaningful existence at this time. Rather, we can say that by the mid-800s there were people being called Sufis whose teachings would gradually (and, moreover, retrospectively) be sifted and appropriated in the following generations as growing numbers of people came to call themselves Sufis and to formulate rituals, doctrines and dress to distinguish themselves from others and to construct a self-conscious historical pedigree to give weight to their truth claims. By maintaining this distinction between the label and the person, between the word and the referent, we will also be better equipped to navigate the first of the historical problems we need to address: the origins of Sufism.

The Problem of Sufi Origins

It would be scarcely an exaggeration to say that more academic ink has been spilt over the origins of the Sufis than over any other question in Sufi history.

Yet the importance of the question is relative rather than absolute, in that it depends on the model of historical process we bring to bear on our understanding of the past. The longstanding scholarly focus on "origins" developed out of a perspective in which historical process was seen as necessarily vertical, that is, as a set of "inheritances" and "influences" that acted on and were received by each passing generation so as to give cumulative shape to their thoughts, actions and creations. This model was particularly influential in the development of the fields of Religious Studies and Oriental Studies during the nineteenth century in which, under the influence of the new archaeological and textual discoveries concerning early Christian and Jewish history, the practice of the secular investigation of any religious history became an "archaeological" one of stripping away the accumulating strata of influence and inheritance to unearth, as it were, the "foundations" of any historical entity. But historical process is not merely (nor even mainly) a vertical one and with a century of sociological thinking behind us we are now more likely to think in terms of history being made within the horizontal stratum we recognize as "context" and "contemporaries" in which the past is received less as an irresistible agent than as a set of cultural resources to be continued, adapted or abandoned at will. As we will see below in our discussion of the written evidence of the early Sufis themselves, they were very deliberate in their attitudes towards the past of both their own Muslim community and the communities of non-Muslim peoples in their empire.

For this and for other reasons, the Sufis and their writings are best understood as products of their own "horizontal" time. This is not to say that the distinct practices, ideas or even terms the Sufis used did not originate before the ninth century. On the contrary, in the cosmopolitan society of Iraq and the many different contexts in which the Sufis later operated, the ability to make such selective adaptations from the past was one of the factors which lent the Sufis their attractiveness. But to adapt discrete cultural elements is not to surrender the integrity of the final production. Just as early Muslim jurists appear to have borrowed elements of Late Roman provincial law in constructing their own legal systems, and Muslim Kharijites wrote themselves into narrative paradigms of pious violence or martyrdom first embellished in the Byzantine Empire, so do certain early Sufis appear to have likewise adapted elements of Christian thought and practice for their own purposes.[1] But unless we are working on the theological rather than historical criterion that everything that is Islamic must come from the Quran, then such critical and selective adaptations need not render the final creations any less a product of the cosmopolitan Muslim circles of ninth century Iraq. Rather than thinking in terms of "adaptations" or "borrowings," we may be better off seeing the parallels as part of what has been described as a "semiotic *koinè*" that was common to Muslims, Christians and Jews in the early centuries of Islamic rule.[2]

A good example of this shared symbolic (and indeed linguistic) vocabulary is seen in the term *sufi* itself. Despite a range of alternative purported etymologies (including the Greek *sophia*, "wisdom"), the term has now been generally accepted as a derivative of the Arabic word for wool (*suf*), so as we have seen rendering a *sufi* someone who wears a woolen garment. The most thorough investigator of the history of the term has argued that it was first used in a Christian rather than an Islamic milieu to refer to a deviating trend that emerged in the late sixth century among the Nestorian Christians of Seleucia-Ctesiphon, around twenty miles south of where Baghdad would be founded in 762.[3] While the official language of the Nestorian Church was Syriac, over the decades after the Arab conquests of the region in the years after the Prophet Muhammad's death in 632, many Nestorians lost their ability to understand Syriac and so required Church edicts to be made in Arabic. It was this Arabic Christian vernacular that spread the terms *labis al-suf* ("clad in wool") and in turn *sufi* to refer to a particular group of Christian ascetics in Iraq, with whom early Muslim ascetics shared both word and practice as "an identification with a humble, lowly status and a recognition of values other than material."[4]

The weakness in the argument is that key parts of the evidence are either hypothetical, dependent on reconstructed theoretical word usages, or reliant on purported early usages recorded only in later source materials. But there are also larger problems with the argument as well. Firstly, there is the question of the degree of importance we are willing to lend to a name and the sub-question of whether that name and its "original" etymological meaning had a direct or arbitrary relationship to the persons, ideas or activities to which it came to refer in later Muslim contexts. In a classic study of seventy-eight early Muslim definitions of the terms *sufi* and its derivative *tasawwuf* ("to wear wool" or "to become a Sufi"), only one was found that referred to the wearing of wool and few others that referred to ascetic practices more generally, with the vast majority defining the terms by way of moral values and ethical dispositions.[5] This evidence appears to break the link between the Muslim and purported Christian meanings of the word *sufi* so as to suggest that in the different contexts of its usage the "things" to which the word referred were quite distinct. But the problem here too is that while these seventy-eight definitions are attributed to early ninth century figures, they only survive as quotations in much later sources. Again, we are faced with the problem that the further we go back beyond the great explosion of literary production in the ninth century, the sources either become indirect or dry up entirely: we are left with either late quotations from early figures or hypothetical reconstructions of earlier speech patterns.

Secondly, to look beyond the issue of language, there is the more substantive problem of whether there was a Muslim adaptation of Christian practices as well as words and the sub-question of whether that adaptation shaped the actual activities of those Muslims being called *sufi* in the ninth century. Here it is worth returning to the model of a semiotic and in some cases linguistic vocabulary that Muslims and Christians shared rather than exclusively owned. It is important here that we consider the context, in that during the first couple of centuries of Islamic history, the environment in which Muslims lived in such regions as Syria, Iraq and Egypt was one in which they were outnumbered by Christians. More thoroughly Christianized than even Western Europe at this time, the Middle Eastern Fertile Crescent was a landscape of churches, monasteries and saintly shrines. These sites and their occupants were not only given legal protection by the new Muslim empires, but were also in various ways co-opted by their Muslim rulers. Tombs of Christian saints and prophets were recognized as Muslim pilgrimage centers; monasteries served Muslims as wine-serving country clubs for poets and as libraries for literati; and Christian scholars helped translate into Arabic the heritage of Graeco-Roman thought that had been selectively preserved by the Christians' forefathers.[6] There is therefore no question of the variety of Muslim interaction with Christians, at least for the period up to around 850.

It has long been recognized that the wearing of wool points to similarities with the ascetic activities of the Eastern Christians, particularly in Syria, where between 661 and 750 the Muslims had kept their capital at Damascus before the shift to Iraq with the ascent of the 'Abbasid dynasty. Reacting to nineteenth century fashions for seeking the origins of the Sufis in Indian thought, scholars in the 1930s uncovered detailed evidence on the similarities between Christian and Muslim "ascetics" and it was argued that this

Figure 1.1   Ascetic Lifeways: Wooden and Coco-de-Mer Begging Bowls (*kashkul*) (Image: Nile Green)

common ascetic heritage prepared the way for the Sufis' development into fully-fledged "mystics" more concerned with experience and knowledge than with punishing the body.[7] This placing of the early Muslims into their pluralistic contexts has also been seen in the more recent trend towards seeing both early Christian and Muslim developments within their shared social setting. In its simplest form, the method has been to place evidence on Christian and Muslim activities side by side, to point to similarities and wherever possible evidence of direct contact between them, and to use this as evidence for the influence of the Christians on the Muslims, pointing to such similarities as prayer patterns, sayings and attitudes as well as clothing.[8] But here the debate on origins moves in two directions whose different implications need to be carefully separated. For scholars writing in the 1930s, in both the Muslim and Christian case the isolation and self-mortification of asceticism was a natural (indeed, universal) cradle for the development of "mysticism." The latter was regarded in turn as a universal urge aimed at "a knowledge of Ultimate reality, and finally at the establishment of a conscious relation with the Absolute, in which the soul shall attain to union with God."[9] In other words, this interpretation presents a developmental model of history in which asceticism is not an end in itself but must mature and blossom into mysticism, which is what the author cited the Sufis as being involved with. This collapsing of the differences (and, indeed, the potential antagonism) between the two categories of ascetic and mystic affords a somewhat conflict-free narrative. The early Muslim ascetics who had been influenced by the practices of their Christian neighbors are thus seen as feeding seamlessly into the rise of the Sufis who, in developing the more complex metaphysical models of human and divine interaction that "mysticism" required, once again needed to borrow from the Christians, who, having been around longer, were ahead of the Muslims on the same universal scale of spiritual development.

The problem is that when we look at the evidence on the Muslim side, this early progress from asceticism to mysticism does not seem so straightforward. So rather than seeing the Muslim ascetics as the natural forebears of the Sufis, we may be better off seeing them as their competitors. In recent decades, closer investigation into the discussions that surrounded early Muslim "asceticism" (*zuhd*) has cast serious doubt on this notion of a seamless flow between the *zahid* "ascetic" and the *sufi* "mystic" by showing the degree to which self-mortification, seclusion and above all celibacy were denounced as deviations from the *sunna* or Prophetic Example.[10] As we will see when we deal with the earliest clear evidence of the opinions of the people called Sufis, many of them were forthright in condemning ascetic practices as unnecessarily public displays of what amounted to false piety. (Given the popular acclaim that many Late Antique ascetics gained, the ironic implication was that ascetics were actually egotistic careerists.) To put the matter more plainly, even if Muslim ascetics did copy the style of Christian ascetics, this does not necessarily point towards a Christian "origin" for the Sufis, because far from being the direct heirs of the ascetics, the Sufis may be better understood as their rivals and critics. *Zahid* "ascetics" did not maturely blossom into Sufi "mystics": instead the voices of the *zuhhad* were muted by the more successful Sufis' marginalization and eventual replacement of them.

So far we have questioned the significance of the similarities in designations and practices between the Christian ascetics and the Muslim Sufis. The main problem with such searches for traces has been that while there exists plenty of evidence for similarities and even contacts between Muslims and Christians, there exists hardly any direct evidence for the actual "borrowing" that is meant to have underlain the similarities. One could argue that this is not surprising, since being well aware of the richer development of Christian thought and practice in the early centuries of Islam, Muslims were hardly likely to have publicized their need to adapt ideas and techniques from a religion which their own had supposedly superceded. The same might be said for evidence for the flow of the more subtle traffic of metaphysical doctrines and biographical narratives. It is in this most nebulous of areas that an alternative method was proposed for assessing potential Christian influence, which was not to seek the recurrence of the isolated motif or word-borrowing but the more complex – and thereby less likely to be random – reproduction of a "pattern, configuration or structure."[11] Through a form of historical structuralism, it has been argued that the Sufi debt to Nestorian Christianity could thereby be traced through the repetition of doctrinal or biographical patterns found first in Christian works and later in Sufi writings.[12] One example is the writings of the seventh century Iraqi Christian, Isaac of Nineveh, whose threefold model of the soul's ascent through a series of triad clusters of activities and virtues has been interpreted as reappearing in later Sufi elaborations of their own path.[13] As an attempt to bridge the impasse between merely documenting similarities and deciding between which were coincidental and which were evidence of direct adaptation, this method of historical structuralism claims to identify the recurrence of complex patterns too intricate to recur without direct transmission. The fullest exercise in this vein has been carried out on the biographical accounts of Rabi'a (d.801), the celebrated female Muslim ascetic of Basra in southern Iraq whom the Sufis would claim as one of their forerunners, and here the method has shown with some success how the Muslim legends of Rabi'a drew on older Christian narratives of penitent prostitutes.[14] But even if we accept that certain configurations of ideas were transmitted, ultimately we are left with no clearer understanding of how this happened and for historians this need for a clear explanation of how something happened is as important as the evidence that it did. As in the older type of intellectual history that once dominated the study of Sufism, without an understanding of process we are presented with texts which are supposedly connected, but with no sense of the readers who are meant to have connected them. Even if such direct structural parallels can be detected, again this can be just as efficiently explained as being the result of a shared horizontal symbolic imaginary – a "semiotic *koinê*" – than as being the result of the one-way traffic of Muslims "borrowing" from Christians.

If modern scholarship seems to offer no clear picture of Sufi origins, the question arises as to whether the Sufis' own account is any better? Over time the Sufis certainly became very interested in their own past and in their construction of a tradition furnished all manner of biographical stories about their forebears, stretching right back to connect their teachings with the Prophet. As we will see in more detail below, the problem is that the chief sources on these forebears date from much later (in many cases, several centuries later) than their own lifetimes. As in the case of Rabi'a, the biographies of such other purported Sufi forerunners as the Central Asians Ibrahim ibn Adham (d.777), Fudayl ibn 'Iyad (d.803) and Bishr ibn al-Harith (d.841) and the Egyptian Dhu'l-Nun (d.861) became enmeshed with tropes and motifs that drew on folklore as much as fact.[15] As we will see in Chapter 2 when we come to discuss the biographical collections in which the supposed careers of those forerunners were recorded, the retrospective claiming of such a neat chain of forerunners tells us more about the textual consolidation of tradition in the eleventh century than it does about the lives and circumstances of the earliest Sufis three hundred years beforehand. As we have already seen, in the middle 800s there was as yet no Sufi tradition, nor even a coherent movement, merely a group of often quite distinct individuals being nicknamed Sufis. The point is therefore not so much whether men such as Ibrahim ibn Adham existed, nor even whether they were part of an earlier trend towards asceticism. It is rather a question of, first, whether they can be seen as having constituted in any way a coherent group over such vast distances and, second, whether they can be seen as having constituted a trend or trajectory that the Sufis inherited rather than suppressed.

In historicist terms, these problems concerning the origins of the Sufis are therefore magnified by an emphasis on the vertical transmission of cause and influence, which stresses the inheritance of ideas over their rejection and the transformation of movements over their suppression. The fact of the matter is that, as in the early history of Christianity, the first centuries of Islam were a period of intense competition between producers of often radically contrasting versions of the faith in which patterns of political allegiance, economic activity, everyday etiquette and legal restraint were subjects of intensive and at times violent debate. Rather than search for a neat and multi-generational transformation from asceticism to mysticism that has long characterized the study of early Sufi history, by looking at each stratum of time in its own right we can see the discontinuities and differences that allow us to assess whether the ideas and actions of the previous generation were perpetuated or rejected.

Let us take the ascetic *zuhhad* as a case in point. Following the later biographies written by the Sufis themselves, historians have traditionally taken the *zuhhad* to have been "Sufis-in-waiting." But by putting the ascetics into the circumstances of their own time, we can see how they served very different purposes and sought very different goals from the Sufis who emerged in later centuries. The eighth century heyday of the *zuhhad* was a period in which Muslims were still a minority group in their own imperial domains and in which the consolidation of their conquests left frontier regions under the perpetual threat of re-conquest.[16] It was in these border regions that many *zuhhad* ascetics such as Ibrahim ibn Adham flourished, serving in frontier wars in which their religious devotion and robust asceticism brought them not only success in battle but the renown that would pass on their names to future generations. Seen in the harsh realities of their time, such ascetics were less timeless seekers of God than Muslim equivalents to the hardy Byzantine devotees of the Christian warrior saints whose shrines protected the other side of the same imperial frontiers.[17] Operating as they did in these contested cultural borderlands, in terms of their narratives no less than their actions, the militant Muslim ascetics were shaped by a trans-religious value system that they shared with the Christian militant ascetics of the period.[18] Once again, we may be dealing less with a question of Muslim "borrowings" from Christians than with a shared cultural arena and geographical area in which Muslims and Christians competed with one another within a set of overlapping frameworks, whether narrative, moral or metaphysical.

Of course, not all of the early Muslim *zuhhad* ascetics were frontier warriors and many of them probably did spend more time conversing with than fighting with Christians. But what becomes clear by looking at these figures in their own troubled times is that the Muslim ascetics of the eighth century were not only more complicated figures than the teleological role of the "proto-mystic" would make them: they were also plainly distinct figures with quite different social roles and moral agendas from the people who from the mid-ninth century would be called Sufis in the more peaceable cities of Iraq rather than the frontiers in Syria or Central Asia. As the subsequent historical writings of the Sufis themselves show, in which the Sufis sought to present the earlier ascetics as their own forebears, the search for antecedents often tells us more about the quest for legitimacy than the processes by which ideas and movements take shape.[19] Rather than attempt to trace the developments of one period in the quite distinct circumstances of its predecessors, let us instead remain in the "horizontal" period and circumstances in which a small number of Muslims acquired the nickname Sufi and see if we can do better explaining their origin in their own stratum of time rather than in those that preceded them.

The Sufis of Iraq (800–900)

By the early ninth century, asceticism was falling into widespread dispute among the urban scholars who were becoming an increasingly important voice in Muslim society. This was a period in which the early Islamic model of a community led by a single figure belonging to the family of Muhammad (alternatively a caliph or an imam) was being replaced by new notions of authority whose different formulations lent varying weight to reason and piety, mastery of the scriptures and charismatic closeness to God. Taking their lead from their readings of Graeco-Roman philosophy in the championing of reason, the Muslim philosophers called *falasifa* in imitation of the Greek and the rationalist theologians called Mu'tazilites were particularly influential in Baghdad in the ninth century.[20] In the early decades of the century, the rationalist party was sufficiently influential in its championing of reason over revelation to persuade the leader of the Muslim empire, the Caliph al-Ma'mun (r.813–833), to initiate an "inquisition" or *mihna* which for eighteen years sought to enforce the doctrine that the Quran was not a pre-eternal text but was created in the contextual time of history.[21] On the other side of the debate were various scholars who sought to uphold the authority of revelation, not least because it seemed to offer firmer (as it were constitutional) grounds for law-making, which struck many as less amenable than reason to manipulation by the ruling class. They objected in particular to the Caliph al-Ma'mun's claims to authoritative insight into the meaning of scripture. In addition to defending the status of the Quran, these scholars were also concerned with upholding – indeed, with raising in prominence – the thousands of reports of the sayings and deeds of Muhammad known as the Hadith. It was amidst these debates, naturally converging in Baghdad as the capital of empire of the 'Abbasid caliphs, that there began to emerge what we now know of as Sunni Islam. Based on the premise that Muslims constitute a moral rather than a political community united by their commitment to the message of the Quran and the Example or *sunna* of the Prophet as recorded in the Hadith, this "constitutional bloc" nonetheless maintained a special place for the *'ulama* ("men of learning") who had the textual expertise to decide on what the message of the Quran and Hadith actually was.[22] On the other side were those who remained loyal to the older Muslim notion of authority and religious knowledge being vested in a single person and, though their ideas too took many decades to develop, they kept their old nickname of the "partisans" or Shi'a of their first leader, the Prophet's son-in-law, 'Ali. Two centuries after the Prophet left the community of Muslims he had founded, these debates were attempts to work with the resources he bequeathed to that community, by way of his revelation through the Quran, his example through the Hadith, and his family through the descendents of 'Ali.

This context of contentious debates and cultural resources is important because it prevents us from falling prey to the notion that as "mystics" the Sufis were primarily people who sought a direct relationship with God and thereby had little need for the guidance of scripture and Prophetic Example. It will also prevent us from assuming that the Sufis were from their inception in a position of rivalry with the scholars or *'ulama*.[23] On the contrary, from the earliest records we have of them, the Sufis appear as deeply involved with the scriptural and exemplary legacy of the Prophet and it is this very "bookishness" that allows us to write their history. Given that in this period much of these figures' dealings with the Quran and Hadith were through oral memorization rather than regular resort to written codices, the term "discursiveness" would be more accurate than "bookishness," but the overall point remains that the Sufis and *'ulama* were likewise invested in the discourses of oral and written texts, with the Sufis debating the degree to which experience shed light on the true meanings of these texts.[24] There were probably many people in this period who had direct encounters with God that had nothing to do with scripture and there were certainly those among the early Sufis who claimed that their experiential pursuit of *tahqiq* ("realization, verification") rendered their knowledge claims superior to those relying solely on scripture. But with one major exception whom we will meet in the next section, for the most part we know very little about such people because they were either not members of the text-producing class or were unable to win the support of those who were.

In situating the earliest Sufis in their own "horizontal" time, then, we need to recognize their emergence as belonging to the development of a wider scholar class that was not only equipped with knowledge of Quran, Hadith and the specialist skills of interpreting them, but was also gaining increasing social authority by dint of both possessing such textual or discursive knowledge and putting its righteous example into practice. Living in the major towns, these were not the reclusive ascetics of the mountains or frontiers. Nor did they occupy ivory towers in the city itself, because the knowledge of right and wrong and the ability to persuade others to agree through either personal moral authority or legal decree had deeply practical implications. While there would be exceptions, the general rule would remain through future centuries that whether as lawyers, poets, metaphysicians or moralists, successful Sufis were rarely far from pen and paper or from the Hadith and Quran that laid the foundations of Muslim learning. And yet the early Sufis were not only men of the pen and their claims to experiential knowledge should be seen as placing them not wholly distinctly from the emergent scholarly class but as a special sub- or even splinter group with much in common with the scholars but with an additional claim to the authority of direct contact with the divine realms.

If the Quran and the Hadith were resources for the people being called Sufis, then how did they make use of these resources in the creation of their own doctrines and practices and in making sense of their experiences? In brief, they internalized and externalized them: they internalized the Quran by committing its every verse to their memory and they externalized the Hadith by enacting its moral examples in their behavior.[25] Crucially, they also adopted the Quran's vocabulary to create a scripturally-sanctioned terminology for the spiritual exercises and forms of experience that they added to the religious repertoire of other members of the scholarly class. This was therefore not a passive form of knowledge and if we have emphasized the Sufis' relationship with books, then we must be clear about their way of using them: books were tools for contemplation on the one hand and for action on the other.[26] While we have noted that, with the arrival of paper, far more books were being produced in Baghdad than had ever been the case in the western hemisphere, they were still handwritten and valuable objects. These material factors fed into the culture of reading that developed around them, albeit with the proviso that religious texts took longer to be committed to paper than such secular texts as poems, scientific works and cookbooks. As in other manuscript societies in which book-use existed within a larger framework of oral forms of learning, books were read deeply and repeatedly, a process sometimes compounded by the requirement of either writing out one's own copy of a text or wholeheartedly memorizing it in order to acquire it. While scholars were literate themselves, some of their followers were not and so books were listened to as often as they were read. Rather than marking a page with a highlighter, such auditory readers were in the habit of storing and absorbing their contents mentally. As we will see later, this culture of reading books aloud even affected the shape of their contents, so that a few centuries later most Sufi books contained the kind of anecdotal stories or key points in rhyme that could easily be remembered by their listeners. But before the Sufis took to writing their own books, they were reading the Quran and Hadith in this active and internalizing mode, like other learned men of their period.

This sense of reading as an active engagement with the scripture enables us to tackle another of the key debates around the origins of Sufism. Often seen as the "internalist" counterpart to the "externalist" accounts of Sufi origins in Christian or other non-Muslim influences, the idea that Sufism originated in the Quran has found its greatest proponents among Francophone and more recently American scholars.[27] Tracing the origins of the technical vocabulary or Sufi lexicon that the first generations of Sufis developed in their writings has demonstrated that this was overwhelmingly a vocabulary of Quranic origin. This has in turn been used to argue that Sufism was a consistent and coherent "internal" product of Islam rather than the result of outside influence.[28] Of course, the argument has some basic flaws that relate to the distinction made earlier between words and things: just because Sufis chose to label their practices or doctrines with Quranic terms does not necessarily imply that the actual practices or doctrines themselves came from the Quran. Critics of the theory have used what they see as the dry, sectarian or narrative tone of the Quran to argue that even on its own evidence, the Quran cannot have been the source for the doctrines of the Sufis: "the [Quranic] text is noteworthy for its rigour and severity, and the mystics of Islam have had to work hard to produce inner meanings which reflect personal communion with God."[29]

Yet the answer to the problem may lie in the very words of its critique: the Sufis did indeed have to work hard on the text, for this contemplative and active engagement with its meaning was precisely how they treated scripture. Rather than phrase the debate around what we as later readers may see in the Quran ("rigour and severity"), and demand that the text itself in some way possess agency to create doctrines and movements in the outside world, we are better off shifting our perspective towards asking what the early Sufis themselves saw in the Quran and to ask how their active modes reading produced meanings through the creative interaction between their own life circumstances and the text. So the question becomes not whether Sufism "originated" in the Quran in the passive sense of the verb, but whether the Sufis of the ninth century used the Quran as a resource to understand the world around them and to create ways of morally, intellectually and practically interacting with it.[30] There is nothing wrong with asking whether the Sufis made their ideas originate from the holy book, since this is precisely

Figure 1.2 Contemplating the Quran: Folio of Sura 2.119 from Ninth Century Iraq (Freer Gallery of Art, Smithsonian Institution, Washington, D.C.: Purchas, F194217, F1937.6.7b)

how scriptures are read. The Hadith was used in similar ways, with different groups using the many thousands of often contradictory reports of the Prophet's words or deeds to defend or criticize their own and others' actions. Like the Quran, the Hadith was not an "agent" or necessarily even a "source" of religious movements in its own right, but rather a resource which like their other contemporaries the Sufis deployed in the elaboration and defense of their teachings. Finally, the Quran also found use among the Sufis as a source of the chanted phrases that made up the Sufi practice of chanted "remembrance of God" or *dhikr* (a term itself taken from the Quran). In such contexts, its words functioned not so much as purveyors of linguistic meaning than as sonic provokers of altered states.

In this way, we can see how the early Sufis used the distinct discursive resources of the past (scripture and the Prophetic Example) to create their own "way" and to root it in the legitimate sources of authority which were recognized by their contemporaries. Words have histories and so change meaning over time, and in the different times and places in which they are read, the preserved words of scripture are used to point to different referents in the world than those to which they pointed in the time and place in which the scripture was written. So in the Baghdad of the middle 800s, the Quran was used as a lexical source for a terminology which had different meanings and referred to different activities, virtues and emotions than it did for the Muslim readers of earlier generations. Since the Iraq of this period was a far more complex and cosmopolitan society than the Arabia in which the Quran had taken shape, the actions and ideas to which its vocabulary was attached at that later time were necessarily different. Given the day-to-day cultural exchanges that went on in ninth century Iraq, it would be surprising if some of the actions or ideas to which the Quran's words were attached were not adapted from the many non-Muslims of the region. This is the way scripture operates. When a modern American Christian responds to the Biblical recommendation of charity by writing a check, she is not being any less Christian because such banking procedures were invented in the Dutch Republic rather than Roman Palestine. Ultimately, then, the problem of whether Sufism originated in the Quran or in Christian borrowings is a false one that simplifies the way in which scripture was read and religious ideas and actions were produced.

Among the circles of specialist interpreters of the Quran and Hadith, the early Sufis were closer to the trend defending revelation and tradition over reason. Far from being rule-breaking libertines or spirit-filled radicals, we should probably picture them as a broadly conservative crowd. Instead of fleeing from society like the earlier ascetics, they were often fierce upholders of the emerging moral and legal order. Like the nascent Sunni movement in which they participated, they followed the Quranic injunction to "command the good and forbid the wrong" (*al-amr bi-al-maʿruf wa-al-nahy ʿan al-*

munkar), even if this upset those who didn't wish to be tirelessly moral.[31] Like many of the other major Muslim thinkers of the period, the early Sufis were as much concerned with humanity's proper actions and attitudes in the social world than with humanity's knowledge of and interaction with what lay beyond it.

Perhaps the most important – certainly the best known – among these figures who rejected the showiness (*riya*) of the ascetics in favor of the mastery of the moral rather than the physical self was Muhasibi of Baghdad (d.857).[32] A case has been made that Muhasibi could not have been a Sufi because he was a moralizing theologian rather than a mystic, and indeed in his extant writings he never referred to himself as a Sufi.[33] However, this is to overlook both the context of strong concerns for visible (if not ostentatious) righteousness in which the Sufis emerged and from which they drew sustenance. Muhasibi was also important in terms of providing intellectual resources for the construction of Sufi tradition, for the Sufis of subsequent generations would claim Muhasibi as one of their own. This was a crucially important part of the process we are tracing of the development of a Sufi "tradition" that was at times a retrospective act of claiming prestigious persons and respectable or otherwise useful ideas. For these purposes, Muhasibi was important for developing the key idea and practice that would gradually set the Sufis apart from the other pietists among whom we have positioned them. This practice – which lent him his name as the "self reckoner" (*muhasibi*) – was the scrupulous inspection of the lower, carnal self that the Quran referred to as the *nafs* (note the resort to Quranic vocabulary).[34] Here in discursive as well as practical terms was the "inward turn" that set Sufis apart from their more externally demonstrative rivals, whether the ascetic *zuhhad* or the moralizing People of the Hadith. As we will now see as we turn towards the teachings of the early Sufis proper, it was this creation of a convincing framework for understanding the self and of effective methods for exploring it that brought the Sufis the fame and following that over the following generations was to spread their new method far and wide. Since the doctrines of the Baghdad Sufis of the ninth and tenth century would form the foundations of subsequent Sufi tradition, the following pages trace these doctrines in some detail, since the key concepts and the Arabic vocabulary to which they were attached would later be transmitted to Sufis as far away as the oases of the Sahara and the spice islands of the Indian Ocean.

Kharraz of Baghdad (d.899)

By the middle of the ninth century, in Baghdad as well as in Basra to the south, there were a good many people being called Sufis. But in terms of both contemporary fame and posthumous emulation, one of the most important was Abu Sa'id, known as al-Kharraz ("the cobbler").[35] We know very little with certainty about the life of Kharraz, except that he travelled widely, visiting not only the holy cities of Jerusalem and Mecca (where he remained for eleven years), but also Egypt and the city of Kairouan in what is now Tunisia. His name tells us that at least at some point in his life he worked as a cobbler, pointing towards the urban artisanal milieu that we will see recurring among other early Sufis. But for the most part, we have very little biographical data to work with and so the only kind of contextualization possible with Kharraz and similar figures of the period is a discursive one, placing his ideas and writings among the wider patterns of debate and book production we have seen going on in Baghdad at this time, albeit bearing in mind that we are still in a period when such "books" consisted of something more like manuscript notes than formally arranged codices. Kharraz's main work was the *Kitab al-Sidq* (Book of Truthfulness), which seems to have been composed for a broader scholarly than a narrowly sectarian readership, though he also penned a number of shorter treatises or *risalas* devoted to more specific and complex questions and probably intended for a smaller and more like-minded readership.

Given the tendency of many accounts of Sufi thought to strip away the cultural shell in search of the mystical kernel, it is worth first pointing out the distinctively Islamic character of Kharraz's writings. As in countless other Sufi works of future generations, Kharraz proved his points by presenting supporting quotations from earlier Muslim authorities, whether from the Quran and Hadith or from the scholars and ascetics of the previous two centuries, so using the past that we have already described as a resource for such writers to draw on. Although there was not yet a distinctly Sufi tradition to draw on – the writings of Kharraz's generation would themselves serve as the earliest resources for such a distinct tradition to be created over the next few generations – there was already an abundant Islamic tradition to draw on in support of one's ideas. Recognizing this Islamic, discursive context is important because it prevents us from falling too easily into line with older tendencies in understanding the early Sufis as mystics in search of raw experience. On the one hand, keeping in mind the Islamic content of Kharraz's writings prevents us from too easily stripping away what were to Kharraz and his readers the Islamic foundations of his teachings to present his work as a naked structure of ideas in order to make possible the claim that "his work reads very much like the [Christian] treatises of Isaac of Nineveh."[36] On the other hand, recognizing the intertextual process by which Kharraz and other Sufis constructed their own texts by drawing on (and in some cases, as we will see later, by baldly plagiarizing) authoritative earlier texts, we can avoid the assumption that as "mystics" the Sufis constructed their writings primarily from the raw material of their own transcendental experiences. For, experience was interpreted and gained its meanings through resort to the vocabulary and concepts developed through the Sufis' active reading of Quran and Hadith, such that experience and text formed part of a creative continuum.

Yet the concern for defending the authority of collective Islamic tradition over individual experiential charisma is seen in many of Kharraz's works, which far from overriding the basic requirements of Muslim ritual included an earlier book devoted to the proper performance of formal worship. By the same token, Kharraz defended the authority of the Prophets (who were dead) over that of the self-proclaimed *awliya allah* or "Friends of God" (many of whom were living). We will speak more of these mysterious but key figures later, but for now the point is to recognize Kharraz's traditionism and conformism. While drawing on and positioning himself within this normative background, Kharraz did make important contributions to the development of what would soon become the distinct proprietary method of the Sufis. In the *Kitab al-Sidq*, he outlined a series of moral attributes that the sincere Muslim must acquire if (in the words of the Quran as cited by Kharraz) he "hopes to meet his Lord."[37] Kharraz's concern with "truthfulness" (*sidq*) was an echo of the critique of ostentatious asceticism we have already seen emerging and as he recorded it himself his aim was to show truthfulness as at once a "theoretical knowledge" (*'ilm*) and a "practical science" (*fiqh*), both of these designations conceived within the framework of Islamic categories that were emerging at this time among Muslim scholars of all persuasions, including the law-makers.[38]

Although we are now more used to speaking in terms of "spiritual development," we are perhaps better off thinking of the principles Kharraz outlined as moral conditions, in that to speak of "spiritual" development in the absence of action in the world would be to misconstrue the whole tenor of his message in which spiritual development was meaningless if not accompanied by good action. Outward action and inward intention must be harmonized with one another and scrupulous truthfulness helps ensure that this is the case. But this was only the beginning of the matter and the *Kitab al-Sidq* was dedicated to expounding the subtle implications and nuances of the pursuit and mastery of this guiding principle. In doing so, Kharraz used what would become the central metaphor of Sufi doctrine: that the Sufi method can be understood as a "Path" (*tariqa*) that guides one safely on the journey towards the state of harmony with God that is Islam. Like any other long journey, along the way the traveler passes through a variety of "places" (*maqamat*, sometimes translated as "stations"). And so in order to become truthful – in intention as well as action – one must travel through many such metaphorical "places" in which the different aspects of truthfulness may be acquired: repentance, self-knowledge and self-control; knowledge of the wiles of Satan; knowledge of what is lawful and forbidden; abstinence; trust in God; godfearingness; shame; gratitude towards the creator; boundless love of one's lord; fatalism; longing for God; and finally the place of intimacy with God.

The metaphor of the path was important because, as on any journey, no place can be reached without first passing through the previous places along the road. This method of delineating such "places" on the path towards intimacy with God would become one of the classic characteristics of Sufi writing and, we must presume, proof of possessing the kind of special familiarity with that journey that brought disciples to writers' doors. Nonetheless, we must assume that these teachings were not merely theoretical, as they appear in summaries such as this, but were also practical and effective. Like medicine, they were not only a formal branch of knowledge but also a method that brought about a cure. The Sufis not only showed people how to do good, but also how to feel good by way of the contentment brought by complete reliance on God (*tawakkul*).

If the path and the places along it were one foundational element of the Sufi method to which Kharraz contributed, another was the joint concept of "passing away" (*fana*) and "surviving" (*baqa*). As with any other Sufi doctrine, support for the idea of the death of the ego before the body was found in the Hadith of Muhammad, who was claimed to have advised his followers to "Die before you die." If walking the path was the method, then the procedure itself was the wiping out of the base and lowly instincts of the lower soul (*nafs*) so that at the journey's end nothing remained but the higher spirit (*ruh*) in a state of loving intimacy with its divine creator.

Kharraz discussed the characteristics of that state of intimacy, and the type of people who reached it, in his more specialist *risala* treatises. The language of these works was more dense and obscure, suggesting the emergence of the kind of specialist jargon that not only characterizes closed communities of readers but also requires the oral commentary of a teacher to clarify their meaning. In the circle of Kharraz at least, we should not then imagine the early Sufis as populists: like the occultist Neo-Platonic *Ikhwan al-Safa* ("Brothers of Purity") who emerged in Basra half-a-century later, the early Sufis had a penchant for the arcane and even pedantic. Their critique of the *zuhhad* ascetics whose showy and at times gruesome austerities certainly did win popular support suggests that if anything the likes of Kharraz and Muhasibi beforehand represented a distinctly anti-popularist circle of urbane litterati who sought dignity in mastering their books rather than their bodies.

In Kharraz's treatises, the urge towards classification that we have already seen in the *Kitab al-Sidq* thus found expression in an account of the seven "classes" (*tabaqat*) among the spiritual elite whom he designated as the "people of bafflement and bewilderment." Each of these classes sought God in a different way, from the pondering of abstruse allusions (*isharat*) of those of the lowest class to those higher souls who have been brought into such proximity (*qurb*) to the divine essence as to have entirely lost all of their own attributes in those of God.[39] For all his attempts to avoid controversy through upholding the importance of outwardly observing Muslim social norms, Kharraz was unable to avoid controversy in this dilution of the distinction between God and mankind, even if it was a tiny elite among them. Despite arguing for the existence of seven elite classes of humankind, in other respects Kharraz sought to reduce the status of persons whose proximity and absorption in God led them to be considered his special "Friends" (*awliya*).[40] While like other Muslims of his day, Kharraz certainly accepted the existence of such saintly figures, he was adamant that their status did not exceed that of the Prophets (*anbiya*). The implication was that whatever God revealed to his Friends was lower in authority and status to what he revealed to his Prophets: even a Friend of God could not command one to break the laws or deny the revelations brought by the Prophets. While expanding the ways and numbers of people who might have direct contact with God, Kharraz was therefore at the same time restricting the authority that such contact granted over other members of society.

Tustari of Basra (d.896)

By the second half of the ninth century, the question of the relationship between Prophets and Friends (and thence of the ordinary Muslims in fealty to them) was already a pressing one. Around three hundred and fifty miles to the south of Baghdad in the city of Basra, the question was also being addressed by Kharraz's contemporary, Sahl ibn 'Abdullah Tustari (d.896). Like Kharraz and many other Muslim scholars of the period, Tustari traveled widely in his lifetime and, though he grew up in the Iranian town of Tustar that gave him his name, he made the pilgrimage to Mecca, resided in several towns in Iraq and possibly traveled through Egypt as well.[41] While as evidence historians have the texts that such men as Tustari left behind, it is much harder to assess the impact on their thought of the conversations and meetings that must have taken place during their travels. Later claims that Tustari learned from the semi-legendary Egyptian master, Dhu'l Nun ("He of the Fish," d.861), are not intrinsically unlikely, but simply hard to verify. We do know rather more about the development of ideas in Basra over the decades prior to Tustari's arrival there in 877, when he was already an old man approaching sixty, even if it seems likely that his ideas were already mature by this stage.[42] While we can point to his connection to discussions and modes of writing in the generation or two before him, and while it seems likely that he was influenced by an earlier Quran commentary by the Shi'i *imam* Ja'far al-Sadiq (d.765) that is no longer extant, we are probably better off seeing him as a creative figure in his own right than seeking sources for his ideas among Gnostics and Neo-Platonists.[43]

What is most fascinating about the source of Tustari's creativity is its appearance in the fertile interpretive ground between the Quran and his own experiences. It is important that we do not lose sight of either side of this balance of input, for Tustari was neither solely a freethinking mystic drawing on his own sublime thoughts nor a derivative exegete dealing in simple paraphrases of scripture. Instead, he was a Muslim for whom the Quranic words of God provided an inexhaustible source of knowledge for the contemplative reader in active engagement with his scripture. With the Quran as his guide, Tustari explored the meaning of his own experiences that came from years spent in the intense chanting of incantatory formulas such as those he learned during his youth from an uncle, a well-known scholar of Hadith. While parallels and sources for this practice of chanting have been sought in the lengthy Jesus prayers of the Nestorian Christians, for Muslims such as Tustari and his uncle, the source was wholly Islamic. Not only did the formulas themselves often consist of words from the Quran, the generic term for such exercises – *dhikr* or "remembrance" – was itself taken from the several Quranic recommendations to remember God. Tustari was the first person we know of who connected this practice of chanting *dhikr* with the notion of the heart as the organ of knowledge, the purification of which allowed it to become host to God's primordial light.

Although Tustari's *tafsir* or Quran commentary was more a rambling collection of notes than a step-by-step exegesis, it does provide both an overview of his teachings and a sense of the role of the scripture within them. Between text and contemplation, Tustari developed the Quranic idea that there existed a pre-eternal covenant (*mithaq*) between God and his creatures in which the souls of every human who would ever be created were summoned before God and then accepted him as their master.[44] However, Tustari's version of the Covenant stretched back even further into the dawn of creation, teaching that before God created humankind, he had first created Muhammad.[45] This was not quite the Muhammad of history but a cosmic Muhammad created from pure light brought out of the primordial light of God himself. From this Muhammadan Light (*nur muhammadi*) God then brought out the rest of creation in ranked order: the Prophets, the Friends and then the more ordinary souls of the rest of humanity. Not all of the humans God created were equal; no less important, the Friends were not close to God by merit of their special efforts but because of their preordained status at the moment of creation. While ordinary Muslims could certainly be brought closer to God by using such techniques as chanting *dhikr* to purify themselves of the distractions of the lower soul, there was no chance for them to be promoted in this celestial hierarchy of Friendship (*wilaya*). Indeed, Tustari presented this hierarchy of God's Friends as a closed club dominated by a fixed number of truthful ones (*siddiqun*), substitutes (*abdal*) and cosmic tent-pegs (*awtad*). As we will see in Chapter 2, in social and spatial terms this

Figure 1.3 Sharing Sacred Geographies: Medieval Shrine of Shaykh Yusuf Abu al-Hajjaj in Luxor Temple, Egypt (Image: Nile Green)

theology of Friendship would over time feed a vibrant cult of Sufi saints whose shrines, such as that built for Shaykh Yusuf Abu al-Hajjaj in the former pharaonic temple of Luxor in Egypt, would gradually transform the Middle Eastern landscape into a sacred Islamic geography.

Although Tustari openly taught that there were four levels to the meanings of the Quran (literal, symbolic, ethical and eschatological), it was only the Friends who could truly understand it. While we see again the concern for ranking and enumeration that also characterized the writings of Kharraz, there is no doubt that the Friends loomed far larger in the cosmos of Tustari. At the same time that many Muslim scholars were forming an egalitarian (or at least a meritocratic) Islam in which knowledge and authority were acquired through mastery of scripture and concordance with the Prophetic Example, in the circle of Tustari we see the re-emergence of an older hierarchical Islam in which knowledge and authority were vested by divine election in a small number of people. Because this was not an elite defined by bloodline, as it was in the Shi'i formulation of authority lying solely in the family descendants of Muhammad, it was a more protean and thereby a more manipulable model that was likely to attract more supporters as a result. Since only the Friends themselves knew they were Friends, there was in principle no method of verifying whether a self-proclaimed Friend was really such a one or not. Unsurprisingly, Tustari claimed to be himself the *qutb* or "axis" of the universe who stood at the center of this cosmic hierarchy of Friends whom God had selected in pre-eternity.

Although Tustari's commentary of the Quran abounds in extraordinary visions and insights, his teachings also therefore provided an ideological resource for the highly authoritarian trends which we will see flowering as the Sufis sought greater influence in centuries to come. In his own lifetime, Tustari's claims to Friendship won him as much approbation as support and he seems to have been forced to flee at least one city as a consequence. While he was able to gain a considerable following in Basra, after his death his followers moved in different directions, some founding what became seen as a distinct theological rather than Sufi school called the Salimiyya and others moving to Baghdad to join the circle gathering around the next Sufi we must examine, Junayd the "sober." What we are seeing is therefore not quite yet a coherent Sufi movement, but rather a series of distinct but intersecting circles gathered around individual masters. As we see with the followers of Tustari and Junayd, in Iraq at least these circles had a fair degree of social interaction with one another and it was this interaction which in the course of the ninth and tenth centuries would gradually create a more coherent Sufi movement sharing common ideas and practices.

By around 900, we have certainly moved beyond a position where Sufi was merely a nickname for an assorted medley of seekers, and many of the foundational ideas, terms and practices that would constitute a proprietary Sufi method were being formulated. But, as we will see with the next few figures we examine, the debates and disagreements were such that we are still short of a coherent movement, still less a tradition.

Junayd of Baghdad (d.910)

Unlike Kharraz and Tustari, who traveled widely despite spending the most active parts of their careers in Iraq, Junayd was very much a long-term citizen of the imperial capital at Baghdad.[46] Junayd's nickname of al-Khazzaz tells us that he earned his living as a silk merchant, pointing again to an urban occupational background. Even more than the other figures we have discussed, his early training in the emerging discipline of Islamic jurisprudence placed him squarely in the intellectual mainstream of the Baghdad of his day. These scholarly credentials are clear from both the number of treatises he wrote – over thirty according to one account – and the familiarity with wider discussions they reveal. Like Kharraz and Tustari, Junayd sought to ground his teaching in (indeed, to draw it from) the very same sources being used to create the legal restraints of Shari'a, namely the Quran and Hadith.[47] Just as scores of later Sufis writing in his wake would emphasize the harmony between the internal/esoteric (*batini*) and external/exoteric (*zahiri*) dimensions of existence, so Junayd's teachings on the nature of the soul were a counterpart rather than an alternative to the rules of Shari'a. For Junayd, the "Path" or method was no more and no less than the full realization of the basic principle of Islam as announced in the call to prayer: "there is no god other than God." Known as the doctrine of *tawhid* – the "oneness" or unity of God as opposed to the "threeness" or trinity of the Christians – for Junayd this most fundamental of Muslim principles laid the basis for all Sufi endeavor. It was not sufficient to merely attest to God's unity with the tongue, or accept it with the intellect, but to live or experience it as a reality.[48] Drawing on the same Quranic notion of a covenant being discussed by Tustari in Basra at the same time, Junayd claimed that human souls longed for this original state of being in which their souls were in a state of pre-individual existence in God.[49] Like Tustari again, he taught that the way to recover this original state was through a process of dying to oneself through the *fana* or destruction of the lower individual soul. Speaking of his own experience of such self-destruction, Junayd described how "an overpowering vision and a refulgent brilliance took possession of me and induced in me a state of *fana*, creating me anew in the same way He had created me when I had no existence."[50]

Developing another key concept which would later be harmonized with the model we have already seen of the way being marked by a series of "places" along the Path towards *fana*, Junayd explained that the seeker would pass through a transient but progressive series of "states" (*ahwal*, sing. *hal*). But in the doctrine that would mark Junayd out for future generations of Sufis, he also taught that while states of ecstasy and bewilderment were part of the Path, the seeker who experienced "surviving" (*baqa*) after having destroyed himself in God did not remain in that transient state of excitement but passed beyond it into a higher and abiding condition of "sobriety" (*sahw*).[51] The highest state of communion with God was therefore accompanied by conformist outward behavior that ordinary Muslims could clearly distinguish from the raving ecstasies or austerities of those less close to the Almighty.

Like other Sufis of his day, Junayd was formulating his teachings in a context of heated debates over proper belief and conduct. At one extreme of the debate was the Baghdad-based preacher Ahmad Ghulam Khalil (d.888), who in 877 is reported to have brought formal charges of heresy (*zandaqa*) against over seventy followers of the Sufis such as Junayd, so providing major disincentives against teachings that appeared to contradict the words of the Quran or particularly the Hadith.[52] The prominence in Junayd's teaching of the doctrine of sobriety – of lawfulness, self-control and restraint – was at least partly also a response to popular stories about and sayings of ecstatic seekers of God that were reaching Baghdad from the provinces of the empire. Many of these rumors of mysterious and charismatic spiritual giants concerned a certain Abu Yazid (d.875) from Bistam, in the distant Iranian countryside far to the east of Baghdad. We know relatively little about Abu Yazid (also known as Bayezid), though many of the "ecstatic utterances" (*shath*) he purportedly exclaimed while in rapturous intimacy with God were collected by his followers, passed on to travelers on the trade route through Bistam, and eventually discussed in the refined religious circles of Baghdad. In a geographical no less than spiritual sense, to the urbane intellectuals of the capital Abu Yazid had the attraction of a frontiersman, unrestrained by the conventions of the city and unafraid to voice the excitement of his discoveries. The kinds of statement he was said to have made – "Praise Me! [as though I were God]" and "I shed my self as a snake sheds its skin and then saw that I was He!" – formed pithy summaries of what the more prolix and cautious Sufis of Baghdad were almost saying in their theory of destruction and remaining in God, but were avoiding saying so bluntly.

The story that Abu Yazid was taught by a man called al-Sindi ("from Sind," in North India) would lead one modern scholar to argue not only that Abu Yazid's teachings was "monism" derived from Indian sources – a "Vedanta in Muslim dress" – but also that this Indian influence permanently changed the direction of Sufi thought.[53] In all likelihood, the Baghdad Sufis were very much men of their own minds and (in the case of Junayd especially) realized that the wild man of Bistam was hardly going to help them in their cause among the urban intelligentsia. If the idea popularized by later Sufis that Abu Yazid and Junayd founded two distinct schools of "drunkenness" and "sobriety" was certainly an over-statement, then we can at least see differences emerging by way of doctrinal trends and modes of behavior.[54]

Here again we are reminded that the Sufis were not merely mystics basing their teachings on sublime experience, but also public intellectuals participating in the leading debates of the day. The written records the early Sufis bequeathed us were discursive productions shaped by their participation in spoken debates and their borrowings from written authorities. But they were also the result of attempts to map the words and ideas of that discourse onto individual experiences in a way that made sense of that experience but (for conformists like Junayd at least) refused to allow private experience to shake the legal and political foundations of collective social life. In line with this sensible middle ground, Junayd was cautious in his discussion of God's Friends. As with Tustari, for Junayd such an elite did exist and occupied a position of authority with regard to the ordinary mass of Muslims. But for Junayd the very sobriety of the state of "remaining" in God rendered the accomplished Sufi externally identical to the teacher of Shari'a:

> He is one of the experts in religious law, and in what is permitted and what is forbidden and one of the best informed in all matters pertaining to Islam. He walks in the footsteps of the prophets and follows the way of life of the saints and righteous, he does not stray after those innovations (which, though

contrary to tradition, have gained a measure of currency in Islam), nor does he refrain from accepting the agreed tradition of Islam... He holds the view that authority must be obeyed, nor will he separate himself from his community. He holds that rebellion against authority is an action of the ignorant...[55]

This conformist stance is not to say that Junayd's career was without its controversies. But rather than seeing the early Sufis' development of their method as intrinsically in opposition to the proponents of law and "orthodoxy," we should recognize that few positions on anything were beyond debate (even the methods by which Shari'a was being constituted were highly variant). In a context in which proponents of the idea of the Muslim community being held together by allegiance to the Prophetic Example or *sunna* had developed the notion of the collective consensus (*ijma'*) of the learned as a mode of semi-egalitarian authority, Junayd tried to bring the notion of authority deriving from a special relationship with God held by an elite of Friends into harmony with an emergent Sunni mainstream. By behaving exactly like any other member of the scholarly *'ulama* class, and keeping consensus with their opinions, the Friend of God would only advise people to reaffirm and deepen their ordinary social and legal commitments. Far from being introspective and self-absorbed mystics, Sufis like Junayd were active participants in the creation of a Muslim society and as such participated in vigorous public debates on the nexus between authority and responsibility, behavior and fulfillment. But as we will see as we turn to some of Junayd's less sober contemporaries, the experience of feeling intimate with God and the sense of election it imbued was not in all cases so easily socialized.

Hallaj of Baghdad (d.922)

The most famous demonstration of this emerging tension between person-ally-inspired and collectively-consulted authority is seen in the life of Husayn ibn Mansur, known as al-Hallaj ("the wool sifter").[56] Born in southern Iran in around 857, Hallaj became a follower of Tustari and then of another Sufi, 'Amr ibn Uthman al-Makki, in Basra, before entering Junayd's circle in Baghdad. He seems to have been unable to commit to the discipleship of any one master, perhaps through ambitions to attract a following in his own right. Even by the standards of his most mobile contemporaries, Hallaj traveled extremely widely, wandering not only through Iran but also venturing into the far reaches of Muslim expansion in Central Asia and India. On these journeys he disappears from the limited historical horizons of documentation and he is chiefly known to us through his presence in the literary and intellectual capital of the Islamic world at this time, where he openly courted controversy for his opinions in Baghdad and was finally executed there in 922. Like other victims of untimely deaths, his execution was the crowning of a career, for it ensured his immortalization by scores of Sufi biographers and poets in later centuries for whom he would be remembered as the great martyr for speaking the truth of divine love.

In prosaic fact, the picture was certainly more complicated and probably less attractive. While ecstatic love of God was part of Hallaj's teachings and is evidenced in the moving poetry which he wrote, his short surviving prose writings suggest a more intellectual aptitude for the ideas being developed by his erstwhile teacher, Tustari. As we have seen, in the Sufi circles of Baghdad and Basra that he frequented, the idea of being destroyed in God enjoyed wide circulation, as did the notion that God had a special relationship with an elite known as the Friends or *awliya*. We have already seen how the doctrine of Friendship created a special model of authority by portraying the Friend as being in such close proximity to God as to have knowledge that no amount of memorizing of the Quran or Hadith could bring. But in terms of the social exploitation of the doctrine, thus far self-proclaimed Friends like Tustari had only used their elect status to gather around themselves small circles of like-minded seekers. With Hallaj, we start to see the playing out of the full social potential of the doctrine through the amplification of the claim to Friendship by its outward demonstration through the performance of miracles (*karamat*). When it came to winning larger number of disciples, such performative proofs of special status had great potential and Hallaj's public performance of such miracles achieved precisely that. Hallaj was not the first Muslim believed to have the ability to work miracles and there already existed compilations of the tales of the wonders worked by earlier Friends and Prophets. But Hallaj was the earliest major Sufi to bring this skill into his repertoire and, like a Marxist moving from the seminar room to the rally platform, in gathering so many followers in the process he radically shifted what was at stake in the Sufis' teachings.

Unsurprisingly, the crowds of followers whom Hallaj attracted brought him to the attention of the state authorities in Baghdad, whose own by now rather tired claims to legitimacy were being whittled away with each generation of new ideas. While the reasons for Hallaj's arrest and eventual execution involved an explosive blend of court politics and intelligentsia rivalry, the gravity of the situation was worsened by his own outrageous statements, some of which survive in his own writings and others in quotations in the works of others. Here, Hallaj went beyond the earlier discussion of the ego as being destroyed in God to claim that, since there was now nothing left of Mansur al-Hallaj, it was God who spoke through his lips. The ego of Hallaj had passed away to leave only the spirit of God inhabiting his body as it walked among the streets and peoples of Baghdad. In his most infamous claim – more important through the later belief that he did say it than through any absolute evidence that he did – Hallaj used one of the ninety-nine names of Allah to declare "I am the Real (*ana al-haqq*)," in effect declaring himself identical with God. Even more extraordinarily, he expressed sympathy for the plight of Satan, whose refusal to bow down before Adam in Islamic legend Hallaj saw as an act of heroic loyalty to God by Adam's refusal to swerve from his absorption in worshiping the divine unity.[57] Even so, the official reason for Hallaj's execution lay in his purported teaching that the pilgrimage to Mecca that was incumbent on all Muslims able to perform it could just as well be performed symbolically around a table at home. By implication, Hallaj was arguing that the symbolic or esoteric dimension of religious duties was more important than their actual or exoteric performance. It was a principle which if generalized threatened the entire fabric of obligations and duties on which Islamic society had been developing over three previous centuries. With increasing numbers of followers, there was indeed now much at stake in the opinions of the Sufis.

Iraqi Sufism by the Late Tenth Century

As the tenth century wore on, more and more teachers called Sufis were attracting followers in Iraq and writing works in which they elaborated on the terms and concepts we have seen developing in the writings of Kharraz and others. As with the teachers we have already examined, in showing how the seeker could come close to God, partake in his knowledge and in some cases in his power, these were doctrines with immense socio-political potential, even if this potential had as yet been scarcely realized except in the negative sense with the execution of Hallaj. A case in point is a biographically obscure Iraqi called Muhammad ibn 'Abd al-Jabbar, known as al-Niffari ("from Nippur") who died after 977.

Building on the Sufi tendency we have already seen emerging to elaborate the many "places" (*maqamat*) or "states" (*ahwal*) on the Path, in his *Kitab al-Mawaqif* ("Book of Staying Places"). Niffari developed the idea that the Path also contained "staying places" (*mawaqif*, sing. *waqfa*), as it were, stopover points, which though they might be bypassed by some travelers were actually places in which God revealed different aspects of himself to the patiently thoroughgoing seeker. Implying that other seekers had missed these "staying places," Niffari went on to describe in astonishing detail the revelations which God gave to him at each of no fewer than seventy-seven places, beginning his discussion of each of these *waqfas* with the frank claim that "God stayed me and said to me...."[58] For Niffari, the visionary experience acquired in these staying places was not only superior to book learning, but also to the more hastily acquired direct knowledge that other Sufis claimed to have of God. In these increasingly elaborate expositions of the nature and scale of the journey towards God, it would not be too wide of the mark to see a kind of spiritual one-upmanship at work. And for Niffari, the mastery of the staying places on that journey held great reward, since at them the seeker could even acquire God's creative power to bring things into existence. Even in this early period, the power of miracles – the power to accomplish things that even the mightiest of men could not – was never far away from the Sufis' concerns.

Before we move on to explore the other main geographical region in which Sufism developed, it is worth ourselves staying a moment to look over the developments that had taken place in Iraq by the end of the tenth century. Firstly, we have seen a development from a period in which *sufi* or "wool-wearer" was merely a nickname for a vague assortment of seekers to a period in which the term was used to denote a distinct method of acquiring knowledge which was now termed *tasawwuf*, which we can fairly translate as Sufism. In other words, the terms have acquired a more substantive and specific meaning: where there were previously only people called Sufis, now there is a practical and theoretical method being called Sufism. The factors enabling this development were several, some of them visible at the distance of centuries, others more obscure. The most visible factor was the production of texts in which the Sufis developed a conceptual vocabulary that not only explained their ideas and made sense of their own and their disciples' experiences, but also rooted them in the legitimate sources of knowledge by way of the Quran and Hadith. By around the year 1000, the types of Sufi texts being produced ranged from commentaries on the Quran to treatises on individual topics, emotive poetry, admonishing letters, suggestive aphorisms and accounts of visionary experiences. Often extremely complex and allusive, these were in many cases the creations of an intelligentsia writing for its own members. In a period in which legal and moral authority over the Muslim community was being acquired by precisely those men who called themselves the *'ulama* or "learned," this social location of the new Sufi method was extremely convenient.

This is not to say that every early follower of the Sufis was a member of this urban intelligentsia, for many of the verses, aphorisms and stories which appeared in writing easily circulated among the illiterate through memory and speech. But it is to say that without the support of this increasingly influential intelligentsia, the survival of Sufism beyond this period and its expansion beyond Iraq would have been far more difficult. The writings which the Iraqi literati produced were themselves agents in the process by which Sufism expanded and survived, not only transmitting ideas through time (where with each passing generation they grew in stature as the products of a spiritually gilded age), but also transmitting them through space (where they publicized the fashionable new method of Baghdad in the provinces of its empire). As much as Sufism can be seen as a form of "mysticism" in which experience was always paramount, in terms of accounting for its success we must therefore recognize that it was also very much a matter of writing. And for the historian at least, the latter is the more important, because when transient experience passes away, writing survives: *littera scripta manet.*

While we should not ignore the importance of individual spiritual experiences and acts of creative interpretation, the "discursive" processes of writing were extremely important, because in basing Sufi doctrine on terminology and texts that were recognizable to other Muslims of the period, the early Sufis ensured that their teachings were both respectable enough and intelligible enough to survive in future generations and to be related to wider branches of recognized knowledge. When experience entered the equation, it was not allowed to remain pure and ineffable, but had to be interpreted and understood through the special vocabulary that the early Sufis created in their writings from the resource of the Quran as a revelation in words.[59] The sheer importance of this early development of a powerful because legitimate vocabulary for doctrine and practice would later be seen in the repeated "diglossic" process by which this original Arabic vocabulary was borrowed and maintained in the many other languages in which later generations of Sufis would speak and write. Whether taken as entire books or as their constitutive elements by way of a legitimate and wide-ranging terminology, the textual output of the early Sufis of Baghdad created one of the crucial resources with which later generations of Sufis would construct a "tradition," which is to say a body of beliefs and practices that draws legitimacy and prestige from its relationship to a venerated past. If texts were one resource, then the personae of their producers were another, and as we will see later, in their own writings later generations of Sufis would use the lives of the early Sufis of Iraq to create genealogical biography chains by which any Sufi of later generations could claim to be the heir to one or more of the masters of Baghdad and Basra. The Sufis of ninth century Iraq were therefore not only important for what they did in their own times, but also as resources for the creation of a tradition, and so for what they bequeathed to future times by way of a corpus of texts and a corporation of ancestors.

By looking in the opposite temporal direction and placing the Sufis of this period in relation to the ascetic movement of the previous century, we can also recognize what was along with their search for a legitimate mode of expression perhaps their most important other achievement: the socialization of asceticism. By presenting a convincing alternative path to God from the punishment of the flesh and the renunciation of social life, marriage and ownership of property preached by the ascetic *zuhhad*, the Sufis created a religious product with a far greater chance of replication and survival. This was not only the case because of the general truisms that any society can only support a limited number of economically unproductive renunciants and that the ascetic life will only ever have a limited social appeal. It was also the case for the more culturally specific reason that in a period and place in which the Prophetic Example or *sunna* of Muhammad was becoming the touchstone of social and moral theory, the life of the solitary ascetic began to look less and less legitimately Islamic. Muhammad had been a family man, a leader of his community and a successful merchant, and none of this had prevented him from being chosen as the Prophet of God. In the course of future centuries, the legacy of this early Sufi socialization process – lending Sufis the ability to echo the Prophet by claiming "Friendship" with God while maintaining the opportunities lent by property-owning, social networking and the production of family heirs – was to prove crucial in their ability to embed themselves in almost every corner of the social, economic and political life of their communities.

As yet, we know little of the organizational format of the Sufis of the early period, who seem to have gathered in small circles around their masters in a manner that reflected the gatherings of other Muslim scholars of the time.[60] It is only when we turn towards developments further east that we see evidence for the shift from a Sufi "movement" of like-minded masters and disciples that had developed by 1000 in Iraq to a Sufi "organization" that possessed distinct corporate rules and architectural structures of its own.

Eastern alternatives? Competition and Incorporation in Khurasan

The Sufis were by no means the only Muslims formulating esoteric and mystical models of knowledge in Iraq. But what we have seen is the beginning of their gradual and calculated ascendance there as they replaced a fringe ascetic movement (of authority via bodily mastery) and aligned themselves with a mainstream scholarly movement (of authority via textual mastery). When we turn to the eastern region of the 'Abbasid Empire known as Khurasan ("the land where the sun rises"), we see what were at first a set of parallel and quite discrete religious developments gradually coming into contact with the Sufi movement emanating from the imperial center in Iraq and eventually being absorbed by it. It is important that we make a distinction between these different movements and recognize the processes of competition and collusion by which they interacted, since otherwise we will fall into the trap which led many earlier accounts to portray Sufism as appearing at more or less the same time in a wide range of geographically disparate places. In line with other recent accounts of early Sufism, what is painted here is broadly speaking a picture of the diffusion – or better, the circulation – of religious ideas, practices and (it is here that Khurasan made its own contribution) institutions.

Encompassing regions which we would now consider as eastern Iran, Afghanistan and the Central Asian republics, Khurasan had fallen into Muslim hands during the early decades of conquest that followed the death of Muhammad in 632. Unlike many of the western regions of the Islamic 'Abbasid Empire, which had previously been under Byzantine Christian rule, Khurasan had been subject to Persian Zoroastrian rule and also contained pockets of Buddhist and Christian presence. As in the west, the process of conversion and resettlement was lengthy, and despite the arrival of a new ruling elite of Muslims, in the countryside many of the old Persian-speaking landowners still maintained their influence. With the crumbling of Baghdad's centralizing power in the tenth century, this culturally Persian influence was felt in some of the cities as well.[61] This did not prevent the development in Khurasan's rich mercantile and agricultural oasis towns of properly Islamic modes of social and intellectual life and the survival of any kind of unadulterated pure Persian culture belongs to the imaginary of modern nationalism. But if the towns and country of Khurasan were far from the imperial hothouse of religious production and disputation in Baghdad, then with the sowing of Islamic ideas in their distinctive cultural soil they were nonetheless capable of producing their own new kinds of Muslim movements. The question is: what relationship did these Khurasani movements have with the Sufi movement that was emerging in Iraq and how did they interact with it?

Although later biographical texts from the twelfth century onwards absorbed many early Khurasani masters into the Sufi tradition that they were attempting to construct for their region, modern research has shown that in the tenth century hardly anyone was being called a "Sufi" in Khurasan itself and the few who were had either migrated from or traveled through Iraq.[62] If the early Khurasani renunciants of the ninth century did not call themselves Sufis, then given their distance from the westerly places in which this nickname circulated it is not at all surprising, particularly if we accept the proposition that the term *sufi* was originally used as part of the vocabulary of Iraqi Christians.[63] In their anti-social tendencies, the two most important of the early Khurasani movements resembled (though were not connected to) the ascetic *zuhhad* of Syria and Iraq. Called Karramiyya after the name of their founder Abu 'Abdullah Muhammad ibn Karram (d.874), the members of the first movement were often taunted on account of their rigorous asceticism by their contemporaries with the nickname "mortifiers" (*mutaqashshifa*).[64] Their doctrines combined a literalistic reading of scripture with the claim that work and material gain were obstacles on the path to God. The resulting blend of an appealingly anthropomorphic picture of God and a leadership as materially poor as the most wretched of their peasant followers won them a large popular support base throughout Khurasan. Although like the scholars of Iraq, the leaders of the Karramiyya possessed sufficient scriptural learning to root their doctrines in the Quran and in some cases engage with theological discussions emanating from Baghdad, the Karramiyya was ultimately a movement of the lower classes, who included Muslim converts from the local population whose entry to the Islamic community or *umma* was beginning to challenge the earlier social structure of Islam in Khurasan as the religion of an immigrant imperial elite.[65] From the ninth century through the twelfth century, the Karramiyya remained an important force in the social and religious life of Khurasan. This longevity and influence was enabled by their development of large monastic communities funded by land grants whose residents were thereby able to follow Ibn Karram's command to avoid work and devote oneself exclusively to asceticism and prayer. With residents sometimes numbering as many as four thousand, these monasteries were clearly impressive sites. Although by the twelfth century the days of the Karramiyya would finally be eclipsed with the rising star of the Sufis in Khurasan, the model and even the names of the institutional innovations they interchangeably called *khanaqahs* (from the Persian) and *madrasas* (from the Arabic) would prove to be extremely influential in the Sufis' own development of institutions.[66]

The second rival movement we must reckon with in Khurasan was that of the Malamatiyya or "Blame Seekers" which developed around the city of Nishapur in the circle of Hamdun al-Qassar (d.885).[67] As well as being opposed to the Sufis emanating from Baghdad, the Malamatiyya were on more local ground primarily opposed to the Karramiyya whom (as with the Sufis' opinion of the *zuhhad* in Iraq) they regarded as showy ascetic publicists whose popular acclaim was an obstacle to true piety. By contrast, the Malamatiyya sought to bring themselves closer to God by destroying their egos through the avoidance of any public display of piety likely to attract pride-inducing praise and by the subjecting of their egos to self-humiliating recollections of their own "blameworthiness." Where the Karramiyya seem to have appealed to the lowest sections of society, the Malamatiyya seem to have been popular among the urban artisanal classes, for whom the ability to live piously without giving up either work or social life provided an attractive prospect.[68] The Malamatiyya certainly shared many terms and ideas with the Sufis of Baghdad of the same period, such as avoiding "showiness" (*riya*) and controlling the lower self (*nafs*), but even amid these similarities there were differences. Unlike the Sufis, the Malamatis held that the *nafs* could not be destroyed and claimed that any public expression of spiritual achievement immediately nullified it. If as a result they were skeptical about the claims of Sufis destroying their lower selves and then declaring themselves intimate Friends of God, the Malamatis' avoidance of public piety also left them unwilling to participate in the public moralizing and "commanding the good" that connected the Sufis to the emerging Sunni mainstream.

The third of the Khurasani movements to distinguish from the early Iraqi Sufis was that of the Hakims or "Wise Men" of the oasis towns around Balkh and Tirmiz around what are now the northern borders of Afghanistan. Given the success with which the Sufis subsequently incorporated the leading Hakims, the claims that the Hakims were straightforwardly Sufis rather than a distinct local movement have usually been taken at face value by modern scholars. But there is reason to classify the group of men known by the title Hakim as a separate movement in its own right, albeit one with less impact and reach than those of the Karramis and Malamatis.[69] While broadly speaking the former were peasant and artisanal movements, from what little we know the Hakims seem to have been of a more "aristocratic" character, their leaders being not only hereditary landholders but self-declared Friends of God as well. Indeed, only the leaders were considered Hakims, which was clearly a title of authority rather than fellowship. For our purposes, the most interesting figure among them was Abu 'Abdullah Muhammad, known as al-Hakim al-Tirmidhi ("the Wise Man of Tirmiz"), who died sometime between 905 and 910.[70] One of the reasons Tirmidhi looms so large in later memory was for the sheer fact that he was able to stamp his own personality on history through writing an autobiography, something not only considered poor form among premodern Muslims but also in striking contrast to the self-abasing strictures of his Malamati and Karrami contemporaries.[71] Like the leading Sufis of Baghdad, Tirmidhi had memorized the Quran early in life, mastered the study of Islamic jurisprudence and Hadith, and also visited Basra and Mecca. Like the *Kitab al-Mawaqif* of Niffari in Iraq a generation later, Tirmidhi's Arabic autobiography depicts his personal visionary experiences in fascinating detail, beginning with a dream of the Prophet Muhammad leading him through his home city.[72]

What is most interesting about the autobiography is the way it describes dreams in which Tirmidhi's wife and friends were shown the lofty spiritual rank he himself had attained, such that the dreams of others were presented as a form of third-party evidence for Tirmidhi's status as a Friend, a device which may have been a response to the many detractors we know he had in his home town. Indeed, in providing foundational resources for the subsequent development of Sufi tradition, Tirmidhi was most important for his elaboration of the formal theory of *wilaya* or "Friendship with God," that is, the Muslim doctrine of sainthood.

Displaying the same taxonomic logic as that seen in the Baghdad Sufis' treatment of the places and states on the Path, in his *Kitab Sirat al-Awliya* ("Biography of the Friends") Tirmidhi set out to classify and rank the different classes and kinds of God's Friends. He introduced the idea that just as there was a Seal of the Prophets (*khatm al-anbiya*, a rank occupied by Muhammad), so was there a Seal of the Friends (*khatm al-awliya*, a rank apparently occupied by Tirmidhi himself). While he conceded that the Prophets were still superior to the Friends, in practice the Friends not only possessed most of the Prophets' supernatural attributes but, since prophecy had ended with Muhammad as the Seal of the Prophets, humankind had now in any case to be guided by the living Friends. Yet the Friends were not only on earth to help their fellow men, they were also there to discipline and punish them: the Friend "is the place of God's indulgent glance, as well as God's scourge, amongst His creatures."[73] In the writings of Tirmidhi, we see how claims of visionary experience were not simply testaments of personal salvation but evidence on which to build a starkly hierarchical model of humanity and its rightful leaders.

The Karrami, Malamati and Hakim movements developed sufficiently far away from Iraq as to survive on their own terms well into the eleventh century before being incorporated and effectively suppressed as the Sufi movement spread eastward through its establishment of outposts and pro-selytizers in Khurasan. To examine how this process of competition and incorporation occurred, we must turn to another key time and place in Sufi history: the city of Nishapur between the tenth and twelfth centuries.[74] Nishapur was a major trade and oasis city in what is now the northeastern corner of Iran and, with the impoverishment of Baghdad after its fall to the Shi'i Buyyid dynasty in 945, became increasingly important as a center of moral and religious production. Like the imperial capital in its heyday, the great desert emporium was a marketplace in which the producers and pliers of different models of Islam found themselves in keen competition with one another.

One broad process we can arguably see at work here is the replacement of what we might term frontier expansion movements by interior consolidation movements. As we have seen, one of the most important features of the Karramiyya was its role in the conversion of non-Muslim subject peoples known as *dhimmis*. Growing historical understanding of the eastern marches of Khurasan in the ninth and tenth centuries has also pointed to the role of frontier warrior-teachers who combined war (*jihad*) and preaching (*da'wa*) to expand Islamic rule across the Central Asian steppe lands then being occupied by nomadic Turks.[75] In some ways, this picture of the eastern frontier reflects what we have already seen in the west, where at least some of the ascetic *zuhhad* settled in the troubled frontiers with Byzantine territory. As the external frontier moved further east and the internal social frontier evaporated at the tipping point of conversion and acculturation to Islam, space was opened in the social fabric for new consolidation movements concerned with the deeper Islamization of society through a "permanent settlement" emphasizing law, economic production and maintainable social life for which the renunciant Karramis and the holy warriors of the frontier were no longer appropriate. While the precise contours of these larger rural processes remain unclear, the fuller character of the urban sources means that we have a clearer picture of developments taking place in cities like Nishapur. Here we are looking at two separate but interwoven processes, one discursive and one institutional. Since we have already discussed the ways in which texts and debates helped the Sufis rise to prominence in Iraq, we will turn first to the discursive question of how their books and discussions helped them similarly expand in Khurasan.

As we have seen, many of the texts, terminology and even techniques being used by the "indigenous" movements in Khurasan had much in common with those being employed by the Sufis of Iraq. The Quran and the Hadith were common resources; the language of "Friends" and the "Path" was in widespread use; and formal prayer, the chanted "remembrance of God" (*dhikr*) and for some "listening to music" (*sama'*) were shared practices. The point is not that all of the indigenous Khurasani seekers shared all of these commonalities, nor even that when they did that they agreed on the precise meaning of a common term or the proper performance of a common technique. What was important was rather the mutual intelligibility of the various methods on offer, an intelligibility that enabled productive discussions and interactions between members – and perhaps more importantly between the "swing voters" of potential members – of the different movements. At a more basic level, this intelligibility was enabled by the existence of shared communication tools, including the medium of Arabic as a *lingua franca* of learned exchange and the availability of paper to reproduce books and even write letters. Despite the vast distance between Iraq and many of the cities of Khurasan (the distance from Baghdad to Nishapur is almost as far as from London to Warsaw), these communication tools enabled the learned from these very different regions to share ideas vicariously through writing. As with the role of Latin in medieval Christendom, we must be careful not to take these common communicative tools for granted: when the Sufis later sought to expand in other geographical and social contexts, they would need to acquire other cultural tools such as vernacular languages and popular songs. But in the present context of interaction between the townsmen of Khurasan and Iraq, we are looking at a process by which Iraqi Sufis traveled or dispatched writings east and Khurasani "swing voters" traveled west (typically *en route* to Mecca) and returned home, in both cases carrying what we might now term portable communication devices in their baggage by way of the books they bought (or more likely copied) on their travels.[76]

If this helps us answer the question of how the proprietary Sufi method interacted with its indigenous alternatives in Khurasan, the question of why it was ultimately preferred over them is more difficult to answer. This is not least the case because we are ultimately dealing with many individual acts of choice which, though contributing to an overall pattern of preference, are in their specific rationales long lost in time. Since individual motivations are notoriously difficult for the historian to assess, the evidence presented for the incorporation and replacement of the Malamatis and Karramis is one of more general antagonisms and alliances. In perhaps the most convincing overall theory, the Sufis in Nishapur and its surrounding cities are seen as having attached themselves to the Shafi'i school of Islamic law, which lent them "an institutional framework in which mysticism could be taught and practiced."[77] But before moving on to the "hard" dimensions of this institutionalization, let us first address its "softer" or discursive dimensions.

As we have seen, from the period of their earliest emergence in Baghdad, the Sufis were very much part of the circles of Quranic, Hadith and even legal expertise. For this reason, we must be wary of older interpretations which saw the developments we are now examining as a process which saw the Sufis finally entering the "mainstream," since this interpretation depends on the double fallacy that the Sufis were outside the "mainstream" to begin with and that there even was any such single "mainstream" that flowed evenly through different places during the preceding centuries.[78] If neither Shafi'i law in particular nor Islamic law in general presented a long-term "mainstream" into which the Sufis were baptized for the first time in Nishapur, what legal learning did represent was a more efficient method of acquiring and making practical use of the textual knowledge with which Sufi and non-Sufi specialists had long been concerned, an efficiency which caused Sufis as well as Malamatis to adhere themselves to its practices. The nature of this efficiency lay in the way in which Shafi'i legal scholarship offered scholars a "diploma" or *ijaza* system in which their authority was socially testified by written certification from their teachers and a clear legal methodology to employ in place of memorizing vast numbers of Hadith and constructing idiosyncratic personal methods for making sense of them.[79] This new efficiency, which not only made the practice of law easier but also ensured that the rulings of legal decision-makers were taken seriously, was the product of system-wide prestige rather than personal reputation and drew various individuals and parties to adopt the Shafi'i method, with the result that both Sufis and Malamatis converged in adhering to the Shafi'i law school and the social settings of its schools and study circles.

Having attracted these parties, Shafi'ism provided them with further discursive tools. One of these was the model of knowledge transmission through master-to-disciple lineages that the Sufis called the *silsila* ("chain"), which we will discuss further below. This in turn, encouraged disciples to model their behavior on that of their masters in a way that echoed the notion of the Prophetic Example or *sunna*.[80] The mastery of Hadith also became increasingly important as Shafi'i Sufis of the period such as Sulami (d.1021) wielded this expert knowledge to create compilations and interpretations of Prophetic traditions in support of the Sufi rather than the Karrami method.[81] This is by no means to say that all Sufis in either Khurasan or elsewhere from this point became followers of the Shafi'i law school. But in and around Nishapur through the tenth and eleventh centuries, the Sufi infiltration of an ascendant local establishment of Shafi'i law-makers helped them gain an important foothold in the region of Khurasan previously dominated by Karramis and Malamatis.

Two matters are fairly clear, whatever the extent to which they can be directly related to the expansion of the Shafi'i school in Khurasan: the Sufis of the region were overwhelmingly members of the Shafi'i school and among these Sufis there emerged a similarly efficient model of transmitting and authorizing knowledge. Ultimately it was the consequences rather than the causes of this development that were more important. For what we see emerging in and around Nishapur, and spreading from there not only around Khurasan but also westwards into Iraq and as far as Islamic Spain, was a new master–disciple relationship that would permanently transform the nature of the Sufi method and tie it to a powerful set of new social relationships. This "Nishapur model" has been described as one in which "the shaykh, by means of a pact, binds the novice to practice unquestioning obedience, to carry out every order and to reveal all his secret thoughts and inner states without exception while. . . . [t]he shaykh is not to pass over any mistake on the part of the novice and can assign him whatever punishments he wishes."[82] It seems historically crass to follow an older moralizing interpretation which contrasted a "healthy" early period in which the followers of the Sufis of Baghdad were like students attending the lectures of their professors with a "corrupt" later period of slavish adherence to superstition and master-worship. Any sharp dichotomy between a "teaching master" (*shaykh al-ta'lim*) and a "directing master" (*shaykh al-tarbiya*) is probably a simplification, though there is little doubt as to the increasing intensification of the master/disciple relationship.[83] This binding of the disciple to the master was now accompanied by a solemn vow, designated as a *bay'a* ("oath") after the formal pledges of allegiance made to Muhammad by the first Muslims. And as we will see below when we turn to the more concrete forms of this institutionalization, for many disciples the new "apprenticeship" model involved giving up their family lives for a period of the master's choosing to live in a Sufi hospice, as well as cutting their hair and donning special robes that distinguished them as Sufis.[84] In short, we are entering a period in which it becomes much more feasible to present the Sufis as a distinct corporate movement within society, who marked themselves apart from others and together among themselves by rituals of initiation, pledges of allegiance, modifications of their outward appearance and the use of an arcane idiolect. In social no less than psychological terms, by the eleventh and twelfth centuries, to become a Sufi was becoming a much more totalizing experience.

As Sufism came to mean things that it had not meant before its transformation in Khurasan, the increasingly formal requirements of both participation in a method and membership in a movement found expression in two new types of book that emerged chiefly in Khurasan during the eleventh and twelfth centuries. These were the handbook and the biographical compendium, genres which in practice overlapped a good deal. The most famous early examples of the handbook are the *Kitab al-Luma' fi'l-Tasawwuf* ("Book of Flashing Lights concerning Sufism") of Abu Nasr al-Sarraj (d.988) and the *Ta'aruf li-Madhhab Ahl al-Tasawwuf* ("Introduction to the School of the People of Sufism") of Abu Bakr al-Kalabadhi (d.990 or 995). Further examples produced in the following century included the *Risala al-Qushayriyya fi 'Ilm al-Tasawwuf* ("Qushayri's Treatise on the Science of Sufism") of Abu'l-Qasim al-Qushayri (d.1074) and the *Kashf al-Mahjub* ("Revelation of the Hidden") of 'Ali ibn 'Uthman al-Hujwiri (d. *circa* 1075).[85]

All of these handbooks were produced by writers either in or from Khurasan. Since one of the clearest common characteristics of the handbooks was the legitimacy of the Sufis emphasized through stressing the conformity of their doctrines and practices to the Quran and the Sunna, it was once commonplace to describe them as "defensive" works whose great achievement was to convince the guardians of Islamic legal orthodoxy that the Sufis were not heretics. This apologia was seen as having been all the more pressing after the execution of Hallaj in 922. However, this perspective is probably a false one, since the Sufis were themselves often the very same people as the scholars of Hadith and exponents of law. But even so, these new books and their distinctive purposes do need explaining. It is here that our contextual picture of competing movements and abundant religious productivity proves its worth, especially when combined with what was in the tenth century at least the newness and unfamiliarity of the Sufis in Khurasan compared to the more familiar and better-established Karramis and Malamatis. For with their self-justifying rhetoric, abundant explanations of doctrine and detailed expositions of practice, the handbooks are probably best seen as advertisements and manifestos intended for Muslim scholars throughout Khurasan who were unfamiliar with and even wary of the Sufi newcomers.

This proselytizing intention probably also spurred another important development in the transmission of Sufism which is seen in the last of the handbooks we have listed: the use of Persian rather than Arabic by Hujwiri in his *Kashf al-Mahjub*. We might also see the Sufis' relationship to the obscure urban artisanal movement known as *futuwwa* ("youthful chivalry") as a related strategy for the cooption of regional rivals in which textual production played a similar "rebranding" role, as seen in the case of the *Kitab al-Futuwwa* ("Book of Youthful Chivalry") written by the Nishapuri Sufi, Sulami.[86] As with the move to socialize the frontier warrior-ascetics and the world-renouncing Karramis, in the Sufis' attempt to redirect the lower class violence of the *futuwwa* and related *'ayyar* gangs of the Khurasani towns and countryside, we can see a reflection of the moralizing middle ground sought by the Baghdad Sufis that fits well with the fact that many of Khurasan's chief Sufis were members of the urban legal and property-owning establishment.[87]

The other important new type of book which emerged in this period was the biographical compendium or "book of generations" (*kitab al-tabaqat*).[88] Whether as a separate book or a section within a larger book, it was in this genre of text that we can finally see the emergence of a fully-fledged Sufi "tradition" defined by the historical self-consciousness of its members. For the "book of generations" served as a textual means by which present forms of Sufi knowledge and their practitioners gained legitimacy and prestige through being presented as heirs to a lineal tradition that reached in an unbroken "chain" through every generation to the person of Muhammad. In textual terms, what this involved was the collection (and in some cases we must assume the creation) of biographical notices on the linking figures of every "generation" or *tabaqa*. Here was a process of the invention of tradition which required that the semi-legendary ascetics and pietists of the seventh and eighth centuries be presented as Sufis and that Sufi teachings themselves be seen as the original doctrine of Muhammad as transmitted through the ages.

Unsurprisingly, the writers of these biographical compendia tended to end the chain of reception at their own masters and thence themselves, a process which, once the genre was invented, would be repeated whenever new versions of such texts were written. This repeatable procedure allowed tradition to serve as a form of transferable symbolic capital that could link the Prophet and the early Sufis of Baghdad to eleventh century Khurasan as easily as to nineteenth century India or to whichever time and place in which the biographical handler of tradition happened to be writing. But back in the eleventh and twelfth centuries, when, at the hands of Abu 'Abd al-Rahman al-Sulami in Khurasan and Abu Nu'aym al-Isfahani (d.1038) in central Iran, the earliest extant Sufi biographical compendia were written, the "book of generations" performed two main operations. First, in a consequence of the Sufis' familiarity with the techniques of scriptural learning, it borrowed from Hadith scholarship the method (or rhetoric) by which authentic knowledge of Muhammad's words was verified by means of a chain (*sanad*) of transmitters linked back to the Prophet himself. This was a chain which the Sufis replicated in the chains of transmission they used to authenticate the words of their predecessors and in their concept of the chain of initiatic descent (*silsila*). Second, the "book of generations" genre performed a back-projection into the venerable past of the more recent development of master–disciple bonds of allegiance and initiation. Through creating biographical chains which connected the Sufis of later times and distant places with men considered as their pious ancestors, the biographical compendium afforded the Sufis the comfort that their beliefs and practices were those recommended by none other than the Prophet himself. And between Muhammad in Mecca and men like Sulami in Nishapur, there stood the likes of Junayd in Baghdad a few generations earlier, whose remembered lives and books of advice now served as resources in the construction of a Sufi tradition.[89]

In this way too, writing in a Khurasan in which the Malamatis were still much respected, even fond local memories of the Malamati "blame seekers" could be incorporated into this remembered past in which competition between distinct movements was glossed over. As a result, Malamati masters were inserted into the lineages of the Sufis and their distinct history was elided as the Malamatis became textually remembered as only a sub-group of the Sufis.[90] Even when the biographical texts were not wholly read, Sufis committed to heart the bare structure of their chains of knowledge and verification that in turn became seen as charismatic wires in which not only conscious knowledge was transmitted but also the mysterious blessing power of *baraka* seen as literally handed down from the Prophet through each generation's initiatic handshake in a Sufi form of apostolic succession. Through these discursive means, the backward creation of an at least partially imagined tradition allowed for the forward creation of much more tangible forms of tradition by way of the lineage-creation that we will see coming into full fruition in Chapter 2 in our discussion of the Sufi brotherhoods. Associating with an ascendant legal school, teaching in novel ways, advertising ideas through new types of book and tying living proponents to a venerable past: these were some of the "soft" or discursive methods by which the Sufis won a following in Khurasan. They were helped in this process of expansion and incorporation by the fact that there was now a more tangible Sufi social "body" into which new followers might be incorporated by way of the *madrasa* and *khanaqah*. It is to this "hard" aspect of the Sufis' institutionalization that we must now turn.

What is interesting here is that the acquisition and development of these distinct concrete spaces for Sufi activity not only occurred in Khurasan, and not only occurred through the adaptation of institutions invented by their rival Karramis, but, in then spreading westwards, acted as an institutional counterbalance to the eastward movement of doctrines and persons a generation or two earlier. In other words, we can see a pattern of circulation at work: the Sufism that began in Iraq became something else after moving to Khurasan before then returning to its western homeland in permanently altered form. The first of these new institutions is often not considered to be a Sufi institution at all. But if the *madrasa* ("place of study") was never a uniquely Sufi institution, it was one in which Sufis have operated from its earliest appearance in the eleventh century to the present day. While the earliest *madrasas* appear to have been associated with the Karramiyya, as colleges for the study of the "Islamic sciences," *madrasas* effectively owed their expansion to the collusion of the Muslim scholarly class with the nomadic Saljuq Turks who in the middle of the eleventh century steadily conquered the cities of Khurasan before finally subduing Baghdad in 1055.[91] Needing not only a literate and legally-informed bureaucracy to manage their vast conquests, but also the sanction of legitimacy that came through the public support of Muslim social norms, the Great Saljuq dynasty (1037–1157) channeled part of their material resources into constructing a large network of such colleges right across their domains, so aligning themselves to a trans-regional religious establishment that they themselves substantially (or at least institutionally) created.[92] Although *madrasas* are usually thought of as places for the study of the Quran and Shari'a, as we have already seen in most cases the leading Sufis were themselves recognized experts in these disciplines. Once again, the designation "mystic" robs the Sufis of the multiplicity of skills that helped them succeed.

With the books and treatises it comprised by the eleventh century, "the science of Sufism" or *'ilm al-tasawwuf* could now itself be conceived as one of the religious sciences alongside the mastery of Arabic grammar, the interpretation of scripture and the techniques of jurisprudence. As such, it was able to find a place in the readings of those associated with the new *madrasa* colleges, if probably not being formally taught within them. Of course, this professorial version was very much a bookish brand of Sufism. But in being connected to a salaried official class of bureaucrats and lawyers, this respectable Sufi method of knowledge (respectable by now through its prestige as a "tradition") received the impetus that would finally enable it to incorporate or suppress its competitors.[93] The leading light of this "college Sufism" was Abu Hamid al-Ghazali (d.1111), a public intellectual whose mastery of academic politics and intellectual trends saw him elevated to the position of rector of the great Nizamiyya *madrasa* founded in 1065 in Baghdad.[94] If it is no longer necessary to see Ghazali as the man who finally brought Sufism into the "mainstream" – as if it was ever anywhere else – he does exemplify the power that came with connecting the Sufis to new government-sponsored institutions of learning. While not the most original Sufi book, his massive *Ihya 'Ulum al-Din* ("Revivification of the Religious Sciences") did perform the important function of systematizing many of the ideas developed by earlier Sufis into coherent and intelligible form. As a result, it was read for centuries after his death down to the present day. Among his many other works (which included a short influential commentary placing the Quranic Verse of Lights into line with Sufi ideas of the cosmic Light of Muhammad), the most effective in the propagation of Sufism was a shrewd Arabic autobiography in which this most famous scholar of his day described his own journey towards truth as one in which he pursued every branch of philosophy and book-learning before finally realizing that it was the Sufis who held the true keys to wisdom.[95]

While the *madrasa* was certainly an important area for Sufi influence, the most characteristically Sufi institution which would develop in Khurasan during this period was that of the *khanaqah* or residential Sufi lodge, which in the later eleventh and twelfth centuries the Saljuqs also came to patronize. Although on both the eastern and western limits of Islamic rule, frontier ascetics had previously dwelt in fortified compounds known as *ribats* (a term which in some areas would also later be adopted for Sufi lodges), for the most part the early Sufis of Iraq and Khurasan had met either in the homes of their masters or in public mosques.[96] Their gatherings, like those of the scholarly *'ulama* from whom they were not clearly distinguished, were typically conceptualized through the notion of the *halqa* or "circle" that gathered around a particular master. As we have seen, most of the early Sufis seem to have had day jobs, whether as artisans or practicing lawyers, and although some early figures (such as the *hakim* Tirmidhi) were independently wealthy, they were not wealthy because of their teachings or claims to metaphysical status. In the course of the centuries between approximately 1000 and 1300, this picture would change radically and the first step in this direction was the creation of propertied institutions specifically earmarked for Sufi activity. While we will see the fuller ramifications of these developments in Chapter 2, its foundations were already being laid well before 1100.

More through the serendipities of preservation and archaeological research than through any innate chronological primacy, probably the earliest surviving version of one of these Sufi lodges is found in the far west of the medieval Islamic world in Spain. This is the tenth century *ribat* that was excavated in the late 1980s from the coastal sand dunes at Guardamar in the modern Spanish province of Valencia, what was at the time of the *ribat*'s

Figure 1.4   The First Sufi Institutions: The Ribat at Guardamar, Spain (Image: Nile Green)

construction part of the Muslim caliphate of Cordoba.[97] Established in 944 according to the Arabic inscription on its foundation stone, the *ribat* at Guardamar comprised a communal mosque, a large reception area, lodging rooms for pilgrims, and thirteen cells for the residential hermits.[98] In a pointer to the religious exercises that were practiced there, each of the cells contained its own prayer niche, while Arabic graffiti survive from the late eleventh/early twelfth century in which pilgrims ask for prayers to be said on their behalf.[99] There is considerable debate over the extent to which such *ribats* spread across Islamic Spain and the regions of North and Saharan Africa to which Spain was connected.[100] However, Arabic sources from Muslim Spain do point to the existence of an extensive network by the eleventh century, ranging from Denia and Almeria on the eastern coast to Toledo and Badajoz in the interior and to Silves on the western fringes of the Iberian peninsula.[101] An eleventh century *ribat* has even been located in the Balearic Islands now better known for sunbathing saturnalia than ascetic retirement, as well as in Sicily.[102]

According to some scholars, the *ribats* were linked to a militaristic spirituality that was distinctive to Islamic Spain, though we have already noted the presence of such warrior ascetics on the eastern Byzantine Christian and Buddhist Central Asian frontiers of Islam.[103] It remains unclear how this frontier jihad of the *ribats* was linked to other religious currents in Islamic Spain, including Sufism. However, Arabic biographical dictionaries from Islamic Spain do frequently refer to *ribats* as places of ascetic and other pious practices and these clearly formed the day-to-day life of their residents even if they were at times involved in holy war.[104] As in the emergent *khanaqahs* of Khurasan religious literature was also being created in the *ribats*, as in the case of the renunciant poetry of Ibn Tahir al-Zahid ("the ascetic," d.988).[105] In another echo of what we will shortly see of the commercial links of the Sufi lodges emerging in Iran around the same time, it has also been argued that the coastal *ribats* of Spain and Morocco were multi-purpose institutions that served maritime traders as well as ascetics.[106] In all likelihood, what we see in the *ribats* of Islamic Spain is a regional religious formation, which though echoing the pious warriors of the eastern Byzantine frontier, was particular to the Islamic west and developed its own religious sub-culture there. This would reflect the fact that Sufism followed a different pattern in Spain (or al-Andalus) more generally, where its theorists were often attacked for straying too far from the legal literalism of the Maliki school. However, even if we cannot be sure how closely the "militaristic spirituality" of the early *ribats* was connected with the many Sufis of al-Andalus, the archae-ological excavations of the *ribat* at Guardamar do allow us to examine in detail at an architectural level what an early Muslim ascetic (and perhaps by inference a Sufi) lodge looked like. For as time passed, the *ribats* did lose their early militaristic dimensions and became predominantly places of Sufi retreat. Even if we cannot easily identify the early generations of *ribat* dwellers with the Sufis of Spain, the excavations at Guardamar remain tremendously valuable in presenting us with the earliest physical remains of a Sufi or Sufi-like collective dwelling available anywhere in the world in a period in which such purpose-built lodges were first appearing in various Muslim settings.

Turning back to the Middle East, the earliest significant individual figure whom we can connect to the development of the new expressly Sufi "lodges" lived in southern Iran, which with its closer proximity to Baghdad in the course of the tenth century had developed a brand of Sufism with much in common with the sober moralizing of Junayd.[107] This figure was Abu Ishaq al-Kazaruni (d.1035), named after the southern Iranian city of Kazarun in which he lived and whose deeds were recorded in a Persian biography composed by the son of his successor.[108] While, like other early Sufis in Iran, his teachings do seem to have laid somewhat more stress on the theme of love between humans and God, Kazaruni was also very much a moralist. For present purposes, though, he is important for having established a network of no fewer than sixty-five lodges across southern Iran. While a small residential cadre of his disciples seems to have dwelt permanently in these lodges, the buildings were primarily intended as charitable shelters for travelers and the poor. In this sense, they should be seen as a somewhat distinct development from the model of the *ribat* developing earlier in the Islamic west and of the *khanaqah* developing in Khurasan around the same time, since the latter were primarily intended as training houses for Sufis themselves in which the residents were sworn to abide by increasingly elaborate sets of house rules. Kazaruni left no such system of rules, but even so, his network of lodges does point towards an important development in the Sufis' relationship with wider society in which we see one of the first of the many reciprocal exchanges by which Sufis negotiated to mutual benefit with different social groups. Since Kazaruni's lodges lay on some of the most important trading routes of the Middle East, many of his traveling guests were merchants (here echoing Spain), who in return for his hospitality made the donations that rendered further expansion of the network possible. Within in a short time, Kazaruni lodges reached all the way from central Iran to the port cities of eastern China. With Kazaruni, the Sufis were for the first time attracting significant capital investment to themselves as Sufis, investment which in turn funded further publicity for their movement. Given Kazaruni's characteristic moralism, and his upbringing among Muslim preachers to local Zoroastrians, it seems fair to consider his network as a form of social outreach in which supper came at the price of repeating a few prayers. As the cultural frontier receded, here was another interior consolidation movement deepened the Muslim commitments of the rural inhabitants and passing traders in the deserts and mountains of Iran.

A no less interesting figure who contributed to these "hard" institutional developments was Abu Saʿid ibn Abiʾl-Khayr (d.1049), a Khurasani master who resided for some time in Nishapur but spent most of his life in the semi-rural setting of Mayhana in present-day Turkmenistan.[109] There he established a *khanaqah* which unlike those of Kazaruni held the spiritual training of its inmates as its central purpose. To this end, Abu Saʿid compiled a list of ten rules which his resident disciples were expected to obey. In themselves, the rules were not at all novel – to remain ritually clean, to follow all the formal prayers and perform additional orisons at night, to recite the Quran and perform *dhikr* daily, for example – but placed together they signaled a shift to the more formalized institution of Sufi "training" that we have already seen developing. The shift was all the more significant because with Abu Saʿid, these training rules were also attached to a residential institution. Even at this time, Abu Saʿid's was not a unique case in Khurasan. Further south in the city of Herat in what is now Afghanistan, his contemporary ʿAbdullah Ansari (d.1089) issued a similar set of rules in local Persian dialect which seem to have been intended for easy memorization by his followers.[110] However, Abu Saʿid is a more interesting figure than either Ansari or Kazaruni, since he was not only a wealthy man (which against the Khurasani background of figures like Tirmidhi was not in itself unique) but one who saw no contradiction in flaunting that wealth while remaining a Sufi. For Abu Saʿid, the poverty (*faqr*) that previous Sufis had made much of was an inward and symbolic state and so the possession and even enjoyment of material assets was no obstacle to spiritual progress. In this, he illustrates the moral contradictions and social confrontations that still very much characterized Islam in Khurasan in this period.

While Abu Saʿid was happy to borrow the institution of the *khanaqah* from the Karramiyya, his enjoyment of the good life stood in direct opposition to their vehement stress on poverty. And while in compiling a set of pious rules for the *khanaqah*'s residents, he reflected the outward Sunni conformism we have seen among the Sufis of Nishapur no less than of Baghdad, his emphasis on musical performances and sumptuous dinner parties placed him into disrepute with many of his contemporaries. Although some of the libertine poems on wine, pretty boys and sing-songs may be spurious attributions, there is no doubt that Abu Saʿid laid great emphasis on the practice of "listening" (*samaʿ*), which in this context involved love songs set to drums and lutes which sent audiences into ecstasies expressed through wild dancing. In such practices we can see an important fusion taking place between words and referents in which, with the shift of words to new social locations, the semantic range of the respectable early technical vocabulary developed in Iraq was stretched to refer to and thereby lend respectability to practices which the words' original users probably never had in mind. For example, while the word and concept of *samaʿ* was discussed much earlier in Baghdad, the actual practices we see developing around the likes of Abu Sa'id in eleventh century Khurasan were in all likelihood not borrowed from Iraqi Sufis at all but from the secular hobbies of the rural Khurasani aristocracy who in lifestyle and status Abu Sa'id so closely resembled.[111] This process of the grafting of a linguistic and conceptual superstructure onto the deeper social structures of life in different environments helped Sufism to embed itself into the new communities to which it expanded from the tenth century, first in Khurasan and later in India, Anatolia and elsewhere.

Dwelling in the lodge of which he was master; surrounded by a band of men who had sworn to obey his every command; protecting the poor who sought the safety of his shadow; receiving grandees and princes as though he were one of their rank; enjoying the courtly pleasures of music and verse: all of these activities are found in abundance in the two biographies of Abu Sa'id written in the century after his death.[112] On the one hand, in the biographies' many stories of miraculous aid to the poor, we see a new appeal of Sufism – or at least of powerful Sufis – to peasant social groups. On the other hand, we see the Sufi as founder of a lodge which would be inherited by his successors (often his own family) and survive into future generations as the living Sufi became the dead saint. We have already seen the concept of the "Friends of God" or *awliya allah* developing. In this period, the concept was acquiring the institutional capital that would transform it from a discursive to a social category: into the living Friend as spiritual aristocrat and the dead Friend as venerated saint.

Once again, essential to this development was the interaction of texts with the concrete resources of their contexts. In biographies written by those who inherited the capital and status of the founders of lodges, Sufis like Abu Sa'id and Kazaruni were venerated in the language of Friendship with God, and their spiritual rank and miraculous power were presented in turn as no less inheritable than their property. If these developments had not yet come to fruition in the eleventh century itself, when we are after all only seeing lodges being founded for the first time, it is important that we register from this early stage the implicit and causal connections between lodge-founding and shrine-founding. Teaching lodges did not become saintly shrines by a process of long decay and "spiritual malaise" as an earlier generation of historians once had it, but were from their beginning interdependent aspects of the same institutions.[113] Men like Abu Sa'id, Kazaruni and Ansari were buried in the lodges they founded and even in their own lifetimes in the eleventh century their contemporary Hujwiri could describe his pilgrimages to the tombs of the earlier Sufis in his cautiously conformist handbook on Sufi practice.[114] What we see in the creation of the lodges, then, was the heady fusion of the symbolic capital of Friendship with the material capital of real estate. In the following chapters we will trace the vast repercussions of this development as these shrine-lodges spread from Khurasan to every corner of the Islamic world.

Summary

What we are left with from the earliest centuries of Sufi history is almost exclusively textual evidence, much of it highly arcane and containing little reference to the specific contexts in which it was written. In finding ways in which we can connect this written evidence to the world from which it emerged, our task has partly been one of trying to understand the appeal of writings that allowed Sufism to develop and spread beyond its early core of supporters. In order to do so, over the previous pages we have traced the series of developments which between around 850 and 1100 ensured that the term *sufi* referred to a much larger range of persons, ideas, activities and institutions by the beginning of the twelfth century than it had when it was first used by Muslims three centuries earlier.

The first major development we have seen is what we can call a discursive one, by which the early Sufis used scriptural resources to develop a respectable Sufi lexicon with which to label the ideas and activities they promoted. Whether referring to specific persons as "Friends of God" (*awliya allah*), specific activities as "Remembrance" (*dhikr*) or specific social attitudes as "Reliance on God" (*tawakkul*), this Sufi lexicon connected the Sufis from the outset to wider developments in the mainstream of Islamic thought. As well as being respectable, we must also conclude that the followers who increasingly gathered around the Sufi teachers found this lexicon to be intelligible and useful, allowing them to make sense of their own experiences during their meditations and prayers and so to deepen their commitment to the larger psychological and social visions that Muslims were developing in these centuries. As we have seen, this lexicon and the different types of text that used it to elaborate doctrines on the Path and the Friends were intelligible in Khurasan no less than Iraq, helping what was originally an Iraqi movement to gain followers in eastern regions that had previously developed their own religious movements. It was in these eastern regions that we have the fullest textual evidence for the consolidation of Sufism from a teaching into a tradition, a process in which we have seen a central role played in the late tenth and early eleventh centuries by biographical works that used a genealogical framework to present Sufi doctrine as having been passed down the "generations" (*tabaqat*) from the time of Muhammad to the time of the author in question. In this, we see a process by which the writings and remembered lives of the early Sufis of Iraq (as well as the semi-historical ascetics of an earlier period) served as the "usable past," as history that could be strategically employed to create a prestigious and legitimizing tradition.

Not only did this prestige and legitimacy help Sufis win further supporters and shield them from the potential criticism of having committed deviating "innovation" (*bida‘*). It also placed their methods squarely into a dominant epistemological framework in which tradition and revelation were considered as superior to invention and reason.[115] The Sufis' repeated attempts to link themselves with the authoritative past – whether articulated through their use of Quran and Hadith or through their own lineages of masters – points again to the danger of the notion of the Sufis as "mystics" engaged primarily in the pursuit of experience. While the pursuit of experience – what by the end of this period many Sufis were referring to as "tasting" or *dhawq* – was an important feature of Sufi activity, we must remember that the Sufis were engaged in a perpetual struggle to connect these experiences with the authorized concepts of tradition denoted in the early lexicon. This is not to say that the Sufis somehow "got stuck" in this lexicon and tradition, for in the following chapters we will see that while the early lexicon remained, what it meant and referred to was expanded considerably by later writers. Tradition is, after all, an adaptable resource.

In the process of competition and incorporation through which they expanded from their early arena in Iraq, the Sufis would also be helped by their integration into the institutional frameworks of wider Sunni scholarship (such as the Shafi'i law school and the *madrasa* college) and by their development of institutional mechanisms of their own (such as the authoritarian master–disciple relationship and the *khanaqah* lodges). Compared to the rigorous demands of ascetics such as the *zuhhad* and Karamiyya, the appeal of the Sufi message was probably also helped by its stress on social conformism and moderation. For though there were certainly ecstatic Sufis who won fame in this period, among both scholarly *'ulama* and ordinary people, it was the Sufis' harmonization of their metaphysical teachings with the mundane structures of social, economic and family life that won them the support needed to outlive and outreach the other ascetic and esoteric movements that rose and fell beside them.

By the end of the period between 850 and 1100, we are also seeing the notion of the Sufi as a Friend of God with special access to God's power enabling Sufis to gain a larger following among the ordinary people for whom miraculous intercessions in their ordinary lives was of more pressing importance than a direct vision of God. Seen in the careers of such men as Abu Sa'id of Mayhana, this tentative expansion of the franchise beyond the scholarly and urban to the illiterate and rural should not be seen as a process of "decline." Rather, it saw the playing out of the social ramifications of the notions of Friendship explored by some of the very earliest Sufi theorists. As we will see in Chapter 2, when given full vent, this expansion of the franchise was arguably the most important development in Sufi history. While we have therefore by no means reached the end of the story, for present at least we can say that overall the period between around 850 and 1100 saw Sufism develop from being merely a locally-used word designating "wool wearers" to a method of knowledge elaborated in increasing numbers of texts and finally to a tradition enabled by institutional mechanisms of collective affiliation and reproduction.

Notes

1. T. Sizgorich, *Violence and Belief in Late Antiquity: Militant Devotion in Christianity and Islam* (Philadelphia: University of Pennsylvania Press, 2010).
2. Sizgorich (2010), pp.149, 276–278.
3. G. Ogén, "Did the Term *Sufi* Exist before the Sufis?" *Acta Orientalia* (Copenhagen) 43 (1982), p.45.
4. Ogén (1982), p.48.
5. R.A. Nicholson, "A Historical Enquiry Concerning the Origin and Development of Sufism," *Journal of Royal Asiatic Society* (1906), pp.303–348.
6. E. Key Fowden, "The Lamp and the Wine Flask: Early Muslim Interest in Christian Asceticism," in A. Akasoy, J.E. Montgomery & P.E. Pormann (eds), *Islamic Crosspollinations: Interactions in the Medieval Middle East* (Cambridge: E.J.W. Gibb Memorial Trust, 2007); H. Kilpatrick, "Monasteries Through Muslim Eyes: The Diyarat Books," in D. Thomas (ed.), *Christians at the Heart of Islamic Rule: Church Life and Scholarship in 'Abbasid Iraq* (Leiden: Brill, 2003); and F. Rosenthal, *Greek Philosophy in the Arab World: A Collection of Essays* (Aldershot: Variorum, 1990).
7. M. Smith, *Studies in Early Mysticism in the Near and Middle East* (London: The Sheldon Press, 1931). On earlier claims of Indian influences, see T. Duka, "The Influence of Buddhism on Islam," *Journal of the Royal Asiatic Society* (1904), pp.125–141 and M. Horten, *Indische Strömungen in der Islamischen Mystik* (Heidelberg: O. Harrassowitz, 1927–28).
8. Julian Baldick, *Mystical Islam* (London: I.B. Tauris, 1989), pp.13–33; O. Livne-Kafri, "Early Muslim Ascetics and the World of Christian Monasticism," *Jerusalem Studies in Arabic and Islam* 20 (1996) 105–129; and A. Vööbus, *History of Asceticism in the Syrian Orient: A Contribution to the History of Culture in the Near East* (Louvain: Secrétariat du Corpus SCO, 1958).
9. Smith (1931), p.3.
10. L. Kinberg, "What is Meant by *Zuhd*?" *Studia Islamica* 61 (1985) 27–44 and C. Melchert, "The Transition from Asceticism to Mysticism at the Middle of the Ninth Century CE," *Studia Islamica* 83 (1996), pp.51–70.
11. Baldick (1989), p.17.
12. M. Molé, *Les mystiques musulmans* (Paris: Presses Universitaires de France, 1965), chapter 1.
13. Baldick (1989), pp.15–18.
14. J. Baldick, "The Legend of Rābi'a of Basra: Christian Antecedents, Muslim Counterparts," *Religion* 20 (1990), pp.233–247. For a fuller and more traditional account, see M. Smith, *Rābi'a the Mystic and her Fellow-Saints in Islām* (Cambridge: The University Press, 1928).

15. For attempts to alternatively uncover the earliest historical data and the biographical tropes of these figures, see J. Chabbi, "Fudayl ibn 'Ayyād, un précurseur du hanbalisme (187/803)," *Bulletin d'Études Orientales de l'Institut Français de Damas* 30 (1978), pp.331–335 and M. Cooperson, "Ibn Hanbal and Bishr al-Hafi: A Case-Study in Biographical Traditions," *Studia Islamica* 86, 2 (1997), pp.71–101.

16. M. Bonner, *Aristocratic Violence and Holy War: Studies in the Jihad and the Arab-Byzantine Frontier* (New Haven: American Oriental Society, 1996).

17. C. Walter, *The Warrior Saints in Byzantine Art and Tradition* (Oxford: Oxford University Press, 2003).

18. T. Sizgorich, "Narrative and Community in Islamic Late Antiquity," *Past & Present* 185 (2004), pp.9–42.

19. On these biographical strategies, see M. Cooperson, *Classical Arabic Biography: The Heirs of the Prophets in the Age of al-Ma'mūn* (Cambridge: Cambridge University Press, 2000), chapter 5.

20. For an overview, see M. Fakhry, *A Short Introduction to Islamic Philosophy, Theology and Mysticism* (Oxford: Oneworld, 1997). However, on ascetic trends even among the champions of reason, see O. Aydinli, "Ascetic and Devotional Elements in the Mu'tazilite Tradition: The Sufi Mu'tazilites," *Muslim World* 97, 2 (2007), pp.174–189.

21. M. Cooperson, *Al-Ma'mun* (Oxford: Oneworld, 2005) and J.A. Nawas, "A Reexamination of Three Current Explanations for al-Ma'mun's Introduction of the Mihna," *International Journal of Middle East Studies* 26, 4 (1994), pp.615–629.

22. On the notion of 'constitutional' and 'autocratic' blocs, see W.M. Watt, *Islamic Philosophy and Theology* (Edinburgh: Edinburgh University Press, 1962), p.53.

23. For different approaches to the problem of early Sufi controversialism, see G. Böwering, "Early Sufism between Persecution and Heresy," in F. de Jong & B. Radtke (eds), *Islamic Mysticism Contested* (Leiden: Brill, 1999) and B. Radtke, "Warum ist der Sufi Orthodox?" *Der Islam* 71, 2 (1994), pp.302–307.

24. On debates about whether Hadith should actually be allowed to be written down, see M. Cook, "The Opponents of the Writing of Tradition in Early Islam," *Arabica* 44 (1997), pp.437–530 and G. Schoeler, *The Oral and the Written in Early Islam* (New York: Routledge, 2006).

25. P.J. Awn, "Classical Sufi Approaches to Scripture," in S.T. Katz (ed.), *Mysticism and Sacred Scripture* (New York: Oxford University Press, 2000).

26. For wider discussions of non-Sufi book use at this time, see S. Günther, "Praise to the Book! Al-Jahiz and Ibn Qutayba on the Excellence of the Written Word in Medieval Islam," *Jerusalem Studies in Arabic and Islam* 32 (2006), pp.125–143 and S. Toorawa, *Ibn Abi Tahir Tayfur and Arabic Writerly Culture: A Ninth Century Bookman in Baghdad* (London: Routledge, 2005).

27. L. Massignon, *Essay on the Origins of the Technical Language of Islamic Mysticism* (Notre Dame: University of Notre Dame Press, 1997 [1922]) and

P. Nwiya, *Exégèse Coranique et Langue Mystique* (Beirut: Dar el-Machreq Editeurs, 1970).

28. Massignon (1997 [1922]).
29. Baldick (1989), p.26.
30. On the earliest surviving evidence of Sufi interpretations of the Quran, see G. Böwering, *The Mystical Vision of Existence in Classical Islam* (Berlin: Walter de Gruyter, 1980) and K.Z. Sands, *Sūfī Commentaries on the Qur'ān in Classical Islam* (London: Routledge, 2006).
31. C. Melchert, "The Hanābila and the Early Sufis," *Arabica* 48, 3 (2001), pp.352–367.
32. The fullest study of Muhasibi remains J. van Ess, *Die Gedankenwelt des Hārit al-Muhāsibī anhand von übersetzungen aus seinen Schriften dargestellt und erläutert* (Bonn: Selbstverlag des Orientalischen Seminars der Universität Bonn, 1961); for the best synthesis in English, see L. Librande, "Islam and Conservation: The Theologian-Ascetic al-Muhāsibī," *Arabica* 30, 2 (1983), pp.125–146. On his opponents, see G. Picken, "Ibn Hanbal and al-Muhasibi: A Study of Early Conflicting Scholarly Methodologies," *Arabica* 55, 3 (2008), pp.337–361.
33. On Muhasibi as a non-Sufi, see Baldick (1989), pp.33–35.
34. S. Sviri, "The Self and its Transformation in Sufism, With Special Reference to Early Literature," in D.D. Shulman & G.G. Stroumsa (eds), *Self and Self-Transformation in the History of Religions* (Oxford: Oxford University Press, 2002).
35. The fullest study is N. Saab, "Mystical Language and Theory in Sufi Writings of al-Kharrāz," unpublished PhD thesis, Yale University, 2004. On the Epistles, see Nwiya (1970), pp.234–270.
36. Baldick (1989), p.40.
37. Abu Sa'id al-Kharraz, *The Book of Truthfulness (Kitāb al-Sidq)*, trans. A. J. Arberry (Calcutta: Oxford University Press, 1937), p.4, citing Quran XVIII: 110.
38. al-Kharraz (1937), p.1.
39. Nwiya (1970), pp.234–237.
40. Nwiya (1970), pp.237–242. On the discussion of Friendship (*wilaya*) in the writings of Kharraz and his contemporaries, see B. Radtke, "The Concept of *Wilāya* in Early Sufism," in L. Lewisohn (ed.), *Classical Persian Sufism: From its Origins to Rumi* (London: Khaniqahi Nimatullahi Publications, 1993).
41. For a full elucidation of Tustari's thought, see Böwering (1980).
42. C. Melchert, "Basran Origins of Classical Sufism," *Der Islam* 83 (2006), pp.221–240.
43. Cf. Baldick (1989), p.40.
44. Quran VII: 172 and LV: 26–27. For fuller discussion of the covenant, see Böwering (1980), chapter 4.
45. For a translation of this section of Tustari's commentary, see M. Sells (ed. & trans.), *Early Islamic Mysticism* (New York: Paulist Press, 1996), pp.92–95.

46. For a summary and translation of Junayd's writings, see A.H. Abdel-Kader, *The Life, Personality and Writings of al-Junayd: A Study of a Third/Ninth Century Mystic* (London: Luzac, 1976).

47. Abdel-Kader (1976), pp.1–7.

48. Abdel-Kader (1976), pp.68–75.

49. Abdel-Kader (1976), pp.76–80.

50. Abdel-Kader (1976), p.153.

51. Abdel-Kader (1976), pp.88–96.

52. Ahmet Karamustafa, *Sufism: The Formative Period* (Berkeley: University of California Press, 2007), pp.11–12.

53. R.C. Zaehner, *Hindu and Muslim Mysticism* (London: Athlone Press, 1960), chapter 5. For a reassessment, see Baldick (1989), pp.35–37.

54. On the emergence of the two schools typology, see J.A. Mojaddedi, "Getting Drunk with Abū Yazīd or Staying Sober with Junayd: The Creation of a Popular Typology of Sufism," *Bulletin of the School of Oriental and African Studies* 66, 1 (2003), pp.1–13.

55. Abdel-Kader (1976), pp.142–143.

56. On Hallaj, see (with caution) H.W. Mason, *Al-Hallaj* (London: Curzon Press, 1995) and L. Massignon, *The Passion of al-Hallāj: Mystic and Martyr of Islam*, 4 vols (Princeton: Princeton University Press, 1982 [1922]). For translations of his writings and sayings, see G. Kamran, *Ana al-Haqq Reconsidered, with a Translation of Kitab al-Tawasin* (Delhi: Kitab Bhavan, 1994); L. Massignon & P. Kraus, *Akhbar al-Hallaj: Recueil d'Oraisons et d'Exhortations du Martyr Mystique de l'Islam Husayn Ibn Mansur Hallaj* (Paris: Librarie Philosophique Vrin, 1957); and A. Schimmel, *Al-Halladsch: "O Leute, rettet mich vor Gott"* (Freiburg: Herder, 1995).

57. See P.J. Awn, *Satan's Tragedy and Redemption: Iblīs in Sufi Pyschology* (Leiden: E.J. Brill, 1983), especially chapter 3.

58. A.J. Arberry (ed. & trans.), *The Mawáqif and Mukhátabát of Muhammad Ibn 'Abdi'l-Jabbár al-Niffari* (London: Luzac & Co., 1935). On the depiction of the places on the Path a generation later, see K. Honerkamp, "A Sufi Itinerary of Tenth Century Nishapur Based on a Treatise by Abū 'Abd al-Rahmān al-Sulamī," *Journal of Islamic Studies* 17, 1 (2006), pp.43–67.

59. Massignon (1997), Nwiya (1970). For different interpretations of the later use of this vocabulary, see K.S. Avery, *A Psychology of Early Sufi Samā': Listening and Altered States* (London: RoutledgeCurzon, 2004), chapter 3; C.W. Ernst, "Mystical Language and the Teaching Context in the Early Sufi Lexicons," in S.T. Katz (ed.), *Mysticism and Language* (Oxford: Oxford University Press, 1992); and N.S. Green, "Idiom, Genre and the Politics of Self-Description on the Peripheries of Persian," in N.S Green & M. Searle-Chatterjee (eds), *Religion, Language and Power* (New York: Routledge, 2008).

60. C. Melchert, "The Etiquette of Learning in the Early Islamic Study Circle," in J.E. Lowry, D.J. Stewart & S.M. Toorawa (eds), *Law and Education in Medieval Islam: Studies in Memory of Professor George Makdisi* (Warminster: E.J.W. Gibb Memorial Trust, 2004).

61. On the early Islamization of Khurasan and Central Asia, see R.W. Bulliet, "Conversion to Islam in Iran and the Emergence of a Muslim Society in Iran," in N. Levtzion (ed.), *Conversion to Islam* (New York: Holmes & Meier, 1979) and D.G. Tor, "The Islamization of Central Asia in the Sāmānid Era and the Reshaping of the Muslim World," *Bulletin of the School of Oriental and African Studies* 72, 2 (2009).

62. J. Chabbi, "Remarques sur le Développement Historique des Mouvements Ascétiques et Mystiques au Khurasan," *Studia Islamica* 46 (1977), pp.5–72; on the various designations in use, see pp.29–38.

63. Ogén (1982).

64. C.E. Bosworth, "The Rise of the Karāmiyyah in Khurasan," *Muslim World* 50 (1960), pp.5–14, W. Madelung, *Religious Trends in Early Islamic Iran* (Albany, N.Y.: Persian Heritage Foundation, 1988), chapter 4 and M. Malamud, "The Politics of Heresy in Medieval Khurasan: The Karramiyya in Nishapur," *Iranian Studies* 17 (1994), pp.37–51.

65. On the theological output of various Karrami masters, see J.-C. Vadet, "Le Karramisme de la Haute-Asie au Carrefour de Trois Sectes Rivales," *Revue des Études Islamiques* 48 (1980), pp.25–50.

66. Madelung (1988), p.45.

67. Chabbi (1977), C. Melchert, "Sufis and Competing Movements in Nishapur," *Iran* 39 (2001), pp. 237–247 and S. Sviri, "Hakīm Tirmidhī and the Malāmatī Movement in Early Sufism," in Lewisohn (1993). For a translation of the main primary source on the Malamatiyya by al-Sulami (d.1021), see N. Heer & K.L. Honerkamp (trans.), *Three Early Sufi Texts: A Treatise on the Heart, Stations of the Righteous, The Stumblings of Those Aspiring* (Louisville KY: Fons Vitae, 2003).

68. Karamustafa (2007), pp.48–51.

69. In this I am following the interpretation of Karamustafa (2007), p.47 and B. Radtke, "Theologen und Mystiker in Ḥurāsān und Transoxanien," *Zeitschrift der Deutschen Morgenländischen Gesellschaft* 136 (1986), pp. 536–569. On the theological output of various hakims, see C. Gilliot, "La Théologie Musulmane en Asie Centrale et au Khorasan," *Arabica* 49, 2 (2002), pp.135–203.

70. For the fullest accounts, see B. Radtke, *Al-Ḥakīm at-Tirmidī: Ein Islamischer Theosoph des 3./9. Jahrhunderts* (Freiberg: K. Schwarz, 1980) and Sviri (1993).

71. B. Radtke & J. O'Kane (trans.), *The Concept of Sainthood in Early Islamic Mysticism: Two Works by Al-Hakim al-Tirmidhi* (Richmond: Curzon Press, 1996).

72. The autobiography is translated in Radtke & O'Kane (1996), pp.15–36.

73. Radtke & O'Kane (1996), p.169.

74. On the formation of the Muslim elite among whom the Sufis would locate themselves, see R.W. Bulliet, *The Patricians of Nishapur: A Study in Medieval Islamic Social History* (Cambridge: Harvard University Press, 1972).

75. J. Paul, *The State and the Military: The Samanid Case* (Bloomington: Indiana University, Research Institute for Inner Asian Studies, 1994) and Tor (2009).

76. For details of such figures, see Melchert, "Competing Movements" (2001), pp.237–239. On the interaction between travel, writing and knowledge in this period more generally, see H. Touati, *Islam et Voyage au Moyen Âge: Histoire et Anthropologie d'une Pratique Lettrée* (Paris: Le Seuil, 2000).

77. M. Malamud, "Sufi Organizations and Structures of Authority in Medieval Nishapur," *International Journal of Middle East Studies* 26, 3 (1994), p.430.

78. For a recent version of the critique, see the comments on Malamud (1994) in Melchert, "Competing Movements" (2001), p.242.

79. Melchert "Competing Movements" (2001).

80. Malamud (1994), pp.433–435.

81. G. Böwering, "The Qur'an Commentary of al-Sulami," in W. Hallaq & D. Little (eds), *Islamic Studies Presented to Charles J. Adams* (Leiden: EJ Brill, 1991) and F.S. Colby, "The Subtleties of the Ascension: al-Sulamī on the Miʿrāj of the Prophet Muhammad," *Studia Islamica*, 94 (2002), pp.167–183.

82. F. Meier, "Khurasan and the End of Classical Sufism," in Meier, *Essays on Islamic Mysticism and Piety* (Leiden: Brill, 1999), p.214.

83. Most famously, see A.J. Arberry, *Sufism: An Account of the Mystics of Islam* (London: George Allen & Unwin, 1950), chapter 11 and J.S. Trimingham, *The Sufi Orders in Islam* (Oxford: Clarendon Press, 1971). For the most thorough reassessment of the contrast as it relates to the master/disciple relationship, see L. Silvers-Alario, "The Teaching Relationship in Early Sufism: A Reassessment of Fritz Meier's Definition of the *Shaykh al-Tarbiya* and the *Shaykh al-Taʿlīm*," *Muslim World* 93 (2003), pp.69–97.

84. Meier (1999).

85. For translations, see Abu Nasr al-Sarraj, *The Kitáb al-Lumaʿ fiʾl-Taṣawwuf of Abú Naṣr ʿAbdallah b. ʿAli al-Sarráj al-Ṭúsi* (trans. R.A. Nicholson) (London: Luzac & Co., 1914); Abu Bakr al-Kalabadhi, *The Doctrine of the Ṣūfis* (trans. A.J. Arberry) (Lahore: Sh. Muhammad Ashraf, 1966); Abu'l-Qasim al-Qushayri, *Al-Qushayri's Epistle on Sufism* (trans. A.D. Knysh) (Reading: Garnet Publishing, 2007); and Ali bin Uthman al-Hujwiri, *The Kashf al Mahjúb: The Oldest Persian Treatise on Súfism* (trans. R.A. Nicholson) (London: Luzac & Co., 1936).

86. Ibn al-Husayn al-Sulami, *The Way of Sufi Chivalry* (trans. T.B. al-Jerrahi) (London: East-West Publications, 1983). On the subsequent development of this sub-tradition, see L. Ridgeon, *Morality and Mysticism in Persian Sufism: A History of Sufi-Futuwwa in Iran* (London: Routledge, 2009).

87. D.G. Tor, *Violent Order: Religious Warfare, Chivalry, and the ʿAyyār Phenomenon in the Medieval Islamic World* (Wuŕzburg: Ergon, 2007).

88. J.A. Mojaddedi, *The Biographical Tradition in Sufism: The Tabaqat Genre from al-Sulami to Jami* (Richmond: Curzon Press, 2001). For translated selections from later Sufi biographies, see J. Renard (ed.), *Tales of God's Friends: Islamic Hagiography in Translation* (Berkeley: University of California Press, 2009).

89. On the presentation of Junayd's life by the biographers Abu Nuʿaym al-Isfahani (d.1038) and ʿAbd al-Rahman Jami (d.1492), see J.A. Mojaddedi, "Junayd in the 'Hilyat al-Awliyā' and the 'Nafahat al-Uns'," in Renard (2009).

90. See for example the chapter 'On Blame [*malamat*]' in al-Hujwiri (1936), pp.62–69.

91. For classic if problematic surveys, see G. Makdisi, "Muslim Institutions of Learning in Eleventh-Century Baghdad," *Bulletin of the School of Oriental and African Studies* 24 (1961), pp.1–56 and A.L. Tibawi, "Origin and Character of *al-Madrasah*," *Bulletin of the School of Oriental and African Studies* 25, 2 (1962), pp.225–238.

92. O. Safi, *The Politics of Knowledge in Premodern Islam: Negotiating Ideology and Religious Inquiry* (Chapel Hill: University of North Carolina Press, 2006).

93. H. Dabashi, "Historical Conditions of Persian Sufism during the Seljuq Period," in Lewisohn (1993).

94. For a biographical study of his writings, see E. Ormsby, *Ghazali: The Revival of Islam* (Oxford: Oneworld, 2008).

95. For translations of both texts, see al-Ghazali, *Mishkāt al-Anwār (The Niche for Lights)* (trans. W.H.T. Gairdner) (London: Royal Asiatic Society, 1924) and W.M. Watt, *The Faith and Practice of al-Ghazālī* (London: G. Allen and Unwin, 1953).

96. On *ribat* foundation in Baghdad from this period, see J. Chabbi. "La Fonction du *Ribat* à Bagdad du V Siècle au Debut du VII Siècle," *Revue des Études Islamiques* 42 (1974), pp.101–121.

97. R. Azuar Ruiz (ed.), *El Ribāt Califal: Excavaciones y Investigaciones (1984–1992)* (Madrid: Casa de Velázquez, 2004).

98. M. Azuar Ruiz, "Excavaciones (1984–1992): Espacios, Arquitectura y Estratigrafía," in Azuar Ruiz (2004).

99. C. Barceló Torres, "Los Escritos Árabes de la Rabita de Guardamar," in Azuar Ruiz (2004).

100. H.J. Fisher, "What's in a Name? The Almoravids of the Eleventh Century in the Western Sahara," *Journal of Religion in Africa* 22, 4 (1992), pp.290–317.

101. M. Marín, "La Práctica del *Ribāt* en Al-Andalus," in Azuar Ruiz (2004), pp.192–195.

102. D. Urvoy, "La vie intellectuelle et spirituelle dans les Baléares musulmanes," *Al-Andalus* 37, 1 (1972), pp.87–127, particularly p.88, and A. Metcalfe, *The Muslims of Medieval Italy* (Edinburgh: Edinburgh University Press, 2009), pp. 61–62.

103. For the argument for the distinctiveness of Spanish Muslim militaristic spirituality, see M. de Epalza, "La Espiritualidad Militarista del Islam Medieval: el Ribat, los Ribates, las Rabitas y los Almonastires de al-Andalus," *Medievalismo: Boletín de la Sociedad Espanola de Estudios Medievales* 3 (1993), pp.5–18.

104. Marín (2004).

105. Marín (2004), p.194.

106. P. Cressier, "De un *Ribāt* a Otro: Una Hipótesis sobre los *Ribāt*-s del Magrib al-Aqsà," in Azuar Ruiz (2004).

107. On Ibn Khafif and his disciple Daylami, the most important of the early Sufis in southern Iran, see Abū'l-Hasan 'Alī b. Muhammad al-Daylamī, *A Treatise on Mystical Love* (trans. J.N. Bell & H.M. Al-Shafie) (Edinburgh: Edinburgh

University Press, 2005) and F. Sobieroj, *Ibn Hafīf Aš-Šīrāzī und seine Schrift zur Novizenerziehung (Kitāb al-Iqtiṣād): Biographiche Studien, Edition und Übersetzung* (Beirut: Franz Steiner Verlag, 1998).

108.   D. Aigle, "Un Fondateur d'Ordre en Milieu Rural: Le Cheikh Abû Ishâq de Kâzarûn," in Aigle (ed.), *Saints Orientaux* (Paris: De Boccard, 1995). For Kazaruni's biography, see F. Meier (ed.), *Die Vita des Scheich Abū Isḥāq al-Kāzarūnī in der Persischen Bearbeitung* (Leipzig: Kommisionsverlag F. A. Brockhaus, 1948).

109.   C.E. Bosworth, "An Early Persian Sufi: Shaykh Abū Saʿīd of Mayhanah," in R. M. Savory & D.A. Agius (eds), *Logos Islamikos: Studia Islamica in Honorem Georgii Michaelis Wickens* (Toronto: Pontifical Institute of Medieval Studies, 1984), T. Graham, "Abu Saʿid ibn Abi'l-Khayr and the School of Khurasan," in Lewisohn (1993) and R.A. Nicholson, *Studies in Islamic Mysticism* (Cambridge: Cambridge University Press, 1921), chapter 1.

110.   A.G. Ravan Farhadi, "The *Hundred Grounds* of ʿAbdullāh Ansārī of Herat (d.448/1056): The Earliest Mnemonic Sufi Manual in Persian," in Lewisohn (1993).

111.   On developments in the theory of *samaʿ* in Abu Saʿid's lifetime, especially by Qushayri (d.1074) in Khurasan, see Avery (2004).

112.   For a translation of the later of the two, see Mohammad Ibn-e Monawwar, *Les Étapes Mystiques du Shaykh Abu Saʿid: Mystères de la Connaissance de l'Unique* (trans. M. Achena) (Paris: Desclée De Brouwer, 1974).

113.   The expression belongs to Trimingham (1971), p.71. The influential decline model is most clearly outlined in Trimingham (1971), chapter 3.

114.   al-Hujwiri (1936), pp.68–69, 234–235.

115.   On the links of many Sufis to the most "traditionalist" wing of Sunni Islam, see G. Makdisi, "The Hanbali School and Sufism," in Makdisi, *Religion, Law and Learning in Classical Islam* (Aldershot: Variorum, 1991) and Melchert, "Hanābila" (2001).

Chapter 2

An Islam of Saints and Brothers (1100–1400)

Changing Contexts

In the centuries between 850 and 1100, we have seen the Sufis emerge as only one among many Muslim groups operating in Iraq and gain a following, as well as a conscious sense of tradition and a more institutionalized mode of organization, through their easterly expansion into Iran and Central Asia. While the last chapter focussed on the two main regions of early Sufi productivity in Iraq and Khurasan, by 1100 there was also a substantial Sufi presence in the Islamic west of Spain and North Africa, as well as the beginnings of their tremendously influential expansion into India. Having established their institutional footholds across a wide region, the period between 1100 and 1500 to which we now turn saw the Sufis achieve an extraordinary ascent to a position in which, from Morocco to Bengal, they acted as the social and intellectual linchpins of the very different communities that they penetrated across this vast area. By 1500, not only were Sufis at once the patrons and clients of kings, they were also central to the lives of lower class groups in town as well as country, a position consolidated by their role in the conversion of nomadic and cultivator groups to Islam in expanding frontier regions.

We have already seen how the study of Quran and Hadith was the formative discipline of the early Sufis and how, as time passed, the Sufis ensured their alliance with the emerging norms of Sunni Islam. With the mainstream as their natural environment, rebels like the executed Hallaj were the exceptions rather than the rule. But if the Sufis were rarely far from the norms of the period, in their early centuries they were unable to become dominant religious authorities. However, in many regions, the period

Sufism: A Global History, First Edition. Nile Green.
© 2012 Nile Green. Published 2012 by Blackwell Publishing Ltd.

between 1100 and 1500 saw them do precisely this. In part, this was the fruit of the intellectual and institutional syntheses we have seen beginning in the eleventh century, when a formal "science of Sufism" (*'ilm al-tasawwuf*) developed alongside the curricula and schools that emerged through the orthodoxy sponsored by the Saljuq Turks, a process encapsulated in the teachings and career of al-Ghazali (d.1111).[1] The continued expansion of the *madrasa* and *khanaqah* system certainly helped the Sufis in the centuries after 1100, not only in the various Saljuq domains between Anatolia and Khurasan but also as part of the deliberate "Sunnification" of Egypt and Syria that followed the fall of their Isma'ili Shi'i rulers to the Ayyubid dynasty in 1171.[2] While this nexus between Sufis, Sultans and the institutions of Sunnism remained an important factor, the unprecedented expansion of Sufi influence in the centuries that followed also owed much to new developments. It is on these developments – of diversification and institutionalization, sanctification and vernacularization – that this chapter concentrates in order to navigate a way through the increasing number of peoples and places participating in Sufi Islam between 1100 and 1500. Since historians once saw this period as one of Sufi "decadence" in which genuine mysticism was sacrificed on the altars of sainthood, it is important that we recognize the relationship of each of these processes to what went before. The more formal institutions of brotherhoods and the more elaborate doctrines of sainthood that characterized this second period were once seen as symptoms of spiritual decline. But in seeing their connection to the ideas and practices that Sufis elaborated before 1100, we can see how new developments emerged from the use to which later Sufis put the resources of their tradition as they struggled to make sense and advantage of the new social conditions in which they were operating.

Before turning towards these developments, it is worth emphasizing the degree of difference between the old and the new conditions. We have already seen how from the mid-eleventh century the Saljuq Turks swept westwards in an arc of conquest from Central Asia to Anatolia. Like various Turkic dynasties between the twelfth and fifteenth centuries, the originally nomadic Saljuqs entered an alliance with the settled Muslim scholarly class who served as their bureaucracy, protecting and ultimately championing the legal and learned foundations of urban Islamic life. The same was not true of the next major nomadic group to ride westwards. Under Genghis Khan and his sons, between the 1220s and the 1260s, the armies of the shamanistic Mongols literally obliterated many of the cities of Khurasan (including Nishapur) and ultimately conquered Baghdad, where they put an end to the system of the caliphate which had given an at least symbolic leadership to the Muslim community since the death of the Prophet. The horror and destruction of the Mongol conquests were felt far beyond the immediate spaces of their impact. On both the western and eastern limits of Mongol expansion, Syria, Egypt and India were taken over by the slave soldiers or *mamluks* who were meant to protect their sultans. East and west likewise played host to vast movements of refugees, among whom were many scholarly and Sufi families.

Even as much of the Iraqi and Khurasani cradle of Sufism was laid waste, there were new opportunities. The desire of the slave dynasties to establish their Muslim credentials saw them patronize many a new Sufi lodge in the towns or grant land in the country, while the movement of refugees speeded further the circulation of Sufi teachings. It was almost a century before the new Mongol rulers of the central Islamic lands converted to Islam, but when they did it was among the Sufis that they found their protégés and teachers. If these centuries of turmoil ushered in very different societies from those in which Sufism had first emerged, they also offered opportunities for Sufis to connect themselves to much larger constituencies than had ever been the case, winning the hearts and purses of not only nomadic *khans* but also of the townsmen and peasants they ruled over. By diversifying their spiritual method and vernacularizing their means of communication, and by founding brotherhoods and saint cults, the Sufis reached a point at which Islam became effectively inseparable from the persons, ideas and institutions of Sufism.

The Diversification of Sufi Doctrine

Success breeds success and the establishment status that the Sufis had achieved by the twelfth or thirteenth centuries encouraged even more Muslims to voice their religious ideas through the respectable idioms Sufis had created over the previous centuries. Sufism was now itself a tradition with a lineage pushed back into the time of the Prophet, while the ties to the ruling class of many of its leading representatives cemented their influence in the present and their role of shaping the future of their societies. This "establishment" status did not mean that their movement had run out of steam and if anything we can see the respectability achieved by the Sufis of the first period as having enabled the diversification process that we see in the centuries between 1100 and 1300. For the Sufis, these were centuries of extraordinary textual productivity, because there were not only many more Sufis in existence but they were now also widening their literary ambit beyond Arabic. The panorama of ideas explored in this period was tremendous in its own right, without even speaking of the rejoinders and responses, the ruminations and commentaries, that each significant work triggered. To make sense of what was new amidst this voluminosity, we will look at the way in which the inheritance of the first centuries was diversified by examining such key themes as light, being and friendship, along with the main figures with whom they were associated. Each of these themes and doctrines, and the texts in which they were elaborated, became important materials in the discursive consolidation of Sufi tradition.

Figure 2.1 Doctrine Diversified: Medieval Manuscript from *al-Mashari' wa al-Mutarahat* ("Paths and Conversations") of Yahya Suhrawardi (d.1191) (Image: Hossein Ziai, courtesy of the Universiteitsbibliotheek of Leiden University Library)

The first of these themes was that of light (*nur*). As we saw in Chapter 1, light was already a topic of discussion among such Sufis as Tustari and Ghazali. But in the writings of Shihab ab Din Suhrawardi (d.1191), earlier ideas were systematized and reworked into a coherent philosophical vision in which light became the basis of both ontology and epistemology: everything in the universe existed as light and every act of knowledge was an expression of light.[3] Born in northern Iran, Suhrawardi saw himself as the heir to several traditions of "wisdom" or *hikmat* and presented his system as the elucidation of what was previously known to the pagan Greeks and Zoroastrian Iranians as well as to the early Sufis.[4] Although it is open to question whether he can be considered a Sufi himself, he certainly spent much time in the company of Sufis, drew on their earlier ideas and influenced their later ones.[5] Suhrawardi's *magnum opus* was his *Kitab Hikmat al-'Ishraq* ("Book of Oriental Illumination"). In this he laid out the framework of what (in a pointer to the central theme of light) he termed "oriental" wisdom in the sense that the east is the place where the sun rises over both the inner and outer horizons where the light of knowledge dawns.[6] For Suhrawardi, the universe and its inhabitants consist entirely of light that emanates from God, who is Himself nothing other than pure self-existent light. Beneath God, the universe exists as a hierarchy of light-beings, whose own light (and so being) is merely contingent in emanating from God. Each light-being in this celestial hierarchy both receives light from above and reflects light below, such that from God through the angelic realms to the human world, and then beneath it to the levels of animals, plants and inert matter, everything in the universe exists as a degree of light received from God that is channeled through the cosmic hierarchy of lights. For Suhrawardi, the human quest – whether by Plato in Athens or Junayd in Baghdad – is to ascend that hierarchy by coming into contact with each of its light-beings in turn. These light-beings are what ordinary people call angels, and the most important among them was the angel whom Suhrawardi identified with both the Gabriel who delivered the Quran to Muhammad and the Active Intellect discussed by the philosophers. Here was a refiguring of the Sufi model of a Path with places along the way into a journey through stages of existence which were themselves forms of the increasingly pure light described in the Quranic Light Verse on which we have seen Ghazali writing a commentary less than a century earlier.

Between the physical and the angelic worlds, Suhrawardi placed an intermediary realm which he called the "World of Likenesses" (*'alam al-mithal*). It was this realm, possessing shape but not substance, which acted as the meeting place between human and angelic beings; it was also here that humans moved when experiencing visions and dreams. This crepuscular meeting ground between angels of light and the shadowy souls of men was of central importance to Suhrawardi's system. For it was here that humans could begin to gather the "experiential knowledge" (*'ilm al-huzuri*) that he considered superior to "acquired knowledge" (*'ilm al-husuli*) gathered from books and lessons, because in visions knowledge was not data that was passively learned, but experience that actively happened.[7] Lying somewhere between descriptions of his own experiences and allegories of his philosophical system, in some of the earliest examples of Persian prose writing Suhrawardi penned a series of "visionary treatises" in which he described his meetings with the angelic beings of light.[8] Although his remarkable writings contributed to disciplines as varied as logic and ophthalmology, what is most significant is his elevation of knowledge by mystical experience over the lesser knowledge acquired from books, a potentially radical realignment of the mainstream Sufi attempt to subject personal experience to the authority of tradition as manifested in the Quran, Hadith and their textual elaboration by way of Shari'a. Making these claims in Aleppo, one of the main outposts of the Sunni Revival in which many Sufis were happy to play their conformist part, it is perhaps little surprise that Suhrawardi was put to death at only thirty-eight years of age. His model of knowledge, and thereby authority, threatened the centrality of revealed scripture and the *'ulama* and mainstream Sufis who were its interpreters.

Nonetheless, from Suhrawardi's lifetime, we find an increasing number of Sufis daring to describe their visionary experiences in vivid and what must have been at the time shocking detail.[9] Some earlier Sufis had described their mystical experiences, as we have seen in Iraq with Niffari's *Book of Stopping Places* and with the dream accounts of Tirmidhi's wife. But these descriptions were typically either brief (Tirmidhi) or highly allusive (Niffari), and the rare bolder accounts (such as that of Abu Yazid's heavenly ascension) were tainted with controversy. Yet from the twelfth century, we find descriptions of such experiences not only becoming more explicit, but gaining sufficient prestige as to serve as proof of the visionary's Friendship with God. Such dream and vision accounts have been aptly described as a new "rhetoric of sainthood" which fed into the larger process of sanctification explored below.[10]

In the *Kashf al-Asrar* ("Unveiling of Secrets") that Ruzbihan Baqli (d.1209) wrote in southern Iran, for example, readers were presented with a series of startlingly anthropomorphic visions. In one, God appeared before Ruzbihan in the guise of a fair-skinned Turk who played such tunes on his lute that Ruzbihan cried at their loveliness.[11] In another vision, he met the Prophet Muhammad, whom Ruzbihan saw wearing a golden suit and turban and sitting drunk amid a red sea of wine; scooping up cup after cup, the Prophet supped Ruzbihan till they both sat drunk together.[12] Many other such dream and vision diaries were written, among which were the hundred-and-nine dreams described two centuries later by the Algerian Sufi, Muhammad al-Zawawi (d.1477).[13] What is fascinating about al-Zawawi's dreams is their relationship to the physical world through which he moved, for their most intense period occurred during a journey to Egypt in which al-Zawawi's dreams served to sublimate and somehow accentuate the reality of his waking experiences of the places he was visiting. By this period, Egypt's was a geography dotted with Sufi tombs and after visiting these by day, by night al-Zawawi returned in his dreams to converse with their dead inhabitants, who assured him of his exalted status and invested him with robes of celestial rank.

In such ways, the increased description and theorization of dreams and visions formed a means of acquiring knowledge and authority that might alternatively complement or counter that gained through mastery of the textual legacy of tradition. This is not to say that through such dreams and visions the Sufis rejected their emphasis on tradition, but rather that such experiences formed an alternative and often superior means of accessing and indeed interacting with tradition. As increasing numbers of Sufis would testify in their writings, it was possible to meet any of the Sufis' past masters and even prophets through such visionary means. What we see developing here is the dream and vision as a cultural technology enabling Sufis to transcend the barriers of time and evade the ambiguities of scripture in order to plainly ask questions to the face of God's messengers. The epistemological problem of dreams – that the personal nature of such experiences rendered the knowledge claims they made inherently difficult to verify – was in turn overcome through widespread resort to a hadith in which the Prophet Muhammad had said, "Whoever has seen me has seen me truly," which was taken to mean that Satan cannot imitate the Prophet's form. In other words, any vision or dream of Muhammad was necessarily authentic, such that by this recourse to the textual authority of Hadith dreams and visions became self-affirming. We have seen the wife of Hakim Tirmidhi dreaming that her husband was one of God's Friends as early as the ninth century and in the more abundant visionary literature of the twelfth century onwards, few Sufis were presented as lacking in such visionary proofs of their exalted rank and wisdom.

This was especially true of the most influential of the Sufi theorists of the medieval and probably any other period: the Spanish-born Muhyi al-Din Ibn al-'Arabi (d.1240). Born in Murcia to an elite Arab family in court service, Ibn al-'Arabi spent his formative years among the Sufis of Spain and the culturally contiguous zone of North Africa, before moving to the eastern Mediterranean in his late thirties.[14] There he was received with controversy among scholars and with largesse among princes; reaching Syria a decade after the execution of Suhrawardi, Ibn al-'Arabi was more fortunate in his friendships, dying in Damascus at the ripe old age of seventy-five. This grandest of all Sufi visionaries claimed the ability to summon the presence of any of the souls of the dead before him at any moment and spoke regularly with the souls of Jesus, Muhammad and Moses. In a conscious echo of the Quran's revelation to Muhammad, Ibn al-'Arabi had his own master work, *al-Futuhat al-Makkiyya* ("Spiritual Conquests of Mecca"), revealed to him while circumambulating the Ka'ba in the holy city.[15] Such audacity sounded throughout his ideas and, as we see below, his protracted out-writing of Muhammad's own revelation was echoed in his claim that Friendship was superior to Prophethood, a theory which served well the need to reproduce religious authority in an age when prophethood was seen as having permanently ended.[16] For his own part, Ibn al-'Arabi saw himself as the Seal of the Friends (*khatm al-awliya*) in whose oceanic being God's exploration of his infinite creativity was fully realized.

While Suhrawardi had been important for systematizing ideas of light a generation earlier, it was this notion of being (*wujud*) that represented Ibn al-'Arabi's great contribution. Under his influence, the earlier Sufi emphasis on public morals, supererogatory piety and the search for certain knowledge were subsumed into a grander vision of cosmic existence in which the infinite realizations of creative being now took center stage. Ibn al-'Arabi did not necessarily introduce new concepts and, like other Sufis before and after, he wrote within the discursive framework of Islamic tradition: the raw materials of his work were the Quran, Hadith and the technical lexicon developed by the first generations of Sufis. Using these resources, he explored the implications of the "sacrosanct hadith" (*hadith qudsi*) in which God himself had declared, "I was a jewel that was undiscovered and so I created the world." Using the Quranic term *barzakh* – which, for Ibn al-'Arabi at least, took on the meaning of an "interface" or "isthmus" – he developed the idea that human being was itself this interface between the matter and spirit that were the farthest axes of creation.[17]

Human being, then, was, the place of the Quranic "meeting of the oceans" (*majma' al-bahrayn*) in which all levels of existence, all forms of knowledge, and all possible experiences, could be united in a way that was impossible even for the angels (which was why God had commanded the angels to bow down before Adam).[18] While not all humans contained such lofty possibilities – this is what separated the masses from the Friends and Prophets – those who did were the very reason for creation, for in the words of the sacrosanct hadith, it was they who discovered the divine jewel by realizing all of the possibilities of the Hundred Names of God. Drawing on Suhrawardi's notion of a World of Likenesses that mediated the mystic's encounter with other realms of being, Ibn al-'Arabi dwelt much on the idea that it was through the creative power of imagination (*khayal*) by which God and humanity reached out to one another.[19] Given that he was said to have filled a notebook every day of his adult life and that the *Futuhat al-Makkiya* alone takes up over 15,000 pages, Ibn 'Arabi's own career was no small expression of this faith in the creative power of the imagination. At the center of his thought, holding together the explorations of divine being that he saw all human history as comprising, was the idea that all being was ultimately God's. Although he never seems to have used the expression himself, this vision came to be summarized as that of the Unity of Being (*wahdat al-wujud*), a form of cosmic monism which many a Persian Sufi would subsequently sum up in the epithet, "All is He!" (*hama ust!*).

Arcane as such ideas might seem, there were many potentially concrete social benefits to them. For example, the notion of the Unity of Being has been seen as serving as an enabling mechanism for inter-religious harmony with the different groups whom Muslims encountered. As many a poet (including Ibn al-ʿArabi himself) put it, if God was everywhere, then he could be found in the idol temple as much as the mosque.[20] Of course, the clear danger in the idea that humans were made of the same stuff as God was that it broke down the divide between creator and creature and with it the threat of divine retribution that underpinned moral order. And so while to his followers Ibn al-ʿArabi was the "greatest of masters" (*al-shaykh al-akbar*), to his critics he was the "master of infidels" (*al-shaykh al-akfar*).[21] Yet Ibn al-ʿArabi's thought spread incredibly widely, partly through the piecemeal trickles of influence and partly through the efforts of a studious corps of followers who ranged from Sadr al-Din Qunawi (d.1274) in Anatolia, Fakhr al-Din ʿIraqi (d.1289) in India, Mahmud Shabistari (d.1340) in Iran, Muhammad Wafa (d.1363) in Egypt, ʿAbd al-Karim al-Jili (d.1408 or 1428) in Iraq, and Muhammad ibn Sulayman al-Jazuli (d.1465) in Morocco.[22] In its theoretical expressions, if not necessarily in its social organization and communicational media, Sufism after 1300 was extraordinarily indebted to the profundity and productivity of this son of Muslim Spain.

Ibn al-ʿArabi's migration to the eastern Mediterranean had occurred against the background of the fall of his native Murcia to the crown of Castille and it is fitting that his last decades were safely spent in the capital of the great scourge of the Crusaders, Saladin. The early life of the other great diversifier of Sufi thought in this period was similarly marked by the retraction of Muslim power. For in counterpart to Ibn al-ʿArabi's flight to the east, Jalal al-Din Rumi (d.1273) as a boy undertook a westward flight from the Mongol advance into Khurasan to the safety of the Saljuq capital of Konya in Anatolia. If Ibn al-ʿArabi is often seen as the greatest theorist of Sufism, then Rumi is usually seen as the Sufis' greatest poet.[23] While we will turn to the more literary aspects of his work below in our discussion of vernacularization, what is important here is the way in which Rumi made love central to his version of the Path. Rumi was by no means the first Sufi to propound the importance of love between humans, but we are not dealing with a cultural context in which originality and invention were considered virtues. This is not to say that people were incapable of thinking new thoughts, only that as self-conscious participants in a tradition they presented themselves as extrapolating the same truths recognized by earlier prophets and masters. This is what happened in the case of the love mysticism represented by Rumi, which grew out of the earlier discussions of love by Sufis such as Abu'l Hasan al-Daylami (d.tenth century) and Ahmad Ghazali (d.1126).[24]

The shift in ideas can be summarized as one in which love moved from an acquired attribute which the seeker must cultivate towards God to an absolute attribute of God himself, by being absorbed into which, the seeker reached the furthest point of the Path. Unlike Suhrawardi and Ibn al-'Arabi, Rumi was not a theorist and owed his fame more to his poetic than his doctrinal output, though as we will see below, in his adaptation of narrative verse forms, poetry itself became a vehicle for his teachings. Although Rumi was only one of a number of Sufis who from the twelfth century posited love as the means and end of the Path, through the establishment of a Sufi brotherhood by his successors, he would become the most influential of these love mystics. Even outside the direct influence of his brotherhood, the widespread copying and reciting of manuscripts of his great narrative poem that was later called "the Quran in the Persian language" (*Quran dar zaban-e pahlawi*) ensured that for many Sufis from Anatolia through to India and Central Asia, Rumi's way of love was considered the highest (if most erratic) of the several paths to God.

As they diversified their ideas in the centuries after 1100, the Sufis continued to self-consciously draw on the earlier tradition to which they considered themselves heirs. So assiduous were their attempts to walk in the Path laid out by the earlier generations they knew from their initiatic chains and biographies that the medieval Sufis often studied special dictionaries of sanctioned technical terms.[25] Even when, as we will see below, they began to write in languages other than the Arabic of the Quran and the early Sufis of Iraq, these Arabic terms were adopted as loan words in languages that eventually ranged from Persian and Turkish to Wolof and Malay. Again, this traditionist orientation did not preclude new developments and no-where is this seen more vividly than among the *qalandar* ("clown," "antinomian") groups which developed from around the thirteenth century as bands of wandering Sufi vagabonds.[26] Whether through strolling around naked, openly using drugs and alcohol, or torturing their bodies with spikes and chains, the *qalandars* deliberately rejected all social norms in a way that was antithetical to the conformist Sufi mainstream. Yet in claiming that the true Path lay in renouncing everything from possessions and respectability to family and law, the *qalandars* also drew on what were by now traditional Sufi idioms of poverty and self-abasement to claim that they were the only Sufis who put their words into action. If the same tropes and terminology were handed on, the ways in which they were used could therefore change greatly: tradition was a flexible resource. Nowhere was this seen more clearly than in the transformation of the Path itself which from the twelfth century came to refer to social formations that had previously not existed.

In Chapter 1, we have already seen certain institutional developments taking place in Khurasan which would render tradition a more stable and reproducible resource. But it was between the twelfth and fourteenth centuries that this process would be completed through the conceptual and organizational consolidation of the Path into a series of Sufi "brotherhoods." It is to these new institutions that we must now turn.

The Institutionalization of the Path

In Chapter 1 we have already seen how the early Sufis presented their method as a "Path" or *tariqa* and how in the course of the eleventh century that Path became more formalized through the elaboration of rules and more institutionalized through the foundation of *khanaqah* buildings. Here we will turn to the process by which these developments were both consolidated and expanded, specifically to the related organizational and conceptual developments which allowed Sufi leaders to address the basic obstacles of reproduction through time and space while at the same time maintaining a degree of consistency through developing mechanisms for standardizing practice and doctrine.[27] We have already seen how the creation of a sense of "tradition" encouraged Sufis to conceive of their Path as something inherited from masters who had lived in earlier times and other places. But a sensibility of the traditional is not the same as an actual mechanism of tradition: one can believe one is transmitting the teachings of the ancients without actually doing so. What we see emerging between around 1150 and 1400 are these more formal mechanisms of tradition.

This is not to say that such mechanisms were entirely absent among the Sufis beforehand, who were often very much immersed in the methods of knowledge transmission developed by memorizers of scripture and collectors of Hadith. But these latter were not distinctly Sufi mechanisms of tradition. While the more formal methods of teaching, initiation and organization we have seen emerging around Nishapur were somewhat more (though by no means entirely) distinctive, they were still relatively restricted methods confined to particular teachers in particular places. They had not yet developed into mechanisms of tradition capable of reproducing the standardized and proprietary method of a given Sufi across time and distance. In order to do so, the Sufis would need to develop a more formal geographical distribution network and a cross-generational system of inheritance, as well as more distinctive "branding" mechanisms capable of distinguishing the tradition of one master from that of another. It was the development of such mechanisms that underlay what historians have usually seen as the creation of "brotherhoods" or "orders," a development which is obscured by the fact that the Sufis themselves continued to use the term *tariqa* with reference to both the loosely formulated Path of the early centuries and the organized brotherhoods of the later periods.

   Given the fact that historians have disagreed over when (and even if) such formalized "brotherhoods" came into existence, it is helpful to bear in mind that what we are looking at is primarily the development of reproductive mechanisms of tradition and, for our purposes at least, it is these cultural *mechanisms* to which we refer in speaking of "brotherhoods." For while some aspects of these mechanisms were organizational and corporate in the sense that the term brotherhood usually suggests, they were both enabled by and subject to the intangible but ultimately more weighty operations of tradition as a conceptual and symbolic mechanism. We should not then expect the brotherhoods of this period to comprise complex organizations with card-carrying members and efficient managerial hierarchies. While brotherhoods were certainly better organized in some regions than others, for the most part such more complex modes of Sufi organization belonged to the early modern period of bureaucratic empires explored in Chapter 3. The absence of such complexity does not mean that we cannot speak of brother-hoods at all in the centuries between 1100 and 1400, nor does is mean that there were no organizational developments in these years. But it does mean that we must recognize that what held the members of such brotherhoods together over the generations and geography that divided them were con-ceptual as much as concrete bonds of connectivity. In the medieval period, brotherhoods operated as organizational communities largely on the level of locality or region in which legal or face-to-face authority had a realistic chance of success. When it came to bridging larger distances of either time or space they were forced to operate largely as conceptual communities in which fellowship was built on bonds of memory and imagination rather than bureaucratic ties and direct communication.

   Limited in reach as they were, let us first address the organizational elements of these mechanisms of the reproduction and standardization of tradition that we have termed brotherhoods.[28] We have already seen the inception of a new formalized vision of the Path in the Khurasan of the late tenth and eleventh centuries, from where many of its features were spread west by the administration of the Saljuq and Ayyubid sultans on the one hand and the movement of individual Sufis on the other. Indeed, between the twelfth and fifteenth centuries the lodges and shrines from which the Sufi brotherhoods gathered their followers in town and country acted very much as the hardware of Sunnification, rendering permanent the religious policies of the Saljuq, Ayyubid and Mamluk rulers who from Anatolia to Egypt sought to cement their conquests of the territory of Byzantine Christians and Fatimid Shi'is through the patronage of durable and axiomatically Sunni institutions that included Sufi lodges.[29] What began in Khurasan as a temporary alliance between arriviste Saljuq nomads and an ascendant establishment of scholarly Sufis became a lasting and reproducible alliance between religion and state that would eventually reach from the shores of the Mediterranean to the forests of Bengal. Even as large-scale polities collapsed with the rise of regional sultanates and the repeated disruptions of nomadic conquests, the conceptual and organizational fabric of the Sufi brotherhoods created a recognizable network that would allow travelers like the North African Ibn Battuta (d.1368) to find like-minded fellows and welcoming lodgings in otherwise startlingly different environments between Morocco and India.[30] From limited surviving architectural evidence, we know that by the twelfth century some of these lodges were already being constructed in lavish style, as seen in the delicate stucco decoration that survives at the grandiose lodge of 'Ali ibn Karmakh (c.1180) near Multan in modern day Pakistan.[31]

The elements of this more formal brotherhood Sufism were several, and not all of them were necessarily reproduced together. Most important was the sworn bond of allegiance (*'uqda*) between the master (*murshid*) and disciple (*murid*), a relationship that was in some cases being formalized through charters of "rules' which the disciple was expected to obey. Both the master's authority and the disciple's regulation were in turn linked to the development of specific residential complexes which, as they spread into different regions, were alternatively called *khanaqahs*, *ribats*, *zawiyas* and *takiyyas*. Among the fellow disciples of a master or the erstwhile residents of a lodge, a new sense of corporate identity began to emerge that was consolidated by a socializing ethic of companionship (*suhba*) and a gate-keeping ritual of initiation (*bay'a*). Each of these developments was in turn authorized through their connection to tradition in which through written text and spoken tale the remembered past served as the pedestal of the present. What we see happening here through the foundation of brother-hoods in the twelfth and thirteenth centuries was in part a consolidation and expansion of the "Nishapur model" of the Sufi Path seen in Chapter 1. More particularly, we see a process of the "branding" of discrete versions of this more consolidated Path, their reproduction through "firms" named after purported founders and their distribution to "clients."

The process of the "branding" or proprietary marking of distinct Paths entailed several components. Rules became much more detailed and elab-orate, leading to the development of the new genre of the disciples' etiquette book (*kitab adab al-muridin*), intended not only to ensure the correct training of initiates but, in the manner of a teacher-training manual, also to stan-dardize such training.[32] Proprietary practices were developed by way of distinct *dhikr* chants (some loud, some silent), *muraqaba* visualization techniques and initiation rituals. New mechanisms for marking the corporate identity of members were developed through the modification of outward appearance, whether through donning colored *khirqa* robes, shaving the head, wearing ear-rings or carrying recognizable paraphernalia. In this way, the lack of impersonal and formal methods of group organization was compensated for through acts of personal and informal identification by members of a particular brotherhood. In similar acts of self-identification, disciples inserted themselves into lineages of initiation that stretched through their own masters back through the generations described in the "Book of Generations" genre and so to the Prophet himself. Boundaries with other brotherhoods were marked not only by physical appearance but also by different attitudes towards money, music or even drug use. Properties acquired through patronage were linked to specific brotherhoods, forming residences or meeting houses for fellow initiates, which in larger cities came to include special lodges for female Sufis.[33] Masters began to appoint "deputies" (*khalifas*) to further disseminate the proprietary Path of their brotherhood. With the symbolic capital of authority and the material capital of property, inheritance systems also began to emerge in which birthright competed with initiation as the proper channel of bequest.

These developments afforded the Sufis mechanisms of both horizontal and vertical reproduction that allowed them to expand into new geographical areas and to survive the death of particular masters. The creation of networks of deputies allowed brotherhoods to spread into new regions, while the recognition of heirs allowed them to continue from one generation to the next. In principle if by no means always in practice, the method of master–disciple learning and the reading of training texts ensured some degree of standardization in the doctrines and practices held by fellow members of the same brotherhood at a distance of generations and geography. Once again, what we are seeing here is the ongoing evolution of a self-conscious tradition in which precedent and community were far more important criteria than originality and individuality. Even when mystical experience was sought, it was sought and understood through what the Sufi understood to be long-established practices and conceptual frameworks. None of these developments took immediate effect and, emerging in different times among different brotherhoods, none can be given a single date at which they appeared. As primarily mechanisms of tradition, the brotherhoods necessarily developed through time and so their consolidation and expansion was an inherently multi-generational process in which different generations relied on one another to play distinct but nonetheless necessary roles as founders and perpetuators, heirs and distributors. It would be easy to see the men after whom the major brotherhoods were named as genuine founder figures and so date the emergence of the brotherhoods to their actual lifetimes: Abu Najib al-Suhrawardi (d.1168), 'Abd al-Qadir al-Jilani (d.1166), Ahmad ibn al-Rifa'i (d.1182), Ahmad al-Yasawi (d.1166?), Najm al-Din Kubra (d.1221), Mu'in al-Din Chishti (d.1236), Abu'l Hasan al-Shadhili (d.1258), Jalal al-Din Rumi (d.1273) and Baha al-Din al-Naqshband (d.1389). In the case of some of these men, we do have evidence for new kinds of organizational activity, but on the whole we are looking at men who, through writing or preaching, achieved a fame and following in their lifetimes which their disciples and very often their families inherited and perpetuated after their deaths.[34] They did not simply found brotherhoods whose continued existence then simply rolled on through the ages. Rather, the "founders" are better seen as men who amassed resources – whether patrons and property or teachings and charisma – that could be inherited and used by their successors to found the brotherhoods which were named after them. They thus only became founders through time when that which was developed from their legacies and survived after their lives was connected back to them by later generations who saw themselves as the followers of the "founder's" Path.[35]

By way of example, let us look at one of the most important brotherhoods to emerge in the twelfth century from the fertile ground of Baghdad. This was the Suhrawardi brotherhood which was named after Abu Najib al-Suhrawardi (d.1168), one of several important Sufis who originated in the Iranian town of Suhraward. What is immediately striking about Abu Najib is his similarity to Ghazali, whom we have seen in Chapter 1 riding the crest of the Saljuqs' *madrasa* patronage to publicly promote a conformist model of Sufism that sat comfortably within the intellectual and institutional norms of his time.[36] While Abu Najib's own public career was more checkered than Ghazali's, he still occupied an important position teaching jurisprudence in Baghdad's great Nizamiyya *madrasa* and, after losing his appointment through a dispute at court, continued to teach legal and Hadith studies in a *madrasa* which he founded next to his own Sufi lodge in the city. A famous public figure in his own day (he was a celebrated preacher no less than a consort of caliphs), in addition to his writings on Hadith, Abu Najib was most important for his version of the Sufi rule book genre we saw developing in Chapter 1. Entitled *Kitab Adab al-Muridin* ("Book of the Disciples' Etiquette"), Abu Najib's introduction to the Sufi life showed little concern for Sufism as metaphysical doctrine and mystical experience and instead focused on the outward behavior – the "etiquette" or "manners" (*adab*) – which the disciple was expected to display.[37] For Abu Najib, the gathering of a circle of disciples appears to have been primarily a vehicle for socialization into mainstream norms of Islamic behavior, pointing us less to the history of mysticism than to the history of manners. While later initiates would regard Abu Najib as the founder of the Suhrawardi brotherhood, the latter was more truly the project of his heirs (particularly of his nephew, Abu Hafs 'Umar al-Suhrawardi (d.1234)) who were able to capitalize on the resources Abu Najib bequeathed them by way of a circle of influential supporters, a book of rules, and a widespread reputation for piety. Inheriting something of the public profile of his uncle, 'Umar likewise entered the circles of the court and became so close a confidante of the 'Abbasid caliph, al-Nasir (r.1180–1225), as to serve as his official ambassador and work on his project to socialize the boisterous young men of Baghdad into *futuwwa* or "chivalry" clubs, whose character bore much in common with the emerging Sufi brotherhoods themselves.[38] Gathering a circle of followers, and patronized by his admirers at court, like his uncle, 'Umar also wrote a book of rules, in which the prescribed duties and beliefs of the disciple were laid out in far greater detail than had been the case with the nascent rules of Abu Sa'id and Ansari a century and a half earlier in Khurasan.[39] From among these disciples, it was the nephew 'Umar rather than the uncle Abu Najib who laid the organizational and conceptual foundations of the brotherhood by founding a network of lodges and arguing for the Sufis as the sole legitimate heirs of the Prophet.[40] Even then, the founding was only beginning, and it needed the next generation of his followers, particularly Najib al-Din Buzghush (d.1279) and Baha al-Din Zakariya (d.1262), to distribute the Suhrawardi proprietary version of the Path eastwards into Iran and northern India.[41] Each successive generation would play its part in consolidating and contributing to the symbolic and material resources of the brotherhood, inflating the charisma of the founder and gathering the patronage to found new lodges.

When after six centuries the institutionalized inheritance of the "deputies" or caliphs of Muhammad was extinguished by the Mongol sack of Baghdad in 1258, Suhrawardi's initiatory network of brothers was already spreading far and wide. Even though 'Umar did not himself refer to his successors with the term caliph (*khalifa*), in his brotherhood as in others like it, in the course of a few generations the franchise-founding deputies of his heirs would certainly do so.[42] If there was no longer a single caliph in Baghdad, in growing numbers of towns from Morocco to India there were now many such "deputies" or *khalifas*, whose initiation into the *silsila* chain of their brotherhoods presented them as charismatic transmitters connected directly to the Prophet, their authority demonstrated through the wearing of special ceremonial robes.[43] While the context of the "founder" was an important shaper of any brotherhood, the contexts of the first few generations of heirs who reproduced and effectively shaped his legacy were therefore even more important, pointing to the way in which trans-regional and trans-generational brotherhoods like the Suhrawardiyya emerged out of an organizational and conceptual interplay between different times and places. In setting up shop in the distant north Indian city of Multan, 'Umar's disciple Baha al-Din Zakariya brought with him not only the prestige of a Baghdad that was all the more powerful at so great a geographical remove. Through the apparatus of the brotherhood, he also brought the initiatory and pedagogic mechanisms to reproduce the blessing and behavior of its lineage's most famous holy men.

To transform the brotherhoods from the creation of individual genius into the collaboration of communal process is not to reduce them. It is rather to point to the collective nature of the investments of emotion and action that allowed the brotherhoods to function so effectively in the expansion of Sufism into new areas. For the initiation, rituals and teachings by which any new disciple entered into and indentified with a brotherhood were intrinsically portable and reproducible, allowing deputies to move into new areas and establish new "franchises" of a brotherhood. In some cases, where there were regular patterns of communication, these networks possessed a degree of concrete organizational coherence, particularly along trade and pilgrimage routes or within well-defined geographical or political regions. But in most cases, the founders and heirs of such franchises were their own masters for whom the brotherhood served more as a resource for their own reproduction than as an organizational chain of command to which they were answerable. Once again, we are reminded that in this period the brotherhoods offered a conceptual cultural mechanism as much as a concrete organizational apparatus. By similar means of multi-generation collusion, the Qadiri brotherhood named after another Sufi public moralist, 'Abd al-Qadir al-Jilani (d.1166), emerged from a Baghdad that was imagined as much as it was real to spread, in the century after the caliphate's end, into Syria, Egypt and Yemen and in later centuries to India, Southeast Asia and Africa.[44]

Given that the "chain" or *silsila* into which a new disciple entered on their initiation was regarded as constituting a metaphysical channel which transferred the blessing power or *baraka* of the Prophet Muhammad, whether in the jungles of India or the steppes of Turkestan, the brotherhoods offered a way for initiates to conceive themselves as being meaningfully connected to the teachings and power of a Prophet who had lived centuries ago among a foreign people who resided thousands of miles away. Even in regions closer to the Muslim holy land of Arabia such as Syria and Egypt, mass illiteracy meant that religious knowledge was sought through persons rather than books and the brotherhoods afforded mechanisms by which people could decide which Muslims were the rightful heirs of the Prophet. If the theory that the brotherhoods emerged in response to the Mongol termination of the caliphate in 1258 places too much weight on what was already a long defunct and for most Muslims a very distant Caliphal institution, in the absence of any institution like the Church in Christianity, the brotherhoods gave the ordinary Muslims who joined them both the conceptual and institutional framework with which to connect themselves to a contemporary community of fellow believers and a past tradition of blessed forerunners.[45] In embodying the charisma and the teachings of Muhammad in the physical presence of a living master with whom one could speak and whose hand one could clasp in a pledge of initiation, and in providing shrines for pilgrimages that were infinitely closer than Mecca, the local representatives of the Sufi brotherhoods were able to bridge the distance of time, space and culture that separated the Muslims of the middle ages from the distant age and homeland of the Prophet. What the brotherhoods transmitted was ultimately

الشيخ عبد القادر الجيلاني

Figure 2.2   Building Brotherhoods: Devotional Portrait of 'Abd al-Qadir Jilani (d.1166) (Image: from the author's collection)

Islam itself, a process that becomes all the more clear when we bear in mind that their first requirements were almost always conformity with the formal beliefs and practices of the faith.

One of the striking elements in this process of the transmission of tradition is the way in which the brotherhoods served to distribute and reproduce to places as distant as India, Africa, Turkestan and the Malay archipelago, doctrines and practices that had originally emerged in the early Sufi "production centers" in Iraq and Khurasan. This was by no means a swift development (indeed, it is one that continues to this day); nor was it a seamless one. To gather some sense of its operation, let us look at the example of the expansion of the Chishti brotherhood to India. Named after the Khurasani town of Chisht (in modern Afghanistan) in which it originated, the Chishti brotherhood was effectively constructed from the legacy of Mu'in al-Din Chishti (d.1236), who, in the wake of the Ghurid conquests of the 1190s, migrated to Ajmer in the western Indian region of India's Rajasthan.[46] Within a century of Mu'in al-Din's death, his heirs in the next few generations spread his *tariqa* over an extraordinary geographical range, following the expansion of the Delhi Sultans to found franchises of their brotherhood as far apart as Rajasthan, Punjab, Delhi, Bengal and the Deccan.[47] This pattern of frontier expansion saw the Chishtis establish themselves not only in the commercial and administrative settings of India's cities but, through the receipt of rural land grants, also in the expanding agrarian environment of cleared forests.[48] The Chishtis' impact on these diverse environments was correspondingly varied. Among non-Muslim tribal and forest peoples in rural areas, the Chishtis' introduction of Islamic institutions as part of a package that included agriculture on their landholdings and trade at their shrine festivals triggered a process of conversion through rural people's gradual acculturation to Islamic norms of diet, dress, law and naming as much as worship.[49] By contrast, among the Muslim merchant and administrative elites of the towns, the Chishtis provided moral guidance as scholars of Quran and Hadith, in addition to, as we will see in the next section, inspiring the poets and bureaucrats of the Delhi Sultanate to write down their teachings and transform Muslim precepts into locally recognizable idioms.[50] By perpetuating their physical presence through time, the grave sites maintained by the institutional surety of their *khanaqahs* enabled the deceased Chishti masters to become the focus for pilgrimages. In forming the basis for new devotional forms of Islam, these rendered the Sufis in some sense more important in death than in life. Over the generations, such devotional practices developed not only around the shrines of Chishti Sufis but around those of many other brotherhoods in India. This was to create a distinct regional version of Islam which owed its very existence to the brotherhoods that, through maintaining shrines, hosting festivals and perpetuating saintly biographies, rendered Sufis a permanent presence in the social landscape even after their deaths. Shaping their Indian environment no less than they were shaped by it, the Chishti brotherhood presented their Path as a distinct brand of Sufism with characteristics that marked it is separate from the other brotherhoods that entered India. In this way, they cultivated an association with music, an antipathy for royal associations and an openness for inter-action with Hindus that made their brotherhood attractive to some Muslims in India and unattractive to others.[51] Whereas in 1100, the Chishti broth-erhood consisted of little more than a gathering of men in the mountainous village of Chisht itself, through its reproduction among generations of migrant deputies, by the mid-1400s it could count outposts in the cities and small towns of almost every corner of the Indian subcontinent.

Our picture of a Sufi brotherhood looks rather different if we turn to the case of the Khwajagan-Naqshbandi brotherhood in Central Asia.[52] Where-as the Chishtiyya emerged in India during a period of the expansion of Muslim rule, the Khwajagan masters (whose traditions would later be subsumed into the more famous Naqshbandi brotherhood) by contrast emerged after the death of the "founder" figure 'Abd al-Khaliq al-Ghij-duwani (d.1220) during the century of pagan Mongol rule over Central Asia between the 1220s and the early 1300s. While the Chishtis were establishing socially prominent formal lodges sponsored by the Muslim elites of the towns of India, the early members of the Khwajagan broth-erhood, acting in a region governed by non-Muslims, were more likely to consist of the "decent poor" who were taught to abhor possessors of wealth and high office and follow the far less socially visible practice of "retreat within society" (*khalwat dar anjuman*).[53] The Khwajagan sought to increase their following through a stern critique of other Sufi groups, presenting their rivals as morally lax and arguing that possession of *khanaqahs* was proof of a concern with material things.[54] Of course, we have to be aware that such Khwajagan-Naqshbandi representations of their rivals were strategic uses of rhetoric rather than objective factual descriptions and historians have struggled to piece together a sequence of events from the mutually contested sources on the period. However, in outline it appears that as conditions changed after the Mongols' conversion to Islam, and amid the rise and fall of a tumultuous series of tribal Muslim dynasties, a more organized and socially-engaged brotherhood emerged which gradually co-opted the following and prestige of the Khwajagan and absorbed it in a similar way that the Sufis had previously absorbed the Karramis in Khurasan.[55] Under the leadership of the brotherhood's "second founder," Baha al-Din Naqshband (d.1389), and more particu-larly under his own heirs in the next few generations, this new Khwajagan-Naqshbandi brotherhood radically shifted its doctrinal position to one of actively seeking connections with political leaders and encouraging the acquisition of wealth, which now came to be seen as a sign of God's favor to his Friends.[56] Through a series of affiliations with Central Asia's fragile rulers, whose own traditions and legitimacy were by now far shallower than those of the longer-established Khwajagan-Naqshbandi masters, the branch of the brotherhood led by 'Ubaydullah Ahrar (d.1490) reached the extraordinary status of being the largest landowner in Central Asia. In a physical act of the making of tradition, the shrine of the "second founder" Baha al-Din Naqshband was beautified in the process.[57] At the same time, the brotherhood maintained its own distinctive "brand," laying heavy emphasis on Shari'a, criticizing the religious use of music, and promoting its proprietary forms of silent *dhikr* chants.

While both the Chishtis and the Khwajagan-Naqshbandis were Sufi brotherhoods, they therefore espoused very different approaches to basic questions of wealth and organization, practice and doctrine. The one avoided rulers, sought God through music and accommodated Hindus, while the other cultivated connections at court, condemned music and regularly promoted *jihad* against infidels. At the same time, both brotherhoods shared the basic organizational and conceptual fabric of a chain of charismatic descent from the Prophet Muhammad. In both cases, this was used to create an association of "brothers under the master" through rituals of initiation and sworn allegiance to the living representative of the Prophet and the Friends whose grace, across hundreds of years and thousands of miles, flowed down their respective chains to reach their initiates in either India or Central Asia.

Between 1100 and 1400, the Sufi brotherhoods had penetrated societies as far apart as Spain and Mauretania in the west and Bengal and Turkestan in the east, with a firm concentration in the wealthy mercantile middle regions of Egypt and Syria.[58] In the many regions in which they flourished, local circumstances led them to adopt methods and techniques as varied as those of the Khwajagan-Naqshbandis and the Chishtis. But each of them shared the same basic characteristics we have described, mechanisms of reproduction and standardization that allowed the brotherhoods to endure and expand while maintaining the meaningful consistency that they cherished as their proprietary traditions. While the history of each brotherhood varied greatly, it is fair to say that between the twelfth and fifteenth centuries the multi-generational process of the formation of the brotherhoods led to an overall pattern of greater and more centralized organization by the 1400s than had existed four centuries earlier. In the next chapter, we will return to the brotherhoods to see how they reacted to the development of more ordered and centralized societies under the early modern empires that conquered much of the Muslim world after 1500. For now, we must turn to the second major process after the organization of brotherhoods that characterizes the medieval period: the veneration of the Sufi masters as saints.

The Sanctification of God's Friends

It was once common for historians to discuss the evolution of Sufi teaching and the brotherhoods and lodges through which it occurred without reference to the transformation of leading Sufis into saints. Indeed, the latter process was once considered a quite separate one belonging to a later period of decline from "mysticism" to "superstition."[59] However, as a result of new research over the past few decades, it is clear that neither dichotomy nor decline fit the facts as they now appear. As we saw in Chapter 1, in terms of the doctrinal fabric of Sufi teaching, the notion of certain Sufis being God's special "Friends" (*awliya*) - a relationship possibly preordained and certainly bringing special knowledge and powers – had been a matter of controversy from the earliest period, with the sometimes fierce debate suggesting that there was already a great deal at stake in gaining such status in the earliest period.[60] Even as sober and mainstream a figure as Junayd of Baghdad had written on the theory of Friendship (*wilaya*) and we would do well to note that, of all the early Sufis, it was Junayd who was most commonly incorporated into the chains of forerunners later developed by the brotherhoods.[61] In terms of the institutional fabric of the Sufi brotherhoods, the notion of the Friend was central to the brotherhoods as both conceptual and concrete entities, through the veneration of the past masters of the *tariqa* chains and the construction of mausolea in the midst of the lodges.

While the theory of Friendship had therefore been around for a long time, what was new from around 1100 was a more multi-layered process of sanctification which involved not only a theoretical model of Friendship but a much fuller apparatus of shrine building, hagiographical writing and pilgrimage making. What was previously an idea among the erudite developed into places, stories and actions among the masses: it is this process that we are terming sanctification.[62] Given the existence of so many Christian saintly institutions in the Islamic west, and their recognition as pilgrimage sites by Muslims from an early period, it is possible that the existence of such saintly practices had a much earlier existence in Islam.[63] New work on the early history of Islam shows that the veneration of graves, relics and holy persons has a much older history among Muslims than was once thought.[64] But even if such earlier practices existed by which Muslims venerated the graves and memory of the Christian saints and the founders of the Muslim community, what is important for our purposes is the way in which from the twelfth century they came to be increasingly concentrated around Sufis. In understanding how this came about, we are once again confronted with the role of the Sufi brotherhoods as mechanisms for reproduction. For, as chains of descent and capital-gathering institutions, the brotherhoods were able to both reproduce new masters in every generation and provide them with public spaces to be buried in on their deaths. There were, of course, several sets of components involved in this process. One set comprised the conceptual components by which a given Sufi was initiated into a chain of descent (*silsila*) and afforded recognition as a Friend of God: the latter status was either achieved through personal accomplishments (preaching, praying, writing) or simply inherited through the emergence of family dynasties of brotherhood leaders. Another set of components comprised the spreading of rumors of miracles, which were frequently lent official sponsorship through the writing of hagiographies whose narratives spread into the oral sphere through the work of professional guides who escorted pilgrims through expanding numbers of shrines.[65] A third set of components comprised the development of cult rituals by which pilgrims were able to access the blessing power or *baraka* that the saint transmitted, rituals which, depending on the integration of a given shrine into wider networks of pilgrimage (*ziyara*), might be trans-regional or local in character. A final set of components comprised the financial mechanisms by which money was raised for the construction of the mausolea that served as the focus of cultic activity – mausolea which by 1400 were coming to rival those built for courtiers and rulers.

Possessing abundant access to the necessary components of charisma, commemoration and capital, the brotherhoods thus operated as highly effective institutions for saint-making. After our earliest detailed evidence for the development of these components around such men as Abu Sa'id in eleventh century Khurasan, with the expansion of the brotherhoods over the next few hundred years the pattern was reproduced to reach a point at which the cult of the saints had sponsored whole suburbs for the holy dead – al-Qarafa in Egypt, Shah-e Zinda in Central Asia, Khuldabad in South India – where the wealthy competed to build their own mausolea close to the shrines of the saints.[66] While by no means every venerated saint was a Sufi in medieval Islam any more than every Sufi was a saint, the ideas and institutions of Sufism nonetheless became inextricably interwoven with the saintly practices that came to play a central part in the Islam of the ordinary believer. As with the brotherhoods' own creation, this process of sanctification was typically a multi-generational project, seeing shrines acquire increasing prestige and capital as the centuries passed.[67] While there were also many shrine cults that failed, what this generational process more generally implied was that older shrines tended to be more famous and wealthy than younger ones. In other words, many of the shrines that emerged in the medieval period we are discussing have dominated the younger shrines in their regions of influence down to the present day.[68]

While the organizational and conceptual structure of the brotherhoods played a central part in the spread of this cult of Sufi saints, they were not the only enabling factors at work. Two other factors were of crucial importance, namely, the further elaboration of doctrine, which created a powerful ideology of a divinely-ordained hierarchy of mankind, and the making of political contacts, which brought major Sufis access to capital through relationships of patronage. The most celebrated spokesman for this increasing elevation of God's Friends was the great Spanish Sufi, Ibn al-'Arabi (d.1240), whose voluminous writings and varied disciples spread his ideas through Arabia, Syria, Anatolia, Iran, India, and Southeast Asia. For present purposes, Ibn al-'Arabi is important for promoting the ideas that sainthood was ultimately more important than prophethood and that the universe was held together by a hierarchy of saints and, indeed, owed its *raison d'être* and continued existence to the existence of a saintly "axis" or *qutb* known as the Perfect Man (*insan al-kamil*).[69] Ibn al-'Arabi was by no means the only person promoting such ideas, and over the next century his ideas on sainthood and the Perfect Man were publicized and elaborated by many other Sufis, particularly Muhammad Wafa (d.1363) in Egypt and 'Abd al-Karim al-Jili (d.1408 or 1428) in Iraq. Soon every corner of the Islamic world had its claimants to be the living cosmic axis who held the power to hold the universe together; some were recognized, others were not. And the graves of those who during their lifetimes were recognized as such by influential parties frequently became pilgrimage centers after their deaths.

Working alongside this doctrinal elaboration was an increasing pattern of allegiances between Sufis and members of the ruling elite, the very people with the financial means of raising a particular claimant of Friendship to the

Figure 2.3 Nomads into Muslims: Mongol-Patronized Shrine of Shaykh Muhammad ibn Bakran (d.1303) (Image: Nile Green)

position of wider fame that sanctification required. In many respects, this was a continuation of the Saljuq practice of patronizing scholarly Sufis with *madrasas* and charismatic Sufis with *khanaqahs*. When the Mongols finally converted to Islam in the 1330s, they too recognized the prospective dividends of such patronage.[70] It was in the eastern regions of the Islamic world in Iran and Central Asia ruled by the Mongols and their tribal successors that some of the largest and most stunningly decorated Sufi shrines ever constructed were built in the fourteenth and fifteenth centuries, shrines that in some cases served as the only sedentary institutions with which nomadic groups had any interaction.[71] One of the most impressive and stylistically typical surviving buildings the Mongols patronized for the Sufis was the shrine complex of Shaykh Muhammad ibn Bakran (d.1303, also known as Pir-e Bakran), which was completed around 1312 around twenty miles from the Iranian city of Isfahan.[72] As these associations with ruling groups became more and more commonplace, and the Sufis' claims of cosmic elevation became ever more grandiose, the mausolea of the Sufi saints came to borrow the style of royal tombs. In some cases, rulers even began to abandon their own ancestral burial sites to be interred at the feet of the saints.[73] From one group among many Muslim claimants to religious leadership before the eleventh century, the Sufis became, between 1100 and 1400, not only God's spokesmen on earth but also the confidantes of kings.

There is no need to see this development through the nostalgic lenses of regret or decline. For the historian if not necessarily for the theologian, when seen in the social settings in which it occurred, the Sufis' transformation into saints makes a good deal of sense. This become more clear when we look at the kinds of belief, action and emotion that the sanctification of the Sufis made possible, not just for the ruling elite but also for the ordinary people of their time. Let us turn to these consequences of sainthood in turn, first by looking at how the lives of the elite and then the lives of the masses were shaped by their relationships with the Sufis as saints. As we have seen above, from the Saljuq period onwards, the Sufis entered into bonds of patronage with the rulers of the time through which they acquired the material resources necessary to build concrete institutions in which to live and teach. Yet it is important to grasp the two sides of this relationships and, in order to see what sultans and other elites received in return for their patronage, we must turn to the special type of resources that leading Sufis, both in life and death, were believed to possess. For the Sufis were not merely meant to act as propagandists channeling religious legitimacy to the state through publically serving in its *madrasas* or receiving gifts in its *khanaqahs*. No less important was the belief that, as the Friends of God, leading Sufis possessed the mysterious but tremendously effective power of *baraka* ("grace, life-force, blessing") that they could channel in whichever direction they chose through their ability to work miracles or *karamat*.

The relationship between saint and sultan was, then, one of reciprocal exchange, albeit an exchange of the dissimilar resources of cash and land for miracles and blessing. In almost every corner of the Islamic world, from the twelfth century on we begin to hear more and more stories in which the Sufi saints were seen to use their *baraka* as a means of intervention in what in secular terms would be seen as political affairs. They cured kings and courtiers of life-threatening illnesses; they decided on the outcome of king-making battles; they promised heirs to rulers who had no sons; they caused one town to founder and another to flourish; they brought pestilence or plenty on taxable fiefdoms. Unsurprisingly, our richest sources of such stories are the hagiographical writings composed by the followers (and in many cases, the family descendants) of the saint in question. There is no small sense in which (to borrow a term from Peter Brown's depiction of the Christian cult of saints) these story-spreading heirs acted as the "impresarios" of their relatives and masters. We have already seen this developing in the saintly biographies written by the family of Abu Ishaq al-Kazaruni (d.1035), stories which were successful enough to attract local dynasts. As a result, the Inju ruler of southern Iran, Sharaf al-Din Mahmud Shah (d.1336), named his younger son Abu Ishaq after the saint and in 1334 the Inju dynasts paid for a *madrasa* to be built beside Kazaruni's tomb.[74] Such traffic with kings was nothing to be ashamed of: the family of Abu Sa'id ibn Abi'l-Khayr (d.1049) in Khurasan recorded with pride dozens of stories of their saintly ancestor's supernatural dealings in affairs of state.[75] More interesting, perhaps, is the spread of such stories away from the hagiographical productions of the saintly families and into the realm of the books of "history" or *tarikh* sponsored in the royal palace rather than the Sufi lodge. This is not to suggest a clear divide between courtiers and Sufis, because the richer picture researchers are building of social interaction in such medieval capitals as Shiraz, Herat, Konya, and Delhi suggests that, aside from a hard corps of full-time Sufis, there existed larger bodies of followers who drifted between court and *khanaqah*.[76] Magnified by gossip and expectation, the stories spread by this growing number of influential fellow travelers served to increase the prestige of the Sufis and the belief in their powers. If a certain saint was known to be capable of defeating whole armies on behalf of the sultan, then the average Muslim lower down the social spectrum could be reasonably confident that the saint had the wherewithal to cure his sick daughter. While our evidence is primarily that of texts from the writing circles of relatively small groups of religious or courtly elites, their contents also drew from and added to a wider oral repertoire of stories so as to reach the larger populus.[77]

The consequences of this belief in the Sufis as saintly wonder-workers comprised not only the production of stories. As with 'Umar Suhrawardi in Baghdad no less than among the fissiparous tribal polities further east, the saintly status of Sufi families rendered them inviolate blessed men perfectly suited to act as diplomats and go-betweens.[78] Elsewhere, as with the migrant Iranian Ni'matullahi family in the south Indian capital of the Bahmani Sultans (1347–1527), we find Sufis acting as symbolic king-makers in rituals of royal investiture. United in death as in life, both the Bahmani sultans and their saints were buried in grand neighboring mausolea on the outskirts of the capital at Bidar.[79] In such contexts, miracle stories should be seen as functional as much as praise texts, serving as narrative charters which explained all manner of relationships between the Sufis and their courtly allies: Why did such-and-such a dynasty marry its daughters to the sons of a certain saint? Why did such-and-such a tribe always pay homage to a certain shrine? Many saintly miracle stories served to answer such questions, giving credence and sanction to the perpetuation through time of specific alliances between saints and their clients, so that the bond between a particular prince and a particular Sufi might be inherited by both sets of heirs, even when they moved on to pastures new. Between the twelfth and fifteenth centuries, the ties established in Central Asia between powerful Turkish tribes and the saints of the Yasawi brotherhood were introduced into Anatolia as the descendants of both saints and tribesmen rode westwards, although this twin-migration interpretation has recently been challenged.[80] The same process saw the ties established in the fifteenth century between the Naqshbandi saints and the Timuri rulers of Central Asia reproduced over distance and time when, as we will see in the next chapter, a branch of the

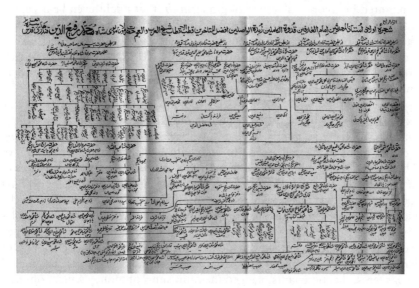

Figure 2.4 Genealogies of Tradition: A Sufi Brotherhood's "Chain" of Masters (Image: Nile Green)

Timuri dynasty (known commonly as the Mughals) conquered India in 1526 and invited the saintly protectors of its forefathers to join them in their new dominions.[81]

Through their links to these larger communities, miracle stories fueled the wider mechanisms by which Sufism was able to perpetuate itself through time, since such stories of past saints served no purpose if there were no living inheritors of their power through future generations, no permanent site of pilgrimage at which it could be accessed, or no surviving community or dynasty to which a saintly lineage was attached. All such heirs had an interest in ensuring that those stories were remembered and passed on. Yet despite its potential rewards, the relationship between Sufi and sultan was also a potentially ruinous one and becoming too close to one dynasty inevitably made a saintly family suspicious in the eyes of the dynasty which replaced it. Different Sufis dealt in different ways with this dilemma between the inevitable need for material patronage and the inherent dangers in too close an association with a particular dynast. As we have seen with the Chishtis and the Naqshbandis, in some cases different brotherhoods developed distinctive approaches to the problem. But for those Sufis who swore to abhor the company of kings, the basic fact of their institutional existence meant that they needed at least a basic operational budget.[82] The theoretically court-avoiding Chishtis of medieval north India thus found themselves developing complicated ethical guidelines by which they hoped (perhaps vainly) to avoid compromising their principles. Earning a living (*kasb*) was denigrated in favor of a system of gifts (*futuh*) that might even be accepted from kings so long as they were not asked for and were channeled into the shared activities of the *khanaqah*.[83] Even so, while we know the Chishtis made much of avoiding kings in their public writings, from their private archives we know that they were far from averse to receiving the royal endowments that allowed their institutions to function.[84]

Even so, kings were not the sole source of material support for the expanding Sufi institutions of the period and while the process is as yet little understood there is good evidence of at least some *khanaqahs* growing wealthy through the patronage of merchants. In the case of the shrine of Abu Ishaq al-Kazaruni, located on one of the most important trade routes of medieval Iran, we know that merchants from as far away as India and China lodged at the *khanaqah* when passing through the region. According to the North African traveler Ibn Battuta, in the mid-1300s Muslim house rules obliged these merchants to stay a minimum of three days, during which they were fed delicious *keskek* stew made with meat, wheat and the rich flavors of lamb's fat. Offered a form of supernatural insurance for the safe passage of their wares, the merchants pledged the saint sums of money which, on their safe arrival home, they dispatched to Kazarun with the next merchant going there.[85] In the drier regions around the central Iranian trading city of Yazd a century later, the *khanaqahs* of the Niʿmatullahi brotherhood are similarly known to have hosted merchants from as far as Arabia and Central Asia. To make up for the fact that their founding saint was buried in distant Mahan rather than in one of the *khanaqahs* of the Yazd plain, the Niʿmatullahis attempted to attract such merchants by constructing restful gardens at the *khanaqahs* to shelter from the desert sun and even a replica tomb of the saint himself which offered vicarious blessings.[86] While such techniques of attracting merchants were probably widespread, more seems to have been made in the written sources of royal than mercantile patronage. Again, there is no need to pass moral judgment on the matter, because no religious institution can survive long without a regular source of material support and, in the period we are looking at, wealth was concentrated in small portions of society. Of course, there were Sufis who avoided any contact with elite groups, and whose tombs were chiefly the resort of the urban poor and peasantry. But such limited constituencies lacked the literacy for text-producing and the wealth for shrine-building, and so unless one of the saints attracted a new following, such patrons of the poor emerge rarely from the shadows of history. Even when we do know of individual Sufis from this period who wrote themselves into history by their own literary efforts – whether it was Shihab al-Din al-Suhrawardi (d.1191), Ibn al-ʿArabi (d.1240) or ʿAla al-Dawla al-Simnani (d.1336) – this was often through their acceptance of royal patronage and protection.[87] Even if such help was neither sought nor accepted, it was a rare Sufi who dared to openly defy the rulers of his day. One case was that of ʿAyn al-Qudat (d.1131) of Hamadan in western Iran, who from his imprisonment on grounds of heresy wrote his *Shakwa al-Gharib* ("Stranger's Complaint") in defence of his teachings.[88] But if such defiance offered one road to remembrance, it was one that few Sufis chose to take.

If rebellion was rarer than alliance with the ruling classes, there was still a good deal of room for the middle way of rivalry.[89] While the precise origins of the practice are unclear, from the fifteenth century in the region stretching between Anatolia and India we find more and more saints being described through the terminology of kingship. Saints were termed "emperors" (*shah*), their shrines called "royal courts" (*dargah*), and their headgear considered "crowns" (*taj*), designations which may have begun among the followers of "Shah" Niʿmatullah Wali (d.1431) in eastern Iran. As over a period of generations the great medieval shrine complexes acquired more and more status, in many regions saintly dynasties became a more permanent and long-lived "establishment" class than the shorter-lived dynasties of kings. In the next chapter we will see how after 1500 this conflict of status played out in several different directions, from Sufis overthrowing sultans to become rulers themselves to new sorts of early modern state seeking closer control of the Sufis in their domains. But in the medieval period we are dealing with here, the overall picture was one of an unassailable ascent of the Sufis as saints acquiring the influence and in some cases the wealth that made their followers' description of them as emperors by no means the exaggeration of piety.

It seems likely that beneath the common theory and terminology of Friendship across wide areas, there lay substantial differences in the way in which saints, their descendants and their institutions functioned in the Turco-Persian east and the Turco-Arab west, with the former regions seeing the saints reach their greatest social and economic impact. But as yet no substantial comparative work has been carried out between the process of sanctification in the Islamic east and west. To some degree at least, part of the explanation for this variation lies in the greater impact on the societies of the Islamic east of the tribal and nomadic groups for whom Sufi saints were so important. This was most clearly seen through the conversion of whole tribes as a consequence of the alliance between a tribal leader and a Sufi. Here we have to bear in mind that, with the exception of North Africa, for much of the medieval period the Islamic world from Anatolia to India was ruled by Turkic and Mongol tribal groups. In many cases what we are dealing with in these links between saint and tribe is as much saintly stories as saintly acts, narratives of the kind we have already seen greatly influencing popular attitudes towards saintly shrines and families. Of particular importance here are the conversion narratives through which a whole range of tribal groups across Central Asia, Iran and India constructed their ethnic identities around stories of the conversion to Islam of their founding ancestor at the hands of a Sufi.[90] Even in agrarian settings in such regions as Egypt, Sufi saints were looked on as founding ancestors by the villagers who lived around their shrines.[91]

Moving from saintly narrative to saintly action, what evidence we have suggests that such interactions between saints and tribesmen were far from purely "spiritual" and in many cases comprised the physical interactions of marriage, sex and procreation. Although the process is not fully understood – not least because tribes did not generate written documents until they settled, came under urban influences and sponsored others to write their histories for them – we find many tribal groups recounting their ethnic origins as lying in the offspring of either a tribal elder and the daughter of a Sufi saint or a Sufi saint and the daughter of a tribal elder. The Timuri branch of the Chahar 'Aymaq tribe of what is now western Afghanistan thus considered themselves as descendants of the union of the Naqshbandi Sayyid Amir Kulal (d.1370?) and a daughter of the great tribal conqueror Timur (d.1405), a tradition in this case bolstered by its appearance in the medieval Persian hagiography, *Maqamat-e Amir Kulal* ("Spiritual Stations of Amir Kulal").[92] Among the Mongol tribes of the Golden Horde in what is now southern Russia and Kazakhstan, a similarly obscure fourteenth century Sufi by the name of Baba Tükles was considered to have been the convertor or even ancestor of the

Golden Horde.[93] What we are looking at in either case is not an abstract mysticism of rarified metaphysics, but a Sufism of marriage, procreation and community-building in which the blessing of *baraka* and the protection of a saintly ancestor was transmitted through no lesser physical means than birth and blood. In such ways, Sufis were sanctified through their integration into myths of ethnogenesis and structures of tribal life, becoming saints through the commemoration and veneration of tribesmen who considered themselves their collective descendants. We should not necessarily imagine these Sufis as the bookish figures we have met in the *madrasas* of the Islamic west. In many cases we are dealing here with wilder, charismatic figures more likely to be seen wearing the skins and horns of animals than the plain cloak and turban of the scholar. It has been widely argued that such Sufis were much closer to the traditional shamanism of the steppes than to the Islam of the cities and that their "shamanized Islam" helped sugar the pill of conversion for their tribal followers.[94] However, while the theory certainly has its appeal, closer inspection of the kinds of Sufis connected with the tribes has shown that many of them were in fact formal initiates of the Sufi brotherhoods, suggesting that their Islam was more than the cosmetic camouflaging of shamans.[95]

Not all features of the sanctification process were unique to the Turco-Mongol sphere. The spread of Islam into the Malay world in the fourteenth and fifteenth centuries was linked to the conversion of local Malay rulers by seafaring Sufis who traveled from Arabia and Iraq. However, it has to be said that the accounts are far later than the events and so again we may be dealing with saints as narrative as much as physical actors.[96] Even among the more sedentary polities of the Islamic west, we find the notion of *baraka* ("blessing power") being transferred through blood being eventually drawn into the social structure of the agricultural landlords along the rim of the Sahara, for whom such blessed bloodlines served to bolster the ethnic boundary between Arab landowner and African slave.[97] If saintly charisma is often seen as an intangible and symbolic resource, through connecting *baraka* to blood in many such settings from Central Asia to Africa, *baraka* became a physical and reproducible asset.

Looking beyond the elite to the masses, the sanctification of the Sufis had its greatest impact in laying the foundations for a devotional Islam in which the veneration of saints deemed more accessible than a distant God provided a vehicle for popular religious expression. As with any other aspect of medieval popular culture, our sources are largely limited to the observations on popular practice made by the learned, whether scornful critics of *hoi polloi* like the Sufi legal scholar Ibn Taymiyya (d.1328) or else Sufi biographers with an eye for local color.[98] Even so, the fact that the existence of God's Friends was part of popular as much as elite religion means that we should not imagine any sharp dichotomy between "popular" and "elite"

Islam in which saint veneration belonged solely to the masses.[99] What we have seen of the formation of the doctrines and institutions of sainthood betwixt scholar and sultan suggests that, if anything, saint veneration emerged at the top of the social spectrum and trickled down from there. Nonetheless, the reproductive mechanisms of the Sufi brotherhoods enabled the gradual expansion of an immense network of shrines built to venerate the local representatives of the various brotherhoods. The development of these shrines allowed the God of Islam to be accessed through interactions with physical spaces and not solely with written scripture: it created an Islam that was immanent and tangible in its local environments. Not merely holy scripture, nor even holy persons and places, the cult of Sufi saints enabled a whole gamut of physical objects to serve as the media and hardware of Islam, from strips of grave cloth and dust swept from tombs to such pilgrimage souvenirs as rose water, flowers or even peacock feathers seen to carry *baraka* through their contact with the grave. This expansion of the ways to articulate and interact with Islam allowed the greater involvement of social groups with relatively little access to scripture, not least women.

It was not only women who were given access to Islam by such means. While it has long been debated whether Islam is primarily an urban religion, from Morocco to Palestine, Central Asia and India, the practice that emerged in the medieval period of bestowing rural land grants on Sufis meant that the initial contact that many country people had with Islamic institutions was through Sufi channels.[100] In the country if not always in the town, Islam effectively was Sufism; and Sufism was in turn an Islam in which access to Allah was mediated through God's local saintly representatives. In such contexts, the veneration of saints took on distinct local forms through the fusion of pan-Islamic concepts with more local idioms of language and ritual. Although such veneration of the saints was surely expressed in vernacular languages, little if anything survives of this folk literature before 1400. But from what is known, it appears that the saints were imagined in ways that fitted closely to the folkways of their clients. In southern India, for example, we find devotion to the saints being expressed through rustic vernacular lullabies and cheerful work shanties for grinding wheat.[101]

In other cases, the close proximity in which Muslims lived with Christians and Hindus saw the development of "syncretistic" idioms of ritual and speech that enabled non-Muslims to participate in saint-veneration without formally accepting Islam.[102] As Anatolia fell from Byzantine to Saljuq rule in the twelfth and thirteenth centuries, Sufi lodges acted as spaces of mediation between older Christian communities and newly arrived Turkoman nomads.[103] In sites connected to other regions by busy trade routes, we typically find such syncretism and localization being expressed without losing sight of the saints' connections to the wider practices of

Islam. But in regions which were more remote or poorly connected, it was not uncommon to find high levels of variation from trans-regional Islamic norms and, as the Sufis spread into such rural settings, they or their followers at times lost their earlier Sufi commitment to the Shari'a and scripture. In some cases, as with the veneration of Shaykh Adi by the Yezidis in the mountains of Kurdistan, such disconnected localization saw the veneration of Sufi shrines gradually fuel the creation of new and independent religions.[104]

However, for the most part, through their transformation into saints whose presence was rendered permanent in their host communities through the building of shrines, the Sufis provided a means for countless ordinary people to express devotion to God and to ask favors of his Friends. Ultimately, the reciprocal cycle of devotion and favor were two sides of the same coin: through providing access to miraculous power, the Sufis as saints performed extremely practical purposes. While princes begged the favor of victory in battle, peasants begged for the return of water to their wells. As the earlier doctrine of Friendship gathered institutional momentum from the eleventh century onwards, its practical implications lent the Sufis wide appeal at every level of the social spectrum. While the status of the Sufi saints would certainly change in future centuries (particularly in the modern period discussed in Chapter 4), it is important to recognize that this veneration of the Sufi saints still forms the basis of the religious life of many millions of Muslims through to the present day.

The Vernacularization of Sufi Teachings

So far this chapter has looked at two processes by which between 1100 and 1400 the Sufis were able to massively expand their status and following through developing the conceptual and organizational institution of the brotherhood and becoming the focus of saintly veneration. In reflection of the vast geographical and social range on which the Sufis were now operating, the medieval period also saw a third important development by way of the increasing vernacularization of Sufi ideas into the regional languages of the many regions they had now entered. Whether in Iraq or Khurasan, almost without exception the founding Sufi theorists discussed in Chapter 1 had written in Arabic. Even setting aside the restrictions of literacy, we must remember that Arabic was only spoken in the regions south of Iraq, and even there it competed outside the towns with languages ranging from Kurdish to Turkish and Berber. Further east, Arabic served only as the language of the learned, with the vast majority of Muslims speaking languages that, despite borrowing a good deal of vocabulary from Arabic and (when they were eventually written down) the letters of the Arabic alphabet, were structurally as distinct from Arabic as English. Clearly, if Sufism was to evolve into something more than the Islam of the elite, it would need to develop inroads into the vernacular language worlds in which the vast majority of Muslims east of Iraq in South and Southeast Asia especially lived and thought. Throughout this process of translating Sufi teachings into the range of languages being spoken by new Muslim communities, a core vocabulary of religious terms was passed on either in the original Arabic or in a modification of the Arabic according to local phonology, so creating "a transregional, standardized Islamic vocabulary across South and Southeast Asian Muslim societies."[105] In addition to basic Quranic terms for prayer and the divinity, this core vocabulary consisted in large part of words from the Arabic Sufi lexicon we saw developing in Chapter 1.[106] Given that Sufis were instrumental in the creation of new Muslim communities in various regions in this period, it has recently been argued that these acts of vernacular translation should be seen as integral to the parallel process of conversion as "through translation, [new] communities gradually created, adopted, and accumulated the cultural resources that made memories of an Islamic past and a lived Islamic presence possible."[107]

Even so, this process of vernacularization was by no means the unique achievement of the Sufis. If in some regions the Sufis do seem to have been literary pioneers of the vernaculars, then in other regions they were copying the fashions of the court in adopting local tongues. Overall, we can therefore posit three broad modes of vernacularization: a courtly one emerging through the patronage of polished literary productions by regional dynasts; a scholarly one of Sufis translating works of doctrine and etiquette for local followers; and a folkloric one emerging through the adaptation of low status folk genres. In the centuries before 1500, the courtly mode effectively meant Persian (and, in one brief period, Hindi); the scholarly mode Dakani Urdu and possibly Malay; and the folkloric mode various other languages in which at least some Sufis interacted with their followers but from which the only surviving evidence is in certain forms of Turkish and again Dakani Urdu and possibly Malay. Such are the connections between language, power and script that Persian was by far more successful in entering the written record and so while literally hundreds of Sufi texts from prior to 1500 survive in Persian, for other vernaculars we are looking at no more than the occasional collection of verses.

The use as a literary language of what was up to this point the unwritten vernacular of Persian was already under way before 1100, having begun as early as the ninth or tenth century in the local Muslim courts that emerged with the fragmentation of the 'Abbasid Empire in Khurasan.[108] By the year 1010, the poet Abu'l Qasim Firdawsi (d.1020) had completed his epic *Shahnama* ("Book of Kings") in which he recounted the heroic deeds of the ancient rulers of Iran in easily memorizable Persian couplets. Although

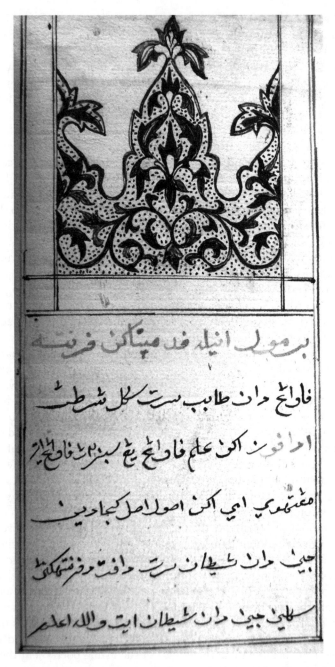

Figure 2.5 Vernacular Expressions: A Sufi Manuscript in Malay (Single unpaginated manuscript text page from Malay 106 (Maxwell collection, Royal Asiatic Society). Unpaginated 1st page of ms. Reproduced by permission of the Royal Asiatic Society)

Persian poetry developed first, prose soon followed. Sufis in Iran and Khurasan were already using Persian in Firdawsi's lifetime: in Chapter 1 we have already mentioned the earliest Persian prose manual in the *Kashf al-Mahjub* ("Revelation of the Hidden") written by Hujwiri in the new Turkish capital of north India at Lahore. With the validity of this pioneering vernacular having been recognized, more and more Sufis over the following centuries chose to write in Persian, borrowing both the genres and the technical language of their Sufi predecessors who had written in the more prestigious Arabic of the scripture and the other religious sciences. While the development of a Persian prose literature widened the social reach of Sufi ideas, and provided a more accessible means with which Sufis from the eastern Islamic world could contribute ideas, in terms of explaining the growing success of the Sufis in the medieval period we must turn to the more popular and memorizable medium of verse. Although Sufis were surely already composing poems in Persian in Firdawsi's day, we have relatively little evidence except for the collections of quatrains (*ruba'iyyat*) attributed to such figures as Baba Tahir (d.1020?) of Hamadan in western Iran and Abu Sa'id (d.1049) of Mayhana, whom we have earlier seen organizing musical *soirées* at his Khurasani *khanaqah*.[109] Such poems are what we would now think of as lyrics, since they were intended to be sung to musical accompaniment and formed the basis of the Sufi practice of "listening" (*sama'*), whose legitimacy we have already seen being debated. The controversial character of *sama'* becomes all the more clear when we look at the themes and topoi with which many such quatrains dealt by way of drunkenness, passion, wayfaring, madness and, not least, the physical beauty of slave-boys and cup-bearers.

While it later became standard practice for Sufi commentators to explain that the "true" meaning of such early Persian poetry was inward and spiritual – drunkenness meant absorption in God and not wine, the beautiful youth was a metaphor for divine perfection, and so on – there seems little point in doubting that many (perhaps even most) of the medieval audiences of these songs enjoyed them for what they appeared to be: celebrations of wine, sex and song. Comparing the themes of worldly pleasure that characterized the first generations of Persian poetry with the esoteric themes that subsequently came to dominate all but panegyric genres of Persian verse, one scholar has gone so far as to speak of a Sufi "colonization of Persian literature."[110] In social terms, such poetry served to justify the at times aberrant behavior of the Sufi poets by draping their actions in the obscuring but nonetheless respectable rhetoric of metaphysics.[111] The larger point is that such poems owed their aesthetic as well as social power to the multiple ways in which their meanings could be understood. For the very ambiguity and double-entendre of the passionate performance of such sung poetry lent the Sufis a highly effective means of community outreach and propaganda. Here we have to bear in mind that in pre-industrial societies, in which music necessarily meant live performance, for most people the opportunity to hear music was a rare pleasure and so the increasing tendency of *khanaqahs* to sponsor musical concerts or *mahfil-e sama'* formed an important attraction for their surrounding communities.

Of course, the obsession with formal etiquette that we have seen as being highly characteristic of the Sufis meant that formal rules were devised for the proper listening to music (often including banning women from attending), though it seems reasonable to surmise that some gatherings were less formal than others. In Iran and Khurasan, between the twelfth and thirteenth centuries, the Sufis adapted from the courts the genre of the secular love lyric or *ghazal* in which the relationship between the Muslim and God was presented as one of lover and beloved, allowing poets to imagine the Almighty in vivid physical terms: a fair-skinned slave, a hat-tilting coquette, an androgynous beardless boy. Borrowing from the romance poetry popular at court, the Sufi himself was painted in similarly new guise, as lover, fool or madman, alternatively teased and tortured in the alternating presence and absence of his lover. Increasingly, the Sufi was depicted in the form of the *qalandar*, a shady and rule-breaking figure of whom we will have more to say later.[112] Such was the earthiness of the imagery that in the finest examples of such "Sufi" *ghazals* in the work of poets such as Sana'i (d.1131) of Ghazna and Sa'di (d.1292) and Hafiz (d.1390) of Shiraz, it is hard to say whether their verses were intended for esoteric interpretation or plainly for the pleasure of young princes. In other cases, as with the lyrics produced by such thorough-going Sufis as Fakhr al-Din 'Iraqi (d.1289) and Jalal al-Din Rumi (d.1273), there is less ambiguity as to the poet's intentions. Ultimately, though, the question of authorial intention is less important than the fact that the Sufis co-opted the genre and imagery of the court poets for their own purposes. Once again, we see how the Sufis were capable of incorporating people and their writings into their own tradition and in so doing to lend meanings to others' works that were in line with their own doctrines. Just as the earliest Sufis had made mystical meanings from the Quran, so later did they find similar affirmation in the intoxicating love songs of medieval Persia.

From the time of Rumi in the thirteenth century, the ambiguous possi-bilities of the Persian lyric became well-established as the preferred medium for daring ideas. In Rumi's case, this included nothing less than the decla-ration that the glory of God shined from the face of his beloved boon pal, Shams al-Din of Tabriz. But despite the ardor and excitement of Rumi's *ghazals*, in which the Sufi path was presented as one of the bewilderment and ecstasies of love, it was in his vast and rambling narrative poem or *mathnawi* ("rhyming couplets") that he made his greatest contribution to the spread of Sufi ideas. While the shorter verse forms of the quatrain and lyric were suitable for the musical settings whose purpose was to summon the ecstatic "finding"(*tawajud*) of God, such short verses were poor media for the exposition of doctrine. For this purpose, the Sufis adopted the genre of the Persian narrative poem. Like other forms of Persian poetry, narrative verse emerged in the courts of Khurasan and in terms of the development of the religious and more specifically Sufi narrative the key figure was again Sana'i at the court of the Turkish sultans of Ghazna (modern Afghanistan) in the early twelfth century.[113] While Sana'i is better viewed as a court poet than a mystic – singing to the moods of his patrons, his poems ranged from celebrations of drinking to moralizing homilies on good conduct – his extended poem laid the foundations for verse as a didactic vehicle. In such works as his *Hadiqat al-Haqiqa wa Shari'at al-Tariqa* ("The Garden of Truth and Law of the Path") and *Sayr al-'Ibad ila al-Ma'ad* ("Journey of God's Slaves to the Place of No Return"), Sana'i rendered rhymes into allegorical maps of the cosmos, revealing the journey of the soul through the various cosmic spheres.[114]

The abundance of technical concepts and terminology in Sana'i's poems has often led them to be seen as "encyclopedia" of Sufi doctrine. But as a canny and creative artist, Sana'i was more eclectic than systematic. Though his poems were taken up by the Sufis and given esoteric glosses, his own sources were more varied, reflecting the hotchpotch of philosophers, scientists, and mystics who hovered round the Ghaznavid court. A century later, still in Khurasan, Farid al-Din 'Attar ("the druggist," d.*circa* 1220) brought greater doctrinal consistency to the didactic Persian narrative poem, of which he wrote several important examples.[115] The most significant was his *Mantiq al-Tayr* ("Speech of the Birds") in which different avian species formed similes for the types of mankind and their search for the "sultan of the birds" across seven valleys with names like "Love" and "Bewilderment" formed an allegory of the places on the Path towards God. In perhaps the most famous pun in all Persian literature, the thirty birds (*si murgh*) who made it to their final destination realized that they were themselves identical to the fabulous griffin (*simurgh*) who was their bird-king: when the Sufi destroys his lower self through following the Path, at journey's end all that remains is God.

In terms of measuring the successful expansion of the Sufis that was so central a feature of medieval Islam, the main point to grasp about such poems is that in their pre-industrial cultural contexts they were a form of entertainment. Committed to memory by professional bards, such poems formed hours of entertainment that could be easily transported and reproduced for audiences who would be edified no less than amused. Seen within his own time, this is especially true of the greatest of the Sufi narrative poets, Jalal al-Din Rumi, whose *mathnawi* drew so freely on the folklore, idioms and humor of the people that, not to put too fine a point on it, one allegory centered on a slave-girl's fascination with a donkey's penis.[116] As in the case of lyrical poems set to music, through the jokes and stories they wove into their poetry, the Sufis were able to tie their message to vehicles that the ordinary and unlettered would welcome to their villages. Compared to the dogmatic handbooks, and even to the heady but complicated treatises, these poems had a more immediate appeal and accessibility. If the Arabic prose literature we have seen the Sufis developing from their early days in Baghdad helped them maintain their position in the religious establishment, then it was through their co-option of such vernacular entertainments that the Sufis were able to reach a more general audience. If sanctification brought the Sufis a mass following based on power and respect, then vernacularization ensured that it was also a relationship which was warmed with affection and informed by at least a measure of understanding.

The actual lives of such poets as 'Attar and Rumi point us to another important feature of the spread of Persian in the exodus of refugees fleeing Khurasan in the wake of the Mongol invasions.[117] 'Attar was not so fortunate, and like thousands of his fellow townsmen in Nishapur, some time around 1220 the poet disappeared in the anonymity of the general massacre. As a child growing up in the Khurasani towns of Vakhsh and then Balkh, the young Rumi was more fortunate and his scholarly father had the connections to find a position in the new capital of the Turkish Saljuqs in the Rum (literally "Rome") or Anatolia that was to lend Rumi his name. When the Sufi theorist of light visions and "founder" of the Kubrawi brotherhood, Najm al-Din Kubra, was slaughtered by the Mongols, some of his followers also fled to Anatolia, where in the city of Kayseri his disciple Najm al-Din Razi (d.1256) summarized his master's teachings in his Persian prose treatise, *Mirsad al-'Ibad min al-Mabda ila al-Ma'ad* ("The Path of God's Slaves from their Origin to their Return").[118] Kubra's other followers fled to India, where they propagated the teachings and brotherhood named after him to an audience eager for the now famous wisdom of Khurasan.[119] In such ways, the Mongols did not put an end to either the Sufis or their new fondness for Persian. As we have seen, when the Mongols began to convert to Islam from the end of the thirteenth century, they too became assiduous patrons of the Sufis like the former Saljuq nomads before them. But in the period between the Mongols' appearance on Khurasan's horizons in the 1220s and their acculturation to Islam after the conversion of the Mongol leader Ghazan Khan in 1295, they triggered a refugee crisis which fed a Khurasani diaspora whose customs and culture sparked highly creative syntheses in their various new homelands. Whether to the west in Anatolia or to the south in India, many thousands of people fled the Khurasan that had not only reared its distinct traditions of Sufism but had also pioneered the literary use of Persian.

While Persian was already present in north India, the role of Delhi as the protective "canopy of Islam" (*qubbat al-islam*) protecting these refugees saw the city develop a rich Persian prose literature cast very much in the clay of Khurasan. Again, there is no sense in seeing this as a lack of originality, since insofar as originality was even a recognizable concept, it was abhorred in

favor of tradition, and the Indian Sufis of the Chishti and Kubrawi brotherhoods saw themselves very much as the heirs to the traditions of the Khurasan
in which their distinct Paths were founded. Even so, the Indian heirs to this
Khurasani exodus did push the genres they inherited in new directions, not
least in expanding the older practice of quoting masters verbatim into a
whole new genre of the "recorded conversation" or *malfuzat*. From the time
of the Delhi-based Chishti Sufi Nizam al-Din Awliya (d.1325) onwards,
malfuzat served as a paper technology for reproducing the precise living
words of the inspired master long after he died. As the Sufis of the Delhi
Sultanate spread into southern and eastern as well as northern India, they too
became vigorous producers and judicious popularizers of Persian. By inspiring such court poets as Amir Khusraw (d.1325), the Sufis succeeded in
bending the literary fashions of the Delhi court to their own purposes in a way
that echoed what had happened earlier in the courts of Khurasan before the
Mongol invasions.[120] In doing so, they laid the foundation for a rich body of
literature that, from saintly biographies to technical treatises and collections
of letters (*maktubat*), recreated for a new environment the forms of Persian
Sufi expression that had developed earlier in Iran and Central Asia.[121]

Although in literary terms the period before 1100 belonged mainly to
Arabic, and the centuries between 1100 and 1500 mainly to Arabic and
Persian, there were certain situations in which other languages were put into
writing. For if Persian served as a vernacular in large parts of Central Asia and
Iran, and was widely understood among the educated or immigrated in
Anatolia and India, in the latter regions it was never truly a vernacular. Just
as, under the shadow of Arabic, Persian took several centuries to establish its
credentials as a literary language, so did the various forms of Turkish and
Hindi/Urdu need time to emerge from the shadows of Persian. While this
second phase of vernacularization was certainly under way in the medieval
period, it would not be completed until as late as the seventeenth century. But
even if the Sufis' use of Indian and Turkic languages was rarely written down
in this earlier period, there survives just enough evidence for us to see that the
Sufi technique of spreading their ideas in the languages of the ordinary people
had already begun to be expanded from Persian into Hindi and Turkish and
even Malay. Of course, it had taken the patronage of royal courts to give
Persian the status of a written language and it would ultimately be sultans
and states rather than Sufis and peasants that were responsible for properly
putting Turkish and Hindi into ink. Nonetheless, if usually only as inter-
polations in Persian texts, we do possess enough examples of Sufis using these
less prestigious vernaculars to suggest they were willing to adopt any
language necessary to reach a larger audience. There was often a linguistic
compromise involved, in that in many cases we find Sufis introducing into
these other languages the Arabic terms for their concepts which we saw
developing as the technical lexicon of the Baghdad Sufis. This compromise

was a reflection of the diglossic power relationship between Arabic and the vernacular languages which from Persian right through to Hindi, Turkish, Malay and eventually other languages carried over what was by now the esteemed vocabulary of the founders of Sufi tradition.[122] Even so, many Sufis were willing to use not only local languages but also the idioms and stories with which their audiences were familiar. In India the earliest evidence relates to the master of the Chishti brotherhood, Farid al-Din Ganj-e Shakar (d.1265), whose verses in an early form of Punjabi were transmitted orally for generations before eventually finding an incongruous home in the Sikh holy book, the Adi Granth.[123] In the next generation, the Chishtis' courtly disciple, Amir Khusraw (d.1325), turned his hand to writing devotional Sufi songs in an early form of Hindi, though again these verses were not written down for centuries.[124] It was among the Chishtis again that the first Hindi/ Urdu prose work on Sufism appeared, this time in south India, with the *Mi'raj al-'Ashiqin* ("Ascent of God's Lovers") written by the north Indian migrant Muhammad al-Husayni "Gisu Daraz" ("long-haired"). The text was composed in the capital of the Bahmani sultans, who built a huge stone mausoleum for Gisu Daraz after his death in 1422.[125] The court was to play an even closer role in the first Sufi narrative or *mathnawi* poem written in Hindi before 1500, for its very author was a courtier patronized by the governor of a regional court in eastern India. Echoing the way Rumi had exploited the local folk tales of Anatolia, in Awadh the Chishti disciple and courtier Mulla Da'ud borrowed not only one of the region's most popular romances, but also its dialect, to write his *Candayan* in 1379.[126] By now the Sufi quest was being seen not only through 'Attar's Persian allegories of birds, but also through tales of romance and adventure that appealed not solely to the warring lords of the palaces but were also intelligible to the ordinary folk of the countryside, where we can assume Da'ud's poems circulated second-hand with all the cachet of the court. Although no other Hindi *mathnawis* have survived from this period, in the sixteenth and seventeenth centuries many other Sufi romances would be written in Hindi.[127] Steeped in the landscape, the heroes and the fantasia of India, by the 1400s the Sufis were vernacularizing their teachings to an extraordinary degree. For many Sufis, such rustification appeared to be diluting Islam with paganism. But with the greater accommodation the Chishti brotherhood afforded to their cultural environment, this was a risk which the likes of Amir Khusrow and Mulla Da'ud were willing to take.

The third major move towards the vernaculars that we find in this period was in Turkish. Given the political strength of the various Turkish groups, it is initially surprising that so little literary production was sponsored in the different versions of their language. But such were the links formed between Turkish warriors and the older learned establishment that it was mostly the more prestigious languages of Arabic and Persian that the Turks chose to patronize. Installed in the Anatolian Saljuq capital at Konya, Rumi is himself the prime example. Nonetheless, some evidence does survive of medieval Sufis using Turkish, even though these verses were not written down for several centuries. The most important examples are the quatrains known as *hikmet* ("wisdom"), attributed to the Central Asian Sufi Ahmad Yasawi (d.1166?), which championed the life of the ascetic and celebrated the miracles of the saints. If much of the so-called Yasawi corpus of poetry was probably of later date and falsely attributed to the saint, the collective purpose of these verses still seems to have been to spread Islam (albeit in its Sufi version) among the unconverted nomadic Turks of the steppe, a process in which the poems were aided by their links with the great pilgrimage shrine built round Ahmad Yasawi's grave in what is now Kazakhstan.[128] A century and a half later, when the Turks were well established in Anatolia, the poetry of Yunus Emre (d.1321?) served to transmit a Sufism of humility and love through the often complex oral verse forms Yunus Emre introduced to Anatolian Turkish.[129] Another important case was 'Ashiq Pasha (d.1333), whose monumental *Gharib-name* ("Book of the Poor") comprised around 12,000 Turkish verses which served to transmit complex theological doctrines into the vernacular arena.[130] Although Yunus Emre seems to have been a wandering dervish rather than a settled master of high formal status, Turkish was also occasionally used by the wealthy custodians of the shrines being founded in Anatolia as part of the Saljuq and early Ottoman sponsorship of Muslim institutions. The most important example was that of Sultan Walad (d.1312), the son and impresario of Rumi, whose recorded output included several dozen poems in Turkish and a smaller number of verses in the Greek still spoken by most of the region's Christians.[131] Although the number of Sultan Walad's Turkish poems pales besides his almost forty thousand lines of Persian verse, its very existence is proof of the deliberate attempt the medieval Sufis made to reach audiences with no command over Arabic or Persian. And the strategy was a success, for through their move into vernacular forms of expression, especially into the oral and performative genres of poetry and song, the Sufis were able to reach a far larger audience than would otherwise have been possible, shifting their following beyond the towns and the learned to the unlettered nomads and peasants who first found Islam through their words.

Summary

At the same time that Sufis were increasingly using the more accessible vernaculars to explore the finer implications of their ideas, learned Sufis in all regions continued to use Arabic. From an earlier period dominated by short treatises and lengthier handbooks, after 1100 we enter a period in which Sufi Arabic literary production expanded in terms of both length and genre. In Arabic and its Persian handmaiden, the expansion into the unwritten vernaculars was therefore matched by a massive literary profusion by way of biographies, pilgrimage manuals, letter collections, recorded conversations, epic poems and dream diaries, to name just a few examples. In genre and complexity no less than temperament and theme, between 1100 and 1400 the core vocabulary of terms and concepts developed in the first period of Sufism became a far more diversified idiom in which a much wider range of Muslims from across the geographical and social spectrum found their needs answered and their worlds reflected. Yet in expanding from their early use of Arabic into Persian and more local vernaculars, the Sufis effectively shifted the entry requirements to their fellowship from close knowledge of the Quran and specialist methods of chants (*dhikr*) and retreats (*khalwa*) to a far more accessible curriculum that progressed from singing the vernacular melodies of Yunus Emre to pondering renditions of the allegories of 'Attar. Like the rumors of miracles that circulated among pilgrims to the shrines of Sufi saints, over time these orally-transmitted verse forms were able to penetrate and shape the imagination of the masses in a way that the Quran could not. As with each passing century the Arabic of the Quran became ever more distant from the many spoken languages of Islam, the songs and the shrines of the Sufis served to bridge the growing distance between the believer and the moment of Muhammad's revelation. And for increasing numbers of Muslims in their far-flung locales, what they knew of Islam was what was brokered through the tongues and tombs of their community's Sufis.

The cult of the saints by which Sufis were venerated in architecture, ritual and narrative therefore served as the crucial bridgehead between Sufism as an esoteric method belonging to an inevitably limited movement of committed spiritual aspirants and Sufism as an everyday idiom appealing to the religious needs of a mass clientele. As approachable grandees in their accessible shrines, the "sanctified" Sufi saints could act as intermediaries between the limited reach of human agency and the limitless power of God. Reproduced in shrine buildings from Morocco to Turkestan, this was an arrangement that was as useful to peasants as it was to sultans, each of whom contributed to the coffers of the shrines, placing Sufis into the patterns of reciprocal exchange that tied them to their communities of clients by a mutual web of favors. Given the distance of these developments from a model of Sufism as a personal mystical quest for union with God, they were once seen as heralding a medieval end of "true" Sufism. But such an interpretation is to miss both the internal logic of Friendship and the social strategies by which the Sufis were able to survive and reproduce their tradition through time. For shrines were not separate institutions from the teaching rooms, lodges and retreats in which "mysticism" took place but were rather one element in larger complexes shared by day-visiting pilgrims and permanently-resident Sufis. It makes sense to think of the holy graves in such complexes as the pilgrim-gathering public interface to the wider societies on which the Sufis depended for material support.

As we have seen, the sanctification of the Sufis did not emerge from nowhere and had its doctrinal foundations in the theory discussed in the earliest Sufi writings that God had special "Friends" (*awliya*). Between 1100 and 1400, as the resources of tradition these older ideas were drawn on to explain a socio-religious order based on an articulate hierarchical "hidden government" of saintly finders. It makes sense to see the development of the cult of saints as a logical consequence of the growing material investment in this ideology that occurred as the Sufis gained a larger elite following from the twelfth century onwards, through their alliance with settling nomadic rulers in the east and the royal patrons of the Sunni revival in the west. Such sanctification did not occur in an institutional vacuum. The public services of the Sufis as saints were matched by their more private services to the new brotherhoods in which sanctification occurred as part of the corollary of institution-building, whereby the founders of brotherhoods were sanctified through the veneration of the brotherhood members. The mechanisms of sanctification and of tradition operated hand-in-glove as the prestige of the knowledge and blessing passed down through the brotherhoods' chains of descent required each figure in the chain to be regarded as a Friend of God, because otherwise the chain of saints was incomplete and the knowledge and blessing it transmitted rendered worthless. The logic of tradition and its use for the conceptual foundation of the brotherhoods was thus in itself an engine for the production of saints.

Linked to popular and wealth-generating shrine complexes, as both organizational and conceptual institutions the brotherhoods formed a means of attaching Sufi ideas and practices to the actual communities whose membership could be expanded and reproduced through simple rituals of initiation at the hands of a master. While it would be anachronous to see such brotherhoods as akin to modern organizations with integrated hierarchies of efficient communications between their many geographical outposts, in functioning as conceptual if not always organizational networks they were able to construct parallel (if not necessarily inter-connected) institutions in the many different environments in which medieval Muslims were living. By reproducing such parallel institutions across distances of thousands of miles, the Sufi brotherhoods created mechanisms of interaction, coherence and fellowship between Muslims who were otherwise increasingly separated by political disunity and ethnic difference. By making such saints and brothers, and labeling them with the same Arabic lexicon in regions as far apart as the Bay of Bengal and the North African coast of the Atlantic, the Sufis rendered

Islam both tangible in their local settings and consistent across the wider world. In so doing, for many millions of medieval Muslims, these developments rendered Sufism inseparable from Islam itself.

Notes

1. For overviews, see H. Dabashi, "Historical Conditions of Persian Sufism during the Seljuq Period," in L. Lewisohn (ed.), *Classical Persian Sufism: From its Origins to Rumi* (London: Khanaqahi Nimatullahi Publications, 1993) and O. Safi, *The Politics of Knowledge in Premodern Islam: Negotiating Ideology and Religious Inquiry* (Chapel Hill: University of North Carolina Press, 2006), especially chapter 2.

2. D. Ephrat, "Religion in the Public Sphere: Rulers, Scholars, and Commoners in Syria under Zangid and Ayyubid rule (1150–1260)," in M. Hoexter, S.N. Eisenstadt & N. Levtzion (eds), *The Public Sphere in Muslim Societies* (Albany: State University of New York Press, 2002) and Y. Tabbaa, *Constructions of Power and Piety in Medieval Aleppo* (University Park: Pennsylvania State University Press, 1997).

3. For contrasting readings of Suhrawardi as mystic or philosopher, see M. Amin Razavi, *Suhrawardi and the School of Illumination* (Richmond: Curzon Press, 1997) and H. Ziai, *Knowledge and Illumination: A Study of Suhrawardī's Hikmat al-Ishrāq* (Atlanta: Scholars Press, 1990).

4. I.R. Netton, "The Neoplatonic Substrate of Suhrawardi's Philosophy of Illumination: *Falsafa* as *Tasawwuf*," in L. Lewisohn (ed.), *The Legacy of Medieval Persian Sufism* (London: Khanaqah Nimatullahi Publishing, 1992) and J. Walbridge, *The Leaven of the Ancients: Suhrawardī and the Heritage of the Greeks* (Albany: State University of New York Press, 1999).

5. On later Sufi light mysticism, see H. Corbin, *The Man of Light in Iranian Sufism* (Boulder: Shambhala, 1978) and J.J. Elias, "A Kubrawī Treatise on Mystical Visions: The *Risāla-yi Nūriyya* of 'Alā' ad-Dawla as-Simnānī," *Muslim World* 83, 1 (1993), pp.68–80.

6. Shihâboddîn Yahya Sohravardî, *Le Livre de la Sagesse Orientale* (trans. H. Corbin) (Paris: Gallimard, 1986).

7. R.D. Marcotte, "Reason (*'Aql*) and Direct Intuition (*Mushahada*) in the Work of Shihab al-Din Suhrawardi (d.1191)," in T. Lawson (ed.), *Reason and Inspiration in Islam: Essays in Honour of Hermann Landolt* (London: I.B. Tauris, 2004).

8. W.M. Thackston (trans.), *The Mystical and Visionary Treatises of Suhrawardi* (London: Octagon Press, 1982). For an interpretation of the symbolism of two of the treatises, see G. Webb, "An Exegesis of Suhrawardi's The Purple Intellect (*'Aql-i Surkh*)," *Islamic Quarterly* 26, 4 (1982), pp.194–210 and A.K. Tuft, "Symbolism and Speculation in Suhrawardī's the Song of Gabriel's Wing," in P. Morewedge (ed.), *Islamic Philosophy and Mysticism* (New York: Caravan, 1981).

9. N.S. Green, "The Religious and Cultural Roles of Dreams and Visions in Islam," *Journal of the Royal Asiatic Society* 13, 3 (2003), pp.287–313.

10. C.W. Ernst, *Ruzbihan Baqli: Mysticism and the Rhetoric of Sainthood in Persian Sufism* (Richmond: Curzon Press, 1996).

11. Ernst (1996), p.118.

12. Ernst (1996), p.20.

13. J.G. Katz, *Dreams, Sufism, and Sainthood: The Visionary Career of Muhammad al-Zawāwī* (Leiden: E.J. Brill, 1996).

14. On Ibn 'Arabi's life, see C. Addas, *Quest for the Red Sulphur: The Life of Ibn 'Arabi* (Cambridge: Islamic Texts Society, 1993). On his connections to Spanish and North African Sufis, see G. Elmore, "Poised Expectancy: Ibn al-'Arabī's Roots in Sharq al-Andalus," *Studia Islamica* 90 (2000), pp.51–66 and A. Shafik, "Los Šādiliyya e ibn 'Arabī tras las huellas de Abū Madyan," *Revista de Ciencias de las Religiones* 14 (2009), pp.117–132. For Ibn al-'Arabi's own account of his teachers in Spain, see Ibn 'Arabi, *Sufis of Andalusia: The Ruh al-Quds and al-Durrah al-Fakhirah of Ibn Arabi* (trans. R.W.J. Austin) (London: George Allen & Unwin, 1971).

15. Ibn al-'Arabī, *The Meccan Revelations: Selected Texts of al-Futūhāt al-Makkiya* (trans. M. Chodkiewicz, W.C. Chittick & J.W. Morris) (New York: Pir Press, 2002–).

16. On medieval discussion over the finality of Muhammad's message, see Y. Friedmann, *Prophecy Continuous: Aspects of Ahmadi Religious Thought and its Medieval Background* (Berkeley: University of California Press, 1989), chapter 2 & 3.

17. S.H. Bashier, *Ibn al-'Arabī's Barzakh: The Concept of the Limit and the Relationship between God and the World* (Albany: State University of New York Press, 2004).

18. W.C. Chittick, *The Sufi Path of Knowledge: Ibn al-'Arabi's Metaphysics of Imagination* (Albany: State University of New York Press, 1989).

19. S. Akkach, "The World of Imagination in Ibn 'Arabi's Ontology," *British Journal of Middle Eastern Studies* 24, 1 (1997), pp.97–113 and H. Corbin, *Creative Imagination in the Sūfism of Ibn al-'Arabī* (Princeton: Princeton University Press, 1969).

20. W.C. Chittick, *Imaginal Worlds: Ibn al-'Arabi and the Problem of Religious Diversity* (Albany: State University of New York Press, 1994).

21. On his critics, see A.D. Knysh, *Ibn 'Arabi in the Later Islamic Tradition: The Making of a Polemical Image in Medieval Islam* (Albany: State University of New York Press, 1999).

22. See W.C. Chittick, "Notes on Ibn al-'Arabi's Influence in the Indian Sub-Continent," *Muslim World* 82 (1992), pp.218–241; J. Clark, "Early Best-Sellers in the Akbarian Tradition: The Dissemination of Ibn 'Arabi's Teaching through Sadr al-Din al-Qunawi," *Journal of the Muhyiddin Ibn 'Arabi Society* 33 (2003); V.J. Cornell, *Realm of the Saint: Power and Authority in Moroccan Sufism* (Austin: University of Texas Press, 1998), chapters 6 & 7; L. Lewisohn *Beyond Faith and Infidelity: The Sufi Poetry and Teachings of Mahmud*

Shabistari (Richmond: Curzon Press, 1995); and R.J.A. McGregor, *Sanctity and Mysticism in Medieval Egypt: The Wafā' Sufi Order and the Legacy of Ibn 'Arabī* (Albany: State University of New York Press, 2004).

23. Amid the voluminous literature on Rumi, the outstanding survey is F.D. Lewis, *Rumi: Past and Present, East and West* (Oxford: Oneworld, 2000).

24. W.C. Chittick, *The Sufi Path of Love: The Spiritual Teachings of Rumi* (Albany: State University of New York Press, 1983) and J.E.B. Lumbard, "From Hubb to 'Ishq: The Development of Love in Early Sufism," *Journal of Islamic Studies* 18, 2 (2008), pp.345–385. Ahmad Ghazali is not to be confused with his brother, the more respectable *madrasa* Sufi, Abu Hamid Ghazali.

25. C.W. Ernst, "Mystical Language and the Teaching Context in the Early Sufi Lexicons," in S. Katz (ed.), *Mysticism and Language* (Oxford: Oxford University Press, 1992).

26. A.T. Karamustafa, *God's Unruly Friends: Dervish Groups in the Later Middle Period 1200–1550* (Salt Lake City: University of Utah Press, 1994).

27. For alternative approaches to the definition and emergence of the brotherhoods, see J.M. Abun-Nasr, *Muslim Communities of Grace: The Sufi Brotherhoods in Islamic Religious Life* (Columbia University Press, 2007), chapter 3 & 4, C.W. Ernst & B.B. Lawrence, *Sufi Martyrs of Love: The Chishti Order in South Asia and Beyond* (New York: Palgrave Macmillan, 2002), chapter 1 and J.S. Trimingham, *The Sufi Orders in Islam* (Oxford: Clarendon Press, 1971), chapter 2 & 3.

28. For an overview of organizational patterns, see M. Gaborieau, "Les Modes d'Organisation," in A. Popovic & G. Veinstein (eds), *Les Voies d'Allah: Les Ordres Mystiques dans le Monde Musulman des Origines à Aujourd'hui* (Paris: Fayard, 1996), pp.205–212.

29. L. Fernandes, *The Evolution of a Sufi Institution in Mamluk Egypt: The Khanqah* (Berlin: Klaus Schwarz, 1988), Y. Tabbaa, *The Transformation of Islamic Art during the Sunni Revival* (Seattle: University of Washington Press, 2001) and E.S. Wolper, *Cities and Saints: Sufism and the Transformation of Urban Space in Medieval Anatolia* (University Park: Pennsylvania State University Press, 2003).

30. See V.J. Cornell, "Ibn Battuta's Opportunism: The Networks and Loyalties of a Medieval Muslim Scholar", in M. Cooke & B.B. Lawrence (eds), *Muslim Networks from Hajj to Hip Hop* (Chapel Hill: University of North Carolina Press, 2005) and I.R. Netton, "Myth, Miracle and Magic in the *Rihla* of Ibn Battuta," in Netton, *Seek Knowledge: Thought and Travel in the House of Islam* (London: Routledge, 1996).

31. H.F.C. Edwards, "The Ribat of 'Ali b. Karmakh," *Iran* 29 (1991), pp.85–94.

32. On brotherhoods and etiquette, see G. Böwering, "Règles et Rituels Soufi," in Popovic & Veinstein (1996), pp.139–156.

33. On women as patrons in this period, see R.S. Humphreys, "Women as Patrons of Religious Architecture in Ayyubid Damascus," *Muqarnas* 11 (1994), pp.35–54 and E.S. Wolper, "Princess Safwat al-Dunyā wa al-Dīn and the Production of Sufi Buildings and Hagiographies in Pre-Ottoman Anatolia," in

D.F. Ruggles (ed.), *Women, Patronage and Self-Representation in Islamic Societies* (Albany: State University of New York Press, 2000).

34. On the popular preaching as a means of social influence for Sufis and others, see J.P. Berkey, *Popular Preaching and Religious Authority in the Medieval Islamic Near East* (Seattle: University of Washington Press, 2001).

35. For a case study of this posthumous process as related to Abu'l Hasan al-Shadhili (d.1258), see D. Gril, "Le Saint Fondateur," in Popovic & Veinstein (1996), pp.104–120.

36. For overviews of Abu Najib's career, see A. Bigelow, "The Sufi Practice of Friendship, the Suhrawardi Tariqa and the Development of a Middle Road," *Jusūr: UCLA Journal of Middle Eastern Studies* 15 (1999), pp.14–49 and I.R. Netton, "The Breath of Felicity: *Adab, Ahwāl, Maqāmāt* and Abū Najīb al-Suhrawardī," in Netton (1996), pp.71–92.

37. M. Milson (trans.), *A Sufi Rule for Novices: Kitāb Ādāb al-Murīdīn of Abū al-Najīb al-Suhrawardī* (Cambridge: Harvard University Press, 1975).

38. On his relationship with the caliph, see A. Hartmann, "La Conception Gouvernementale du Calife an-Nasir li-Din Allah," *Orientalia Suecana* 22 (1973), pp.52–61. On his overall career, see E.S. Ohlander, *Sufism in an Age of Transition: 'Umar al-Suhrawardī and the Rise of the Islamic Mystical Brotherhoods* (Leiden: Brill, 2008), chapter 2.

39. For translations, see R. Gramlich (trans.), *Die Gaben der Erkenntnisse des 'Umar as-Suhrawardī ('Awārif al-Ma'ārif)* (Wiesbaden: Steiner, 1978) and Shahāb-u'd-Dīn 'Umar b. Muhammad Suhrawardī, *The 'Awārif-u'l-Ma'ārif* (trans. H. Wilberforce Clarke) (Lahore: Sh. Muhammad Ashraf, 1973). Note that the latter translation is of a later Persian recension.

40. Ohlander (2008), chapters 3 & 4.

41. On the expansion into India, see S.A.A. Rizvi, *A History of Sufism in India*, 2 vols (Delhi: Munshiram Manoharlal, 1978–1983), vol. 1, pp.190–226.

42. Ohlander (2008), p.314.

43. J.J. Elias, "The Sufi Robe (*Khirqa*) as a Vehicle of Spiritual Authority," in S. Gordon (ed.), *Robes and Honor: The Medieval World of Investiture* (New York: St. Martin's Press, 2000).

44. On 'Abd al-Qadir's own career, see J. Chabbi, "'Abd al-Kadir al-Djilani, Personnage Historique," *Studia Islamica* 38 (1973), pp.75–106. On subsequent Qadiri expansion into Africa and India, see A.S. Karrar, *The Sufi Brotherhoods in the Sudan* (London: C. Hurst & Co, 1992), pp.20-35 and Rizvi (1978–1983), vol. 2, pp.55–150.

45. On this theory, see Abun-Nasr (2007), p.82.

46. P.M. Currie, *The Shrine and Cult of Mu'īn al-Dīn Chishtī of Ajmer* (Delhi: Oxford University Press, 1989).

47. S. Abdul Latif, *The Muslim Mystic Movement in Bengal, 1301–1550* (Calcutta: K.P. Bagchi, 1993), pp.18–40, R. Aquil, "Hazrat-i-Delhi: The Making of the Chishti Sufi Centre and the Stronghold of Islam," *South Asia Research* 28, 1 (2008), pp.23–48 and C.W. Ernst, *Eternal Garden: Mysticism, History, and Politics at a South Asian Sufi Center* (Albany: State University of New York Press, 1992).

48. S. Digby, "Before Timur Came: Provincialization of the Delhi Sultanate through the Fourteenth Century", *Journal of the Economic and Social History of the Orient* 47, 3 (2004), pp.298–356 and R.M. Eaton, *The Rise of Islam and the Bengal Frontier, 1204–1760* (Berkeley: University of California Press, 1993).

49. R.M. Eaton, "The Political and Religious Authority of the Shrine of Bābā Farīd", in B.D. Metcalf (ed.), *Moral Conduct and Authority: The Place of Adab in South Asian Islam* (Berkeley: University of California Press, 1984); Eaton (1993); and B.B. Lawrence, "Islam in India: The Function of Institutional Sufism in the Islamization of Rajasthan, Gujarat and Kashmir," *Contributions to Asian Studies* 17 (1982), pp.27–43. On parallel processes among Christians in Anatolia, see S. Vryonis, *The Decline of Medieval Hellenism in Asia Minor and the Process of Islamization from the Eleventh through the Fifteenth Century* (Berkeley: University of California Press, 1971), chapter 5 and Wolper (2003), chapter 5.

50. S. Babs Mala, "The Sufi Convent and its Social Significance in the Medieval Period of Islam," *Islamic Culture* 51, 1 (1977), M.A. Khan, "*Khanqahs*: Centres of Learning," in M. Haidar (ed.), *Sufis, Sultans and Feudal Orders: Professor Nurul Hasan Commemoration Volume* (Delhi: Manohar, 2004) and I.H. Siddiqui, "The Early Chishti Dargahs", in C.W. Troll (ed.), *Muslim Shrines in India: Their Character, History and Significance* (Delhi: Oxford University Press, 1989).

51. On Chishti Sufism as a vehicle of Muslim 'integration' with Hindus, see M. Alam, *The Languages of Political Islam* (London: Hurst, 2004), chapter 3.

52. For overviews of the brotherhood's history, see H. Algar, "The Naqshbandi Order: A Preliminary Survey of its History and Significance," *Studia Islamica* 44 (1976), pp.123–152 and I. Weismann, *The Naqshbandiyya: Orthodoxy and Activism in a Worldwide Sufi Tradition* (London: Routledge, 2007).

53. J. Paul, "Solitude within Society: Early Khwajagani Attitudes toward Spiritual and Social Life," in P.L. Heck (ed.), *Sufism and Politics: The Power of Spirituality* (Princeton: Markus Wiener Publishers, 2007).

54. D. DeWeese, "Khojagani Origins and the Critique of Sufism: The Rhetoric of Communal Uniqueness in the *Manaqib* of Khoja 'Ali 'Azizan Ramitani" in F. De Jong & B. Radtke (eds), *Islamic Mysticism Contested: Thirteen Centuries of Controversies and Polemics*, ed. Frederick and Bernd (Leiden: E.J. Brill, 1999), pp.492–519.

55. D. DeWeese, "The *Mashā'ikh-i Turk* and the *Khojagān*: Rethinking the Links between the Yasawī and Naqshbandī Sufi Traditions," *Journal of Islamic Studies* 7, 2 (1996), pp.180–207.

56. J. Gross, "The Economic Status of a Timurid Sufi Shaykh: A Matter of Conflict or Perception?" *Iranian Studies* 21, 1–2 (1988), pp.84–104 and J. Paul, *Doctrine and Organization: The Khwājagān/Naqshbandīya in the First Generation after Bahā'uddīn* (Berlin: Das Arabische Buch, 1998).

57. T. Zarcone, "Le mausolée de Baha al-Din Nakshband à Bukhara (Uzbekistan)," *Journal of Turkish Studies* 19 (1995), pp.231–244.

58. On the latter regions in this period, see D. Ephrat, *Spiritual Wayfarers, Leaders in Piety: Sufis and the Dissemination of Islam in Medieval Palestine*

(Cambridge, MA: Harvard University Press, 2008), E. Geoffroy, *Le Soufisme en Egypte et en Syrie sous les Derniers Mamelouks et les Premiers Ottomans: Orientations Spirituelles et Enjeux Culturels* (Damascus: Institut Français de Damas, 1995) and R. McGregor & A. Sabra (eds), *Le Développement du Soufisme en Égypte à l'Époque Mamelouke* (Cairo: Institut Français d'Archéologie Orientale, 2006).

59. See e.g. Trimingham (1971), p.70: "This development into orders, and the integral association of the saint cult with them, contributed to the decline of Sufism as a mystical Way." For a more sympathetic survey of the evolution of Islamic sainthood, see J. Renard, *Friends of God: Islamic Images of Piety, Commitment and Servanthood* (Berkeley: University of California Press, 2008).

60. M. Fierro, "The Polemic about the *Karāmāt al-Awliyā'* and the Development of Sūfism in al-Andalus (Fourth/Tenth-Fifth/Eleventh Centuries)", *Bulletin of the School of Oriental and African Studies* 55, 2 (1992), pp.236–249.

61. A. Karamustafa, "Walayah According to al-Junayd (d.910)," in Lawson (2005), pp.62–68.

62. For contrasting positions on whether we can speak of 'sanctity' in Islam, see J. Baldick, *Mystical Islam* (London: I.B. Tauris, 1989), pp.7–8 and F.M. Denny, "God's Friends: The Sanctity of Persons in Islam," in R. Kieckhefer & G.D. Bond (eds), *Sainthood* (Berkeley: University of California Press, 1988). For a fuller comparative survey, see N. Amri & D. Gril (eds), *Saint et Sainteté dans le Christianisme et l'Islam: Le Regard des Sciences de l'Homme* (Paris: Maisonneuve & Larose, 2007).

63. On such shared shrines and practices, see M. Ayoub, "Cult and Culture: Common Saints and Shrines in Middle Eastern Popular Piety", in R.G. Hovannisian & G. Sabagh (eds), *Religion and Culture in Medieval Islam* (Cambridge: Cambridge University Press, 1999) and J.W. Meri, *The Cult of Saints Among Muslims and Jews in Medieval Syria* (Oxford: Oxford University Press, 2002).

64. L. Halevi, *Muhammad's Grave: Death Rites and the Making of Islamic Society* (New York: Columbia University Press, 2007) and C. Robinson, "Prophecy and Holy Men in Early Islam", in J. Howard-Johnston & P.A. Hayward (eds), *The Cult of the Saints in Late Antiquity and the Middle Ages* (Oxford: Oxford University Press, 1999).

65. For of a study of such guides, pilgrims and the literature surrounding them, see C.S. Taylor, *In the Vicinity of the Righteous: Ziyāra and the Veneration of Muslim Saints in Late Medieval Egypt* (Leiden: Brill, 1999). For translations from a wide range of hagiographies themselves, see J. Renard (ed.), *Tales of God's Friends: Islamic Hagiography in Translation* (Berkeley: University of California Press, 2009).

66. On these sites, see Ernst (1992), R. Marefat, "Beyond the Architecture of Death: The Shrine of the Shah-i-Zindah in Samarkand" (unpublished Ph.D. dissertation, Harvard University, 1991) and Taylor (1999).

67. This multi-generational process is traced with regard to two of the most famous Sufi saints of Egypt in H. Hallenberg, *Ibrahim al-Dasuqi (1255–1296):*

A Saint Invented (Helsinki: Finnish Academy of Science and Letters, 2005) and T.E. Homerin, *From Arab Poet to Muslim Saint: Ibn al-Farid, His Verse and His Shrine* (Columbia: University of South Carolina Press, 1994).

68. For Indian and Egyptian examples, see Currie (1989) and Hallenberg (2005).

69. M. Chodkiewicz, *Seal of the Saints: Prophethood and Sainthood in the Doctrine of Ibn 'Arabī* (Cambridge: Islamic Texts Society, 1993) and M. Takeshita, *Ibn 'Arabī's Theory of the Perfect Man and its Place in the History of Islamic Thought* (Tokyo: Institute for the Study of Languages and Cultures of Asia and Africa, 1987).

70. R. Amitai-Preiss, "Sufis and Shamans: Some Remarks on the Islamization of the Mongols in the Ilkhanate," *Journal of the Economic and Social History of the Orient* 42, 1 (1999), pp.27–46, V.F. Minorsky, "A Mongol Decree of 720/ 1320 to the Family of Shaykh Zahid," *Bulletin of the School of Oriental and African Studies* 16 (1954), pp.515–527 and L.G. Potter, "Sufis and Sultans in Post-Mongol Iran", *Iranian Studies* 27, 1–4 (1994), pp.77–102.

71. S.S. Blair, "Sufi Saints and Shrine Architecture in the Early Fourteenth Century", *Muqarnas* 7 (1990), pp.35–49 and L. Golombek, "The Cult of Saints and Shrine Architecture in the Fourteenth Century," in D.K. Kouymjian (ed.), *Near Eastern Numismatics, Iconography, Epigraphy and History: Studies in Honour of George C. Miles* (Beirut: American University of Beirut, 1974).

72. E.J. Grube, "Il-Khanid Stucco Decoration: Notes on the Stucco Decoration of Pir-i Bakran," in G. Scarcia (ed.), *Isfahan: Quaderni del Seminario di Iranistica, Uralo-Altaistica e Caucasologia* (Venice: La Tipografica, 1981), pp.88–96.

73. Z.A. Desai, "The Major Dargahs of Ahmadabad," in Troll (1989), C.-P. Haase, "Shrines of Saints and Dynastic Mausolea: Towards a Typology of Funerary Architecture in the Timurid Period," *Cahiers d'Asie Centrale* 3–4 (1997) and M.E. Subtelny, "The Cult of 'Abdullah Ansari under the Timurids," in A. Giese & J.C. Bürgel (eds), *Gott ist Schön und Er Liebt die Schönheit: Festschrift für Annemarie Schimmel* (Bern: Peter Lang, 1994).

74. F. Çagman & Z. Tanındı, "Manuscript Production at the Kāzarūnī Orders in Safavid Shiraz", in S.R. Canby (ed.), *Safavid Art and Architecture* (London: British Museum Press, 2002), p.44.

75. For fuller discussion, see Safi (2006), chapter 5.

76. See e.g. D. DeWeese, "Yasavi Şayhs in the Timurid Order: Notes on the Social and Political Role of Communal Sufi Affiliations in the 14th and 15th Centuries," in M. Bernardini (ed.), *La Civilità Timuride come Fenomeno Internazionale* (Rome: Oriente Moderno, 1996).

77. On this overlapping process, see N.S. Green, "Stories of Saints and Sultans: Remembering History at the Sufi Shrines of Aurangabad", *Modern Asian Studies* 38, 2 (2004), pp.419–446.

78. N.S. Green, "Blessed Men and Tribal Politics: Notes on Political Culture in the Indo-Afghan World", *Journal of the Economic and Social History of the Orient* 49, 3 (2006), pp.344–360 and Hartmann (1973).

79. See M.S. Siddiqi, *The Bahmani Sūfīs* (Delhi: Idarah-i Adabiyat-i Delli, 1989), chapter 3 and G. Yazdani, *Bidar: Its History and Monuments* (London: Oxford University Press, 1947), pp.114–148.

80. A. Karamustafa, "Early Sufism in Eastern Anatolia", in Lewisohn (1993) and I. Mélikoff, *Hadji Bektach, un Mythe et ses Avatars: Genèse et Évolution du Soufisme Populaire en Turquie* (Leiden: Brill, 1998). For the counter-argument, see A. Karamustafa, "Origins of Anatolian Sufism", in A. Yaşar Ocak (ed.), *Sufism and Sufis in Ottoman Society: Sources, Doctrine, Rituals, Turuq, Architecture, Literature and Fine Arts, Modernism* (Ankara: Turkish Historical Society, 2005), pp.67–95.

81. R. Foltz, "The Central Asian Naqshbandi Connections of the Mughal Emperors", *Journal of Islamic Studies* 7, 2 (1996), pp.229–239.

82. For an Anatolian case study in a slightly later period, see S. Faroqhi, "Agricultural Crisis and the Art of Flute-Playing: The Worldly Affairs of the Mevlevi Dervishes", *Turcica* 20 (1988), pp.43–70.

83. R. Islam, *Sufism in South Asia: Impact on Fourteenth Century Muslim Society* (Karachi: Oxford University Press, 2000), chapter 3.

84. Ernst (1992), chapter 10.

85. Çagman & Tanındı (2002), p.44.

86. M.P. Connell, "The Nimatullahi Sayyids of Taft: A Study of the Evolution of a Late Medieval Iranian Sufi Tariqah" (unpublished PhD dissertation, Harvard University, 2004), pp.166–170.

87. On the links between several generations of Simnani's family and the Khwarazmian and Mongol elite, see J. Elias, *The Throne Carrier of God: The Life and Thought of 'Alā' ad-Dawla as-Simnānī* (Albany: State University of New York Press, 1995), chapter 2.

88. F. Papan-Matin, *Beyond Death: The Mystical Teachings of 'Ayn al-Quḍāt al-Hamadhānī* (Leiden: Brill, 2010).

89. See e.g. S. Digby, "The Sufi Shaykh and the Sultan: A Conflict of Claims to Authority in Medieval India," *Iran* 28 (1990), pp.71–81.

90. D. DeWeese, *Islamization and Native Religion in the Golden Horde: Baba Tükles and Conversion to Islam in Historical and Epic Tradition* (University Park: Pennsylvania State University Press, 1994), chapters 3 & 4.

91. C. Mayeur-Jaouen, "Maîtres, Cheikhs et Ancêtres: Saints du Delta à l'Époque Mamelouke", in McGregor & Sabra (2006).

92. A. Singer, "Ethnic Origins and Tribal History of the Timuri of Khurasan", *Afghan Studies* 3–4 (1982), pp.65–78.

93. DeWeese (1994).

94. M.F. Köprülü, *Influence du Chamanisme Turco-Mongol sur les Ordres Mystiques Musulmans* (Istanbul: Imp. Zellitch Frères, 1929) and T. Zarcone, "Interpénétration du Soufisme et du Chamanisme dans l'Aire Turque," in D. Aigle, B. Brac de la Perrière & J.-P. Chaumeill (eds), *La Politique des Esprits: Chamanismes et Religions Universalistes* (Nanterre: Société d'Ethnologie, 2000).

95. Amitai-Preiss (1999) and Karamustafa (1993).

96. R. Jones, "Ten Conversion Myths from Indonesia", in N. Levtzion (ed.), *Conversion to Islam* (New York: Holmes & Meier Publishers, 1979).

97. R. Ensel, *Saints and Servants in Southern Morocco* (Leiden: Brill, 1999).

98. S.H. Askari, *Maktub and Malfuz Literature as a Source of Socio-Political History* (Patna: Khuda Bakhsh Library, 1976) and M.U. Memon, *Ibn Taimīya's Struggle Against Popular Religion* (The Hague: Mouton, 1976).

99. B. Shoshan, *Popular Culture in Medieval Cairo* (Cambridge: Cambridge University Press, 1993).

100. For Morocco, India and Palestine respectively, see Cornell (1998), chapter 2, Digby (2004) and Ephrat (2008), chapter 3.

101. R.M. Eaton, "Sufi Folk Literature and the Expansion of Indian Islam", *History of Religions* 14 (1974), pp.117–127.

102. On Syria and India, see Meri (2002) and H. van Skyhawk, "Nasīruddīn and Ādināth, Nizāmuddīn and Kāniphnāth: Hindu-Muslim Religious Syncretism in the Folk Literature of the Deccan", in H. Brückner, L. Lutze & A. Malik (eds), *Flags of Fame: Studies of South Asian Folk Culture* (Delhi: Manohar, 1993).

103. Wolper (2003), chapters 3 & 4.

104. For an overview of Yezidi history, see P.G. Kreyenbroek, *Yezidism: Its Background, Observances, and Textual Tradition* (Lewiston: Edwin Mellen Press, 1995).

105. R. Ricci, *Islam Translated: Literature, Conversion, and the Arabic Cosmopolis of South and Southeast Asia* (Chicago: University of Chicago Press, 2011), p.167.

106. For more discussion of the Sufi lexicon, see N.S. Green, "Idiom, Genre and the Politics of Self-Description on the Peripheries of Persian," in Green & Searle-Chatterjee (2008).

107. Ricci (2011), p.271.

108. J.S. Meisami, *Medieval Persian Court Poetry* (Princeton: Princeton University Press, 1987).

109. For an overall survey up to *circa* 1500, see J.T.P. de Bruijn, *Persian Sufi Poetry: An Introduction to the Mystical Use of Classical Persian Poems* (Richmond: Curzon, 1997).

110. Dick Davis, "Sufism and Poetry: A Marriage of Convenience?" *Edebiyat* 10, 2 (1999), pp.279–292.

111. Davis (1999).

112. J.T.P. de Bruijn, "The Qalandariyyāt in Persian Mystical Poetry," in Lewisohn (1992).

113. J.T.P. de Bruijn, *Of Piety and Poetry: The Interaction of Religion and Literature in the Life and Works of Hakīm Sanā'ī of Ghazna* (Leiden: Brill, 1983).

114. On the cosmological models that Sufis borrowed from earlier philosophers, see S.H. Nasr, *An Introduction to Islamic Cosmological Doctrines: Conceptions of Nature and Methods Used for its Study by the Ikhwān al-Safā, al-Bīrūnī and Ibn Sīnā* (Albany: State University of New York Press, 1993).

115. L. Lewisohn & C. Shackle (eds), *'Attar and the Persian Sufi Tradition: The Art of Spiritual Flight* (London: I.B. Tauris, 2007).

116. For fuller discussion, see M. Tourage, *Rūmī and the Hermeneutics of Eroticism* (Leiden: Brill, 2007), chapter 3 and Appendix 1. On Rumi's use of folk stories more generally, see M.A. Mills, "Folk Tradition in the Masnavi and the Masnavi in Folk Tradition", in A. Banani, R. Houanisian & G. Sabegh (eds),

Poetry and Mysticism in Islam: The Heritage of Rumi (Cambridge: Cambridge University Press, 1994).

117. For a study of Persian texts written the wake of the Mongol invasion in the safety of Anatolia, see W.C. Chittick, *Faith and Practice of Islam: Three Thirteenth Century Sufi Texts* (Albany: State University of New York Press, 1992).

118. Najm al-Dīn Rāzī, *The Path of God's Bondsmen from Origin to Return* (trans. H. Algar) (Delmar: Caravan Books, 1982).

119. Rizvi (1978–1983), vol. 1, chapter 4.

120. B.B. Lawrence, *Notes From a Distant Flute: The Extant Literature of Pre-Mughal Indian Sufism* (Tehran: Imperial Iranian Academy of Philosophy, 1978).

121. For one fourteenth century Indian Sufi letter collection, see Sharafuddin Maneri, *The Hundred Letters* trans. P. Jackson (New York: Paulist Press, 1980).

122. On this process, see Green, "Idiom, Genre and the Politics of Self-Description on the Peripheries of Persian", in Green & Searle-Chatterjee (2008).

123. S. Singh et al (ed. & trans.), *Hymns of Baba Fareed Shakar Ganj* (Lahore: Suchet, 2005). More generally, see C. Shackle, "Early Vernacular Poetry in the Indus Valley: Its Contexts and its Character", in A.L. Dallapiccola & S.Z.-A. Lallemant (eds), *Islam and Indian Regions* (Stuttgart: Steiner, 1993), vol. 1.

124. P. Machwe, "Amir Khusrau's Hindi Poetry", in Anon. (ed.), *Amir Khusrau: Memorial Volume* (Delhi: Govt. of India, 1975). For the sake of simplicity, I have used the generic term Hindi ("language of India") to group together the regional vernaculars of Hindwi, Awadhi and Dakhani.

125. S.S.K. Hussaini, *The Life, Works and Teachings of Khwajah Bandahnawaz Gisudiraz* (Gulbarga: Sayyid Muhammad Gisudiraz Research Academy, 1986). For more on early Dakani Urdu, see O.R. Bawa, "The Role of Sufis and Sants [*sic*] in the Development of Deccani Urdu" (trans. S. Kugle) *Journal of Deccan Studies* 7, 2 (2009), pp.69–81.

126. N.A. Hines, *Maulana Daud's Candayan: A Critical Study* (Delhi: Manohar, 2009).

127. For the two most important, see A. Behl, "The Magic Doe: Desire and Narrative in a Hindavi Sufi Romance, circa 1503", in R.M. Eaton (ed.), *India's Islamic Traditions, 711–1750* (Delhi: Oxford University Press, 2003) and Manjhan, *Madhumālatī*, trans. A. Behl & S. Weightman (Oxford: Oxford University Press, 2000).

128. M.F. Köprülü, *Early Mystics in Turkish Literature* (London: Routledge, 2006), chapters 5 & 6.

129. T. Halman (ed.), *Yunus Emre and his Mystical Poetry* (Bloomington: Indiana University Turkish Studies, 1989) and Köprülü (2006), chapter 9.

130. A. Karamustafa, "Early Turkish Islamic Literature", section 10 of article "Turk," *The Encyclopaedia of Islam*, 3rd edition (Leiden: Brill, 2007), vol. 10, pp.715–716.

131. Lewis (2000), pp.239–240. On the Arabic-script Greek poems, see P. Burguière & R. Mantran, "Quelques Vers Grecs du XIIIe Siècle en Caractères Arabes", *Byzantion* 22 (1952), pp.63–80.

Chapter 3

Empires, Frontiers and Renewers (1400–1800)

Introduction

In Chapter 2 we have seen the influence and reach of the Sufis expand in a multitude of directions, social no less than geographical. In ranging from cycles of metaphysical systems and vernacular songs to social networks and miraculous protection, the different things that Sufism came to mean in the medieval period assured its reception among princes and peasants, nomads and townsmen, the lettered and unlearned. Of course, such an influential proliferation of personnel no less than practices meant that there were critics of certain forms of Sufism and their practitioners, most famously by the Syrian scholar Ibn Taymiyya (d.1328). But such criticisms were largely of particular (and especially popular) aspects of shrine devotion rather than of the entire metaphysical and moral edifice connected to the saints. Ibn Taymiyya was especially vehement in his castigation of festivities around the tombs of Sufi saints, seeing them as "innovations" from the Prophetic Example.[1] Nonetheless, he may still have been a Sufi himself and was an admirer of the great Baghdad Sufi, 'Abd al-Qadir al-Jilani (d.1166).[2] The critiques made by others tended to be *ad hominen* attacks on individual Sufis rather than on corporate groups of Sufis at large, taking the form of attacks by particular Muslims (often Sufis themselves) against other particular Muslims.

While in a few cases such attacks came from sufficiently influential corners to draw on the powers of the state (as in the execution of Shihab al-Din Suhrawardi in Aleppo in 1191), for the most part the medieval period saw representatives closely supporting the persons and institutions of Sufism. In no small measure, the vast influence which Sufism achieved came through

Sufism: A Global History, First Edition. Nile Green.
© 2012 Nile Green. Published 2012 by Blackwell Publishing Ltd.

the alliance of its representatives with the regional sultanates whose own legitimacy was dependent on public support for Islam. This triggered massive investment in the shrines and lodges that through the medieval era saw Sufism become physically embedded in landscapes and townscapes from the Atlantic coastline of Africa to the Bay of Bengal. If criticism of certain Sufis was part of the tempo of medieval religious debate, then there was no wholesale attack on Sufism. Nor could there be, since "Sufism" had no discrete existence as a category in the modern sense, meaning that to attack Sufism as a whole would be to attack Islam itself. It is important to recognize, then, that to a very large extent, Sufism *was* Islam in its medieval form, an Islam of saints and miracles supported by the intellectual efforts of scholars no less than the rustic enthusiasms of tribesmen. Despite the customary usages of both academics and publishers, "Sufi Islam" is probably a more helpful term than "Sufism."

Although it would be simplistic to offer a single trajectory for the fortunes of Sufism in the very different regions to which this "Sufi Islam" spread, certain common or otherwise large-scale developments can be observed in the centuries between 1400 and 1800. In large part, these relate to major changes in the relationship between Sufism and the state, changes which were themselves dependent on the emergence of new kinds of "early modern" state which were more bureaucratized, centralized and confident of their own authority. With such a rapid turnover of dynasties in the centuries of tribal incursions between around 1100 and 1500, state interactions with religion were not only of a stop/start character. They were also predominantly in favor of the independence of the religious classes as tribal dynastic newcomers sought legitimacy through the patronage of the Sufis who held sway among the populace. Combined with the use of the *waqf* endowments that ensured such investment continued to support its designated Sufi families through future generations, what this practically meant was that Sufi institutions were often much more stable than those of the state. Along with their palaces and policies, tribal dynasties rose and fell in fairly rapid succession, but the endowed shrines and lodges of the Sufis outlived them as the more permanent feature of the physical and social landscape. Through their often grandiose and durable shrine architecture, Sufis acquired a kind of petrified immortality, their flesh turned into the stone of shrines that became a permanent part of the urban and rural landscapes in which more mortal Muslims lived and died.

Against this background, it is little wonder that the idea became widespread that since the "sainthood" (*wilayat*) of a given holy man also expressed itself through his supernatural authority over his territorial "domain" or "jurisdiction" (*walayat*), the Sufis were the true rulers of the regions surrounding their shrines, an ideology played out in scores of narratives describing saints bestowing kingdoms onto sultans who were merely their visible rulers. The comparative permanence of Sufis compared to sultans was also manifested in dynastic terms. We have already seen the Sufi brotherhoods promoting the model of a "chain" or "lineage" of masters, each inheriting his blessing, knowledge and authority from his predecessors. In an age in which lineage (whether manufactured or genuine) was essential to any claim of authority, whether political or religious, the great families of saints that emerged in the medieval period could claim lineages of impeccable descent. These were articulated through the same vocabulary as that used by sultans, for the Sufi term *silsila* could be applied to a royal no less than a religious "dynasty." Wealthy in property and feared for their strange powers, the great Sufi families and brotherhoods that emerged through the medieval period were major players in their societies. They were, in short, the establishment. And like all establishments, their status was secured by their central place in the web of relationships that tied them to disciples in every section of society.

What we will see in this chapter is the gradual giving way of this older set of conditions as larger, more successful state polities emerged whose longevity and more efficient control of their resources allowed them to enact institutional changes in the religious structures of their societies over longer periods. Although each of the early modern empires pursued these policies towards different ends, in each case they affected a change in the relationship between the Sufis and the state. In coinciding with a concomitant deepening of the previously weak ties between state and society compared with the previously stronger ties of the Sufis and society, these changes effected a gradual shift in the balance of power between religious and state elites. This did not necessarily weaken the Sufis, who, as we will see, in many cases became major beneficiaries of the state's more efficient command of its resources. Since these resources included the employment of larger numbers of civil servants, in several contexts we will see Sufi brotherhoods becoming closely identified with selective organs of state. An important dimension of this process is seen in the increasing role of Sufis as frontiersmen, expanding and settling new territories on the fringes of state control. This not only occurred on such medieval frontiers as the mountains of southeastern Europe and the jungles of Bengal, but now spread to expanding new frontiers in Africa and Southeast Asia as the new Muslim states that emerged as the brokers of the growing global trade in gold, spice and slaves employed Sufis as settlers and administrators of their new territories. If the new picture was therefore more one of realigning the Sufis' position between state and society than a simple reversal of fortunes, it did see them enter relationships that made them more dependent and ultimately more vulnerable to shifts in the policies or fortunes of the states to which they were tied.

In the following pages we will trace the ambivalent role of Sufism in the major empires and regional sultanates of the early modern period by examining the ways in which Sufism offered these states means of ideological authority, social coherence and imperial expansion, while at the same time providing vehicles for sedition and localizing fracture. The first general pattern to be discerned is the use of Sufi ideas and personnel as state-building resources, a pattern expressed most vividly in the parallel assumption of Sufi forms of authority by rulers and of royal forms of authority by Sufis. As even emperors strove to model themselves as Sufis, it is probably fair to say that the sixteenth and early seventeenth centuries witnessed the zenith of Sufi influence to date, with the English loanword "sophy" (derived from the name of the Safawi brotherhood) trickling even into the vocabulary of Shakespeare and the authors of *The Travels of the Three English Brothers* as a title for Persian kings rather than religious figures. But this very success contained the need for its own dilution as those outside these cliques of the Sufi establishment chafed at the Sufis' access to state coffers and contacts. So as time passed, this collusion between royal and Sufi authority was viewed as counterproductive and even threatening to the longer term maintenance of state power as opposed to the original seizing of power. This manifested itself through the growing ability of certain states to construct a model of Islamic "orthodoxy" and impose it on their citizens.

The second general pattern to be discussed is the growing legalistic critique of certain forms of Sufism which, though in large part a result of the entry of legal specialists into state positions, was also a reflection of a larger "crisis of conscience" that surrounded the turning of the Islamic millennium in 1591. The cultural agency of this latter event was magnified through its connection to a longstanding discourse hailing the religious "renewal" (*tajdid*) and "renewers" (*mujaddid*) who were meant to accompany each passing century, and especially the millennium.[3] Of course, this turning of the millennium marked a point in cultural time rather than in the more neutral or processual time of the historian. But what made the millennium significant was that the century that followed it – the first century in the second millennium of Muslim cultural time – coincided with a host of developments in the processual time of the historian. Affecting different Muslim regions in sundry but nonetheless significant ways, these developments included increases in population that shifted the demographic relationships between different social groups; growing urbanization that increased contacts between townsmen, peasants and nomads; expanding trade that empowered merchant communities and heightened interactions with non-Muslim peoples; natural or man-made ecological changes that resulted in migrations and the settlement of new regions; a renewed bout of military encounters with pagan and Christian polities in Eurasia and Africa; and, by no means of least importance, the formation of new imperial states with bureaucratic agendas that increasingly brought religious leaders and discourses into the remit of government. Each of these developments in social history had its effect on developments in religious history, creating a sense among certain Sufi individuals or groups acting in a wide variety of regions that the Muslims around them had lost their moral or spiritual grounding. Even as the new Muslim millennium's occurrence was uneven and its unfolding complex, the coincidence of the cultural time of the new Muslim millennium with the processual time of early modernity was of vast significance. However problematically, the phrase "crisis of conscience" is therefore used in this chapter in an attempt to recognize at a general and comparative level the significance of this broad if multifarious coincidence of temporalities.

In most cases, the crisis of conscience that accompanied the manifold social changes of the early modern era was not explicitly voiced in millennial terms but in the multiple calls for self-reflection or renewal that were heard from Southeast Asia to West Africa. Nor did the crisis of conscience occur in a single moment in all regions: its timing depended on local factors of social change and individual action. And when the millennium was explicitly invoked, its semantic weight was used for strategic and rhetorical ends in the pursuance of particular agendas. Even so, certain broad trends can be discerned. In almost all areas, this crisis of conscience saw attempts to diminish the influence of individuals or movements increasingly being considered "unorthodox" in the eyes of the state, especially charismatic movements that had the potential to fuel rebellions against the ruling power. By the same token, when excessive legal zeal threatened social harmony, early modern states were no less willing to repress the Sufis' legalistic critics. Whether in terms of charisma or legalism, the larger pattern was one of increasing state regulation of the religious sphere which, in the different periods and places we will examine, alternatively favored or disfavored different Sufi or anti-Sufi groups. In broad terms, what we will see in this chapter is a picture of the early modern Islamic empires first associating themselves with charismatic forms of Sufism in the sixteenth century and then increasingly distancing themselves from them in favor of a more legalistic Islam (whether Sufi or otherwise) in the seventeenth century.

Nonetheless, by looking through the opposite end of the telescope from this "state's eye" perspective, there is much to be learned from the smaller scale perspective of small group and individual Sufi actions. While the early modern era saw states become more influential players in Sufi history than in previous centuries, this did not mean that Sufis ceased to be historical agents in their own right. By shifting the perspective to look at the activities of Sufi brotherhoods and even families (it seems possible that we can also discern Sufi figures who resemble "individuals" more than "types" around this time), we can see how Sufis adapted to the new circumstances of the early modern period. Once again, ambivalence was the keynote as, on the one hand, Sufis colluded with states as willing (if often freelance) "imperialists" in state service and, on the other hand, used the more abundant opportunities of the period to carve out their own spheres of supra-state influence as mobile inter-regional elites.

Finally, in a context of imperial contraction and widespread social disorder from the mid-eighteenth century, we will trace in this chapter the emergence of a series of new sub-brotherhoods that sought to impose order on societies they saw as collapsing. Their success in doing this was itself the result of the increasing mobility of the early modern era and the legitimacy carried from the medieval period of the continuous tradition that the Sufis claimed to transmit into an uncertain eighteenth century. Once again, the notion of Sufism as an adaptable mechanism of "tradition" capable of reproducing itself over time and space helps us understand how Sufism acted as a highly efficient response to the collapse of other logistical and ideological forms of social organization.

Ambivalent Relationships: Empires and Brotherhoods, c.1400–1600

The period between around 1100 to 1400 was one in which much of the Middle East and Central and South Asia saw state-making dominated by mobile tribes or tribal confederations. Most of these tribal groups had their distinct affiliations with particular Sufi families or brotherhoods. However, there was a difference between the types of Sufi with whom these tribal rulers chose to associate at different points in their careers. Through their connection with the two "career stages" of the successful state-making tribe, we can loosely designate these types as "tribal" and "settled" Sufis. In Chapter 2 we have seen the most famous example of such a literate and learned "settled Sufi" being patronized by a tribal polity in its settled period in Jalal al-Din Rumi (d.1273), who rose to prominence with the support of the Saljuq Turks after they had settled into their capital at Konya. Here, however, we are more concerned with the kind of "tribal Sufi" who associated with the next generation of tribes who were still in their nomadic stage. We have already briefly encountered such Sufis in Chapter 2 in the discussion of how one aspect of the vernacularization of Sufism was found in the emergence of charismatic holy men clad in animal skins and horns serving as the protectors of particular clans or tribes. The association was a convenient one, in that many such Sufis specialized in deploying their supernatural powers for typically tribal demands, such as discovering water sources or intervening in skirmishes over pasture land.[4] Given that successful tribes were rich in the portable wealth of livestock, slaves and bullion, such associations were beneficial to both parties. In numerous cases, we find tribesmen pledging allegiances of loyalty to these Sufi protectors, who as a result were able to oust the authority of tribal elders. As much a product of the fissiparous social structure of the tribes than a result of the independent operations of "charisma," this process was particularly important through its ability to unify different tribal groups under a common Sufi leader. For the Sufi's position as an "outsider" born out of the folds of tribal genealogy allowed him to unite the members of different tribes more effectively than any "insider" who belonged to any one of the rival tribal groups in question could. Even where tribal Sufis did not attract such coalitions, many of them emerged as leaders of the nomadic tribal bands or the semi-pastoral highland communities that populated the steppes and mountains between Anatolia and Central Asia.

It is important to grasp the consequences for the social life of religion of such a context of segmented and independent social units. For in such environments there was no overarching person or institution of religious authority, no common touchstone of doctrine, and in many cases no common access to the written word of the Quran. As each tribal group possessed its own religious patron, what emerged amid these scattered and disconnected communities was a system of religious anarchy in which each tribal holy man was his own authority. How, then, did the Sufi doctrines and brotherhoods we have earlier seen developing fit into this picture? An answer can again be found in the model of Sufism as a "tradition" and of the brotherhoods as not primarily organizations but as mechanisms for reproducing and authenticating tradition. While the rhetoric (indeed, the purpose) of tradition is to present its content as unchanging, tradition is in fact a highly flexible resource, as sociologists have long recognized. When we put this into the mobile and fissiparous tribal societies beyond the towns, what such a model suggests is that while the holy men of the tribes did partake in Sufi tradition – using its terminology, adapting its rituals, giving initiations into its brotherhoods – they did so on their own terms rather than under the command of a master elsewhere and in accordance with the needs of their tribal clients. After all, in such "anarchistic" milieu there was no-one to prevent tribal Sufis from creating their own idiosyncratic medleys from the resources of tradition they inherited, just as there was no Sufi "Vatican" to ensure a common catechism to abide by.[5] While many scholars have described tribal Sufis as "unorthodox" or "heterodox," the fact is that in their own period there was no centrally empowered "orthodoxy" with which to compare them. As we will see later in this chapter, such "orthodoxies" (with the terms of orthodoxy varying in each imperial state) were only to emerge as by-products of the centralization of the early modern empires that followed the more fluid tribal era of the 1400s.

From the Balkans to India, the half-century either side of 1500 saw the tribal founders of new states struggle to transform themselves from conquerors to rulers. This transition also involved a transformation of the kinds of Islam they supported, as they became responsible not only for the fortunes of their tribal kinsmen but also for the more complex and diverse populations they now ruled over. The ruling elites of the Safawi, Ottoman and Mughal empires each had to make this transition and the different ways in which they did so had important consequences for the fortunes of Sufism in their dominions. With its abundance of ambitious tribes, and its rapid turnover of settled polities, it was the mobile, fractious and religiously anarchistic environment of the steppes and mountains that gave birth to both the Ottoman and Safawi empires. This was an environment whose religious forms the new rulers would ultimately have to confront in their attempts to rule over the unruly spaces from which they had themselves emerged. While the case of the Mughals is more complex, in that their rise to power saw them move out of the mobile steppe to conquer the settled agrarian society of India, when they came to rule over the more pluralistic domain of India, the Mughals too faced the problem of how to divorce themselves from their old steppe loyalties to the Naqshbandi brotherhood.

The Mediterranean: The Early Ottoman Empire

To see how this uneasy transition was made from the support of "tribal" to "settled" forms of Sufism, let us first turn to the Ottoman case. Between the fourteenth and sixteenth centuries, the rise of the Ottoman state from a petty tribal chiefdom to a complex bureaucratic empire joining southern Europe with Anatolia, Egypt and ultimately Arabia involved a precarious transformation from tribal and settled forms of religious loyalty. As we have seen in earlier chapters, the learned and literary dimensions of Sufism had developed hand-in-glove with the study of the Quran and the application of Islamic law. Like the Saljuq, Ayyubid and Mamluk rulers before them, the Ottomans considered the institutional fabric of the Sufi brotherhoods in the towns to be an important fillip in the maintaining of social order.[6] As a result, Ottoman expansion saw a reaffirmation of the role of the learned and orderly brotherhoods in urban life, whether through support to pre-existing brotherhoods or through the introduction of new brotherhoods or sub-brotherhoods with closer ties to the Ottomans themselves. The Khalwatiyya ("Seclusionist") brotherhood is a case in point as an example of a legally-conformist brotherhood with little previous connection with Anatolia.[7] The Khalwatiyya developed close connections with both the Ottoman sultans and their highest officials, leading to the establishment of a grand convent for the brotherhood in 1574 in the heart of Istanbul by the grand vizier, Sokollu Mehmed Pasha.[8] The new empire also sponsored the expansion of Rumi's Mevlevi brotherhood of "whirling dervishes," which became the favored affiliation of the Ottoman bureaucracy. This in turn saw the Mevlevi brotherhood's organization become more efficiently centralized around the shrine complex constructed around Rumi's grave in Konya. Naturally, this sponsorship of favored brotherhoods did not take place in a social vacuum and the rising influence of these favored brotherhoods saw a corresponding diminishing in the influence of brotherhoods favored by the Ottoman's predecessors. The Ottoman conquest of Syria and Egypt from the Mamluk dynasty in 1516–1517, for example, saw the gradual replacement of the Sufi notables linked to the Mamluks with a new Sufi order with closer affiliations to the new regime.[9] This "colonizing" agenda was no less apparent when, after moving from Anatolia to Egypt in the wake of the Ottoman conquest, Hasan al-Rumi dictated the terms of the endowment for a new lodge built in Cairo in the Ottoman style: he specified that none of its employees should be local Arabs.[10]

By sponsoring the construction of new Sufi lodges and mausoleums, even the sacred geography of these areas of conquest was gradually "Ottomanized."[11] Indeed, the imperial patronage of new Sufi foundations in the newly conquered territories of the Ottomans in southeastern Europe no less than the Levant has led several historians to describe Sufis as playing the roles of "colonists" and "settlers."[12] In such urban contexts as Aleppo or Cairo, this effectively entailed a privileging of one set of Muslims over another, as in the case we have seen of Sufi brotherhoods or individuals affiliated to the Ottomans replacing those favored by the Mamluks. But in other (particularly rural) contexts, it appears to have entailed the establishing of what amounted to Sufi bridgeheads by way of Muslim settlements in predominantly Christian regions. The main apparatus for this settlement policy was the endowment or *waqf*, by which either a sultan or imperial notable granted a Sufi shaykh sufficient property to not only support himself but also attract a larger community of followers.

The fact that, as followers of the Prophetic Example, Sufis were typically expected to marry and procreate meant that such original settler populations gradually expanded over time. An example is seen in 1516 in the granting to a Sufi by Sultan Selim I of a Christian monastery and its surrounding vineyards and olive groves in the predominantly Christian village of Dayr Bi'na in Galilee.[13] Since Sufi lodges often contained hostels, and in some regions constituted a more or less formal network for supporting travelers, they also attracted Muslim merchants who stimulated the economy of the surrounding region.[14] This was not a policy directed solely at Christian areas and, as in the case of the Bektashi brotherhood's outposts in Anatolia, it was also used to control rural areas with unstable populations of tribal Muslims.[15] The imperial patronage of Sufism was therefore not only a question of supporting institutions whose role in the "civilizing process" made for a more orderly and governable population. It was also a question of supporting institutions that helped settle new territories in the wake of conquest. It would be a mistake to see such settlements as part of a long-term trajectory of Muslim/Christian opposition. While there were presumably in many cases Christians who became unhappy and even disenfranchised by the arrival of

Sufis with friends in high places, as had already happened in the case of earlier Sufi settlements in the medieval period, over time the different religious communities came to accommodate one another and create new syntheses of religious practice.[16] As we will see again with regard to the Mughal Empire, the early modern period was therefore not only one of confrontation but also one which brought about new forms of religious fusion in which the Sufis played an important part.

While the Ottoman attempt to appoint selected Sufis in town and country was in part an echo of the earlier pattern of state-sponsored "Sunnification" seen in Chapter 2, in the Ottoman case it evolved into a much more concerted policy to centralize religious appointments and control potentially subversive Sufi groups, particularly those of the tribal kind. It has been suggested that the Ottomans encouraged the settling of legally-inclined Naqshbandi Sufis in their domains as part of their attempt to disseminate a more standardized and legally-codified adherence to Sunni Islam among the Turkoman tribes of the countryside.[17] While more recent research has questioned this, there is little doubt that the patronage given to Naqshbandis did contribute to the more staunchly Sunni character of Ottoman society that emerged over the longer term.[18] For between the fifteenth and seventeenth centuries, there emerged a formal religious bureaucracy in which appointments – whether as teachers in madrasas, preachers in mosques or masters in Sufi lodges – were controlled by a centralized administration reaching back to the imperial capital of Istanbul.

Thanks to this administration's existence, historians have been able to use the imperial Ottoman archive to gather statistical data on economic life in the lodges of both Istanbul and the rural provinces, where the landholdings and wealth of the lodges appear to have been much greater than was the case in the cities.[19] Such was the expansion of data-gathering that even groups of wandering, antinomian dervishes found their lodges falling into the purview of the imperial bureaucracy, with even the world-renouncing activities of begging and wandering becoming in some degree regularized in the process.[20] But even such a relatively developed state as that of the Ottomans was never able to gain control over all the Sufi lodges in its dominions, let alone over individual Sufis. Perhaps because it was a relative latecomer to Anatolia, the Naqshbandi brotherhood generally maintained a less regulated institutional framework in the Ottoman domains, operating through informal circles in mosques or lodges funded by Central Asian merchants rather than by means of imperial land grants.[21] On an individual level, the career of Niyazi-e Misri (d.1694) showed that there remained Sufis who were willing to use their social influence to voice explicit denunciation of the Ottoman rulers.[22] While the ruling powers decided it was unwise to execute such a critic, they did have the power to do so: in Niyazi's case they chose to exercise their power through the more discreet mechanism of exiling him to the island of Rhodes and then Lemnos. The sheer resources, organizational acumen and longevity of the Ottoman state therefore meant that it did overall bring an unprecedented degree of state control over the hierarchical Sufi assemblies of the towns and the lodges by which it could reach out to the country. It is little wonder that Bali Efendi (d.1553), an eminent Khalwati Sufi with close ties to the imperial order, acquired the nickname "the spy of the shaykhs" (*jasus al-masha'ikh*).[23]

The Ottomans were not the first dynasty to sponsor a literate and orderly Sufism in the lands they governed. But in their attempts to also control rural and tribal religiosity, they signaled the new ambitions (if not always the ability) of the state. It is in these tribal contexts that the ambiguous dynamic between Sufism and the imperial enterprise best reveals itself. For in the period of their initial expansion in the fourteenth and fifteenth centuries, the Ottomans had been quite happy to rely on the help of mobile warrior groups led by the kind of "tribal Sufis" we have described. Much of the Ottoman conquest of the Balkans and Rumelia (that is, modern central Greece and European Turkey) was sub-contracted in precisely this fashion.[24] Such freebooting Sufi warriors drew on the notion of *ghaza* or "raiding" the lands of Christian infidels, an ideology of legitimate violence that was more flexible than the more legally restricted doctrine of *jihad*.[25] In some cases, we hear of a formalization of these Sufi raids into the more structured armies of the Ottomans, with particular Sufis being attached to regiments through the office of "army shaykh" (*ordu shaykhi*).[26] Those Sufis were not only influential frontier figures in their own lifetimes but also after death, as their legends were written down and their tombs transformed into pilgrimage centers. This helped spread their fame beyond the time and place of the frontier societies in which they served their original imperial purpose, so perpetuating their disorderly and idiosyncratic visions of Islam into the period of settlement in which the state was promoting a more orderly Sufism that was substantially standardized throughout its domains.[27]

This attempt to contain the very forces that had helped to establish their empire was one of the lasting dilemmas of Ottoman history. It was by no means unique to the frontier with Christian Europe and the most vivid illustration is seen in the history of the Bektashi brotherhood that was named after a classic tribal Sufi, Hajji Bektash Wali (d.1337).[28] Like other products of the religiously anarchistic environment beyond the towns, the Sufism promoted by Hajji Bektash comprised an idiosyncratic blend of various elements from Sufi tradition and his tribal environment, with input from the Sufi repertoire blending with the shamanic heritage of the Turkoman tribesmen, popular Shi'ism and the peasant Christianity of Anatolia.[29] Like the frontier cults of such similar figures as Sarı Saltuk (d.1298) in the Balkans, the cult of Hajji Bektash was initially only associated with new Turkish-speaking settlers, whether warrior tribesmen or newly-settled agriculturalists.[30] As time progressed, from the late sixteenth century onwards the cult of Hajji Bektash maintained (or acquired) its military association through connections with the more regularized Ottoman army. However, attempts to then centralize and control the Bektashis began as early as 1501 with the state appointment as head of the Bektashis of the Ottoman loyalist Balım Sultan (d.1516), who was designated the "second master" (*pir-e sani*) in the manner of an official heir to the "founder," Hajji Bektash.[31] Far from resulting in the suppression of the cult (which would have been too risky a policy), this attempt to bring the Bektashis under state control took the form of regularizing its organization from tribal Sufi fellowship into formal Sufi brotherhood with a centrally-appointed leadership and a hierarchy of lodges in the towns rather than countryside. While earlier sultans had been generous and enthusiastic patrons of Hajji Bektash's shrine, after the reign of Bayezid II (r.1481–1512) such imperial support was far less regular.[32] Somewhat ironically, in a period in which the Ottoman state was attempting to promote a more standardized and orderly Islam, this policy ensured that many features of the old anarchistic Islam of the tribes were spread and perpetuated through the Bektashi lodges established in every city of the empire. But in the larger picture of Sufi history, the intervention of the centralizing Ottoman state in Sufi affairs meant that the Bektashi brotherhood was transformed from an eclectic blending of tribe and tradition into a more bureaucratic organization of tradition. From the sixteenth century onwards, this pattern would be repeated in the Ottomans' systematization and bureaucratization of the other major brotherhoods in their domains.

Such attempts to rein in the authority and independence of tribal Sufis were not simply part of an innate trajectory of state-building and were very much shaped by events of the period. While the fifteenth century had seen tribal Sufis lead many successful expansions of Ottoman territory, it had also seen rebellions led by the same kinds of figures (most notably that of Shaykh Badr al-Din in 1416) and as the century progressed such rebellions became more frequent.[33] The physical mobility and anarchistic religiosity of such movements meant that they were as likely to resist as assist imperial objectives. In 1493, a Sufi of the antinomian Haydari brotherhood even attempted to assassinate the emperor, Bayezid II.[34] The tension between tribal and settled forms of Sufism was a reflection of the various elements of a heterogeneous society comprising different communities of nomads and townsmen. In such contexts, Sufi brotherhoods provided important tools for social cohesion and interaction between different groups. So, for a centralizing government, the idea of appointing Sufi leaders and promoting firmer structures of brotherhood organization beneath them was therefore clearly attractive. Even if such attempts remained partial and incomplete, over the course of the sixteenth and seventeenth centuries they did bring the brotherhoods into closer relations with the Ottoman state, even if those relations were never characterized by outright fealty.

Figure 3.1 The Saint as Iranian Emperor: Shrine of Safi al-Din at Ardabil
(Image: Nile Green)

Iran: The Early Safawi Empire

The fortunes of Sufism in the Ottoman domains were not only a reflection of internal concerns, but were also shaped by the need to respond to developments in neighboring regions. In this respect as in others, no single event in the early modern period was of greater importance than the rapid conquest of Iran by a tribal Sufi group who originated in the mountainous eastern frontiers of Ottoman rule. In 1501, with the help of an army of tribal followers, a teenaged hereditary Sufi master conquered the Iranian city of Tabriz. Over the next decade, he conquered the remainder of Iran to lay the foundations for an empire which at its greatest expanse would stretch from eastern Anatolia to the borders of India. Right up to its collapse in 1722, the imperial dynasty that the teenage Isma'il Safawi (1487–1524) had founded bore the name of his own Safawi (or Safavid) Sufi family.

The Safawi family and brotherhood originally garnered its following among the tribes of the regions around the mausoleum of the brotherhood's founder, Safi al-Din (d.1334), in the highlands of what is now north-western Iran, though its wealth and prestige also lay in landholdings and influential urban followers. However, it was the Safawis' tribal following that was to prove most influential in its rise. As in the case of other tribal Sufi movements, in the fifteenth century Safi al-Din's descendants Junayd and Haydar gained the following of increasing numbers of Turkoman tribesmen, whose energies they channeled into the kind of religiously-sanctioned raiding or *ghaza* that we have also seen characterizing the Ottoman frontier in the same period.[35] Referred to as the *qizilbash* or "red-turbaned," the tribal followers of the Safawi shaykhs were fiercely loyal to their masters. While, as in the case of other tribesmen, we have no record of their side of the story, from the poetry of the founder of the Safawi Empire, Shah Isma'il, they appear to have venerated him as a living incarnation of God.[36] Given that the logistical and emotional enterprise of founding a new state and binding its peoples together around the charismatic person of the ruler was hardly unique to Muslim states of the early modern period, it is perhaps worth comparing the "political theology" of the early Safawis with European formulations of the king's sacred body from the same period.[37] Perpetuated by ritual performance as much as written doctrine, disseminated through rumors of the miraculously curative powers of the royal touch, and rendered permanent through the building of religio-dynastic mausolea, such *rois thaumaturges* were not unique to the European experience and emerged from common political demands on the leaders of the more complex societies emerging across Eurasia in this period. Against the view that Shah Isma'il claimed to be God in human form, the objection has been made that his poetry invoked less a deliberate new doctrine of incarnation (*hulul*) than the poetic license lent to a more acceptable older doctrine of the Sufi reaching a state of temporary co-identity with God through the "destruction" (*fana*) of his own attributes.[38] While Isma'il's ideas were certainly similar to those of earlier times, the rural and tribal context in which they were deployed was quite distinct from that in which we have seen the terminology and ideas of Sufism previously emerge.

The unregulated religious environment in which the Safawis emerged was one that allowed such intellectual resources of Sufi tradition as the idioms of the master's authority and the powers of God's Friend to be deployed towards such self-aggrandizing ends without effective challenge. Indeed, a number of near-contemporary accounts report how on several occasions the Qizilbash tribesmen cannibalized the enemies of their master Isma'il.[39] According to an Indian Muslim ambassador to the Safawi court, "it was decreed that whoever was a convinced believer [*mu'taqid*] among the great fighters of faith [*ghazis*] must partake a morsel of the roasted [human] body as his share. A terrifying crowd of man-eaters swarmed in and ate the body up such that not a trace of flesh or bone remained."[40] Here was a physical demonstration of the tribesmen's unswerving loyalty to a God who in incarnating himself in the body of Isma'il was himself no less material in form. In the settings in which Isma'il presented himself as God's instrument on earth, there was no central state or religious authority to prevent him from doing so. And if his tribal followers chose to interpret his poems as assurances of his divinity that would protect them on the field of war, then there were no representatives of a Sufi or other Muslim "orthodoxy" at hand to tell them their beliefs were "heterodox." In historical terms, the Safawi movement was very much a product of its tribal and mountain environments in which there existed no state institutions to regulate a person-centered Islam of charismatic Sufi holy men.

Here the early Safawis had much in common with the early Baktashi and similar tribal movements we have seen in the territories of the Ottomans. And this was precisely the problem. For the Safawi brotherhood not only emerged on the fractious eastern fringes of Ottoman territory, but its appeal to tribesmen nominally loyal to the Ottomans found expression in anti-Ottoman uprisings in support of the Safawis. This raised the possibility that the eastern Ottomans provinces would secede to the neighboring new Safawi polity. Since in 1501 Isma'il had also declared that his state would follow the ordinances of Shi'i rather than Sunni Islam, the rivalry between the Ottomans and Safawis also afforded each empire the rhetoric of defending the true version of Islam against its Sunni or Shi'i corrupters. The effectiveness of the Safawi family in channeling the loyalty of the Qizilbash tribesmen into the founding of a new state led to a corresponding attempt to suppress not only direct sympathizers but any similar movements among the tribesmen of Ottoman Anatolia. As part of their policy to contain the Safawi threat, the Ottoman sultans Bayezid II (r.1481–1512) and Selim I (r.1512–1520) made

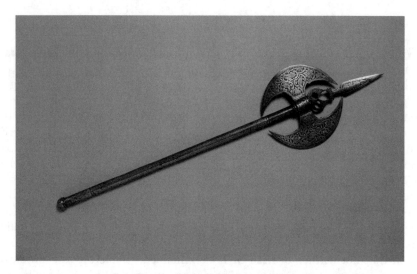

Figure 3.2 The Sufi as Soldier: Axe of an Early Modern Iranian Dervish (Dervish axe (Iran, 18th c.), Inv. No. 3376. Reproduced by permission of the Munich State Museum of Ethnology (photographer: Marietta Weidner))

several attempts to suppress the Qizilbash tribesmen present in their own domains.[41] Yet when we compare the trajectories of Sufism under the Ottoman and Safawi empires, what emerges is not a simple picture of the triumph of a tribal Sufism in the Safawi realms triggering a corresponding suppression of tribal forms and a patronage of settled forms of Sufism in the Ottoman Empire. For just as we have seen the Ottoman state itself struggling to contain the bands of tribal Sufis that had contributed so effectively to their every expansion, so did the creation of a stable state structure require the Safawis to reassess the usefulness of their own tribal Sufi followers. In the Safawi case, the result would be immeasurably more catastrophic for the Sufis than the Ottoman attempt at simply regulating the brotherhoods through greater organization. For, in the course of the sixteenth century, this shift transformed Safawi Iran from a state brought to power by Sufism to a state that persecuted its Sufis into near-extinction.

If the Qizilbash had been effective in supplying the violence necessary to bring the heads of the Safawi brotherhood to the throne, in the longer term they were far less helpful in the maintaining of settled rule over their empire. For as each of the new empires of the period found, the mobility, violence and loyalty required to conquer a territory were never sufficient to govern it. And this in turn required that religious affiliations be adjusted in the shift from conquering to ruling. At the beginning of the Safawi period, the Qizilbash were more or less secure in their special status as the spiritual disciples of the man they made king. But over the following decades, for their part the Safawi rulers not only realized that this special relationship was alienating to the sedentary notables and other power-holders whose loyalty they needed, but they also realized that the framework of a Sufi brotherhood was ultimately insufficient to hold together an entire population.[42] For the Qizilbash tribesmen, this led to the gradual demotion of their role at court to the point at which they eventually found their loyalty exploited to the point of becoming court executioners devouring the noses and ears of the condemned.[43] For Iran at large, it meant gradual implementation of Shi'i Islam as a "state religion," a term which begins to take on genuine meaning from the early modern period.

As a result, Sufis who refused to accept Shi'ism were brutally suppressed, leading in the early 1500s, for example, to the massacre of around four thousand members of the Kazaruni brotherhood in southern Iran. Within a few generations, a new state-sponsored "orthodoxy" would emerge as the forms of Islam promoted by the Safawi state shifted towards a more scholarly and clerical form of Shi'i Islam. Looking back onto the Qizilbash's zeal, violence and veneration for the Safawi family, this ascendant clerical class denigrated the Qizilbash's tribal Sufism as "extremism" or "exaggeration" (*ghuluww*). Unlike the tribal Sufism of the Qizilbash, which like other products of the highland frontier appeared rustic and even heretical to the urban elites with whom the Safawis now dealt, Shi'i Islam possessed the legal scholars, the systematic vision of social order and the international recognition to offer the by-now-settled empire a more respectable alternative to the inheritance of the frontier.

India: The Early Mughal Empire

When we turn to the early modern Muslim empire of the Mughal rulers of India, we see both commonalities and differences to the situation of the Sufis under the Ottomans and Safawis of the sixteenth century. While the Mughals did not come to power as a Sufi family themselves like the Safawis did, like other Turco-Mongolian rulers, their earlier history in Central Asia had seen them enter alliances with the holy men of the Naqshbandi brotherhood.[44] Yet, as with the Ottomans and Safawis, the area over which the Mughals came to rule after the conquests of the dynasty's founder Babur (r.1526–1530) included Sufi groups with influential ties to the population, who could not be easily marginalized in favor of the conquerors' Naqshbandi allies. Recognizing the power of the Sufi establishment that had already been in India for centuries, Babur's first move on conquering Delhi was to make a public pilgrimage to the shrines of its Chishti Sufi saints.[45] Even so, there is evidence that when Babur's son Humayun was overthrown by an uprising of the Afghans whose association with the previous regime saw them marginalized under the new dispensation, Sufis played an active role in enabling and then ultimately disabling the Afghan interregnum that followed.[46] If the beginning of Mughal rule therefore presented a picture of continuity with what we have seen emerging in Chapter 2 of Sufi saints being on a comparable footing with sultans, as the Mughals' hold over India settled, the balance of power shifted in favor of the state. While the Mughals were never to attempt anything like the centralizing organization of brotherhoods seen under the Ottomans, important parallels do appear with both Ottomans and Safawis in the ways in which the Mughals came to interact with the personnel and the symbols of the Sufis. As in the case of other early modern states, the tradition of the Sufis presented a valuable resource for the state to appropriate. Nowhere is this sense of Sufism as a state resource more apparent than in the great Mughal gazetteer of empire '*A'in-e Akbari* (c.1590) in which the Sufi shrines and holy men in the territories of the Mughals were catalogued alongside every other category of imperial possession.[47]

Akbar (r.1556–1605), the emperor who commissioned this work, represents the Mughals' most audacious attempt at channeling Sufism towards imperial ends. This was first seen in his decision to build a new imperial capital at Fatehpur Sikri around the home (and, shortly, the tomb) of Salim Chishti (d.1572), the Sufi who had miraculously granted him a son and heir.[48] In its echo of the Safawi patronage of a shrine-palace complex around the tomb of Shaykh Safi al-Din during the previous decades, the Mughal construction of a parallel complex around the tomb of a saint was in some respects a sign of the Sufis' elevated status.[49] But in surrounding the shrine with high walls of sandstone, it was also a kind of besiegement, and, as such, a vivid pointer to a policy of the containment and integration of the more important Sufis of the realm. As the conqueror of Bengal, Rajputana, Gujarat and Kashmir, Akbar's ambitions were even grander than this, leading him (or his chief courtier, Abu'l Fazl) to promote a new socio-religious organization in which elements of Muslim and Hindu religiosity were synthesized to form a new "divine religion" or *din-e ilahi*.[50] At heart, the *din-e ilahi* was an imperial cult in which the now long-established idioms of the Sufis were co-opted for the emperor himself, who was designated as the perfect man (*insan-e kamil*) and spiritual director (*murshid*) of a circle of loyal Sufi disciples (*murids*) who were none other than his courtiers.[51] Given Akbar's varied millenarian concerns, there is also reason to connect his inception of the *din-e ilahi* with the turning of the Islamic millennium in the middle of his reign. While many other Muslims would see the new millennium as an occasion to return to the Prophetic Example, for the richest emperor of the age, it was an occasion to create an altogether new religious synthesis.

Even so, there was a series of precedents for the Mughals' imperial Sufi ideology, particularly in Iran. A century earlier a poetic Sufi parable

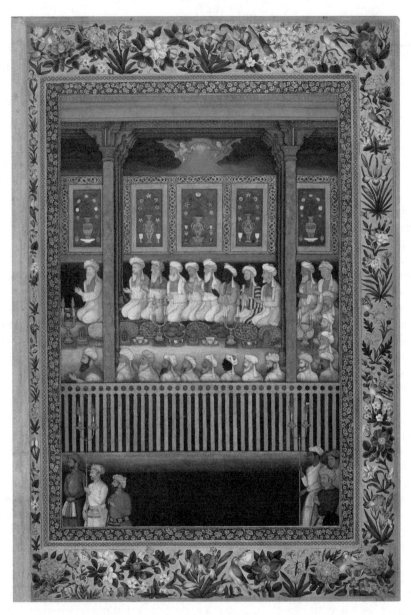

Figure 3.3 The Sufi Establishment: Gathering of Sufis and Scholars before the Mughal Emperor, c.1635 (Freer Gallery of Art, Smithsonian Institution, Washington, D.C.: Purchas, F194217, F1937.6.7b)

entitled *Salman va Absal* addressed by Jami of Herat (d.1492) to his Aq Qoyunlu patron Sultan Ya'qub (d.1490) had similarly presented the tribal ruler in the guise of the Sufi "perfect man" who was as such an ideal ruler over other, existentially-lesser Muslims.[52] Another precedent was the courtly *chub-e tariq* ("rod of the way") ritual of the early Safawi rulers of Iran in which Qizilbash tribesmen were symbolically beaten into submission to their royal and spiritual master.[53] Echoing such court-oriented poems and rituals, the Mughal *din-e ilahi* and its *murshid-murid* template were more intended as a means of consolidating loyalty at the court than as a system intended to be promulgated through Indian society at large. Even if the short lifespan of the *din-e ilahi* has seen it belittled as a princely caprice, the Sufi language of the emperor as the *murshid* and the courtier as *murid* would continue under subsequent Mughal rulers.[54] In the reign of Akbar's successor, Jahangir (r.1605–27), for example, the courtier 'Abd al-Satar collected the emperor's conversations in the form of a *malfuzat* text of the kind usually reserved for the speeches of Sufi shaykhs.[55] In Sufi language, 'Abd al-Satar expressly referred to this conversational compendium as the *malfuzat-e jahangiri*, in addition to describing Jahangir as a miracle-worker bearing the Sufi titles of "master and guide" (*pir u murshid*).[56] Nor were the Mughals the only early modern rulers in South Asia to adapt these models of Sufi authority to their own courtly purposes. From his small mountain kingdom to the north of Delhi, a century after the reign of Jahangir the Indo-Afghan ruler Muhammad Khan Bangash (r.1713–1743) formulated a similar persona that blended the imagery of the Sufi master (*pir*) and the holy warrior (*ghazi*), and encouraged his courtiers to think of themselves as his Sufi disciples (*chelas*). Sufi models of authority were therefore highly transferable.[57]

As with the Safawis and Ottomans, the new confidence of the early modern Mughal state expressed itself in the willingness to confront no less than contain groups whose deployments of Sufi tradition threatened imperial authority. Just as the Ottomans and Safawis eventually sought to suppress the tribal Sufism of the Qizilbash, so in the reign of Akbar the tribal-unifying Rawshani movement led by the charismatic Sufi Bayazid Ansari (d.1585) among the Afghan tribes of the northern frontier was met with fierce suppression.[58] Overall, the dealings of the Mughal court with Sufism reflected the different roles that Sufism played in Indian society at large during the Mughal era.[59] Even more than the other empires of the period, that of the Mughals brought together a variety of ethnic and religious groups, and though their identities were subject to change over time, there existed vivid senses of difference and factionalism between them. The plurality and complexity of Mughal society channeled Sufi brotherhoods and shrine cults into two different directions, one seeing Sufi affiliations effectively mapping onto and replicating forms of ethnic, linguistic or class association and the other seeing them act as socially-inclusive brokers of interaction between different groups. On the one hand, we find that the people who gathered around a given Sufi were predominantly of the same ethnic group as the Sufi himself, a factor which emerged from a context of the migration and displacement that was a feature of imperial society.[60] On the other hand, we find many cases of living Sufi masters or their shrines acting as vehicles of social integration by bringing together members of different ethnic and even religious groups.[61] It has been argued that the key role was played here by the doctrine of the Unity of Being (*wahdat al-wujud*), which we saw in Chapter 2 originally developing in the teachings of Ibn al-'Arabi (d.1240). In the Indian context, the doctrine may have served as an enabler of social unity that allowed Muslims and Hindus to recognize their different gods and practices as part of a greater cosmic unity.[62]

While it is difficult to know how to prove such a generalization, the doctrine of *wahdat al-wujud* did enable many Muslim poets (and their listeners) to imagine themselves entering temples and bowing down before their statues. Insofar as such an ideological role can be granted to *wahdat al-wujud* in India, it is significant that the doctrine also enjoyed state support in the similarly multi-religious empire of the Ottomans. But it was not only the message but also the medium that afforded such accommodation between members of different religious groups. We should not underestimate the role of Persian in enabling the dissemination of Sufi idioms among the different groups exposed to its literary culture in Mughal India, where Persian was promoted among all groups connected with the state, including the many Hindus of the writer castes who formed the bulwark of the Mughal bureaucracy.[63] Looking beyond Persian, we have already seen how vernacularization spread Sufi teachings through various local languages and this was no less the case in India. In the case of such Punjabi poets as Shah Husayn (d.1599), Sultan Bahu (d.1691) and Bulleh Shah (d.1757) and such Sindhi poets as Shah 'Abd al-Latif (d.1752), the Mughal period saw the trickling down to the rural level of Sufi idioms that before 1500 were largely the preserve of the urban classes.[64] This rural outreach not only brought religious ideas to a rural audience, but also mechanisms of arbitration and control, for whether in admonishing lawbreakers, settling disputes or teaching seemly behavior, the Sufis became important pillars of the rural social order. If in Mughal India they never became as closely connected to the state as in the Ottoman Empire, and even if it was at a greater distance from the state, the Sufis did much to maintain social order and harmony in India.[65] While there remained many mendicant Sufis who subsided on the fringes of society no less than state, it would be no exaggeration to say that for the most part Sufism was very much a part of the Mughal establishment.

Another important parallel between between Sufi-state relations in the Ottoman and Mughal domains is seen in the Sufi role in expanding the imperial frontier. We have already seen the importance of Sufi "settlers" to Ottoman expansion in southeast Europe and the Levant and there was a parallel process in Mughal India. The process in itself was not new to India and Sufis had helped expand Muslim settlement along the fertile Ganges plain throughout the period of the Delhi Sultanate (1206–1526), whether as self-helping frontiersmen or as recipients of lands granted by the sultan.[66] This older mode of employing Sufis to expand the agricultural frontier was continued under the Mughals, whose conquest from 1574 of the great forest region of Bengal provided them with an inexhaustible supply of land to grant to pious and loyal subjects. On receiving grants of forestland, Sufis employed local woodsmen to clear the land for agriculture. In so doing, they introduced the indigenous peoples of the rainforest to Islam in its Sufi form, expanding not only the frontiers of the empire but also bringing about a process of "conversion by the plough."[67] While this in part expanded the reach of formal Islamic learning, it also pushed the process of vernacularization to new levels of fusion, with Middle Bengali Sufi literature cross-fertilizing themes drawn from Tantrism and the old legends of the forests.[68]

This pattern of early modern states appropriating and redirecting either the personnel or idioms of Sufism was not unique to the three great empires of the period and can be seen in a variety of other settings. In many cases, this involved the mobility of elite Sufi families, moving from prestigious older centers to frontier environments in which the symbolic capital of their learning and existential status as Friends were scarce resources. The incorporation of such mobile holy men into new states on the maritime frontier of the Indian Ocean helps us tie together the history of Sufism in different areas. The regional sultanates of the south Indian Deccan region are one example. As part of a larger policy of sponsoring immigrant over local elites, the Deccan's Bahmani sultans attracted the family of the sanctified Iranian Sufi, Shah Ni'matullah (d.1431), to their capital at Bidar.[69] Lavishly patronized and allied in marriage to the royal family itself, the Ni'matullahis became key figures at court, not only leading the sultans' coronation ritual but granting the sultan Ahmad Shah (r. 1422–1436) the Sufi rank of *wali* or Friend of God to add to his official royal titles. A rare Persian biography of Shah Ni'matullah from the Bahmani period describes how even before Ahmad Shah came to power, he had a dream in which he saw Shah Ni'matullah placing a crown on his head; after waking, he received a letter from the saint further assuring him of his future success.[70] Continuing these ties between saint and sultan into the following generations, the great south Indian historian, Firishta (d.1620) repeated the story, while another biography of Shah Ni'matullah was dedicated to the next Bahmani ruler, 'Ala' al-Din Ahmad Shah II (r.1436–1458), who was described in the dedication as the "sultan of

Gnostics" (*sultan al-'urafa*).[71] Other south Indian sultanates also saw a tightening of the relationship between Sufis and the state, as in the case of the great increase in the bestowing of land-grants (*in'am*) and pensions (*yawmiyya*) to Sufis by the 'Adil Shah sultans of Bijapur in the seventeenth century.[72] As in other early modern contexts, the motivation seems to have been the creation of a stable and uniform religious establishment that was loyal to (because dependent on) patrons representing the state.[73]

Southeast Asia: The Malay Sultanates

If the Deccani picture most closely resembled the Ottoman model, then there were also examples of smaller regional polities following the more radical co-option of Sufi idioms seen under Shah Isma'il in Iran and Akbar in India. Such presentations of the king as Friend of God and Perfect Man also occurred in the sultanates of Southeast Asia, making *rois thaumaturges* for the spice islands of Java and Sumatra. Early Malay sources such as the *Hikayat Raja-Raja Pasai* ('Tales of the Kings of Pasai') show how even in the earliest Islamic sultanates established in the region, sultans were being presented as sharing the power to work miracles (*karama*) in common with the Sufis.[74] Just as India itself hosted mobile Sufis from prestigious earlier centers in Central Asia and Iran, so in turn did the little kingdoms of the Malay-Indonesian archipelago welcome those who embodied the prestige and power of distant spiritual places. While Southeast Asia has often been depicted as the passive partner at the "receiving end" of these Sufi migrations, it is worth bearing in mind that Muslim scholars from Southeast Asia were reported as teaching in Arabia as early as the fourteenth century, as in the case of Abu 'Abdullah Mas'ud al-Jawi.[75] Fashionably exotic in the distant towns of Arabia, in later praise poems Mas'ud's vaguely understood "Javanese" homeland was used to metaphorically link him with the costly spices and fragrances for which Southeast Asia was chiefly known.[76] Not only devotional hyperbole, such imaginative associations point to the interdependence of religious and trade networks that allowed the Sufi "imports" of the early modern era. While the process can only be glimpsed through miraculous narratives preserved in royal chronicles, the conversion of the Malay rulers of the new mercantile states that emerged in Southeast Asia in the fifteenth and sixteenth centuries was widely attributed to the charisma and teachings of such mobile Sufis who sailed to the region from such older centers as Baghdad, though more recent research suggests India to have been a more likely source for these holy men.[77] The conversion accounts preserved in the Malay chronicles are often highly colorful, with kings being miraculously circumcised as they slept or being rescued while drunk from devils pissing in their wine cups. The evidence for the spread of Islam deeper into Southeast Asia shows similar developments at work, with the conversion of Java associated with stories and shrines of the famous "nine saints" (*wali sanga*). The earliest significant literary evidence on Javanese Islam, such as a sixteenth century Javanese *primbon* or "handbook," similarly documents the spread into Java of an Islam that was inherently Sufi in form.[78]

From sixteenth century Southeast Asia, evidence survives of writings by Sufis themselves, whose works testify to what was already a highly sophisticated grasp of metaphysical subtleties on this oceanic frontier. This sophistication reflected the emergence of a class of peripatetic Sufi scholars in the region.[79] In the case of Hamza Fansuri (d.1527 or 1590), we find a Sufi who was born in Southeast Asia travelling to Mecca, Baghdad and even Palestine before returning to teach in his home region, again suggesting a model of two-way circulation more than simple center-to-periphery transfer.[80] A recent reappraisal of the evidence on Fansuri's career suggests he was a member of the Baghdad-founded Qadiri brotherhood who recruited disciples at the Pasai court on Sumatra, whose ruler had converted to Islam in around 1270.[81] Fansuri's presence echoed the cosmopolitanism afforded by the region's trade rates. When the North African traveler Ibn Battuta (d.1368) visited Pasai, he described two Iranian experts in Islamic law in the sultan's service.[82] By Fansuri's lifetime a century later, Pasai had developed into a religious no less than a commercial carrefour from which Fansuri and his disciples transmitted Sufi tradition to new geographical areas. Through their adoption of Malay as a written language, the teachings of the great Spanish Sufi Ibn 'Arabi (d.1240) reached audiences of whom he could never have dreamed expanding to new horizons the vernacularization process we have seen in Chapter 2. Poetic as well as doctrinal, Fansuri's own abundant writings in Malay are the great early example.[83] At the same time that Fansuri sought Malay equivalents for Sufi terms, in the midst of this vernacularization, his loaning into Malay of key terms from the original Arabic lexicon of the early Baghdad Sufis helped maintain the continuity of this new Malay Sufism with earlier tradition.[84] Somewhat later, such key words as *wali* ("Friend of God") were also borrowed into Javanese from the Arabic Sufi lexicon.

In line with the larger early modern picture of state–Sufi interaction, the adaptation of Sufi tradition to this new Malay cultural context occurred in partnership with larger ideological agendas. Given that Sufis such as Fansuri were supported by royal patrons, it is scarcely surprising that the Sufism these patrons supported bolstered rather than undermined their own authority. Even so, it has to be said that the circumstances and even date of Fansuri's career remain contested and so, as we see below, it is only in the seventeenth century that we can speak more clearly about the interactions between Sufi and state in Southeast Asia.

Central Asia: Shrine Societies

If the picture in Southeast Asia is hazy during the sixteenth century, we possess much fuller documentation of the traffic between Sufi brotherhoods and the state in Central Asia. As we saw in Chapter 2, in a region where the state structures of tribal dynasts had relatively shallow ties to wider society, the fifteenth century saw a leader of a single branch of the Naqshbandi brotherhood become not only Central Asia's largest landowner, but also the governor of a surrogate state that outlived and outreached the region's Timuri and Shaybani rulers. The case of the Naqshbandiyya is a valuable one, since it shows how the same brotherhood became very different in its various settings, pointing to the interactions between a tradition, its participants and its environment. If in the Ottoman domains the Naqshbandis remained only loosely organized through the early modern period, in the oasis towns of Central Asia the case could not have been more different. After forming a more centralized organization structure under the leadership of 'Ubaydullah Ahrar (d.1490), the brotherhood (or more concretely the followers of Ahrar) effectively constituted a state in their own right, operating a system of "protection" or *himayat* through which the brotherhood's members not only received spiritual blessings but also the more tangible aid of employment on Ahrar's vast agricultural landholdings.[85] This policy of agrarian expansion through using *waqf* endowments to grant under-used arable land to saintly families was promoted was by the Timuri sultans (particularly Husayn Bayqara, r.1469–1506); and when the state itself collapsed, the saintly families held onto their rich agrarian resources.[86] Through the fifteenth and sixteenth centuries, the Naqshbandi brotherhood offered its vast membership among settled peasants and townsmen such state-like services as protection from nomadic raiders or such privileges as immunity from taxation.[87] Wielders of spiritual no less than material power, the masters and deputies of the brotherhood were celebrated in stories that presented them as supernaturally punishing the enemies of those under their "protection."[88] Having emerged in the 1100s as a quietist, poor and loosely-organized brotherhood, by 1500 the Naqshbandiyya had become a vastly wealthy and highly-centralized organization with close ties to every dynasty it encountered. Surviving letters written by 'Ubaydullah Ahrar and the members of his organization document the operation of a highly effective bureaucracy which paralleled and in certain cases outreached the authority of the formal rulers of the region.[89] Startlingly practical in character, the many surviving letters show the brotherhood as a mechanism for solving property and legal disputes, offering "passports" to travelers, giving cash grants to peasants and tax breaks to merchants.

While 'Ubaydullah Ahrar and his Naqshbandi heirs were the most successful operators of this system of "shrine societies," they were by no means the only ones. The early modern period saw the system expand throughout the vast Central Asian steppe lands, with the Sufis' institutional longevity enabling them to manage a fragile agricultural ecosystem far more effectively than the ephemeral dynasties of sultans.[90] Further east along the silk road, Ubaydullah's Naqshbandi descendants were even more successful in their state-making ventures. One of 'Ubaydullah's own sons, Ahmad Kasani (d.1543), expanded the reach of brotherhood as far as Kashgaria in modern western China and ultimately to Tibet, attempting to replicate there the earlier Naqshbandi success in bringing the moral restraints of Shari'a to the Turkic tribesmen of the steppes. In 1531, in what appears to have been a convenient marriage of the missionary expansiveness of the Naqshbandiyya and the attractions of the wealthy trade routes that crossed through the Himalaya, one of Kasani's disciples from the Shaybani dynasty even launched a *jihad* against Tibet.[91] Later in this chapter we will see one of Kasani's descendants founding a new Naqshbandi state in what is now western China.

North Africa: Marini & Sa'di Kingdoms

Under the Marini (1215–1465) and Sa'di (1509–1659) dynasties of Morocco, North Africa saw the Sufis in similarly elevated positions. While Sufism had previously faced many detractors in North Africa, the Marini period witnessed steady gains in the status of the region's Sufis. In part, this came about through the Sufi affiliations of lawyers trained at the great Qarawiyyin *madrasa* that the Marinis funded in their capital of Fes to provide their government with administrators.[92] Even so, the Sufis were not easy instruments of the state and the Marinis' inability to defend their territories from the nascent Spanish and Portuguese empires saw the rise of a war party led by Sufis who denounced the ruling house and called their followers to *jihad* against the Christians. When the Portuguese conquered Tangier, for example, the Shadhili Sufi Muhammad al-Jazuli (d.1465) helped lead a *jihad* in defense of Muslim territory that brought together twelve thousand Sufis and tribesmen under his leadership.[93] The uprising led to the Marinis' replacement by the war party comprising the Wattasi family of descendents of the Prophet and their Qadiri Sufi allies. Not all Sufis were happy with the rise of the Wattasis, particularly those who held positions in the Marini administration, leading such non-Qadiri Sufis as Ahmad al-Zarruq (d.1493) to leave Fes for a long exile in Cairo.[94]

Jazuli's model of political authority resting in a union of Sufi saints and sultans who were *sharifs* (descendant of the prophet) played a key role in the legitimization of the Sa'di dynasty (1509–1659) that replaced the Wattasis.[95] Like the Ottomans and Safawi empires at the same time, the Sa'dis were able to exert power over their tribal frontier to unprecedented degree.

In bringing not only the loyalties of tribesmen but also raising the status of Sufi pilgrimage sites in Saʿdi territory (as opposed to those in Egypt and Arabia), men like Jazuli were important assistants in the making of what would ultimately emerge as the Moroccan nation state. By the sixteenth century, North African Sufis' were so self-conscious of their own political authority as saintly heirs of Muhammad that in a fusing of Sufi and political terminology they were publically referring to themselves as the "axes of the state" (*aqtab al-dawla*).[96] Developing the idea that the Sufi was the "substitute" or *badil* who rightfully held authority in the absence of the Prophet, al-Jazuli and his successors carved out an influential place for themselves not only at court but in North Africa's rural communities as well.

Like the Safawis at the same time in Iran, in its ascent to power the Saʿdi dynasty made use of the millenarian expectations of the period, drawing on eschatological themes in the writings of Jazuli in particular. As in other regions, the decades around the turn of the Islamic millennium in 1591 witnessed millenarian anxieties in Morocco that both Sufis and sultans sought to channel to their own messianic claims.[97] The legitimacy of the early Saʿdis was framed in precisely such terms. Their dynastic name of *al-dawla al-saʿdiyya* ("the salvific state") drew on the notion of *saʿda* ("bliss, salvation") in the teachings of Jazuli. It encapsulated the millenarian promise to found a perfect Muslim community based on the expulsion of the Portuguese infidels and the shared rule of dynastic descendents of the Prophet and the Jazuli saintly "axes."[98] Early on in their reign, the importance the Saʿdis lent to the Sufis was seen in the devotion the Saʿdi founder Muhammad al-Qaʾim (r.1509–1517) held for Jazuli himself; the dynasty's founder even asked to be buried beside the Sufi. This led al-Qaʾim's successor Ahmad al-Araj (r.1517–1544) to exhume al-Jazuli's body and rebury it in a specially constructed mausoleum in the Saʿdi capital of Marrakech in which saint and sultan were interred together in a vivid symbol of their unity.

The rise of the Saʿdis also involved a struggle to control the semi-Islamized southern frontier of Berber tribesmen and prosperous caravan trails. Here too, rural Sufi lodges played an important role in claiming the region for Islam and thence the Saʿdis as the family heirs of the Prophet.[99] As with the rich agricultural lands of Central Asia, such high stakes encouraged attempts to centralize Jazuli's branch of the Shadhili brotherhood, with Jazuli's successor ʿAbdullah al-Ghazwani (d.1529) calling summits in the tribal south to unify the leaders of the various Jazuli lodges behind the Saʿdi throne.[100] The many teaching centers which Jazuli's followers established in the countryside no less than the towns not only spread literacy through the importance they lent to scriptural and legal studies, but also gave Jazulis the qualifications to enter the Saʿdi bureaucracy in a manner that echoed the place of educated Sufis in the Ottoman bureaucracy.[101] Yet as we have seen in other settings in the same period, participation at court had its perils. As with the fate of the Safawi Sufis and their Qizilbash followers in Iran, after around 1550 the Sa'di rulers viewed the lofty Jazuli claims to authority as more threatening than advantageous and so moved to persecute their former Sufi partners.

Even so, such expanding state–Sufi authority was not only achieved in the urban settings of the Moroccan "realm of government" (*bilad al-makhzan*), but also through the establishment of rural lodges among Berber tribes in the frontier "realm of dissidence" (*bilad al-siba'*). As in other regions we have examined, rural Sufi influence was furthered through the agricultural properties that Sufis controlled. Amid the abandoning of farm land and the subsequent famines that accompanied the wars of the fifteenth and sixteenth centuries, these Sufi landholders offered work and charity to displaced peasants and tribesmen. In the process, they brought abandoned and previously uncultivated land under cultivation, developments which, as with the Naqshbandi role in the unsettled tribal/agricultural zones of Central Asia at the same time, made Sufis leaders of what amounted to agrarian Sufi frontier fiefdoms.[102] In time, this early modern development policy would also see African slaves purchased to work the land, forging an enduring religious economy of Arab saints and African slaves that survived into modern times.[103]

Saharan Africa: The Songhay Empire and Funj Sultanate

The fifteenth and sixteenth centuries also saw the introduction of Sufism to new Muslim states emerging in Saharan Africa. This was probably already the case in the earliest African Islamic state of the period, the Songhay Empire (1464–1591) of west Saharan Africa, where Islamic symbolism was used to support a royal cult in which the emperor was endowed with miraculous powers.[104] While the role of Sufis in these developments is unclear due to the lack of early sources on the Songhay Empire, we do know of various North African Sufis settling in the key scholarly and trading outpost of Timbuktu during the Songhay era. Whether at the western or eastern end of Saharan Africa, the direction of Sufism's introduction was from north to south, principally along routes of trade and pastoral migration that reached north through the Sahara to Morocco and Egypt. As a result, brotherhoods with a strong presence in North Africa such as the Shadhilis and Qadiris were also those which were taken south.[105] The Shadhili brotherhood, for example, was introduced to Nilotic Sudan by Hamad Abu Dunana (*fl.*1450), a follower of the North African Sufi Jazuli.[106] Whether merchants or scholars, we are effectively talking here of traveling people who brought back initiations and ideas from the north. The early presence of Shadhili and Qadiri Sufism was therefore in terms of affiliated individual migrants rather than structured brotherhoods. As a result, what we see emerging in Africa were family-*tariqas*, that is, locally powerful holy families affiliated by lineage to but organizationally independent from the wider trans-regional brotherhoods such as the Qadiriyya from which they gained prestige in their local settings.[107] As with the Islamization of other regions of the world in the early modern period, especially important in this process were Sufi migrants belonging to prestigious *silsila* lineages associating them with the brotherhoods of the Muslim Mediterranean, particularly Morocco and Egypt. As one historian has described the matter,

> the characteristic Islamic presence in the Funj and Darfur states [of early modern Sudan] was the holy lineage, which usually traced its origins to an immigrant who intermarried locally. The lineage gains a monopoly over education, medical and magical practice in its locality and frequently consolidates its power by receiving tax-exempt status (*jah*) or landed estates (*hakura, iqta'*) from the rulers.[108]

In Saharan Africa, then, as in other regions in the same period, kings and Sufis negotiated workable alliances. Partly in reflection of the juridical Sufism we have seen flourishing in North Africa in this period, and partly in reflection of the rarity of literacy in an African context at this time, Saharan Sufism was also characterized by a strong emphasis on written learning. In many regions, Sufis were termed *faqihs* or "jurisconsults" in reference to the prestigious legal learning in which they also specialized.

Figure 3.4   Oases of the Saints: Agricultural Shrine Settlement, Northwestern Sahara (Image: Nile Green)

While certain legends survive of Sufis moving into the Sudan region during this period, it is only with the emergence of the Funj sultanate (1504-1821) that the picture of Sufi activities becomes clearer. Islam had first appeared in Nilotic Sudan through the influx of Arab pastoralists in the thirteenth and fourteenth centuries which led to the collapse of the Christian kingdoms of Maqurra and 'Alwa. By the Funj period, scholars from the *madrasas* of Egypt and North Africa to the north of Sudan were widely affiliated to Sufi brotherhoods; and, for scholars willing to make the southward journey through the desert, the establishment of the Funj sultanate created rich opportunities of patronage. Armed with the *baraka* of their holy blood lines and the mystique of their mastery of writing, in Sudan these Sufis acted as mediator figures whose prestige rendered them pillars of social order in a state whose influence over its population was otherwise rudimentary.[109] Funj patronage was typically given in the form of abundant unused land and so, as in the other imperial attempts we have seen at settling frontier regions, in Sudan Sufis similarly received land grants and founded agricultural villages known as *khalwas* ("retreats"). From there, through employment and intermarriage, they brought about the gradual conversion of their surroundings to an Islam that was inseparable from the Sufis who transmitted it.[110] As in other regions, this pattern of the gradual acculturation of Africans to Muslim lifeways was accompanied by a parallel process of the adaptation of Islam to African ways.[111] With their miraculous powers, their skills in writing Arabic talismans and their posthumous transformation into sacred shrines, the Sufis were central to this two-way pattern of Islamization.

A Crisis of Conscience: Legalists and Renewers, c.1600–1800

Whether in terms of persons, institutions or ideas, so far in this chapter we have seen Sufism reaching such a degree of influence that it was either incorporated into state methods of governance or even replaced states entirely. Such was the permeation by the early modern period of Sufi ideas and institutions through all levels of society across most of the Islamic world that it is often difficult to decide who was and was not a Sufi. Whether by paying homage to a shrine, reciting a popular song or taking formal initiation at the hands of a living master, ordinary Muslims were exposed to a Sufism that had largely become indistinguishable from Islam in general. By 1600, the tradition fostered by the Sufis – a tradition they claimed was transmitted from the Prophet Muhammad through such early Sufis as Junayd and the founders of the brotherhoods down to their own time – had sufficiently diversified that there now existed a confusing variety of Sufi practices, doctrines and organizations. Different Sufis did different things, often quite spectacularly so, and this range of doctrine and practice begged the question as to whether all of them could possibly be the true tradition of the Prophet. In the seventeenth century, legalistic debates tested the Sufis in all corners of the Muslim world and the first key question in these debates was which brotherhood's tradition – which *tariqa* or "Path" – best connected Muslims to the Example of Muhammad? And since it was clear that many Sufis were doing things that Muhammad himself never did, the second key question was which practices condoned by the Sufis were praiseworthy innovations (*bid'a hasana*) acceptable even though not part of the Prophetic Example and which were reprehensible ones (*bid'a sayyi'a*) which must be suppressed? This notion of "innovation" or *bid'a* was the main critical tool which both Sufis and non-Sufis used to criticize those they regarded as deviators from the Example of Muhammad and the tradition of the early Sufis who followed him.

There are many reasons why the seventeenth century "crisis of conscience" occurred when it did. As we have already seen in the introduction to this chapter, while its timing can partly be explained by the turning of the Muslim millennium in 1591 (the year 1000 in the Islamic calendar) the cultural time of the Islamic calendar was not the only factor. The processual time of the historian must also be taken into account. As we have already seen, the last century of the first Muslim millennium and the first century of the second Muslim millennium coincided with the processual time of a panoply of social, economic and political changes that have led historians to refer to the period as one of early modernity. It is the considerable effects of this coincidence of cultural and processual time that allows us to speak of the period as characterized by a crisis of conscience which affected many groups and not only the Sufis.

Yet the passing of time also affected the Sufis in more specific ways, particularly through the tension between this more general crisis of conscience and the legacy of passing time in the creation of a superabundance of ideas, practices and institutions that all claimed to represent the true Sufi tradition. We have described this development above as a process of diversification. Amid the period's crisis of conscience, many of these diversified variations of Sufi tradition were criticized as reprehensible "innovations" from the Prophetic Example. This was part of a gradual and cumulative conscience-driven critique that emerged in the seventeenth to blossom most vividly in the eighteenth century when the heightening pressures of early modernity saw the collapse of many Muslim states. One of the reasons why Sufi and non-Sufi scholars could critique so many practices from the seventeenth century was therefore because by this period there simply existed a far greater variety of Sufi practices than had developed in earlier centuries through the vernacularizations traced in Chapter 2. Whatever its theological dimensions, in historical terms the crisis of conscience can be understood as a response to the abundant *success* of Islamization rather than its failure, as many of the clerical critics of the Sufis claimed in their accusations. For rather than being genuine survivals of hoary pre-Islamic antiquity, many of the rituals that were criticized as having "pagan" origins were either localized versions of Islam or earlier Muslim practices that had become suspect by the early modern period. The critique of "innovation" can therefore be partly explained as a theological response to the cumulative historical process of vernacularization that gained momentum from the more general crisis of conscience that affected a wide range of Muslims in the midst of the disruptive changes of early modernity.

The dissemination of the *bida'* innovation critique through the sixteenth to eighteenth centuries can in turn be related to greater *awareness* of this diversity of practices. Such increasing awareness of the troubling diversification of tradition itself occurred as growing numbers of Muslim scholars travelled to other Muslim regions (particularly outside the Middle East) as part of the larger interactions between different regions that characterized early modernity. A connection can also be made between the rise of the innovation critique and the increasing interaction between particular regions that also characterized the period. For as country people moved to the growing cities of the early modern empires, they brought with them their distinctive vernacularized Islams. And as literate urbanites were dispatched on government service to provincial or rural areas, they were in turn confronted with the variations of Sufi Islam in the countryside. Here again, it was social interactions that provoked theological problems, as scholarly Muslims (where Sufis or not) drew on the language of "innovation" in their struggle with the conceptual problem that not every Muslim practice they observed could possibly have been taught by the Prophet. The religious consequences of this increasing traffic between Muslims of town and country can be compared to the rise of a persecuting theory of "witchcraft" in Christian Europe during the same era as a response to parallel interactions of rural and urban peoples. Like the accusations and theory of "witchcraft," which could be uniformly applied to condemn remarkably diverse practices and circumstances in a variety of different places, the discourse of "innovation" was similarly transferable in its applicability and authoritative in its consistency. While this new crisis of conscience did therefore fuel a geographically widespread critique of "innovations," except in a few cases (most notably Iran) it did not involve a wholesale attack on the ability of Sufism as such to transmit the Prophet's legacy. Rather, in the first century of the new Muslim millennium, the crisis remained one of questioning which aspects of Sufi tradition were beneficial and which obstructive to the proper Muslim life. It would have to wait until the great Muslim Reformation in the late nineteenth and early twentieth centuries until large numbers of Muslims saw Sufism in all its forms as failing to connect them to the intentions of the Prophet.

While Western scholars once considered Sufis to be the mystical opponents of the legalistic scholars or *'ulama*, as Chapter 1 and Chapter 2 have shown, Sufis and *'ulama* were in many cases the same persons and even when they were not, there were similar concerns with law and scripture being shared. Even so, in the seventeenth century, there did emerge a new emphasis on legal compliance in each of the early modern empires. But, rather than looking for innate tensions between abstract moralistic and mystical pieties representing legal and mystical authority, in historical terms it is more fruitful to conceive this shift towards legalism and the crisis of conscience behind it as involving particular groups reacting to particular circumstances. By seeing mystical knowledge and legal book-learning as forms of authority which might alternatively be united in a single person or separately championed by rivals, this contextual approach helps us reckon with the inconsistencies of the older static picture of "mystics versus lawyers." For what we are mostly looking at is a picture of Sufis using the law to either criticize one another or else criticize the common people (though we will see important instances of legal specialists with no Sufi affiliations using the law to criticize the Sufis *en masse*). In the following pages, we will turn to case studies of what amounted to a widespread seventeenth century challenge by the lawmakers in almost all corners of the Islamic world. If many of these legalistic challengers were themselves Sufis seeking to undermine brethren who took the law more lightly, in other cases we will see the increasing status of a scholarly class with no Sufi affiliations at all.

The Mediterranean: The Later Ottomans

In this survey of the seventeenth century crisis of conscience, let us again turn first to the Ottoman Empire. There, despite the state's investment in training a class of legally expert *'ulama*, the period between around 1620 and 1685 saw a faction of these scholars use the prestige of their learning not in the service of social integration but in sowing discord in a society they regarded as morally bankrupt. Known as the Kadızadelis, this faction criticized the Sufis who were an integral part of Ottoman society. As such, the polemics the Kadızadelis exchanged with their Sufi opponents represented a struggle between different parties within the Ottoman system.[112] Far from being a simplistic instance of mystic versus lawyer, many *'ulama* retained their membership of the Sufi brotherhoods, particularly of the more legally scrupulous Khalwati and Naqshbandi brotherhoods. In dividing the *'ulama* against themselves, the Kadızadeli disputes have been aptly described as "the heart of the religious establishment ... divided against itself."[113]

The eponymous founder of the Kadızadeli movement, Kadızade Mehmed (d.1635), was the son of a minor provincial judge who came to Istanbul in search of employment in the imperial religious bureaucracy or *'ilmiyye*.

Despite seeking affiliation to the well-connected Khalwati brotherhood, Kadızade Mehmed later came to regard the Sufis as responsible for leading the population of the empire astray from the Prophetic Example. Having scaled the ladder of the official *wa'iz* or "preacher" hierarchy (one of the *'ilmiyye's* lowest tiers), Kadızade Mehmed used his influence as preacher in the largest mosques of Istanbul to disseminate his vision of a decadent age needing a renewal of faith (*tajdid-e iman*). The scope of his critique was wide, taking on not only the doctrine of the Unity of Being but also Sufi musical concerts, the popular rituals of the Sufi cult of saints and a range of degenerate activities (smoking tobacco, drinking wine or coffee) for which he regarded morally lax Sufis as responsible. As we have already noted, the key critical tool was the notion of *bid'a* or "innovation" from the Prophetic Example, which he used to recast the tradition of the Sufis as a deviation of the true faith. A fire and brimstone preacher, Kadızade Mehmed stirred sufficient righteous wrath among his listeners that the faction he inspired effectively became one of moral vigilantism, leading in the 1620s and 1630s (and sporadically for the next half century) to the vandalizing of Sufi properties and the beating and occasional murder of Sufis themselves. Of course, the Sufis answered back and defended the practices the Kadızadelis condemned. But nothing could hide the fact that, after centuries of increasing Sufi influence in both society and state, a new social faction or even party was emerging which used the charge of innovation and the authority of law to place its members in a position to challenge the authority of Sufis who were in many cases privileged pillars of the Ottoman establishment.[114]

Figure 3.5 "Whirling Dervishes": Musical Rituals of the Imperial Ottoman Heirs of Rumi (Image: from the author's collection)

What is interesting about the Kadızadeli faction is the way it shows not only divisions within the imperial religious bureaucracy, but also the ways in which particular forms of Islam were used as vehicles for particular group interests. As we have seen, many of the higher ranks of state officials and *'ulama* were affiliated to Sufi brotherhoods. Moreover, as far as the ruling elite was concerned, the task of the religious bureaucracy was not to strictly enforce Islam but to maintain social order through the pragmatic rather than literal interpretation of Islamic law. Far from maintaining social harmony, the Kadızadelis were at first regarded as upsetting it, though as time went by, the significant following they acquired rendered them political players in their own right, with some high palace officials attempting to use Kadızadelis for their own purposes. Far from being a solely theological struggle over what constituted the true tradition of Muhammad, the conflict between Sufis and Kadızadelis was also a conflict over employment opportunities. Sufis did, after all, hold many of the most comfortable sinecures in the Ottoman system. For example, unlike the lower ranking preachers and judges whose positions were held on an early modern equivalent of the short-term contract, shaykhs of Sufi lodges were typically appointed for life. Statistics show that the Kadızadeli heyday between 1621 and 1685 also saw almost half of the preacher positions granted to members of those Sufi brotherhoods favored by the higher officials who made the appointments.[115] Lower down the ladder, the leading Kadızadelis belonged to the lower preaching ranks of the *'ilmiyye* bureaucracy, with the privileged Sufis capturing even the best preaching jobs. It is little wonder the Sufis were despised and critiqued as lapsed sybarites.

Even so, there was more at stake than government jobs. The resonance the Kadızadelis found in the streets suggests they were more than a disgruntled fringe and tapped into a wider conscience brooding on the twin concerns of moral decline and the need for renewal. For many, the Sufis were regarded as the root of the problem. The popularity of the messianic movement centered on the self-proclaimed Jewish messiah Sabbatai Sevi (d.1676) among Ottoman Jews in the 1650s and 1660s suggests that the desire for renewal was not unique to Muslims and may have sprung from deeper socio-political tensions that affected all groups in the empire.[116] Even after the Kadızadelis petered out in the 1680s, this conscience resurfaced in various Ottoman domains. This dissemination may have been connected to the other Muslim regions in which this conscience spread through networks of texts and teachers which historians have not yet traced. In 1711, for example, a preacher in Cairo declared Sufi saints unable to perform miracles and lacking any special knowledge that was hidden to other Muslims and so encouraged his listeners to prevent Sufi *dhikr* chants, destroy saintly shrines and turn Sufi lodges into *madrasas*.[117] As a result, a group of Arab Sufis were beaten and several shrines destroyed by a mob of a thousand disbanded Turkish soldiers among the preacher's audience. As with the Kadızadelis, this attack on Sufism cannot be separated from the interests of its perpetrators, whether seen through the demand that Sufi property be turned over to *madrasa* students or the disputes over regimental incomes that left four thousand dead in Cairo in the same year as the attack.[118] Even so, as in the case of the Anatolian Halveti/ Khalwati Sufi 'Umar al-Fu'adi (d.1636), Sufis in the Ottoman domains were quite able to overcome the Kadızadeli attacks and find patrons for the new brotherhoods and shrine institutions they established in the 1600s.[119] Yet, while legalistic critiques on Sufi "innovations" and "excesses" were by no means unique to this period, from the seventeenth century they were finding a deeper social resonance as certain groups in society chose to identify themselves with a theological critique that had tangible consequences by way of the distribution of influence, competition and opportunity. If in Mughal India we have seen how a Sufism of social cohesion could draw Hindus and Muslims together, here in the Ottoman context we see how the prominence of wealthy shrines and the influence of well-connected brother-hoods became points of social fracture by serving as rallying points for the dissatisfied and underprivileged.

By the eighteenth century in Egypt, the Ottoman Khalwatiyya Sufis were promoters of a Sufism in which the experience of ultimate reality (*haqiqa*) was in scrupulous harmony with the injunctions of the law (*shari'a*).[120] Far from seeing a divorce between Sufis and *'ulama*, by the mid-eighteenth century this resulted in the rise of the Khalwatiyya to the favorite affiliation of the teachers at al-Azhar, the most important seminary for Sunni *'ulama* in the Middle East.[121] The crisis of conscience was not restricted to cities like Cairo and Istanbul and, on the tribal periphery of Ottoman rule in the Najd region of Arabia, the second half of the eighteenth century also saw the emergence of ultimately the most influential critic of Sufi "innovations": Muhammad ibn 'Abd al-Wahhab (d.1787).[122] The central concern of Ibn 'Abd al-Wahhab was to attack all forms of "innovation" and "idolatry" that divorced Muslims from what he saw as Muhammad's original teachings. This in turn led him to denounce such practices as shrine veneration and the treating of Sufi holy men as intermediaries between man and God. If the larger (and looser) trend of "Wahhabism" would eventually become an attack on all forms of Sufi thought as well as practice, the critique of Ibn 'Abd al-Wahhab himself was rather narrower. Given the fact that by the early modern period Sufism was inseparable from many aspects of Islam as such, such an immediate and wholesale rejection of everything said and done by the Sufis was hardly possible and Ibn 'Abd al-Wahhab in any case did not even use the term "Sufi" in his denunciations.[123] While the modern rise of the Sa'udi family as the rulers of Arabia would see the development of Ibn 'Abd al-Wahhab's ideas into a wholesale anti-Sufi agenda, in his own period Ibn 'Abd al-Wahhab was part of the wider conscience calling for a return to the

Prophetic Example and the rejection of innovations. If Ibn 'Abd al-Wahhab stood at the furthest extreme of this spectrum (bringing him as many critics as supporters), he was still a man of an era in which Sufism might be reformed but rarely completely rejected.

Iran: The Later Safawis

If the Ottoman seventeenth century saw the influence of anti-Sufi *'ulama* wax and wane according to the alliances they fostered against Sufis they identified as enemies, then parallel developments were at work in Iran at the same time. We have already seen how, after coming to power as a tribal Sufi movement backed by Qizilbash tribesmen, the Safawi dynasty found the model of the Sufi brotherhood too restrictive to bind together the varied peoples of their empire. Over subsequent decades, the Safawis "imported" Shi'i legal experts from the Jabal 'Amil mountains of Lebanon, who spread their critique of the Sufis widely through Iranian society by attracting students and writing legal guidebooks in simple Persian.[124] Official state support for this legalistic form of Shi'ism had varying repercussions for the Sufis and while Sufi idioms continued to reverberate through popular and literary culture in Iran, the Sufi brotherhoods themselves were increasingly marginalized as a vehicle of religious authority.[125] The shrines that were so central to the Sufis' popularity and wealth lost their patronage and pilgrim traffic and were gradually replaced by rival and specifically Shi'i shrines known as *imamzadas* ("descendents of the imam").[126] Those brotherhoods with the firmest Sunni commitments (such as the Qadiris and Naqshbandis) were either suppressed or exiled to the fringes of the empire. The leaders of brotherhoods who were happy to declare themselves Shi'i (particularly the Ni'matullahis) were treated better. But in the case of the Ni'matullahis too, their masters were either co-opted as provincial governors or retired to country estates, and so reduced as a source of alternative authority to the Shi'i *'ulama*.[127]

While for most of the sixteenth century these new Shi'i Sufis managed to survive and occasionally flourish in Iran, during the reign of Shah 'Abbas I (r.1587–1629) they became less and less politically useful and so the cycle of their suppression was completed. By building an army of slaves, the Safawis freed themselves from their military dependence on Sufi-affiliated Qizilbash tribesmen, while the importing of Shi'i clerics from Lebanon brought the dynasty authority that no longer depended on the Sufi origins of their Safawi family. While the Ottomans continued to find Sufi brotherhoods useful aids in governance and expansion, in Iran the same organizations became superfluous. In 1593, matters came to a head when followers of the Nuqtawi movement, which a created a millenarian synthesis from elements of Sufi tradition and the incarnationist tendencies of the frontier, rebelled against Safawi rule. The suppression of the revolt was brutal and extended, leading not only to the Nuqtawis' destruction but also to the final execution in 1615 of the last survivors of the old Safawi-Qizilbash Sufi brotherhood. While the shahs held onto their Sufi title of *murshid-e kamil* or "perfect master," from then on their authority was mainly as Shi'i sovereigns allied with legalistic clerics who were only too willing to denigrate their defeated Sufi rivals.[128]

Around the turn of the eighteenth century, the rise of the fanatically anti-Sufi jurist Muhammad Baqir Majlisi (d.1699) and his successor Muhammad Husayn Khatunabadi (d.1739) as the chief state jurist saw Sufis banned from the capital at Isfahan.[129] If such purges were ultimately limited to the institutionalized Sufis of the cities, they concluded a long decline of Sufi influence in Iran and the concomitant rise of a legalistic brand of Shi'i legitimacy, with a plethora of new shrines and popular rituals to replace those of the Sufis. Even so, the collapse of the Safawi Empire in the 1720s afforded new opportunities for the Sufis and the last decades of the eighteenth century saw the migrating return to Iran of several Ni'matullahi masters almost three centuries after their ancestors sought patronage at the Bahmani court in India.[130] As we will see below in Africa and Southeast Asia alike, despite the increasing power of the state, the early modern period thus remained one in which mobile Sufi elites possessed sufficient prestige and charisma to out-manoeuver even their more formidable adversaries.

The Central Asian Frontier and China

In the first half of this chapter we saw the important political role of the Naqshbandis in Central Asia under such figures as 'Ubaydullah Ahrar (d.1490) and Ahmad Kasani (d.1543). The seventeenth century saw one of Kasani's descendants, Afaq Khwaja (d.1694), bring the Naqshbandiyya into an even more influential position in the region. Faced with the westward expansion of the Chinese Qing dynasty from the 1640s and the disintegration of the Mongol khanate of the Chaghtais, Afaq Khwaja drew on the older Naqshbandi role as political mediators to travel to Tibet and enter negotiations with the fifth Dalai Lama, Ngawang Lobsang Gyatso (d.1682), whose own military power base had rendered him the ruler of a united Tibet.[131] With diplomatic support from Buddhist Tibet and military support from Qalmaq tribesmen, Afaq Khwaja was able, in 1680, to seize power from the Chaghtai rulers and establish a system of Naqshbandi political rule over the region of Kashgaria that would survive until its fall in 1760 under the conquests of the Chinese Qing Empire. Known as the *ishanat* after the respectfully indirect "they" by which its leaders were known, during its heyday the Sufi *ishanat* state managed a "veritable economy of spirituality" in which the hierarchy of the brotherhood directed taxes and land-holdings at the same time as administering to the moral and spiritual guidance of its followers through the characteristically Naqshbandi format of the séance (*suhbat*) around the master.[132]

At the same time, the presence of a Sufi court on the fringes of the cultural realm of China supported the eastward transmission of what were by now the classic works of Persian Sufi poetry and prose, such as Rumi's *Mathnawi-ye Ma'nawi* ("Spiritual Couplets") and Jami's *Nafahat al-Uns* ("Breaths of Intimacy").[133] By the seventeenth century, Chinese Muslim scholars working further east in the cultural heartlands of China proper were not only translating such Sufi works into Chinese but also writing original texts on Sufi theory in literary Chinese. In a Chinese playing out of the process of vernacularization we have already seen at work in Turkish, Malay and Indian settings, Wang Tai-yü (d.1657/1658?), from his residence in the Southern Ming capital of Nanjing, grappled with the use of such existing Chinese conceptual terms as *chen* to express such Muslim notions as divine unity (Arabic *tawhid*) and the unique revelation of the Quran. As a result he coined such new terms as "Real Lord" (*chen-chu*) and "Real Classic" (*chen-ching*) in his pioneering work, *Ch'ing-chen ta-hsüeh* ("Great Learning of the Pure and Real").[134] Another Nanjing-based Chinese Muslim writer of the period was Liu Chih (d.1730). In addition to writing his *Chen-ching chao-wei* ("Displaying the Concealment of the Real Realm"), a Chinese version of the Persian *Lawa'ih* ("Flashing Lights") of the Naqshbandi poet 'Abd al-Rahman Jami (d.1492), Liu Chih also wrote a celebrated biography of the Prophet Muhammad in Chinese.[135] What we see in such works is not only the route of transmission of Sufism to China along the Central Asian "book road" from the old Sufi centers of Khurasan. We also see that in Liu Chih's lifetime, instruction about Sufi doctrine was seen as inseparable from instruction about Islam at large. This promotion of a Sufism that was closely linked to the exemplary life of the Prophet echoed patterns that could be seen in the eighteenth century all across the Muslim world.

India: The Later Mughals

Turning to Mughal India, in the seventeenth century we saw certain aspects of Sufi thought (the doctrine of Unity of Being in particular) opening the possibility to interpret non-Muslim religious ideas as part of God's limitless manifestation. In his *Haqa'iq-e Hindi* ("Indian Truths"), for example, 'Abd al-Wahid Bilgrami (d.1608) compiled a dictionary of devotional songs to the god Vishnu in which Hindu hymns were given Islamic meanings so as to render them fit for Sufi musical concerts. In the *Mir'at al-Haqa'iq* ("Mirror of Truths") of 'Abd al-Rahman Chishti (d.1683) a century later, there appeared a sympathetic Persian rendering of the Sanskrit *Bhagavad Gita* in which Krishna's message was seen as no less compatible with the teachings of Islam.[136] Various other Sufis, including the Mughal heir-apparent Prince Dara Shikoh (d.1659), took interest in the teachings of the Hindu sages they regarded as the "Indian unitarians" (*muwahidun-e hind*). Yet such mystical accommodation to the Indian environment created tensions of its own and was widely attacked by the later part of period. For India, too, we see the rise of a legalistic critique presenting certain Sufi practices as "innovations" from the Prophetic Example. Once again, the context was that of the crisis of conscience that followed the turn of the Islamic millennium.

This millennial conscience was seen most vividly in the case of the Indian Naqshbandi Sufi, Ahmad Sirhindi (d.1624). Known to his followers as the "renewer of the second millennium" (*mujaddid al-alf al-thani*), Sirhindi was born in the Mughal province of Punjab in around 1564 and in Delhi initiated into the Naqshbandi brotherhood by its immigrant Central Asian propagator, Baqi B'illah (d.1603).[137] As Sirhindi in turn trained disciples and dispatched them to important outposts of the Mughal Empire, the opening decades of the seventeenth century saw the Naqshbandis acquire a foothold in Indian society as such disciples as Hashim Kishmi (d.1644) established contacts with the imperial elite.[138] Sirhindi wrote no single master text and his ideas were mainly spread through the letters he wrote his followers on a remarkable range of themes. Over five hundred of the letters were collected into an epistolary compendium or *maktubat* from which scholars have struggled to reconstruct a coherent overall doctrine. Nonetheless, certain key themes are apparent. One which we have already encountered elsewhere is the criticism of innovation and the need to return to the Prophetic Example, a theme related to the wider importance which Sirhindi lent to the Law. The present age, he thought, was one in which morals had become lax through the abandoning of Sunna and Shari'a and so required a renewer to bring Muslims back to the path of salvation. Sirhindi had no qualms about declaring himself to be this renewer and his claim to this grand role brought him many disciples.

Another major theme of Sirhindi's letters was the danger of misunderstanding the teachings of Ibn al-'Arabi. Although Sirhindi saw himself as properly interpreting rather than disproving Ibn al-'Arabi's work, he was mindful of the dangers of their misinterpretation. This was particularly the case with the doctrine of Unity of Being which he correctly claimed encouraged some Muslims to minimize the difference between Islam and other religions or the difference between God and themselves. Instead Sirhindi argued for a doctrine of Unity of Witnessing (*wahdat al-shuhud*), which held that while in his highest ecstasies the mystic might feel as though he had become united with God, for those who (like Sirhindi) traveled further on the Path, it was clear that God was always other than his creatures and that the Unity of Being was merely a lofty illusion on the way to the fuller realization of God's otherness. Unlike figures whom we have seen equating Muslim teachings with the higher doctrines of the Hindus, for Sirhindi there always remained a clear division between Islam and the religions of infidels.

Based on the letters that Sirhindi wrote to the members of the Mughal court, it was once thought that he was responsible for a shift in imperial policy which saw the inter-religious experiments of Akbar replaced by the renewed commitment to Shari'a seen in the reign of Awrangzeb (r.1658–1707).[139] As in the case of the Kadızadelis, in reality the picture was a more complex one in which Sirhindi's legalistic enthusiasms and criticism of the non-Muslim majority were seen as a threat to state stability, which depended on the loyalty of its vast numbers of Hindu subjects no less than Muslim civil servants and warriors. In 1619 Awrangzeb's grandfather, the emperor Jahangir, went so far as to imprison Sirhindi and in 1679 Awrangzeb himself banned the circulation of his letters, bolstering his right to do so by seeking legal support from Mecca.[140]

If Sirhindi's ideas caused controversy, they struck a sufficiently attractive note to bring him a considerable following. As in the case of the Kadızadelis in the Ottoman Empire, in the first century of the new millennium the Naqshbandi critique of a society which had gone astray found resonance among a significant segment of India's Muslim elite. Awrangzeb's reintroduction of various aspects of Shari'a into Mughal governance has been shown as having more to do with court politics than Sirhindi's influence. [141] But the new legalistic turn under Awrangzeb can also be connected to the era's crisis of conscience as espoused by such men as Sirhindi and the highly influential Iranian anti-Sufi jurist Muhammad Baqir Majlisi (d.1699), who visited India several times between the 1660s and 1690s and may have corresponded with Awrangzeb.[142] Even as there were many Muslims in India who gravitated towards a Sufism which accommodated Islam to the religious pluralism of the Indian environment, there were also those who found attractive Sirhindi's demand that the Hindus be treated like dogs and insulted through the slaughtering of their sacred cows and the imposition of the *jizya* poll tax.[143] (The early years of Awrangzeb's reign also saw the public execution of the naked antinomian Sufi and reputedly Jewish convert, Sarmad.[144]) As with the parallel disputes among the Ottomans, Sirhindi's critique of the Hindus must be understood within a context in which many key positions in the bureaucracy of what Sirhindi considered an Islamic empire had been given to Hindus rather than Muslims. For all his lofty claims to be the "Renewer of the Age," Sirhindi was not above sending letters seeking stipends and government positions for his followers. Yet, despite Sirhindi's criticisms of Sufis who failed to uphold the Law, he still remained committed to the notion of Sufism itself as a tradition that connected Muslims to the Prophet's teaching, reflecting larger trends in other parts of the Muslim world. His message of renewal for the new millennium was therefore no narrow Naqshbandi *Sonderweg*, but part of a more widespread conscience that he shared with contemporaries elsewhere.

If the Mughal bureaucracy was never as centralized or "Islamic" as the Ottoman *'ilmiyye*, the practical skills in literacy and law-making which many Sufis possessed afforded them entry into the imperial Mughal bureaucracy, which as with the Ottoman case, held an intrinsic preference for a stable and predictable Sufism placing law before inspiration. As the Mughal Empire fell apart in the course of the eighteenth century, these legalistic skills became even more important. In part, this was because the diminishing of the state as a provider of social order magnified the importance of sub-state providers of social control. In part, this was because the collapse of an empire controlled by a Muslim elite was interpreted as divine punishment for Muslim immorality. But if the Muslims were seen to be astray, then the Sufi Path was still seen as offering the solution, albeit the legally conscientious form promoted by the heirs of Sirhindi, 'Abd al-Haqq and their heirs. As the eighteenth century saw the old imperial capital pillaged by a sequence of invaders, Hindu as well as Muslim, prominent Sufis such as the Naqshbandis Shah Waliullah (d.1763) and Mirza Mazhar Jan-e Janan (d.1781) in Delhi and the Chishti Nur Muhammad Maharawi (d.1791) in Punjab pushed forward the legalistic critiques of the seventeenth century, not least through the establishing of *madrasas* to spread their teachings.[145] In preferring to establish *madrasas* rather than *khanaqahs* no less than in the legalistic foundations of their teachings, the eighteenth century revivalists were true to their roots in the century beforehand. Shah Waliullah was particularly concerned with "innovations," and, in the course of a lifetime that saw Delhi repeatedly ravaged by invaders, he became an increasingly stern critic of popular veneration of Sufi shrines.[146] This was not conceived as a denial of Sufi tradition, for Shah Waliullah was fully conscious of his position as the heir to a lineage of past Sufi masters.[147] It was, however, part of the wider pattern we have seen in which the sheer diversity of Sufi practices raised the logical problem that they could not all be equally valid. For Shah Waliullah, too, it was the sure touchstone of Shari'a that distinguished valid tradition from unwarranted accretion. The same logic was found in the Delhi circles of Muhammad Nasir 'Andalib (d.1759) and his son Mir Dard (d.1785), who in founding a form of Sufism they referred to as the "Path of Muhammad" (*tariqa Muhammadiyya*) likewise sought to redirect Sufi practices into harmony with the authority and Example of the Prophet. In line with the increasing focus on the study of Hadith, the Prophet himself came to play an increasing role in spiritual practice: the disciple now sought annihilation in Muhammad before reaching Allah.[148]

Developments in India were again part of the larger international picture, which also saw the notion of a *tariqa Muhammadiyya* being spread in North Africa by such figures as Ahmad al-Tijani (d.1815) a few decades later. But rather than a new eighteenth century phenomenon, a distinct "neo-Sufism" as some scholars have called it, the focus on Muhammad and his Prophetic Example was the culmination of the general conscience of renewal that emerged in the previous century.[149] The links to this wider crisis of conscience are reflected in the fact that the term *tariqa Muhammadiyya* itself was first used by the Ottoman scholar Muhammad al-Birgili (d.1573) in his book *al-Tariqa al-Muhammadiyya wa al-Sira al-Ahmadiyya*, which in its attacks on popular shrine veneration and its exhortations to uphold the Prophetic Example had also inspired the Kadizadelis.[150] Even so, such trans-regional patterns only emerged through the appeal of their message in specific local contexts. Just as in the wide social reach of Sufi ideas and institutions had nurtured a multitude of practices which alarmed the legally conscientious the Ottoman Empire, so in India had the vernacularized adaptation of Sufism to wider patterns of social life and even entertainment brought about a situation in which Sufi shrines hosted performances of Sufi love poetry by low class female prostitute-singers known as *tawa'if* ("tribes, gypsies"). Preserved in the *Muraqqa'-e Dihli* ("Delhi Scrapbook") of around 1750 are descriptions of a shrine culture in which Sufism had become inseparable in its cultural services from a demimonde of late night music concerts and the pleasurable indiscretions of a fading imperial capital.[151] It is therefore important not to overstate the influence of the legalistic Sufis, especially in the vernacular sphere of Sufism which continued to develop in India throughout this period. In rural Sindh and Punjab, the rustic vernacular verses of Shah 'Abd al-Latif (d.1752) and Bulleh Shah (d.1757) included many satirical jibes at the Muslim law makers. As Shah 'Abd al-Latif sang in mockery of those who studied the classics of law and grammar,

> If you have read Kanz, Quduri, Kafiya and understand all of them,
> It is as though a lame ant, fallen into a pit, would regard the sky.[152]

Southeast Asia: Renewal in the Malay States

When we turn to the situation in Southeast Asia in the seventeenth and eighteenth centuries, we see much in common with this Indian picture of legalistic Sufism, which also spread at the courts of the Malay rulers. We have already seen Hamza Fansuri spreading the ideas of Ibn al-'Arabi in Malay at the court of Aceh at the western end of the Indonesian archipelago. In the seventeenth century, his disciple Shams al-Din (d.1630) of Pasai in northern Sumatra received the post of *shaykh al-islam* (placing him second only to the sultan in rank) at the court of Sultan 'Ala al-Din Ri'ayat Shah (r.1588–1604) and acted as the Sufi master of Sultan Iskandar Muda (r.1607–1636), whom he regularly accompanied on state occasions.[153] Such was the fame of these Sufi *éminences grises* that they even found their way into the travel accounts of European sailors in the Indian Ocean. The English navigator John Davis seems to have been referring to Shams al-Din in his 1599 description of the Aceh court when he wrote of "a Prophet in Achien, whom they greatly honor; they say that he hath the spirit of Prophesie, as the Ancients have had. He is dignified from the rest in his Apparell, and greatly imbraced of the King."[154] In sources from Aceh itself, we find the notion of the Perfect Man or *insan al-kamil*, which featured in the teachings of Ibn al-'Arabi and Hamza Fansuri alike, being used to aggrandize Sultan Iskandar Muda.[155] Already seen in Iran and India, this royal co-option of Sufi idioms can be seen at work in a Malay court poem to Iskandar Muda which borrowed from the original Arabic lexicon of the Sufis to describe the sultan as "Royal Axis, completely perfect / Friend of God, in complete union / Gnostic King (*Raja qutub yang sampurna kamil/Wali Allah, sampurna wasil/Raja arif*)."[156] Just as Iskandar Muda seems to have been influenced by the Sufi titles of his Mughal contemporaries Akbar and Jahangir, in the course of the sixteenth and seventeenth centuries this presentation of the king as Sufi cosmic axis (*qutb*) or Friend of God (*wali*) was also put to work in the new Muslim states developing on the archipelago frontier, whether at Mataram in Java or Gowa on Sulawesi.[157]

As one of the earliest Sumatrans to have written in Arabic, in his own writings Shams al-Din similarly showed the influence of Indian Sufi ideas on the Malay imagination, particularly the ideas of Muhammad ibn Fadlullah (d.1620) of Burhanpur in central India, whose *Tuhfat al-Mursala ila Ruh al-Nabi* ("Gift Addressed to the Spirit of the Prophet") subsequently spread even deeper into Southeast Asia through its translation into Javanese.[158] While still centrally concerned with ontological ideas of the true nature of human and divine being, in his *Tuhfat* Fadlullah also aimed to uphold the importance of Shari'a in controlling the actions of even the closest Friends of God. As in the other regions we have surveyed, the seventeenth century in Southeast Asia therefore also witnessed attempts to rein in the unrestrained and wilful authority of God's Sufi Friends through a more legally-restraining vision of Sufi doctrine. Already signaled in the dissemination of Fadlullah's writings, this was also seen in the Southeast Asian teachings of such Sufis as Nur al-Din Raniri (d.1658), who used his own ascent to the state post of *shaykh al-islam* at Aceh to attack various Sufis he considered guilty of heresy, charges he documented in his polemical *Hujjat al-Siddiq li-Daf al-Zindiq* ("Proof of the Truthful in Refutation of the Heretic"). Nur al-Din's up-bringing in the Indian region of Gujarat suggests that his ideas should also be seen in relation to the larger currents we have seen washing through India in his lifetime. Nur al-Din's critique of the teachings of his Sufi predecessor in Aceh, Hamza Fansuri (particularly in relation to Fansuri's version of Unity of Being) may even have drawn on the attack on the same doctrine we have seen carried out by Ahmad Sirhindi in the India of Nur al-Din's youth.[159] More clear is the evidence connecting Nur al-Din to the 'Aydarusi brotherhood from the Hadramawt region of Yemen, whose diffusion through the Indian Ocean consistently disseminated a legally-oriented Sufism.[160]

'Aydarusis such as Nur al-Din were not the only itinerant Sufis preaching this legalistic Sufism in Southeast Asia during the seventeenth century. After studying in Medina with the Kurdish Sufi Ibrahim al-Kurani (d.1690), the Acehnese Sufi 'Abd al-Ra'uf (d.1693) returned to Sumatra to teach a syllabus in which Sufism was inseparable from the study of law and scripture.[161] The early modern intensification of Southeast Asia's connections to Arabia during the eighteenth century saw this legalistic Sufism spread further through the movement of more Sufis from the Hadramawt and the transmission of their teachings as far as North Africa. It was these mobile Sufis who connected Malay Muslims to the wider currents of the age.[162] It seems possible that this more intensified circulation of ideas was linked to the increased sea traffic that accompanied the growth of early modern trade. The rise of mercantile Dutch power in Southeast Asia even brought about the introduction of Islam to South Africa through the deporting of a renowned Malay Sufi, Yusuf al-Maqasari (d.1699), to the Dutch outpost at Cape Town.[163] Even in the shackles of Europeans, the Sufis continued to breach new frontiers in the spread of Islam.

Shari'a in the Sahara

Comparable patterns can be seen in North and Saharan Africa during this period. We have already seen how the fifteenth century saw the emergence in Morocco of a self-consciously legalistic Sufism through the efforts of such figures as al-Jazuli and Ahmad al-Zarruq. While these men must primarily be located in their local contexts, their concerns echoed the wider problem of the sheer variety of Sufi practices that had emerged by the early modern era, provoking concerns that not all could be true to the Prophetic Example. Zarruq, for example, wrote a book entitled *al-Radd 'ala Ahl al-Bid'a* ("Refutation of the People of Innovation") in which he railed against such reprehensible Sufi innovations as head-shaving, the wearing of special cloaks and the ostentation of the entourages who accompanied famous masters.[164] In such writings as his *'Aqida* ("Creed"), Jazuli had likewise displayed concern for outward propriety, calling for the community to raise its moral standards. While he had his particular definitions of what it meant, Jazuli was among the several Sufis of the period who spoke of a *tariqa Muhammadiyya* or "Path of Muhammad" in which the practices of the Sufis were to be constrained by the example of Muhammad's actions. In seventeenth- and eighteenth-century North Africa, these attempts at a union of mystical and legal claims to authority continued through the model of the "juridical Sufi" whose knowledge and behavior combined the traditions of the Sufis and the

Prophet. This was particularly seen in the careers of such figures as Ahmad al-Tijani (d.1815) and Ahmad ibn 'Ajiba (d.1809), who continued the model of legally-constrained Sufism and whose attempt to return Sufi practices to the Prophetic Example saw al-Tijani claim that certain of the special chants he taught had been composed by the Prophet himself and transmitted to him in a vision.[165] By initiating travelers who came to his teaching center in the Moroccan city of Fes, al-Tijani expanded his following southwards into West Africa, where it would form one of the most influential Muslim organizations of the nineteenth century.[166] In North Africa itself, this expansion of a legally conformist Sufism with no place for "innovations" was echoed in the policies of the Moroccan rulers Sidi Muhammad ibn 'Abdullah (r.1757–1790) and Mawlay Sulayman (r.1792–1822), with the latter seeing many Sufi brotherhoods as obstacles to the religious renewal he sought for his kingdom.[167]

Even so, the early modern period in North Africa saw Sufi brotherhoods gain new wealth by becoming major players in the expanding trade between Europe, North Africa and the Sahara, rendering their leaders among the most wealthy and influential figures in their communities. Using its mutually trusting and widely dispersed members as a network, the Nasiriyya brotherhood managed a large proportion of the European trade by arranging caravan protection fees, communicating information on market and travel conditions, and manipulating access to political elites. The wealth it generated was in turn invested in either land purchases or money lending.[168] Whether with the Nasiriyya in the northern Sahara or the Qadiri-affiliated merchants of the Kunta clan in the southern Saharan regions, by providing wide-reaching networks of trust, communication and credit, Sufi brotherhoods acted as enabling mechanisms for the growing trans-Saharan trade that connected Africa to Europe.[169] At the same time, these trade routes were also knowledge routes by which Sufis carried Arabic learning and the Nasiri brotherhood's syllabus of legal and mystical study into the oasis settlements of what is now Mauretania, Mali, Niger and Sudan.[170]

It was in the desert and riverine regions of greater Sudan that we find some of the period's most significant interactions of Sufis with their surrounding environments. For the seventeenth and eighteenth centuries witnessed the great expansion of Sufi influence in Saharan Africa through which an earlier tradition of independent Sufi learned and holy men became incorporated into the trans-regional networks and lineages of such brotherhoods as the Qadiriyya.[171] Even as somewhat haphazard networks, they were still able to connect Saharan Africa to practices and debates that were emerging in North Africa, Egypt and Africa. This southward expansion of the brotherhoods occurred through grafting their lineages and teachings onto existing social structures and teaching groups, seeing trans-regional Sufi affiliations adapted to local contexts by way of clan groups and scholarly families, with affiliations further spread along the merchant routes that criss-crossed the

Sahara and connected its inhabitants to the Mediterranean north. As with such other trans-regional brotherhoods as the Naqshbandis, these new connections were not centralized and until the nineteenth century effectively remained autonomous branches. During the mid-seventeenth century, African affiliations to the Qadiri brotherhood were spread by Taj al-Din Bahari, who was originally from Baghdad and who attempted to bring members of existing Sudanese holy families into the Qadiri fold.[172] Another autonomous branch of the Qadiriyya was established around this time by Idris ibn Muhammad al-Arbab (d.1650), who successfully attracted the elite of the Funj sultanate, while also acting like other Sufis of the period as a diplomatic mediator, in this case in disputes between the Funj and their enemies.[173] In the spread of the sanctification process to Africa, a mausoleum was built over Idris's grave at al-ʻAylafun to the south of modern Khartoum in Sudan, turning it into a pilgrimage center for the semi-Islamized people of the region. Blending pilgrimage, agriculture and instruction, other Sufis such as Hasan wuld Hassuna (d.1665), whose grandfather had migrated through the Sahara from what is now Tunisia, acted as the founders of villages. Over a period of several generations, these villages in the heart of Africa became little Sufi worlds of Islam as their inter-related inhabitants were bound together by common descent from the shaykh and his early followers.

As such autonomous branches of brotherhoods expandeds through the eighteenth century, in some cases we find membership being based on the criterion of common ethnicity or kinship. In other cases, the brotherhoods created new patterns of sociability that transcended ethnic barriers. In all cases, the brotherhoods tied people together into communities based on a common vision articulated by their shaykhs. Many of these leaders belonged to the same holy families, allowing the brotherhoods to act as mechanisms of domination in which particular families or ethnic groups were able to perpetuate their status through time. In Islamic Africa as elsewhere, the leading Sufis constituted an established class, made wealthy by their land holdings and the gifts of their followers. In such ways, Sufi tradition offered the peoples of the Sahara an adaptable set of resources for the construction of social order, from models of authority and organization to unifying communal rituals and the sanction of a historical legacy that connected an African Sufi establishment to such prestigious urban centers as Cairo, Baghdad and Mecca.

As in other regions at the same time, many major Sufis in Saharan Africa during the seventeenth and particularly eighteenth centuries laid especial emphasis on the law. In the Funj Sultanate of Sudan, the seizure of power by Hamaj noblemen in 1762 triggered a crisis of legitimacy that the Hamaj tried to solve by a policy of promoting Shariʻa. This in turn required them to offer positions in the court and bureaucracy to Sufis or other scholars qualified to carry through the policy.[174] As a result, legalistic Sufis ascended in influence and by the end of the eighteenth century there spread through Sudan a sustained attack on Sufi or other popular practices that smacked of "innovation." In a manner that echoed the agendas of Naqshbandi Sufis among the oasis dwellers and tribesmen of Central Asia, Arabic manuscripts which survive from the Sahara's urban enclaves show the period's Sufis as key proponents of Shari'a. One example is the Sudanese Ahmad al-Tayyib (d.1824), who during his travels to Arabia in the late 1750s was initiated into the new Samaniyya branch of the legally scrupulous Khalwati brotherhood which we have already seen as highly influential in the Ottoman Empire. Ahmad propagated Samaniyya teachings on his return to his homeland, where one of the last Funj rulers granted him an agricultural estate in the fertile Sudanese rainlands.[175]

Given these increasing connections between Sufis in Saharan and Mediterranean Africa in the seventeenth and eighteenth centuries, the role of Sufis as law-bringers and community-founders points to ways in which Africa participated in wider early modern developments of standardizing behavior through socializing disparate groups into shared ritual communities that in turn enabled the foundation of larger social units. By the second half of the eighteenth century, these developments reached new levels as such major North African Sufis as Ahmad al-Tijani (d.1815) and Ahmad ibn Idris (d.1837) reached beyond the Arabized peoples of the Sahara to initiate large numbers of black Africans into their new brotherhoods. At the western end of Saharan Africa in what is now Mauretania, the period also saw Muhammad al-Hafiz (d.1830) travel to Mecca and Fes, where he was initiated by al-Tijani before returning through the Sahara to propagate a form of Sufism in which the study of Hadith and the Prophetic Example were given central place.[176] By the late 1700s, all across Saharan Africa Sufis used the model of the Prophet to paint the rulers, morals and customary laws of this vast region as pagan infidelity and "innovations." This more intense Sufi involvement in social reform was often inseparable from political reform, leading the Qadiri Sufi 'Uthman dan Fodio (d.1817) to call his fellow Fulani tribesmen into the series of righteous *jihads* that resulted in the founding of the Sokoto "caliphate" in 1809.[177] Even though it has been argued that dan Fodio regarded Sufism as a means of personal purification which was separate from the sources of his political vision, the fact remains that Sufis if not always Sufism were responsible for the establishing major new states in Africa.[178]

However, we should not only see this as a picture of the Sufi impact on Africa, but also as one of the African impact on Sufism. More specifically, we should recognize the process by which Sufism afforded Africans a religious idiom, organizational model and means of transferring knowledge that enabled them to export elements of African religious practice to the wider Muslim world. In large part, this was made possible by enforced slave

Figure 3.6 A Tribal Sufi? Itinerant Sufi, Provinces of Ottoman or Safawi Empire, c.1600 (© The British Library Board, source Or.2709, f28v)

migration to North Africa, Arabia and India, where Sufism afforded an intelligible and legitimate vehicle for the continuation of traditional African practices of musical trance and spirit possession. The process can be observed among the former slave African-descended Sidis in India and the Hamadsha and Gnawa brotherhoods in Morocco.[179] The Sidis kept the memory of their African past alive through rituals performed at the shrine of their purported African ancestor, Baba Gor, in Gujarat.[180] The Hamadsha explained their distinctive spirit-summoning rituals through legends of their own founder, Sidi Hamdush (d.1718), having traveled to Sudan and brought back their ritual flute (*'awwad*), drum (*daff*) and the female genie, 'Aisha Qandisha.[181] In both cases, the African roots of diasporic communities or practices were kept alive by the remembered traditions of their heirs in the distant towns of Morocco and India. If by the later 1700s increasing numbers of Sufis were denouncing such activities as reprehensible innovations, then the sheer popularity of such musical rituals and the solace they gave to the depressed and displaced meant that, for all the attacks of the reformers, they would survive into the modern age.

Summary

In this chapter, we have seen a period of ambiguous relationships between Sufis and states in which Sufis sometimes themselves founded states and sometimes were drawn into closer control by states. In a period in which Islam was still expanding in large parts of the globe, Sufis also acted as frontiersmen and their institutions served as state surrogates as Muslim societies developed around them. While among the Sufis there naturally remained significant numbers of impoverished wandering dervishes, the larger mark on history was left by mobile Sufi elites whose learning, prestigious lineages, miraculous powers and in some cases ethnic backgrounds enabled them to muster the resources to either found states or acquire important offices within existing polities. Even so, while unified by the continued expansion of Sufi influence on increasing numbers of peoples, the period between 1400 and 1800 can be divided into two periods roughly divided by the turning of the Muslim millennium in 1591. While developments were gradual, the first two centuries of the new millennium saw an emphasis on the law-abiding moral rectitude of the Sufi as a social role model that was attractive to state administrators. If Sufis and sultans had first entered alliances in the medieval period, then the early modern centuries saw Sufis settle into the security of being indispensible players in the social no less than the political order, especially in the more durable empires. If the period saw increasing attempts to regulate the more capricious dimensions of Sufi behavior through uniform standards of law, except in such exceptional settings as Shi'i Iran this was ultimately a sign of the extraordinary influence Sufis had acquired by this period by pointing to how much was at stake when Sufis morally misled their followers.

Taken as a whole, the early modern period saw Sufi tradition being taken in two opposing but inter-related directions. In one direction, it saw the competitive deployment and co-option of tradition by various leaders of tribal or state foundation, many of whom made selective use of discrete elements of tradition according to the needs of their situation. After all, with its claims to authority and its mechanisms of loyalty and affiliation, Sufism had developed into a powerful idiom of collective organization and communal solidarity. In the other direction, the period saw the opposing (but ultimately related) process of the increasing consolidation of these powerful idioms and symbols of tradition into organized and regularized brotherhoods, whose behavior thereby became more predictable and stable. While the process was certainly patchy, from this period the brotherhoods resembled more networked organizations rather than the mechanisms for reproducing tradition of the medieval era. Insofar as the greater regularization of the brotherhoods came partly from their closer interaction with the more ambitious and organized states of the period, the governmental incentive is clear in the promotion of brotherhoods as stable, settled, law-abiding social institutions and the demotion of the nomadic, charismatic and "anarchistic" Sufism associated with rural tribal groups. Even in the major case in which Sufism was suppressed in Safawi Iran, the chief factor was the replacement of an older, fissiparous tribal Sufism with a standardized, legalistic model of Shi'i Islam which, unlike even the largest brotherhoods, could unite an entire population.

The eighteenth century has often been presented as a distinct "age of reform" in which "neo-Sufi" brotherhoods pushed a new, Prophet-centered agenda of legally-circumscribed Sufism. What we have instead seen in this chapter suggests that the millennium of 1591 marked the more significant turning point. Of course, the conscience of decline and the critiques of "innovation" that resounded through almost every Muslim region were not triggered by the calendar alone and in each region the legalists' success was reliant on local social and political circumstances. Although such groups as the Kadızadelis wielded the slur of "innovation" from the Prophetic Example as a way of criticizing their privileged Sufi rivals, it was usually Sufis themselves who used Sunna and Shari'a to criticize other Sufis. In some cases, this was part of longer term doctrinal brands nurtured by particular brotherhoods that had always upheld the primacy of obeying the religious law no matter how intoxicating one's private communions with God. Far from seeing the demise of the Sufis under the assault of a separate class of lawmakers, despite (or even because of) the compromises with more powerful state structures, the early modern period as a whole from Timbuktu to Sulawesi saw more of an expansion than a diminishing of Sufi influence on

Muslim lives. If they were not without their detractors, then the Sufis were nonetheless in large part the religious establishment.

Notes

1. M.U. Menon, *Ibn Taimīya's Struggle against Popular Religion* (The Hague: Mouton, 1976).
2. For the debate about whether Ibn Taymiyya was a Sufi, see G. Makdisi, "Ibn Taymiyya: A Sufi of the Qādirīya Order," *American Journal of Arabic Studies* 1 (1973), pp.118–129 and F. Meier, "The Cleanest About Predestination: A Bit of Ibn Taymiyya," in Meier, *Essays on Islamic Mysticism and Piety* (Leiden: Brill, 1999), note 9, pp.317–318. Thanks to Ahmet Karamustafa for this reference.
3. E. Landau-Tasserson, "The 'Cyclical Reform': A Study of the Mujaddid Tradition," *Studia Islamica* 70 (1989), pp.79–117.
4. N.S. Green, "Tribe, Diaspora and Sainthood in Afghan History," *Journal of Asian Studies* 67, 1 (2008), pp.171–211.
5. For examples, see G. Veinstein (ed.), *Syncrétismes et hérésies dans l'orient Seljoukide et Ottoman (XIVe–XVIIIe siècles)* (Louvain: Peeters, 2005).
6. On Mamluk institutional patronage, see H. Hallenberg, "The Sultan Who Loved Sufis: How Qāytbāy Endowed a Shrine Complex in Dasūq," *Mamluk Studies Review* 4 (2000), pp.147–158.
7. N. Clayer, "Des agents du pouvoir ottoman dans les Balkans: Les Helvetis," *Revue du monde musulman et de la Méditerranée* 66 (1992), pp.21–30 and B.G. Martin, "A Short History of the Khalwati Order of Dervishes," in N.R. Keddie (ed.), *Scholars, Saints, and Sufis: Muslim Religious Institutions since 1500* (Berkeley: University of California Press, 1972).
8. Z. Yürekli, "A Building between the Public and Private Realms of the Ottoman Ruling Elite: The Sufi Convent of Sokollu Mehmed Pasha in Istanbul," *Muqarnas* 20 (2003), pp.159–185.
9. E. Geoffroy, *Le Soufisme en Egypte et en Syrie sur les derniers Mamelouks et les premiers Ottomans* (Damascus: Institut Français de Damas, 1995), pp.128–135.
10. L. Fernandes, "Two Variations on the Same Theme: The Zāwiya of Hasan al-Rūmī, the Takiyya of Ibrāhīm al-Gulšānī," *Annales Islamologiques* 21 (1985), pp.95–111.
11. J. Gonnella, *Islamische Heiligenverehrung im urbanen Kontext am Beispiel von Aleppo (Syrien)* (Berlin: Klaus Schwarz, 1995), pp.97–112.
12. See e.g. N. Clayer, *Mystiques, état et société: Les Halvetis dans l'aire balkanique de la fin du XVe sieècle aè nos jours* (Leiden: E.J. Brill, 1994), pp.113–179 and A. Layish, "*Waqfs* and Sufi Monasteries in the Ottoman Policy of Colonization: Sultan Selim's *Waqf* of 1516 in Favour of Dayr al-Asad," *Bulletin of the School of Oriental and African Studies* 50, 1 (1987), pp.61–89.

13. Layish (1987).
14. Faroqhi (1986), pp.112–113.
15. S. Faroqhi, "The Tekke of Haci Bektaş: Social and Economic Activities," *International Journal of Middle East Studies* 7, 2 (1976), pp.183–208.
16. F.W. Hasluck, *Christianity and Islam under the Sultans* (Oxford: Clarendon Press, 1929) and H.T Norris, *Popular Sufism in Eastern Europe: Sufi Brotherhoods and the Dialogue with Christianity and 'Heterodoxy'* (London: Routledge, 2006).
17. Geoffroy (1995), p.130.
18. D. Le Gall, *A Culture of Sufism: Naqshbandīs in the Ottoman World, 1450–1700* (Albany: State University of New York Press, 2005), chapter 6. Cf. J.J. Curry, *The Transformation of Muslim Mystical Thought in the Ottoman Empire: The Rise of the Halveti Order, 1350–1750* (Edinburgh: Edinburgh University Press, 2010).
19. Faroqhi (1976) and K. Kreise, "Medresen und Derwischkonvente in Istanbul: Quatitative Aspekten," in J.-L. Bacqué-Grammont & P. Dumont (eds), *Économies et sociétés dans l'Empire ottoman* (Paris: CNRS, 1983).
20. A. Karamustafa, *God's Unruly Friends: Dervish Groups in the Later Middle Period 1200–1550* (Salt Lake City: University of Utah Press, 1994), chapter 6.
21. Le Gall (2005), pp.167–172.
22. D. Terzioğlu, "Sufi and Dissident in the Ottoman Empire: Niyāzī-i Misrī (1618–1694)" (unpublished PhD dissertation, Harvard University, 1999).
23. Clayer (1994), p.79.
24. Clayer (1994), pp.113–142 and C. Kafadar, *Between Two Worlds: The Construction of the Ottoman State* (Berkeley: University of California Press, 1995), pp.62–90.
25. On the Ottoman interpretation of *ghaza* and its distinction from formal *jihad*, M.D. Bonner, *Jihad in Islamic History: Doctrines and Practice* (Princeton: Princeton University Press, 2006), pp.144–149.
26. Clayer (1994), p.121.
27. S. Faroqhi, "Seyyid Gazi Revisited: The Foundation as Seen through Sixteenth and Seventeenth-Century Documents," in Faroqhi, *Peasants, Dervishes and Traders in the Ottoman Empire* (London: Variorum Reprints, 1986) and M. Kiel, "Ottoman Urban Development and the Cult of a Heterodox Sufi Saint: Sarı Saltuk Dede and Towns of İsakçe and Babadağ in the Northern Dobruja," in Veinstein (2005).
28. J.K. Birge, *The Bektashi Order of Dervishes* (London: Luzac Oriental, 1994); S. Faroqhi, *Der Bektashi-Orden in Anatolien (vom späten fünfzehnten Jahrhundert bis 1826)* (Vienna: Verlag des Instituts für Orientalistik, 1981); A. Karamustafa, "Kalenders, Abdals, Hayderis: The Formation of the Bektasiye in the Sixteenth Century," in H. Inalcik & C. Kafadar (eds), *Süleyman the Second and his Time* (Istanbul: Isis Press, 1993); and A. Popovic & G. Veinstein (eds), *Bektachiyya: études sur l'ordre mystique des Bektachis et les groupes relevant de Hadji Bektach* (Istanbul: Les Editions Isis, 1995).

29. I. Mélikoff, *Hadji Bektach: Un mythe et ses avatars* (Leiden: E.J. Brill, 1998).
30. I. Mélikoff, "Qui était Sari Saltuk? Quelques remarques sur les manuscrits du Saltukname," in C. Heywood & C. Imber (eds), *Studies in Ottoman History in Honour of Professor V. L. Ménage* (Istanbul: Isis Press, 1994). Thanks to Ahmet Karamustafa for pointing me to the agriculturalist dimension.
31. Mélikoff (1998), pp.145–161.
32. Faroqhi (1976), p.206.
33. M. Balivet, *Islam mystique et révolution armée dans les Balkans Ottomans: Vie du cheikh Bedreddin, le "Hallâj des Turcs," 1358/59–1416* (Istanbul: Isis Press, 1995).
34. Karamustafa (1994), p.70.
35. M.M. Mazzaoui, *The Origins of the Safawids: Šī'ism, Sūfism, and the Gulāt* (Wiesbaden: Franz Steiner, 1972), chapter 4.
36. V. Minorsky, "The Poetry of Shah Isma'il," *Bulletin of the School of Oriental and African Studies* 10, 4 (1942).
37. M. Bloch, *The Royal Touch: Sacred Monarchy and Scrofula in England and France* (London: Routledge & Kegan Paul, 1973 [1924]) and E.H. Kantorowicz, *The King's Two Bodies: A Study in Mediaeval Political Theology* (Princeton: Princeton University Press, 1957).
38. The objection is raised by Julian Baldick, in *Mystical Islam* (London: I.B. Tauris, 1989), p.124.
39. S. Bashir, "Shah Isma'il and the Qizilbash: Cannibalism in the Religious History of Early Safavid Iran," *History of Religions* 45, 3 (2006), pp.234–256.
40. Bashir (2006), p.240.
41. I. Beldiceanu-Steinherr, "La Règne de Selîm 1er: Tournant dans la vie politique et religieuse de l'empire Ottoman," *Turcica* 6 (1975), pp.34–48 and G. Veinstein, "Les premières mesures de Bâyezîd II contre les kizilbaş," in Veinstein (2005).
42. S.A. Arjomand, "Religious Extremism (*Ghuluww*), Sufism and Sunnism in Safavid Iran, 1501–1722," *Journal of Asian History* 15, 1 (1981), pp.1–35 and K. Babayan, "The Safavid Synthesis: From Qizilbash Islam to Imamite Shi'ism," *Iranian Studies* 27, 1–4 (1994), pp.135–161.
43. Arjomand (1981), p.7 and Bashir (2006), p.249.
44. R. Foltz, "The Central Asian Naqshbandiyya Connections of the Mughal Emperors," *Journal of Islamic Studies* 7, 2 (1996), pp.229–239.
45. W.M. Thackston (trans.), *The Baburnama: Memoirs of Babur, Prince and Emperor* (Washington, D.C.: Freer Gallery of Art, 1996), p.327.
46. S. Digby, "Dreams and Reminiscences of Dattu Sarvani, a Sixteenth Century Indo-Afghan Soldier," *Indian Economic and Social History Review* 2 (1965), pp. 178–194 and N.S. Green, "Blessed Men and Tribal Politics: Notes on Political Culture in the Indo-Afghan World," *Journal of the Economic and Social History of the Orient* 49, 3 (2006), pp.344–360.
47. Abū'l Fazl, *Ā'īn Akbarī*, ed. H. Blochmann, 2 vols (Calcutta: Asiatic Society of Bengal, 1875), vol. 2, pp.207–225.

48. A. Husain, "The Family of Shaikh Salim Chishti during the Reign of Jehangir," in K.A. Nizami (ed.), *Medieval India: A Miscellany*, vol. 2 (Delhi: Asia Publishing House, 1972).

49. K. Rizvi, "'Its Mortar Mixed with the Sweetness of Life': Architecture and Ceremonial at the Shrine of Safī al-dīn Ishāq Ardabīlī during the Reign of Shāh Tahmāsb I," *Muslim World* 90, 3–4 (2000), pp.323–352 and A. Petruccioli, "The Geometry of Power: The City's Planning," in M. Brand & G.D. Lowry (eds), *Fatehpur Sikri* (Bombay: Marg Publications, 1987).

50. I.A. Khan, "The Nobility under Akbar and the Development of his Religious Policy, 1560–80," *Journal of the Royal Asiatic Society* 1, 2 (1968), pp.29–36.

51. P. Hardy, "Abul Fazl's Portrait of the Perfect Padshah: A Political Philosophy for Mughal India – Or a Personal Puff for a Pal?" in C.W. Troll (ed.), *Islam in India: Studies and Commentaries*, vol. 2 (Delhi: Vikas, 1985) and J.F. Richards, "The Formulation of Imperial Authority under Akbar and Jahangir," in *idem*. (ed.), *Kingship and Authority in South Asia* (Delhi: Oxford University Press, 1988).

52. C.G. Lingwood, "Jami's *Salaman va Absal*: Political Statements and Mystical Advice Addressed to the Aq Qoyunlu Court of Sultan Ya'qub (d. 896/1490)," *Iranian Studies* 44, 2 (2011), pp.175–191.

53. A.H. Morton, "The Chúb-i Tariq and Qizilbásh Ritual in Safavid Persia," in J. Calmard (ed.), *Études Safavides* (Paris-Teheran: Institut Français de Recherche en Iran, 1993).

54. S.A.A. Rizvi, *Shāh Walī Allāh and his Times: A Study of Eighteenth Century Islam, Politics and Society in India* (Canberra, Maèrifat Publishing House, 1980), p.80.

55. M. Alam & S. Subrahmanyam, "Frank Disputations: Catholics and Muslims in the Court of Jahangir (1608–11)," *Indian Economic and Social History Review* 46, 4 (2009), pp.457–511.

56. Alam & Subrahmanyam (2009), pp.476, 487.

57. J.J.L. Gommans, *The Rise of the Indo-Afghan Empire, c. 1710–1780* (Delhi: Oxford University Press, 1999), pp.131–132.

58. S. Andreyev, "The Rawshaniyya: A Sufi Movement on the Mughal Tribal Periphery," in L. Lewisohn & D. Morgan (eds), *The Heritage of Sufism: Late Classical Persianate Sufism (1501–1750)*, vol. 3 (Oxford: Oneworld, 1999).

59. M. Alam, "The Mughals, the Sufi Shaikhs and the Formation of the Akbari Dispensation," *Modern Asian Studies* 43, 1 (2009), pp.135–174.

60. N.S. Green, *Indian Sufism since the Seventeenth Century: Saints, Books and Empires in the Muslim Deccan* (London: Routledge, 2006), chapter 1.

61. M. Alam, "Assimilation from a Distance: Confrontation and Sufi Accommodation in Awadh Society," in R. Champakalakshmi & S. Gopal (eds), *Tradition, Dissent and Ideology: Essays in Honour of Romila Thapar* (Delhi: Oxford University Press, 1996) and H. van Skyhawk, "Nasīruddīn and Ādināth, Nizāmuddīn and Kāniphnāth: Hindu-Muslim Religious Syncretism in the Folk Literature of the Deccan," in H. Brückner, L. Lutze & A. Malik (eds), *Flags of Fame: Studies of South Asian Folk Culture* (Delhi: Manohar, 1993).

62. M. Alam, *Languages of Political Islam* (London: Hurst, 2004), chapter 3.
63. M. Alam, "The Pursuit of Persian: Languages in Mughal Politics," *Modern Asian Studies* 32, 2 (1998), pp.317–349 and Green (2008).
64. T. Kamran, "Some Prominent Strands in the Poetry of Sultan Bahu," in S. Singh & I.D. Gaur (eds), *Sufism in Punjab: Mystics, Literature and Shrines* (Delhi: Aakar Books, 2009), C. Shackle, "Styles and Themes in the Siraiki Mystical Poetry of Sind," in H. Khuhro (ed.), *Sind through the Centuries* (Karachi: Oxford University Press, 1981) and T.K. Stewart, "In Search of Equivalence: Conceiving the Muslim-Hindu Encounter through Translation Theory," *History of Religions* 40, 3 (2001), pp.260–287.
65. Cf. W. Feldman, "Mysticism, Didacticism and Authority in the Liturgical Poetry of the Halvetī Dervishes of Istanbul," *Edebiyât* 4, 2 (1993) and D. Gilmartin, "Shrines, Succession and Sources of Moral Authority," in Metcalf (1984).
66. S. Digby, "Before Timur Came: Provincialization of the Delhi Sultanate through the Fourteenth Century," *Journal of the Economic and Social History of the Orient* 47, 3 (2004), pp. 298–356.
67. R.M. Eaton, *The Rise of Islam and the Bengal Frontier, 1204–1760* (Berkeley: University of California Press, 1993), chapter 9.
68. D. Cashin, *The Ocean of Love: Middle Bengali Sufi Literature and the Fakirs of Bengal* (Stockholm: Association of Oriental Studies, Stockholm University, 1995) and T.K. Stewart, "Alternate Structures of Authority: Satya Pīr on the Frontiers of Bengal," in D. Gilmartin & B.B. Lawrence (eds), *Beyond Turk and Hindu: Rethinking Religious Identities in Islamicate South Asia* (Gainsville: University of Florida Press, 2000).
69. M.S. Siddiqi, "The Ethnic Change at Bidar and its Influence (AD 1422–1538)," in A.R. Kulkarni, M.A. Nayeem & T.R. de Souza (eds), *Mediaeval Deccan History: Commemoration Volume in Honour of Purshottam Mahadeo Joshi* (Bombay: Popular Prakashan, 1996), pp.41–43.
70. N. Ahmad, "An Old Persian Treatise of the Bahmani Period," *Islamic Culture* 46, 3 (1972), pp.215–216.
71. Ahmad (1972), p.210, Persian text only.
72. R.M. Eaton, "The Court and the Dargāh in the Seventeenth Century Deccan," *Indian Economic and Social History Review* 10, 1 (1973), pp.50–63.
73. Eaton (1973), p.52.
74. Kenneth R. Hall, "Upstream and Downstream Unification in Southeast Asia's First Islamic Polity: The Changing Sense of Community in the Fifteenth Century 'Hikayat Raja-Raja Pasai' Court Chronicle," *Journal of the Economic and Social History of the Orient* 44 (2001), pp.198–229; see especially pp.203 and 208–209.
75. R.M. Feener & M.F. Laffan, "Sufi Scents across the Indian Ocean: Yemeni Hagiography and the Earliest History of Southeast Asian Islam," *Archipel* 70 (2005).
76. Note that the medieval Arabic toponym Jawa referred to the Southeast Asian archipelago more generally rather than the island known in modern times as

Java. See M.F. Laffan, "Finding Java: Muslim Nomenclature of Insular Southeast Asia from Śrivijaya to Snouck Hurgronje," in E. Tagliacozzo (ed.), *Southeast Asia and the Middle East: Islam, Movement, and the Longue Durée* (Singapore: NUS Press, 2009).

77. R. Jones, "Ten Conversion Myths from Indonesia," in N. Levtzion (ed.), *Conversion to Islam* (New York: Holmes & Meier, 1979).

78. M.C. Ricklefs, *Mystic Synthesis in Java: A History of Islamization from the Fourteenth to the Early Nineteenth Centuries* (Norwalk: EastBridge, 2006), pp.21–25.

79. A.H. Johns, "Islamization in Southeast Asia: Reflections and Reconsiderations with Special Reference to the Role of Sufism," *Southeast Asian Studies* 31, 1 (1993), pp.43–61.

80. For variant evidence on Fansuri's biography and death date, see V.I. Braginsky, "Towards the Biography of Hamzah Fansuri: When Did Hamzah Live? Data from his Poems and Early European Accounts," *Archipel* 57, 2 (1999), pp.135–175 and C. Guillot & L. Kalus, "La stèle funéraire de Hamzah Fansuri," *Archipel* 60 (2000). On Fansuri's travels in their larger regional context, see P.G. Riddell, *Islam and the Malay-Indonesian World: Transmission and Responses* (London: C. Hurst & Co., 2001).

81. Guillot & Kalus (2000).

82. Guillot & Kalus (2000), pp.18–19.

83. S.M.N Al-Attas, *The Mysticism of Ḥamzah Fanṣūrī* (Kuala Lumpur: University of Malaya Press, 1970).

84. On Fansuri's language, see Al-Attas (1970), pp.142–175.

85. J. Paul, "Forming a Faction: The *Himāyat* System of Khwaja Ahrar," *International Journal of Middle East Studies* 23, 4 (1991), pp.533–548. For fuller exploration of the socio-political entrenchment of the brotherhood, see Paul, *Die Politische und Soziale Bedeutung der Naqsbandiyya in Mittelasien im 15. Jahrhundert* (Berlin: W. de Gruyter, 1991).

86. M. Subtelny, *Timurids in Transition: Turko-Persian Politics and Acculturation in Medieval Iran* (Leiden: Brill, 2007), chapter 6.

87. Paul (1991), p.541.

88. J. Gross, "Authority and Miraculous Behavior: Reflections on *Karāmāt* Stories of Khwāja 'Ubaydullāh Ahrār," in L. Lewisohn (ed.), *The Heritage of Sufism: The Legacy of Medieval Persian Sufism (1150–1500)*, vol. 2 (New York: Khaniqahi Nimatullahi Publications, 1992).

89. J. Gross, *The Letters of Khwaja 'Ubayd Allah Ahrar and his Associates*, ed. A. Urunbaev (Leiden: Brill, 2002).

90. R.D. McChesney, "Society and Community: Shrines and Dynastic Families in Central Asia," in McChesney, *Central Asia: Foundations of Change* (Princeton: Darwin Press, 1996).

91. T. Zarcone, "Sufism from Central Asia among the Tibetans in the 16–17th Centuries," *Tibet Journal* 20, 3 (1995), pp.96–114.

92. S. Kugle, *Rebel Between Spirit and Law: Ahmad Zarruq, Sainthood, and Authority in Islam* (Bloomington: Indiana University Press, 2006), pp.85–88.

93. Kugle (2006), p.89.
94. Kugle (2006), pp.89–95.
95. M. El Mansour, "Saints and Sultans: Religious Authority and Temporal Power in Pre-Colonial Morocco," in K. Masatoshi (ed.), *Popular Movements and Democratization in the Islamic World* (London: Routledge, 2006).
96. V.J. Cornell, *Realm of the Saint: Power and Authority in Moroccan Sufism* (Austin: University of Texas Press, 1998), p.271.
97. M. Garcia-Arenal, "La conjonction du sufisme et du sharifisme au Maroc: le Mahdi comme sauveur," *Revue du monde musulman et de la Mediterranée* 55–56 (1990), pp.233–256.
98. Cornell (1998), pp.257–271.
99. M. García-Arenal, "Mahdi, Murabit, Sharif: L'Avènement de la dynastie Sa'dienne," *Studia Islamica* 71 (1990), pp.77–113.
100. Cornell (1998), pp.261–271.
101. Cornell (1998), pp.248–249.
102. F. Rodriguez-Manas, "Agriculture, Sufism and the State in Tenth/Sixteenth Century Morocco," *Bulletin of the School of Oriental and African Studies* 59, 3 (1996), pp.450–471.
103. R. Ensel, *Saints and Servants in Southern Morocco* (Leiden: Brill, 1999).
104. J.O. Hunwick, "Religion and State in the Songhay Empire, 1464–1591," in I. M. Lewis (ed.), *Islam in Tropical Africa* (Oxford: Oxford University Press, 1966).
105. A.S. Karrar, *The Sufi Brotherhoods in the Sudan* (London: C. Hurst & Co., 1992), Introduction.
106. N. Grandin, "La shâdhiliyya au soudan nilotique du nord: Notes sur la tradition du xvie au xixe siècle," in E. Geoffroy (ed.), *La Voie Soufie des Shadhilis* (Paris: Maisonneuve & Larose, 2005), p.208.
107. P.M. Holt, "Holy Families and Islam in the Sudan," in *idem.*, *Studies in the History of the Near East* (London: Routledge, 1973), pp.121–134 and N. McHugh, *Holymen of the Blue Nile: The Making of an Arab-Islamic Community in the Nilotic Sudan, 1500–1850* (Evanston: Northwestern University Press, 1994), pp.70–85.
108. R.S. O'Fahey, "Islamic Hegemonies in the Sudan: Sufism, Mahdism and Islamism," in L. Brenner (ed.), *Muslim Identity and Social Change in Sub-Saharan Africa* (Bloomington: Indiana University Press, 1993), p.23.
109. McHugh (1994), pp.57–70.
110. McHugh (1994), pp.116–128.
111. D. Robinson, *Muslim Societies in African History* (Cambridge: Cambridge University Press, 2004), chapter 4.
112. M.C. Zilfi, "The Kadizadelis: Discordant Revivalism in Seventeenth-Century Istanbul," *Journal of Near Eastern Studies* 45, 4 (2008), pp.251–269.
113. Zilfi (1986), p.252.
114. J.J. Curry, "Defending the Cult of Saints in 17th Century Kastamonu: Omer al-Fu'adi's Contribution to the Religious Debate in Ottoman Society," in C. Imber & K. Kiyotaki (eds), *Frontiers of Ottoman Studies: State, Province, and the West* (London: I.B. Tauris, 2005).

115. Zilfi (1986), p.267.
116. J. Hathaway, "The Grand Vizier and the False Messiah: The Sabbatai Sevi Controversy and the Ottoman Reform in Egypt," *Journal of the American Oriental Society* 117, 4 (1997), pp.665–671.
117. R. Peters, "The Battered Dervishes of Bab Zuwayla: A Religious Riot in Eighteenth-Century Cairo," in N. Levtzion & J.O. Voll (eds), *Eighteenth-Century Renewal and Reform in Islam* (Syracuse: Syracuse University Press, 1987), pp.94–95.
118. Peters (1987), pp.103–104.
119. Curry (2010).
120. R. Chih, "Cheminements et situation actuelle d'un ordre mystique réformateur: la Khalwatiyya en Égypte (fin XVe siècle à nos jours)," *Studia Islamica* 88 (1998), pp.181–201.
121. Chih (1998), pp.186–187.
122. N. Delong-Bas, *Wahhabi Islam: From Revival to Reform* (Oxford: Oxford University Press, 2004), chapter 2.
123. Delong-Bas (2004), p.84.
124. R.J. Abisaab, *Converting Persia: Religion and Power in the Safavid Empire* (London: I.B. Tauris, 2004), chapter 1.
125. On the survival of Sufi ideas through coffee house storytelling and other popular media, see Babayan (2002), chapter 12.
126. K. Babayan, *Mystics, Monarchs and Messiahs: Cultural Landscapes of Early Modern Iran* (Cambridge: Harvard University Press, 2002).
127. T. Graham, "The Ni'matu'llāhī Order under Safavid Suppression and in Indian Exile," in Lewisohn & Morgan (1999).
128. A.J. Newman, "Sufism and Anti-Sufism in Safavid Iran: The Authorship of the *Hadīqua al-Shī'a* Revisited," *Iran* 37 (1999), pp.95–108.
129. Arjomand (1981), p.29.
130. L. Lewisohn, "An Introduction to the History of Modern Persian Sufism, Part I: The Ni'matullāhī Order: Persecution, Revival and Schism," *Bulletin of the School of Oriental and African Studies* 61, 3 (1998), pp.437–464.
131. A. Papas, *Soufisme et politique entre Chine, Tibet et Turkestan: Étude sur les Khwajas Naqshbandis du Turkestan oriental* (Paris: J. Maisonneuve, 2005), pp.90–102.
132. Papas (2005), p.144 and more generally chapter 3.
133. T. Zarcone, "Le Mathnavî de Rûmî au Turkestan Oriental et au Xinjiang," in V. Bouillier & C. Servan-Schreiber (eds), *De l'Arabie à l'Himalaya: Chemins croisés en hommage à Marc Gaborieau* (Paris: Maisonneuve & Larose, 2004).
134. S. Murata, *Chinese Gleams of Sufi Light: Wang Tai-yü's Great Learning of the Pure and Real and Liu Chih's Displaying the Concealment of the Real Realm* (Albany: State University of New York Press, 2000), chapter 2.
135. Murata (2000), p.26.
136. S.A.A. Rizvi, *A History of Sufism in India*, 2 vols (Delhi: Munshiram Manoharlal, 1978 & 1983), vol. 1, pp.359–362 and R. Vassie, "'Abd al-Rahman Chishtī and the Bhagavadgita: 'Unity of Religion' Theory in Practice," in Lewisohn (1992).

137. Y. Friedmann, *Shaykh Ahmad Sirhindī: An Outline of his Thought and a Study of his Image in the Eyes of Posterity* (Delhi: Oxford University Press, 2000).

138. I. Sabir, "Khwaja Mohammad Hashim Kishmi: A Famous Seventeenth Century Naqshbandi Sufi of Burhanpur," in M. Haidar (ed.), *Sufis, Sultans, and Feudal Orders: Professor Nurul Hasan Commemoration Volume* (Delhi: Manohar, 2004).

139. K.A. Nizami, "Naqshbandi Influence on Mughal Rulers and Politics," *Islamic Culture* 39, 1 (1965), pp.41–52. Cf. Y. Friedmann, "The Naqshbandīs and Awrangzēb: A Reconsideration," in M. Gaborieau, A. Popovic & T. Zarcone (eds), *Naqshbandis: Cheminements et situation actuelle d'un ordre mystique musulman* (Istanbul: Isis Press, 1990).

140. Friedmann (2000), pp.94–95.

141. S. Chandra, "The Religious Policy of Aurangzeb during the Later Part of his Reign – Some Considerations," *Indian Historical Review* 13, 1–2, (1986–87), pp.88–101.

142. S.A.A. Rizvi, *A Socio-intellectual History of the Isnā'Asharī Shī'īs in India*, 2 vols (Delhi: Munshiram Manoharlal, 1986), vol. 2, p.33.

143. Friedmann (2000), pp.73–74.

144. N. Katz, "The Identity of a Mystic: The Case of Sa'id Sarmad, a Jewish-Yogi-Sufi Courtier of the Mughals," *Numen* 47 (2000), pp.142–160.

145. Green (2006), chapter 3 and Rizvi (1980), chapter 7.

146. J.M.S. Baljon, "Shah Waliullah and the Dargah," in C.W. Troll (ed.), *Muslim Shrines in India: Their Character, History and Significance* (Delhi: Oxford University Press, 1989).

147. M.K. Hermansen, "Contemplating Sacred History in Late Mughal Sufism: The Case of Shāh Walī Allāh of Delhi," in Lewisohn & Morgan (1999).

148. J.M.S. Baljon, *Religion and Thought of Shāh Walī Allāh Dihlawī, 1703–1762* (Leiden: E.J. Brill, 1986). A. Schimmel, *And Muhammad is his Messenger: The Veneration of the Prophet in Islamic Piety* (Chapel Hill: University of North Carolina Press, 1985), chapter 11.

149. R.S. O'Fahey & B. Radtke, "Neo-Sufism Reconsidered," *Der Islam* 70, 1 (1993), pp.52–87.

150. J. Malik, "Muslim Culture and Reform in 18th Century South Asia," *Journal of the Royal Asiatic Society* 13, 2 (2003), pp. 227–243, p.233.

151. Dargah Quli Khan, *Muraqqa'-e-Delhi: The Mughal Capital in Muhammad Shah's Time*, trans. C. Shekhar & S.M. Chenoy (Delhi: Deputy Publications, 1989).

152. A. Schimmel, *Pain and Grace: A Study of Two Mystical Writers of Eighteenth-Century Muslim India* (Leiden: E.J. Brill, 1976), p.202.

153. A.H. Johns, "Reflections on the Mysticism of Shams al-Din al-Sumatra'i (1550?–1630)," in J. van der Putten & M.K. Cody (eds), *Lost Times and Untold Tales from the Malay World* (Singapore: NUS Press, 2009), p.150.

154. Braginsky (1999), p.149. For discussion on whom Davis was actually referring to, see Guillot & Kalus (2000), p.15.

155. T. Gibson, *Islamic Narrative and Authority in Southeast Asia: From the 16th to the 21st Century* (New York: Palgrave Macmillan, 2007), pp.41–42.

156. Gibson (2007), p.42.
157. Gibson (2007) and A.C. Milner, "Islam and the Muslim State," in M.B. Hooker (ed.), *Islam in South-East Asia* (Leiden: E.J. Brill, 1983), pp.39–43.
158. A.H. Johns (trans.), *The Gift Addressed to the Spirit of the Prophet* (Canberra: Australian National University, 1965).
159. G.W.J. Drewes, "Nūr al-Dīn al-Rānīrī's Charge of Heresy against Hamzah and Shamsuddin from an International Point of View," in C.D. Grijns & S.O. Robson (eds), *Cultural Contact and Textual Interpretation* (Leiden: KITLV, 1986).
160. A. Azra, "Opposition to Sufism in the East Indies in the Seventeenth and Eighteenth Centuries," in De Jong & Radtke (1999), p.676.
161. Johns (1993), pp.53–58.
162. A. Azra, *The Origins of Islamic Reformism in Southeast Asia: Networks of Malay-Indonesian and Middle Eastern 'Ulama' in the Seventeenth and Eighteenth Centuries* (Honolulu: University of Hawaii Press, 2004) and R.S. O'Fahey, "'Small World': Neo-Sufi Interconnexions between the Maghrib, the Hijaz and Southeast Asia," in S.S. Reese (ed.), *The Transmission of Learning in Islamic Africa* (Leiden: Brill, 2004).
163. C. Greyling, "Schech Yusuf: The Founder of Islam in South Africa," *Religion in Southern Africa* 1, 1 (1980), pp.9–22.
164. Cornell (1998), pp.230–231.
165. J. El-Adnani, *La Tijâniyya, 1781–1881: Les origines d'une confrérie religieuse au Maghreb* (Rabat: Marsam, 2007), pp.121–123.
166. A.D.O. Abdellah, "Le 'passage au sud': Muhammad al-Hafiz et son héritage," in J.-L. Triaud & D. Robinson (eds), *La Tijâniyya: Une confrérie musulmane à la conquête de l'Afrique* (Paris: Karthala, 2000).
167. M. El Mansour, *Morocco in the Reign of Mawlay Sulayman* (Wisbech: Middle East & North African Studies Press, 1990), chapter 4.
168. D.P.V. Gutelius, "The Path is Easy and the Benefits Large: The Nāsiriyya, Social Networks and Economic Change in Morocco, 1640–1830," *Journal of African History* 43, 1 (2002), pp.27–49.
169. A. McDougall, "The Economics of Islam in the Southern Sahara: The Rise of the Kunta Clan," *Asian and African Studies* 20, 1 (1986), pp.45–60.
170. D.P.V. Gutelius, "Sufi Networks and the Social Contexts for Scholarship in Morocco and the Northern Sahara, 1660–1830," in Reese (2004).
171. Karrar (1992) and K. Vikør, "Sufi Brotherhoods in Africa," in N. Levtzion & R.L. Pouwels (eds), *The History of Islam in Africa* (Oxford: James Currey, 2000).
172. Karrar (1992), pp.21–24.
173. Karrar (1992), pp.25–26.
174. McHugh (1994), pp.111–115.
175. Karrar (1992), pp.44–47; McHugh (1994), pp.136–141.
176. Abdellah (2000), pp.78–83.
177. M. Hiskett, *The Sword of Truth: The Life and Times of the Shehu Usuman Dan Fodio* (Evanston: Northwestern University Press, 1973).
178. L. Brenner, "Muslim Thought in Eighteenth Century West Africa: The Case of Shaikh 'Uthman b. Fudi," in Levtzion & Voll (1987), pp.55–59.

179. P.-A. Claisse, *Les Gnawa marocains de tradition loyaliste* (Paris: L'Harmattan, 2003).
180. H. Basu, *Habshi-Sklaven, Sidi-Fakire: Muslimische Heiligenverehrung im westlichen Indien* (Berlin: Das Arabische Buch, 1994).
181. V. Crapanzano, *The Hamadsha: A Study in Moroccan Ethnopsychiatry* (Berkeley: University of California Press, 1973), pp.32–35.

Chapter 4
From Colonization to Globalization (1800–2000)

Introduction

Sufism is no exception to the general rule that the impact of European colonialism must be factored into understanding any aspect of modern Muslim history. While in the case of the Russian Empire and the "company empire" of the British East India Company, the second half of the eighteenth century saw larger numbers of Muslims fall under European control in the Crimea and Bengal, it was the nineteenth century which saw Europe's greatest expansion into Muslim regions. It is important to grasp the scale of these developments.[1] Under different rubrics of administration, in the British case it involved the gradual absorption of what is today India, Pakistan and Bangladesh, Malaysia and Singapore; and Nigeria, Sudan, Somalia, Zanzibar, Kenya, Uganda and South Africa, Egypt; and, more briefly, Palestine and Jordan. Under similarly varied rubrics, in the French case it involved the absorption of Algeria, Tunisia and Morocco; Senegal, Mauritania, Mali, Chad and Niger; and, more briefly, Syria and Lebanon. In the Dutch case it involved the conquest of the vast archipelago of islands that now comprises Indonesia. And in the Russian case it involved the invasion of the Crimea and Volga regions; the Caucasus (particularly Chechnya); and the vast Central Asian expanses that now make up the republics of Kazakhstan, Turkmenistan and Uzbekistan. In addition, smaller numbers of Muslims lived under Austro-Hungarian rule in the Balkans and under Spanish rule in North and West Africa, while the westward expansion of the Qing Empire into Central Asia saw Han Chinese ruling over the Muslims of what remains to this day the Chinese-controlled Xinjiang Uyghur Autonomous Region. By the 1920s Afghanistan, Iran and the new nation states of Turkey and Saudi

Sufism: A Global History, First Edition. Nile Green.
© 2012 Nile Green. Published 2012 by Blackwell Publishing Ltd.

Arabia were the only large regions to have escaped colonial rule, though European power was keenly if indirectly felt in these places as well.

In Chapter 3, we have seen how the development of new and larger states in the early modern period saw Sufism embedded in various levels of social and political life. No narrowly "mystical" phenomenon, this Sufi Islam had in institutional and ideological terms come to underpin the imperial, agricultural, mercantile, and bureaucratic spheres no less than the religious. We have also seen how in the two hundred years after the Muslim millennium of 1591 there spread a conscience calling for religious renewal in which the Prophetic Example and Shari'a were used to counter the diversification process of the preceding centuries. In some cases (such as the Ottoman Empire), the spread of this more legally conformist Sufism took place within the framework of existing state institutions; in other cases (such as Saharan Africa), it participated in the creation of new frontier states. The retraction or collapse of many of those states and their replacement in the early nineteenth century by trans-regional European empires did not bring about any immediate diminishing of Sufi influence. On the contrary, the shifts in power-holding were accompanied by the redistribution of resources and the forging of new alliances as new powers, whether colonial or indigenous, sought the legitimacy that came through the cooperation of the Sufi heirs of the Prophet. In a period of rapid social and political change, the continuity of tradition which the Sufis represented acquired even greater symbolic capital. Even when modern science began to threaten the old truth claims of Muslim as well as Christian modes of knowledge, there were many Sufis who saw opportunities in the practical technology of the new sciences. In the two most significant examples, the onset of printing in the Islamic world from the 1820s and the expansion of travel from the 1850s through steam-powered ships and trains allowed more entrepreneurial Sufis to reach new audiences in North America and Europe as well as in their older dominions.

However, in the longer term there were multiple outcomes from the massive social and political changes that accompanied the gradual colonization of the greater part of the Muslim world. Colonization was a discursive as well as an institutional project and as such involved a fierce engagement with the forms of indigenous knowledge that Europeans encountered. The knowledge forms of the Sufis – including their epistemological foundations through visions, rituals and intercessions – were no exception. It was in this colonial context that the English term "Sufism" was first coined as Europeans came into increasing contact with Muslims in places like Bengal.[2] At first, among such enthusiastic heirs of the Enlightenment as Sir William Jones (1746–1794) and Johann Wolfgang von Goethe (1749–1832), the definitions and qualities that were attributed to the term Sufism (in German, *Sufismus*) were positive: the Sufis were seen as tolerantly cosmopolitan pantheists with a cultivated taste for poetry, music and wine.[3] Even such Evangelical Christians as the early missionary to Iran, Revd Henry Martyn (1781–1812), viewed the Sufis in a positive light, seeing them as sufficiently enlightened to be likely converts to Christianity. But as colonization expanded as the nineteenth century progressed, European interactions with Sufis were as likely to be on the battlefield as on a page of Persian poetry. As a result, "Sufism" – and particularly such borrowed terms for its adherents as "fakir" and "dervish" in English, "marabout" in French and "myurid" in Russian – acquired darker connotations of fanaticism and fraudulence.[4] Yet even at the height of the colonial era, European attitudes to Sufism were not uniformly negative and in the late nineteenth century the disagreements of different Europeans concerning Islam created a definition of "Sufism" that has survived to this day. For as the mass of colonial representations portrayed Muslims as fanatics, a more liberal wing of late Victorian and Edwardian intellectuals used the fashionable new discourse of "mysticism" to portray Sufis as Muslim equivalents to the more amiable sages of Yoga and Buddhism. In doing so, these sympathetic colonial scholars emphasized the comparative and universal rather than the contextual and specific. Moreover, in the polemically anti-Islamic environment in which they were writing, they sought sympathy for Muslims by paradoxically downplaying the Islamic dimensions of Sufism. This focus on the mystical and transcendental also involved the downplaying of Sufi rituals and institutions that to Protestant or other anti-clerical Europeans seemed unappealingly "superstitious" or "popish." Ironically, the factors which these well-intentioned apologists downplayed to make Sufism more congenial to a European and American audience were precisely those which at the same time were being highlighted by anti-Sufi Muslim reformists as reasons for Muslims themselves to abandon Sufi tradition. For by the early twentieth century, both the disparaging and apologetic dimensions of the colonial construction of Sufism found echoes among anti-Sufi reformists on the one hand and modernizing Sufi revivalists on the other.

If the opportunities that came with colonial cooperation and industrial technology suggest that Sufis should no longer be seen as the straightforward losers in the age of colonization and modernity, they were certainly not the only Muslim group to seize the opportunities that the new conditions presented. As the nineteenth century progressed, what had begun as an early modern pattern of legally-minded Sufi reformism gradually divorced itself from its Sufi origins under the pressures of colonialism to become a movement of vehemently anti-Sufi reform presenting Sufis as the principal obstacle rather than the means to a renewal of the faith.[5] Partially in response to a religious reading of history that saw colonization and the collapse of Muslim power as a punishment for straying from the true path of Islam, the earlier attacks on "innovations" increased in the late nineteenth century into a loud call for a wholesale "reform" (*islah*) of the faith. In many early cases, the leaders of these reform movements were themselves Sufis and their organizational vehicles the Sufi brotherhoods. Building on the developments of the eighteenth century through the advantages of steam travel, some of these reformist brotherhoods became truly global in scope, connecting Africa, Arabia, Southeast Asia and Europe within the career of single individuals.[6]

As shifting colonial patterns of global commerce created corresponding slumps in regions beyond colonial control, or as the conditions of colonial rule fed disenchantment with established Sufi leaders, the reformist brotherhoods were able to take advantage of the new demand for religious change while promising at the same time to provide the authentic version of Sufi tradition.[7] However, reflecting back on the historical experience of the collapse of Muslim power, in the early 1900s the spokesmen for other and ultimately more successful reform movements took the drastic step of abandoning Sufi tradition entirely. Given the Sufi backgrounds of all of the major founders of the anti-Sufi reform movements, a case could be made for the reformist brotherhoods of the nineteenth century serving as Trojan horses that allowed a gradual hollowing out of Sufism from the inside. In a period which saw "fundamentalist" movements appearing among a range of world religions, the renewal movements that appeared in various Muslim regions claimed that to return to the scriptural and prophetic foundations of Islam meant wiping the slate of all that stood between the modern day Muslim and the Quran and Hadith. As the aggregate of the rituals, ruminations and institutions that had developed during these intervening centuries – in other words, as a tradition – Sufism was the sacrifice required for this direct reformist return to the sources.

This rejection of tradition found many supporters, especially among middle class urban and educated groups who resented what they saw as the pomp and privilege, the inertia and indolence, of Sufis who lived from begging on the streets or from pensions on their estates. By the early twentieth century, the transformations of modernity were creating new Muslim populations who were either alienated from or unconnected to the old Sufi institutions of shrines and brotherhoods. By way of modern schools and scientific ideas, new institutions and forms of knowledge that either ignored the Sufis or challenged the epistemological foundations of their teachings were also spreading among Muslims, partly under colonial influence. For many Muslims brought up in these new conditions, the Sufis represented a form of Islam that was irrelevant or even bogus. With the rise of anti-colonial nationalist movements, the anti-Sufi dimensions of this disenchanted mode of religiosity were amplified by the proximity of many prominent Sufis to either the colonial powers or the discredited elites of the few independent Muslim regions.

Even so, this somewhat familiar trajectory of an anti-mystical modernity was only part of the story and despite the secularizing and disenchanting predictions of the modernization theorists of the mid-twentieth century,

Sufism did not disappear in the century's postcolonial second half. Through the dialectical arguments of Sufis with their reformist and modernist critics, there also emerged a counter-reform movement that attempted to reform or modernize Sufism in turn. In many cases, these counter-reform movements chose no longer to define themselves as Sufis belonging to brotherhoods but, as with the highly successful Barelvi movement in India and Pakistan, as normative Muslims belonging to the "People of the Sunna and the Community" (*ahl al-sunnat wa jama'at*) who were educated in *madrasa* schools rather than distinctively Sufi lodges.[8] In tracing the contemporary heirs to the centuries-long tradition of the Sufis, we have therefore to bear in mind that many of these heirs chose not to designate themselves as "Sufis." As the colonial era was transformed into an age of postcolonial globalization, there not only remained old Sufi institutions that had weathered the storms of the previous two centuries through clever alliances and profitable investments, but also in California as much as Cairo there also emerged new forms of Sufism that appealed to modern needs and tastes. One of the crucial appeals of this new Sufism was its new presentation as a purely "mystical" practice, as a set of techniques for the individual to make personal contact with the divinity without the distractions of formal ritual and dogma. Such a de-politicized and deracinated Sufism, rendered purely mystical through shearing its ties to superstitious saint cults and "corrupt" state sponsors, was therefore itself the product of a historical process of the accretional momentum of tradition that was finally rejected combined with the impact of modernist ideologies by way of colonial critique and Muslim reform. As we will see over the following pages, from the rejection to the reinvention of Sufism, each of the outcomes of the nineteenth and twentieth centuries emerged in response to the historical experience of their own and the previous period.

From Resistance to Accommodation: Sufism Under Colonialism, c.1800–1950

Since the colonial impact on Sufism can most effectively be traced through imperial interactions with Sufi institutions and personnel, the following pages largely focus on these more tangible exchanges before turning to the attitudes of both the Europeans and Muslims who came to variously appropriate, reject or reinvent Sufism in the postcolonial era. In broad outline, the history of colonial interactions with Sufis can be seen as a two-way pattern of anti-colonial rebellions and pro-colonial alliances, a pattern which can in many cases be seen as a processual development of failed rebellions giving way to negotiated alliances.[9] At different moments, the European empires therefore not only suppressed but also at times patronized

Sufis. As with the earlier interactions we have traced between Sufis and precolonial Muslim empires, to make sense of the two colonial policies we need to register the internal differences among the Sufis themselves, since different types of Sufi reacted differently to the colonial presence and were treated differently by colonial administrators in return. In broad outline, rebellion and resistance policies tended to be initiated by relatively marginal Sufis who led few followers or had little inherited authority before leading their rebellions. In a pattern of continuity with the eighteenth and early nineteenth centuries, such rebel Sufis also tended to belong to the legalistic trend which was often as critical to the Muslim as the colonial establishment. By contrast, alliance and accommodation policies tended to be pursued by well-established Sufis who already possessed authority and status among their host communities, along with property granted them by precolonial powers. At times, a process of transition can be observed amid these two parties as the heirs of Sufis who acquired followers and status through leading what were ultimately unsustainable rebellions entered alliances with the same colonial powers who had defeated their fathers or grandfathers.

The British Empire

As British power crept across the Muslim regions of northern India in the early nineteenth century, the most notable "resistance" movement to confront them directly was the *jihad*, led by Sayyid Ahmad Barelwi (1786–1831). While sometimes seen as an anti-Sufi – or "Wahhabi" – Sayyid Ahmad received a Sufi education from the Naqshbandi Sufi Shah 'Abd al-'Aziz (d.1823), the son of Shah Waliullah of Delhi (d.1763) whom we saw in Chapter 3 promoting the position of Shari'a in the Sufi life.[10] What is important about Sayyid Ahmad was his adaptation of the resources of Sufi tradition towards the foundation of a new movement, which (in an echo of the earlier uses of the phrase) he called the *Tariqa-ye Muhammadiyya* or "Path of Muhammad." Although Sayyid Ahmad was initiated by his master into several pre-existing brotherhoods (such as the Chishtiyya and Naqshbandiyya), his aim in founding the *Tariqa-ye Muhammadiyya* seems to have been to establish a kind of umbrella organization capable of drawing followers from any of the existing brotherhoods by claiming to be the original "Path" of the Prophet. Despite Sayyid Ahmad's declared break with the existing brotherhoods, and the fierce accusations of "innovation" which he and his followers leveled at their Sufi rivals, the *Tariqa-ye Muhammadiyya* adopted many Sufi organizational techniques and doctrines. Its members were initiated through the classic Sufi pledge of allegiance or *bay'at* and introduced into the spiritual lineage or *silsila*. If the law was presented as the foundation of Muslim piety, then the Sufi meditations or *dhikr* were still taught.[11] In organizational terms, the *Tariqa-ye Muhammadiyya* echoed the structure of pre-existing brotherhoods through being directed by the central charismatic saint, Sayyid Ahmad, and his appointed deputies or *khalifas*. Due to the establishment of British control over Delhi in 1803, and the travels of Sayyid Ahmad and his key followers to the chief colonial cities of Calcutta and Bombay, the members of the *Tariqa-ye Muhamma-diyya* were fully aware of the rise of the new "Christian" power over the old Mughal territories and in the middle of Sayyid Ahmad's career this loss of Muslim power came to occupy center stage in his thought. When Sayyid Ahmad returned from a pilgrimage to Mecca in the early 1820s with a renewed zeal to suppress the "innovations" that had crept into the faith, he therefore vowed to establish a new Muslim state based on conformity to Shari'a. While he was in Mecca, two of his followers had already traveled to Calcutta to access the colonial technology which was developing there for printing in Islamic languages and in 1823 they published the *Sirat al-Mustaqim* ("Straight Path") which contained Sayyid Ahmad's teachings.[12] A breakthrough in the means of transferring Sufi knowledge from the old patterns of face-to-face teaching and controlled manuscript circulation, the printing of *Sirat al-Mustaqim* points to the complex traffic between even anti-colonial Sufis and the new opportunities laid open for religious groups by colonial rule. Given that much of *Sirat al-Mustaqim* was devoted to attacking the impious innovations of Sayyid Ahmad's more popular Sufi rivals, there was a certain irony in the strategic use of a new technology that other Muslim scholars regarded as an innovation in its own right. But while happy to borrow such printing technology, the position that Sayyid Ahmad took with regard to British expansion (and the rise of the Sikh kingdom of Ranjit Singh in Punjab) was one of confrontation rather than accommodation. Like the other *jihad* states which we will see below emerging at the same time on the frontiers of French and Russian rule, in the mid-1820s Sayyid Ahmad established himself on the limits of colonial state power in the north-western fringes of the Indian subcontinent. From there, he launched a war against the Sikh kingdom with the eventual aim of moving on to the British territories that now included the old Mughal capital of Delhi. The *jihad* was a failure and, in 1831, Sayyid Ahmad died a martyr's death in battle against the forces of Ranjit Singh. Even so, his followers believed that he had not died but had retreated to a cave whence he would soon re-emerge as the messianic *mahdi* who heralded the end of the world. Both in life and death, Sayyid Ahmad's transformations from Naqshbandi Sufi to founder of the *Tariqa-ye Muham-madiyya*, holy warrior and eventually messiah show the new directions in which Sufi tradition could be taken on the edges of colonial expansion.

In the following decades, Sayyid Ahmad's spirit of resistance to "infidel" rule over Muslims found several other (albeit increasingly marginal) outlets in India. Although the great Indian rebellion of 1857 involved a range of Hindu and Muslim participants with quite different objectives, there were also Sufis who participated. While the scale of Sufi involvement is lost in the fog of war and propaganda, the most notable Sufi known to have fought was the Chishti master, Hajji Imdadullah (d.1899), who like a number of other rebels sought refuge in Mecca after the rebellion's failure. In exile, Imdadullah wrote Persian treatises on Sufi meditation such as his *Ziya al-Qulub* ("Brilliance of the Hearts") and, in a signal of the inward turn of resistance to the private space of the Muslim's own body, he penned Urdu poems praising the "inner *jihad*" against one's own flesh and spirit.[13] In India itself, many leading Sufis linked to Shah Waliullah, Hajji Imdadullah and the Delhi Naqshbandis we saw founding the earlier "Path of Muhammad" in Chapter 3 adopted a strategy of avoidance rather than cooperation. Some followed Imdadullah to Mecca or moved to Muslim-ruled Indian princely states such as Hyderabad; some developed theories disconnecting Shari'a (and through it Muslim life more generally) from any links to the colonial state; some went so far as forbidding their followers from wearing British-style hats and boots.[14] In the case of the Deoband *madrasa* network in South Asia that gradually developed out of the school established by students of the anti-colonial Sufi reformist Hajji Imdadullah in 1867, the Sufi origins and affiliations of the schools founders were gradually written out of its history as an attack on popular festive and shrine-based aspects of Sufi tradition gradually developed into an attack on Sufism *en somme*.[15] If in the towns of the plains, avoidance was more feasible then rebellion, on the mountain edges of the subcontinent, the Sufi shaykh 'Abd al-Ghafur (d.1877) was able to resist British expansion for almost forty years in what he managed to turn into his private Sufi fiefdom in Swat. As late as the 1930s, the charismatic Sufi "Faqir of Ipi" led a rebellion of the tribes of Waziristan on the British Indian border with Afghanistan.[16] However, in the more controlled Indian heartland, after 1858 there was no significant Sufi resistance through violence and, like Imdadullah in Mecca, India's Sufis instead consolidated their control over the private sphere of the bodies and minds of their disciples.[17]

If direct or indirect resistance was one side of the picture in India, then cooperation was the other. In a multi-religious region in which the hereditary Sufi families who maintained the shrines of their saintly ancestors had happily received patronage from Hindu and Sikh rulers, then before the rise of a new Indian nationalist consciousness from the 1900s there was nothing exceptional in their willingness to receive either direct patronage or security for their interests from the Christian British.[18] Since all colonial states sought influential local middlemen to mediate their authority to the general population, in northern India especially Sufi hereditary shrine families appeared perfect candidates. Through the characteristically Sufi pledge of allegiance, such hereditary Sufis commanded the loyalty of many thousands, as entire families made the pledge of *bay'at* as part of the fabric of ancestral practice. In many cases, these bonds of loyalty were reinforced by the fact that many of these followers also owed their livelihoods to their Sufi masters, being employees on their agricultural landholdings. By the late nineteenth century, the shrine of the medieval Chishti Baba Farid at Pakpattan in Punjab controlled no less than 43,000 acres of land in one district alone.[19] In turn, the pressing need of these Sufis to maintain their landholdings through the state's continued recognition of their legality meant that they needed the British as much as the British needed them. For both parties (if not necessarily for the peasants in the background) it proved an excellent partnership. As time passed, the alliance was sealed by the appointment of hereditary Sufis to colonial provincial councils; the education of Sufi heirs in elite colonial colleges and law schools; and their entry into modern party politics when many Sufi families joined the Unionist Party that supported British rule.[20]

Like earlier Muslim states, in such alliances the British Empire in India favored a certain kind of Sufi. Whether in reaching the rural masses of Punjab or in upholding the morale of the colonial Muslim soldier, there was a distinct profile to the types of Sufi whom the empire encouraged: sober, predictable and bookish.[21] If for many colonial commentators (and for the Muslim reformists who echoed them) shrine-centered Sufism represented a decadent decline from an idealized golden age of true mystics, the reality was that shrines and landholdings were the crucial institutional foundations required to uphold the transmission of Sufi tradition.[22] Shrines - and the libraries, lodges and *madrasas* that were typically attached to them – were the concrete embedding of tradition in the living urban landscape. Yet tradition is fragile and so when, whether through the violence of 1857 or the gradual devaluation of endowments, certain Indian shrines were dispossessed or destroyed, then the centuries of local Sufi knowledge they had passed down disappeared with them. When a friend of the Urdu poet Ghalib (d.1869) wrote a letter asking him for the Sufi books of Shah Kalimullah, Ghalib answered that, since Kalimullah's shrine had been looted during the 1858 siege of Delhi and its occupants had fled in the chaos, "whom should I ask for the saint's writings?"[23] As Ghalib was all too aware, the traditions of the Sufis were maintained and transmitted by living people and in order to do so those people needed the security of their institutions in turn. Between the violence of the recapture of Delhi in 1858 and the alliances with the Sufi landholders of the countryside, colonization therefore alternatively overturned and reinforced different elements of Sufi tradition in India.

Even where colonialism did not directly aid or hamper the Sufis, the larger set of social conditions brought about by colonial rule created significant new opportunities for them. An example we have already mentioned was the spread of printing, which in significant degree helped overcome the breakdown of some of the old shrine-based forms of personal contact and manuscript-copying through which Sufi teachings were transmitted in the precolonial era. The money that Indian publishers found they could make in printing classic Sufi works meant that copies of the poetry of Rumi or the saintly biographies of Jami could now be bought for a fraction of the former cost of a handwritten manuscript. Such were the profits to be made that businessmen of all backgrounds became ready investors. The most important printer of Sufi works in nineteenth century India (and possibly in the entire Muslim world) was the Hindu publisher, Nawal Kishore (1836–1895), whose books were also exported as far as Iran, Africa and Central Asia.[24] Over time, Sufis in India (and eventually elsewhere) created new printed genres to transmit their ideas to the new reading audiences of the printed public sphere. One new genre was the Sufi "magazine," such as the Urdu *Anwar al-Quds* ("Lights of Holiness") published between 1925 and 1927 by the entrepreneurial Chishti Sufi, Muhammad Zawqi Shah (d.1951).[25] These cheap new outlets for discussion fueled the spread of new ideas and practices, such that the tradition of the masters of old was not only passed on but reinterpreted and added to, seeing such formerly marginal practices as *tasawwur-e shaykh* or meditating on the image of one's master being promoted as never before through the spread of photographs of Sufi masters.[26] Even attempts by Christian missionaries to convert India's Muslims were turned to advantage as the portable harmonium organs which the missionaries used to sing their hymns were adapted for Sufi *qawwali* songs, breathing new life into the "musical concert" or *mahfil-e sama'* we have seen emerging in Khurasan a thousand years earlier. By the 1920s and 1930s, Sufi *qawwali* music reached even larger audiences through the recording of records and the use of festive *qawwali* in India's emerging musical cinema.[27] Carried by the innate attractions of the music and the Western curiosity for the "mystic east" that was itself a by-product of empire, in the case of 'Inayat Khan (1882–1927) we find an Indian Sufi musician using the new industrial travel routes to sail from Bombay via London to New York. There he became one of the first bearers of Sufi doctrines to an American audience.[28]

A case study of the opportunities for Sufis brought about by colonial change is found in the great industrial city of Bombay. There the mass migration of a rural Muslim workforce to work in its mills and dockyards coincided with the arrival of Sufi masters from all around the Indian Ocean and the availability of steam travel and vernacular printing to disseminate their message.[29] Bombay's industrial infrastructure enabled Iranian and Arabian as well as Indian Sufi masters to mass-produce vernacular summaries of their teachings and hagiographical advertisements of their powers that attracted not only the devotions of the wage-earning workers of Bombay itself, but the larger Muslim audiences reached by the city's communication networks in places as far away as South Africa and Iran. Whether from Bombay or from such other colonial British ports as Singapore, the Sufis oversaw a veritable enchantment of the industrial technologies through which they reached (and increasingly competed for) the loyalties of new followers. In an era of mass labor migration, these new followers included Indian plantation workers and miners for whom the creation of overseas branches of their ancestral Sufi shrines or the printed reproduction of comforting miracle stories offered solace for the discomforts of hard labor so far from home. Examples are seen in the early twentieth century constructions of a shrine at Penang in Malaysia to Shah al-Hamid, the famous Sufi patron of Tamil Muslims, and a mausoleum in Durban for Soofie Saheb (d.1911), the Sufi missionary to the indentured Indian laborers of Natal.[30] In such ways, the spread of capitalism under colonial management created both new demands and opportunities for the Sufis as the rapid changes in ordinary people's lives fueled hunger for the stability of tradition and the links it lent to a heritage that seemed to be slipping over the horizon.

Moving to the British colonies in Africa, we find similar patterns of resistance and cooperation that in turn created opportunities for new Sufi masters. Somalia, for example, saw the rebellion of Muhammad 'Abdille Hasan (1856/1864?–1920) lead to the establishment of a short-lived "dervish state" in which, as in the precolonial *jihad* states in other African regions, the institutions and authority of a Sufi brotherhood were used to create a hierarchical and centralized state system based around the master and administered through his interpretation of Shari'a.[31] It was not only British influence that Muhammad 'Abdille opposed. For having been re-cruited during a pilgrimage to Mecca into the new Salihi brotherhood founded by the exiled Sudanese Sufi Muhammad ibn Salih (d.1917/1919?), he also opposed Somalia's pre-existing Qadiri Sufi establishment. He regarded their members as lax in their observation of Shari'a and too accepting of the mediation of dead saints.[32] Given that Muhammad al-Baraawi (1847–1909), the main Qadiri target of Muhammad 'Abdille's vitriolic, was gathering followers to lead the resistance against Germany's colonization of Tanganyika (modern Tanzania), such internecine feuding may seem counter-productive. But it was part of the local ethnic rivalries and the competition for followers that formed the backdrop to the struggle against the Europeans.[33] Even so, Muhammad 'Abdille's charisma was ultimately insufficient to withstand a renewed colonial assault in which, by way of Vickers machine guns and Havilland DH 9 bombers, weapons developed during the First World War were redeployed to the dusty theater of the so-called "Mad Mullah." But even with his defeat, the poetry he composed in Somali allowed his memory and inspiration to play a leading role in the construction of Somali nationalism.[34] In a pattern we will see reflected below in other colonial contexts, the political tensions brought by colonization provided avenues for such Sufi "upstarts" seeking to challenge the religious establishment. For example, the rapid social change experienced in the more cosmopolitan ports of the Somali coast and the spread of trading routes to the interior also provided new audiences for ambitious Sufi teachers who supplied "pious remedies" for the social breakdowns that accompanied Africans' entry to the arena of global capitalism.[35]

In North and West Africa, British arbitration with influential Sufis managed to avoid rebellion through the pursuit of mutual interests that echoed what we have seen in India. In Egypt, even before the British arrived an official state-sponsored hierarchy of leading Sufis had been established by the Egyptian ruler Muhammad 'Ali as early as 1812.[36] Already used to working alongside rather than against the ruling powers, on Egypt's quasi-colonization by the British in 1882, 'Abd al-Baqi al-Bakri, the official head of the hierarchy of the Egyptian brotherhoods, hosted a grand banquet in honour of General Sir Garnet Wolseley, the commander of British forces.[37] Unsurprisingly, the status and perks of the Sufi hierarchy's members were confirmed in British regulations issued in 1895 and 1903. The privileges brought by this established position afforded new kinds of interactions between Sufi elites and their colonial counterparts, interactions which as in India lent Sufi tradition new forms of expression. In the case of Qut al-Qulub

Figure 4.1 Dervishes and Imperialists: The Battle between the Sudanese Mahdi and the British, 1885 (Credit: Gordon's Last Stand, illustration from 'Cassell's Illustrated History of England' (engraving) (sepia photo), English School, (20th century)/Private Collection/The Stapleton Collection/The Bridgeman Art Library)

(1899–1968), the pen-name of the Egyptian female heir to the Demirdashi Sufi family, this led to the composing from exile in a luxurious hotel in Rome of a series of French novels. In such works as *La Nuit de la Destinée* ("Night of Destiny," a reference to the Quranic *laylat al-qadr*), Qut al-Qulub celebrated popular Sufi festivals as the nostalgic essence of Egyptian national culture.[38] Yet for all her nostalgia, her links to the old Sufi establishment saw her exiled by fellow Egyptian nationalists as a cultivated but corrupted epitome of lavish Sufi decadence.

In neighboring Sudan, many Sufis became followers of the millenarian Mahdist movement that between 1881 and 1898 established a hierarchical new state managed on charisma and Shari'a. Then, in an African example of the process of the gradual colonial incorporation of Sufi rebels, defeat and surrender allowed the Mahdists' heirs in the next generation to negotiate a high degree of influence in the political endgame of decolonization and independent rule in Sudan.[39] In West Africa by contrast, the British conquest of the Sokoto Caliphate in 1903 in what is now Nigeria saw Tijani Sufis actually help the British in battle, before receiving appointments in the colonial administration through the system of indirect rule.[40] While on the eastern side of the Sahara we have seen Muhammad 'Abdille draw on the doctrine of *jihad* to preach rebellion in Somalia, in Nigeria to the west the Tijani Sufi Seydou Nourou Tall drew on the alternative doctrine of *maslaha* ("best interest") to argue that to rebel against so strong an invader was against the Muslims' best interests, and so against the will of God.[41] What we see here is not only that Sufis were capable of protecting the interests of their wider communities rather than solely their own interests, but also that Islam offered a sufficiently wide repertoire of doctrines for Sufi authorities to argue in favor of cooperation or resistance. While there were common processes at work in the Sufi responses to colonialism, there was therefore no single Sufi doctrinal position as to whether to resist or accept colonial rule.

The French Empire

A similar range of Sufi positions confronted French imperialism in North and West Africa.[42] In 1830 the French conquest of Algeria was met with an effective resistance movement led by the Qadiri Sufi, 'Abd al-Qadir al-Jaza'iri (1808–1883).[43] Like many other Sufi resistance leaders, rather than emerging from an establishment Sufi family 'Abd al-Qadir began his career as a marginal figure and only won his fame during a decade spent defying the French. In using the structures of the Sufi brotherhood to establish a Shari'a-based administration in the desert hinterland of French control, 'Abd al-Qadir reflected wider patterns of Sufis founding states in tribal frontier environments that had never been successfully absorbed by the early modern

Muslim empires. After his eventual surrender in 1847, 'Abd al-Qadir spent five years of imprisonment in France and during this time corresponded with leading French scholars, through whom he learned much of scientific advances in Europe. On swearing an oath against further rebellion, he was released in 1852 with a generous pension and allowed by the Ottoman authorities to settle where he would cause less trouble in provincial Damascus rather than the better-connected capital of Istanbul. There, he devoted the remaining decades of his life to writing his *Kitab al-Mawaqif* ("Book of Stopping Places") in which he sought to reinvigorate the teachings of the great medieval Sufi theorist Ibn al-'Arabi for an age in which knowledge inspired by God was being tested by the demonstrated proofs of science.[44] On 'Abd al-Qadir's death in 1883, he was buried beside Ibn al-'Arabi in the shrine constructed three centuries earlier by the Ottoman emperor Selim. Building on and eventually inverting his teachings, his followers in the next generation were among the founders of the new Islamic modernism that eventually abandoned the tradition that 'Abd al-Qadir endeavored to make meaningful for the modern era.[45] In spite of his defeat and exile, 'Abd al-Qadir was by no means the last North African Sufi to oppose French colonization of the region. In neighboring Morocco, which avoided French rule until 1912, a propaganda program of moral and physical resistance to French encroachment was initiated in the mid-1890s by the Sufi Muhammad al-Kattani (1873–1909).[46] Seeing Sultan 'Abd al-Hafid slipping through loan debts and alliances into the closer reliance on the French that brought about the 1912 Treaty of Fez by which the sultan acceded to French rule over Morocco, al-Kattani became a leading voice of religious and political opposition to both the French and their Moroccan royal lackeys. Al-Kattani expanded his following through printing twenty-seven of his works, and even founded a newspaper called *al-Ta'un* ("The Pestilence"), so turning the print technology only introduced to Morocco from Europe in the mid-1860s into an effective method of anti-colonial propagation.[47] Up to a point, it was a highly effective strategy of mobilization, encouraging large numbers of Moroccans to prepare for *jihad*. But ultimately this Sufi-led resistance movement collapsed after al-Kattani was executed on royal orders in 1909 and his successor as leader of the Kattani brotherhood chose to cooperate with the new French rulers.[48]

If 'Abd al-Qadir and al-Kattani demonstrate the dynamics of resistance to the French, then other Sufi figures opted like al-Kattani's successor for the rewards of cooperation. By managing to be cooperative while not appearing subservient to the French, in Tunisia Sidi Muhammad (1823–1897) managed to create a large *zawiya* complex at a crossroads of trans-Saharan trade routes on the limits of French rule. The complex contained a large *madrasa* and lodge for his followers, many of whom offered their labor on the *zawiya*'s well-irrigated landholdings in exchange for their spiritual edification.[49] Attached to the relatively new Rahmani brotherhood, Sidi Muhammad was not merely another upwardly-mobile Sufi but also represented new directions for the transmission of Sufi tradition. Instead of through the printing or writing of novels, here the new direction was female leadership. For in allowing his daughter Lalla Zaynab (c.1850–1904) to succeed him as head of the *zawiya*, Sidi Muhammad made a pragmatic if nonetheless significant step in the challenging of the old Sufi patterns of patriarchy. Passing this female inheritance from the limits towards the center of French colonial culture, Lalla Zaynab in turn transmitted certain Sufi teachings to the Swiss *artiste vagabonde*, Isabelle Eberhardt (1877–1904), whose short stories in French formed the European counterpart to the novels of Qut al-Qulub.[50]

Zaynab and Eberhardt were by no means the sole example in the French Empire of the transferring of Sufi doctrines to European sympathizers or converts. For capitalist modernity reared new enthusiasts for the Sufi message in the cosmopolitan capitals of Europe as well as in the industrializing ports of the Indian Ocean. As with the transfer of the medium of the Sufi message to the purchasable printed book in India, in Europe too the publishing industry played an important role in the process by means of such bookshops as the Librairie du Merveillieux managed in Paris by the Swedish Sufi convert, Ivan Aguéli ('Shaykh 'Abd al-Hadi Aqili', 1869–1917). Around Aguéli's bookstore in the early 1900s there gathered a romantic cadre of European seekers for whom the teachings of the Sufis were interchangeable with those of Hindu Vedanta and the *Tao Te Ching*. From their cosmopolitan and at times confused ruminations there emerged a hybrid and in some cases "de-Islamized" version of Sufism that filtered the tradition of old through to a new Western audience.[51] In some cases there was some genuinely direct transmission of tradition to the Europeans, as with the meetings between Eberhardt and Zaynab and between the Swiss Sufi popularizer Frithjof Schuon (1907–1998) and the Algerian Sufi, Ahmad al-Alawi (1869–1934). In other cases, most famously the French "Traditionalist" writer René Guénon ('Abd al-Wahid Yahya', 1886–1951), first-hand interaction with non-European Sufis seems to have been minimal, with printed books forming his main sources. The postcolonial trajectories of this "Western Sufism" are discussed in a later section of this chapter. However, the main point here is the way in which, in the French-controlled territories of North Africa, the imperial joining together of Muslim and Christian communities brought greater awareness of the Sufis in Europe through new opportunities for travel and interaction. If there was a good deal of romanticism (even "orientalism") in the attitudes of European seekers, there was also a good deal of earnestness and in some cases anti-colonial political sympathy. For not only did the Swedish painter Aguéli fully convert to Islam, but, after moving to British-controlled Cairo in the early 1900s, he joined the

Italian anarchist Enrico Insabato and an Egyptian nationalist and associate of the Algerian rebel 'Abd al-Qadir, called 'Abd al-Rahman Illaysh, in publishing an Arabic/Italian bi-lingual magazine *al-Nadi/il Convito* ("The Club"). In its forbidden pages, the teachings of Ibn al-'Arabi blended with anarchist theory and anti-British politics.[52]

In French West Africa, this interplay of resistance and compromise found its most interesting example with Amadu Bamba Mbacké (1853–1927) in Senegal.[53] Born into an established Qadiri Sufi family in a region which in Chapter 3 we saw Sufis establish a series of *jihad* states in the same decades in which the French were expanding their control over the Senegalese interior, Amadu Bamba grew up to acquire the allegiance of a series of local chieftains and notables. In the wake of the Algerian rebellion and the system of suspicious intelligence-gathering it bequeathed to French administrators, colonial officials were reared to see the often hereditary "marabout" leaders of Sufi brotherhoods as implacably opposed to French rule. As a result, in the 1890s and 1900s Amadu Bamba was sent into exile in Mauritania and Gabon.[54] His prestige grew in response. In the 1344 poetic verses of the *Jazaau Shukuur* ("Tribute of Recognition to the Worthy") written in the early 1900s in the Wolofal language by Amadu Bamba's follower Musa Ka, the old miracle stories that we have earlier seen developing through the Arabic genre of the *manaqib al-awliya* ("feats of the saints") were adapted to a new African colonial context.[55] As in British India, where rumors spread of Sufis miraculously escaping from colonial asylums, the news of Amadu Bamba's imprisonment was transmuted into stories of his taunting his keepers by jumping overboard from the prison-ship to worship on a prayer rug that floated on the waves or of his casually sipping tea in a flaming furnace into which the French wickedly thrown him.[56] Yet Amadu Bamba's story was not only one of miraculous resistance, but also one of pragmatic accommodation in which both he and his captors saw the benefits of cooperating with their French rulers. After returning from exile in 1912, Amadu Bamba led his Mouride followers in establishing a religious center in the Senegalese interior at Touba ("Repentance"), a new city which grew rich through the cultivation of peanuts and their export through the railways that connected the plantations to the French colonial economy.[57] This was no simple strategy of self-enrichment, but rather a project putting Sufi ideals into practical form. And such practicality inevitably involved a margin of compromise. The overall result saw Amadu Bamba forge an attractive alternative to the French *mission civilizatrice*. For while the French quietly allowed the local chiefs through which they controlled the countryside to continue holding onto their slaves, Amadu Bamba's agrarian community at Touba offered a refuge for runaway slaves. In so doing, it created a practical and new religious alternative to indigenous no less than colonial models of government.[58]

Figure 4.2   Rebel and Saint: Colonial French Photograph of Amadu Bamba of Senegal

The Russian Empire

Similar patterns can be seen in the history of the Sufis in the Russian Empire. In the same period that the French were facing the rebellion of 'Abd al-Qadir in Algeria, in the 1820s and 1830s Russian expansion into the Caucasus was met by fierce resistance from the Naqshbandi followers of Ghazi Muhammad (c.1795–1832) and Imam Shamil (1797–1871). Like 'Abd al-Qadir in North Africa, the two leaders of the Caucasian resistance were not born into the Sufi religious establishment of their mountain homeland. After attracting followers through their erstwhile success in keeping the Russians at bay and channeling the frustrations and energies of the young men of the valleys, they managed to establish a short-lived *jihad* state that between 1828 and 1859 flourished on the edge of the Russian Empire. Using the hierarchical structures of the Sufi brotherhood, Shamil established an effective system of administration based on the familiar delegation of authority to sixteen deputies or *na'ibs*, who were allotted control over the four zones into which his Sufi mountain state was divided.[59] No simplistic act of the resistance of a static indigenous culture, the project of Ghazi Muhammad and Shamil was an innovative one which, in its mission to impose the authority of Shari'a over local customary law, had many opponents among local Muslims no less than among Russians.[60] Sending emissaries far and wide from his mountain stronghold, Shamil was rebuffed by the Ottomans and Iranian rulers, who regarded him with suspicion. Among all the established Muslim powers, he only won a degree of support from the Egyptian ruler Muhammad 'Ali (r.1805–1848), who was likewise struggling to keep the Europeans at bay.[61]

Even if by the mid-nineteenth century it was Russian policy to incorporate Muslim religious institutions into the bureaucratic fabric of their "confessional state" wherever possible, Russia's eventual and hard-won defeat of Shamil left a legacy of mistrust of the Sufi brotherhoods among the Russian authorities.[62] Yet in many cases, the Russian attempt to encourage religious "orthodoxy," as part of the confessional state model of rendering more orderly and controllable subjects, played into the hands of Sufis seeking to expand the observance of Shari'a.[63] In a comparable albeit distinct pattern to what we have seen in the agrarian provinces of British India, many of the local religious leaders or *imams* appointed by the Russians were Sufis (or followers of Sufis) who supported both the closer observation of Shari'a and the Russian state as its enforcer, so bringing together a union of the disparate agendas of Sufis and imperialists.[64]

As in British India again, one of the most important contributions of Russian rule to Sufi and Muslim intellectual life more generally was the introduction of printing. As early as 1797 a printing press for Muslim texts was established in Kazan, the administrative capital of the Volga-Ural region.[65] Under the direction of the Russian-appointed printer Abu al-Ghazi

Buraš-uglï, the year 1802 saw what was probably the first ever publication of a Sufi work by a Muslim printer by way of the Chaghatai Turkish narrative poem, *Thabat al-'Azizin* ("The Constancy of the Beloveds"), originally written a century earlier by the Central Asian Naqshbandi, Sufi Allahyar (d.1713).[66] In the nineteenth century, even aside from printing, Russian rule over the Volga-Ural region saw a revitalization of the copying and composition of regional histories by Tatar and Bashkir Muslims. In such works on the landscape and its peoples as the *Tarikh Nama-ye Bulghar* ("History of the Bulgars"), composed in 1805 by Taj al-Din Yalchighul oghli (1768–1838), older Sufi shrine narratives were used to connect the Volga-Ural's inhabitants to the land which they inhabited through stories of ancient convertor saints who lay buried in the shrine town of Bulghar after which the people were named.[67] In a period in which the former Muslim khanates of the Russian Empire saw the influx of German and Russian settlers, and in which Russian Orthodox Christians were writing corresponding sacred histories that used purportedly abandoned Christian shrines as evidence of the ancient hold of Russian Orthodoxy over their southern Muslim imperial provinces, these nineteenth century shrine-histories used the region's architectural and narrative Sufi inheritance to claim the land as the Muslims' own in the face of the new Christian settlers.[68] Here too was a kind of Sufi resistance. Building on these textual claimants of territory, the later nineteenth century saw the region's Sufis take a more nationalistic position in the modern sense, as the poetry of the Naqshbandi intellectual Muhammad 'Ali al-Chuquri (1826–1889) celebrated a new "Volga-Bulgar" patriotism. Unwilling to upset the fearsome Russian ruling system, the poet nonetheless connected his patriotism to the peaceful reign of the tsars.[69]

While consolidating their hold over the Volga-Urals and the Caucasus in the second half of the nineteenth century, the Russians also conquered the cities and steppes of Central Asia that we have previously seen as the early modern strongholds of the great Naqshbandi brotherhood. There the negotiated politics of conquest saw a variety of local Sufis claim to be the true descendants of Ahmad Yasawi (d.1166?) and so have a stake in the vast landholdings of his shrine.[70] Even though in the early decades of Russian rule, the landholdings of the region's shrines remained intact, the wealth locked up in these medieval endowments triggered investigations by the new rulers, who were keen to free up land for the Russian and German settlers they saw as vital to maximum economic extraction from the region.[71] When the Russian Empire was transformed into the Soviet Union after 1917, these vast landholdings were finally wrested from their Sufi custodians. Combined with the official Soviet suppression of the Sufi brotherhoods and the banning of "feudalistic" Sufi literature, the loss of these sources of material support caused a decisive rupture in the transmission of Sufi tradition in Central Asia.[72] As the great shrines of the Naqshbandi saints were transformed into museums of anti-religious propaganda, to a far greater degree than their co-religionists in any of the other European empires, the Muslims of the Soviet Union were divorced from their Sufi heritage.

A Crumbling Establishment: Beyond the Colonial Sphere, c.1800–1950

While colonization had a tremendous impact on both the Sufis and their rivals during the nineteenth and the first half of the twentieth centuries, we should be wary of exaggerating the global reach of colonial power. In the remote high mountains of the Pamir on the borders of Russian rule, the Sufi poet Mubarak-e Wakhani (c.1840–1903) lived in such isolation that he had to invent a huge nineteen-stringed *rubab* lute to accompany the singing of his poems and was forced to develop his own paper-making machine to write the poems down. Russian colonialism was far from his mind and his struggles are instead reflected in such verses as "My senses and thoughts are preoccupied by paper".[73] While it is certainly the case that members of Sufi brotherhoods who entered alliances with colonial rulers were kept under surveillance by the authorities, ultimately this did not prevent the Sufis from making use of the new travel networks on which European rule and commerce was also dependent. The opening of trans-colonial routes put Muslims in distant regions of the world into easier and more regular global contact with one another.[74]

In some cases, this new travel infrastructure enabled the establishment and rapid dissemination of energetic new Sufi brotherhoods from what had previously been peripheral Muslim regions. In the case of the Rashidi-Ahmadi brotherhood, we find the Sudanese shaykh Ibrahim al-Rashid (1813–1874) reinvigorating the tradition he had inherited from his own teachers through a new brotherhood that quickly spread to Arabia, Syria, Egypt, Sudan, Libya, West Africa, the Malay states, Borneo, Singapore and ultimately Thailand and Cambodia.[75] In part, these wide disseminations were enabled by access to printing presses, through which the new brotherhoods' books could be mass produced for international distribution. Often these presses were located in such transport hubs as Istanbul, Bombay or Singapore and their books distributed at such global pilgrimage destinations as Mecca.[76] Such trans-colonial movements show that Sufism offered sufficiently robust forms of inspiration and organization to withstand colonial pressures. Perhaps more important than such trans-colonial diffusions of new brotherhoods was the fact that there also remained Muslim parts of the world which Europe did not colonize. It is important to set what we have seen of the colonial experience beside the fortunes of Sufis in these uncolonized regions. For looking at the history of nineteenth and early twentieth century Sufis in the Ottoman Empire,

Iran and Afghanistan there emerge several general patterns that bear certain similarities with the policies of colonial states. This suggests in turn that the colonial scenarios we have examined need to be situated in the longer historical patterns of interaction between powerful Sufis and state powers, whether the latter were "colonial" or "indigenous."

In the most important of all Muslim regions to at least avoid colonization until after the First World War, the shrinking but nonetheless vast Ottoman Empire remained a crucial arena for the Sufis. It was also one in which the interactions of Sufis and the state show parallels with regions under colonial control. In the early nineteenth century, the most important Sufi event was the official abolition in 1826 of the Bektashi Sufi brotherhood, along with the janissary military corps that had been its main support base for over three hundred years.[77] In the wording of the imperial *firman* order that announced the joint abolition: *birisi düşmanı devlet, birisi düşmanı din* ("the one is the enemy of the state, the other the enemy of the faith").[78] Given that the Bektashis' rituals had long incorporated such suspicious practices as wine-drinking, the abolition can partially be seen as part of the longer term promotion of legally conformist forms of Sufism. This perspective is confirmed by the coincidence of the Bektashis' demise with the rapid rise in elite Ottoman circles of the new legalistic branch of the Naqshbandi-Mujaddidi brotherhood founded by the itinerant Kurdish master, Shaykh Khalid (d.1827).[79] The political factors involved in this change of status between Bektashis and Naqshbandi-Mujaddidis were related to the colonial conquests we have seen leading to the increasing status of legalistic Sufi brotherhoods in the North India, Algeria and the Caucasus in the same decade. For what directly prompted the Bektashis' suppression was the outbreak of the Greek Revolution in 1821 and the subsequent series of defeats of Ottoman armies that culminated in Greece's independence a decade later. Given that parts of Greece had been under Ottoman control for four hundred years, the sudden loss of the western portions of the empire triggered tremendous anger against not only the armies but against what was widely perceived as a moral malaise that had weakened the empire from the inside. With their dubious rituals, their institutionalized wealth and their affiliation with the elite imperial soldiery, the Bektashis were the obvious targets for both popular and courtly resentment. Their abolition also had the advantage of allowing the state to seize the many *waqf* endowments which the brotherhood had accrued over the centuries.[80] In an Ottoman reflection of responses to European expansion in other Muslim regions, the following decades saw the rise of Sufis who publically denounced the lapse morals of the Bektashis, in particular members of Shaykh Khalid's Naqshbandi-Mujaddidi brotherhood. Right through to the 1870s, Shaykh Khalid's heirs occupied the chief religious rank of *shaykh al-islam* in the imperial bureaucracy, as well as preaching positions at the major mosques of Istanbul.[81]

In the 1850s, another Ottoman crisis – this time of the Crimean War – helped the rise of another group of reformists for whom not even law-abiding Sufis offered a solution to the scientifically-empowered victories of Europe.[82] But the brief heyday of these Tanzimat ("Re-ordering") reformers between 1839 and 1876 by no means signaled the demise of Sufi influence in the Ottoman realms. For defeat by the Russians in the war of 1877–78 discredited the Tanzimat reformists in turn, leading to the reactionary reign of 'Abd al-Hamid II (1876–1909). After the constitutional reforms of the previous decades, the latter's need for legitimacy in his attempt to monopolize power into his own hands as sultan saw him turn to the Sufis for help. The master of ceremonies in this policy of legitimization through the patronage of the old Sufi Islamic institutions was the Rifa'i Sufi master, Abu al-Huda al-Sayyadi (1850–1910). He oversaw a highly effective mobilization of Sufis through an "integration politics" in which the Sultan 'Abd al-Hamid was able to draw on the earlier Ottoman centralizing religious developments traced in Chapter 3.[83] Overseeing a so-called "black cabinet" comprising three other Sufi shaykhs with links to North Africa and South India, Abu al-Huda orchestrated a trans-national propaganda project in which the Sultan 'Abd al-Hamid was presented as the caliph or leader of all the world's Muslims.[84]

Another of the leading figures in this renewal of the old alliance between Sufi and sultan was the Palestinian Qadiri Sufi, Yusuf al-Nabahani (1850–1932), who after spending two years at the court in Istanbul in the 1880s rose quickly through the Ottoman judicial service.[85] From his office in Beirut, al-Nabahani wrote propaganda pieces in celebration of the sultan's achievements and in defense of his autocratic goals, while denouncing anti-Sufi and modernizers as the thin end of a Europeanizing wedge that would undermine the Muslim foundations of Ottoman society. In a series of polemical works, al-Nabahani denounced the intellectual leaders of the emerging anti-Sufi Salafi reform movement: Jamal al-Din al-Afghani was an "apostate," Muhammad 'Abduh an "active devil," and Rashid Rida a "perpetuator of evil."[86] Yet al-Nabahani was more than the stooge of an unstable emperor and through his many publications he formulated a conservative but nonetheless coherent response to the social and religious changes that accompanied the Ottoman Empire's contraction. While for reformists like 'Abduh, the appropriate response to these conditions was the abandoning of Sufi tradition by means of a thoroughgoing new "interpretation" or *ijtihad* of Islam's scriptural foundations, for al-Nabahani such desperate times rendered this "re-opening of the gates of interpretation" more dangerous than ever.

Al-Nabahani's was no lone voice. Supported by state appointments or stipends in various provincial cities throughout 'Abd al-Hamid's reign was a larger conservative bloc of late Ottoman Sufis, for whom tradition was not simply a status quo to be defended at all costs: it was a body of doctrinal and institutional resources that might confront the challenges of the modern age just as well as the modernists' teachings. Nor did such conservatism put a stop to new developments. From the 1880s in Damascus, the followers of the exiled former Algerian rebel 'Abd al-Qadir were at the forefront of the revival of literary and historical interests that would culimate in the Arab *nahda* or "renaissance."[87] In the case of the Salafi ("Forerunners") movement that emerged in Ottoman Syria and Egypt and around the turn of the twentieth century, the Sufi upbringings of men like Muhammad 'Abduh (1849–1905) in Tanta and of the followers of 'Abd al-Qadir in Damascus were renounced in maturity in favor of a rationalized Islam in which the rituals and miracles of the Sufis were denounced as incompatible with a modern world of scientific knowledge in which religion should be based on the rational exegesis of scripture rather than on the acceptance of distorting tradition.[88] The resulting rapid replacement of Sufi Islam by Salafi Islam in many regions of the world (the Middle East especially) has been one of the major social and religious changes in modern Islamic history.

By the second generation of the Salafi movement, from the early 1900s leading Salafi figures such as Muhammad Rashid Rida (1865–1935) became still more vehement in their denunciation of the corruption, egotistical excesses and libertinism of the Ottoman Sufis. In one influential printed article, Rida depicted the decadent sensuality of a Sufi performance of "handsome beardless youths... dressed in snow-white gowns like brides' dresses, dancing to the moving sound of the reed pipe."[89] From their Middle Eastern headquarters, the Salafis spread their anti-Sufi critique far and wide through the travels of their students and the publishing of such journals as *al-Manar* ("The Lighthouse").[90] The oppositional politics of an agonistic era meant that when the reformists gained the upper hand with the Young Turk Revolution of 1908, they viewed the Sufi more than ever as self-serving enemies of progress and destroyers of the Prophet's true teachings. In 1909, al-Nabahani was dismissed from his post in the judiciary. Still, even as full-blooded a modernizing Turkish nationalist as Ziya Gökalp (1876–1924) was able to view the intellectual if not the social dimensions of Sufism as valuable assets, arguing that the teachings of Ibn al-'Arabi (d.1240) anticipated the philosophy of Berkeley, Kant and Nietzsche.[91] By 1918 every Sufi shaykh in Istanbul had been sent a printed questionnaire in which they were asked to detail their qualifications, employment history, number of followers and pledges of allegiance.[92] When the Ottoman Empire was formally disbanded in 1922 as a corollary of fighting on the losing side in the First World War, the founder of the Turkish Republic, Mustafa Kamal Atatürk (1881–1938), finally took the drastic step of banning the Sufi brotherhoods altogether in 1925.[93] While many Sufis quietly accepted the new dispensation, there were those who, by refusing to take government posts and practicing their rituals in the privacy of their homes, defied Atatürk and his new secular republic. One of these was the Naqshbandi Shaykh Sa'id of Palu, who led a rebellion of the Kurdish Zaza tribes, before being captured and executed in 1925.[94] But, despite the stridently defended secularism of the Turkish Republic, the disappearance of Sufism from public life in the high republican era by no means brought about the end of Sufi influence in Turkish life.

Turning to Iran, in Chapter 3, we saw how the rise of a Shi'i clerical class in the Safawi Empire saw the eventual suppression of the Sufis in Iran. However, the very last years of the eighteenth century saw the return to Iran from India of the heirs to the Ni'matullahi brotherhood that we previously saw spreading from Iran in the sixteenth century to the Bahmani Sultanate of south India.[95] Through such itinerant teachers as Nur 'Ali Shah (d.1797), and their followers in the next generation, these migrant Sufis oversaw a considerable Sufi revival in Iran. To do so, they propounded an appealing theology centered on ecstatic experiences of rarefied emotions of love (*hubb*), passion (*'ishq*), devotion (*wadd*) and ardor (*hawa*) which could be summoned by the singing to musical accompaniment of the old Persian love poems of Rumi and Baba Tahir.[96] Such was their appeal that by the 1830s the Sufis even gained a following among the Jewish community of Mashhad. There Jewish Rabbis brought Sufi ideas into their readings of the Torah and made visionary connections with the medieval Sufi tradition of the surrounding Khurasan region through visions of Abu al-Qasim al-Qushayri (d.1074).[97]

Although Iran's Sufi revivalists met with much opposition from the Shi'i clerical establishment, leading to the execution of several Ni'matullahi "missionaries," the Sufis found sufficient support among wealthy merchants to spread rapidly through the trading towns of Iran's interior. By the mid-nineteenth century, the Sufis had also found support at the Iranian royal court, most crucially through the rise of the Ni'matullahi Sufi, Hajji Mirza Aqasi (1783–1848), to the position of grand vizier of the Qajar ruler, Muhammad Shah (r.1834–1848). Under Aqasi's patronage, the dilapidated shrines of the great medieval Sufis of Iran – such as Abu Yazid Bistami and Shah Ni'matullahi Wali – were restored and extended, while individual Sufis were granted stipends or endowed with landholdings.[98] Through such strategic alliances with the new Qajar dynasty of erstwhile Turcoman tribesmen that was not entirely dissimilar to the colonial powers in its lack of legitimacy, the Ni'matullahis won back for the Sufis a stake in Iranian society that they had not held for two hundred years. As the century progressed, the Ni'matullahis held onto this renewed profile by maintaining ties with Iranian merchants, not least the rich community of Iranian traders that emerged in colonial Bombay.[99] As in previous centuries, Sufis made use of international global networks to outstrip the control of national powers.

Changes in colonial regions therefore had knock-on effects for the Sufis in areas outside colonial control, effects which were in some cases to the benefit

Figure 4.3   Saints of the Colonial Seaports: Shrine of Ahmad ibn ʿAli at Steamer Point, Aden (author's collection)

of particular groups of Sufis. After a provincial upbringing in Isfahan, Safi ʿAli Shah (d.1899), the leading Iranian Niʿmatullahi of the later nineteenth century, launched his career through a period of residence in Bombay, where he not only won the support of its Iranian merchant diaspora, but also printed the book-length poem *Zubdat al-Asrar* ("Quintessence of Secrets") that established his reputation on his return home.[100] In the new age of printing, Safi ʿAli's verse represented both an appropriation and an extension of earlier Sufi tradition by self-consciously imitating the style of the medieval verses of the great Jalal al-Din Rumi.[101] But, within months of Safi ʿAli's death in 1899, his brotherhood was transformed into a self-consciously modernizing organization known as the *anjuman-e ukhuwwat* ("Fraternal Society") that blended Sufi tradition with the imported mystique of freemasonry.[102] Through the charity dinners of the *anjuman-e ukhuwwat* and through such other modernizing venues as magazines and philosophical academies, the Iranian Sufis of the early 1900s in an era of modernization linked themselves to the aspirations of a new national elite. Through reconfiguring their legacy of writing in Persian to the new ideology of Iranian nationalism, and through adapting the old Sufi role of moral admonition to address modern anxieties about drug consumption and women's rights, right up until the Islamic Revolution of 1979, the Sufi masters of Iran continued to find patronage at the highest levels of state, including the Empress Farah.[103]

In South and Central Asia, meanwhile, the survival of princely and "buffer" states on the fringes of British India allowed the old alliance between Muslim rulers and establishment Sufis to survive well into the twentieth century. In Hyderabad (an Indian princely state about the size of France), the existence of a ruling Muslim class afforded the continued patronage of Sufi activities, particularly by the ruling Nizam Mahbub 'Ali Khan (r.1869–1911), whose generosity saw Hyderabad hosting Sufis from far beyond the shores of India. Sheltered from the colonial upheaval of the old social order, Sufis in Hyderabad continued their old literary tradition by writing such biographical compendia as the Arabic *Mishkat al-Nabuwwa* ("Lantern of Prophethood") of Ghulam 'Ali Qadiri (d.1842), which through textual chains of initiatic descent connected the living Sufis of Hyderabad to the ancient saints of Khurasan and Baghdad.[104] If the anti-Sufi reform movements of British India slipped across the border into Hyderabad, then with the support of local mill-owners such Hyderabadi Sufis as Mu'inullah Shah (d.1926) were able to adapt themselves to the new idiom of reform and pass on their teachings even after Hyderabad was absorbed into independent India in 1948.[105]

In Afghanistan, just over the northwestern frontier of British India, the struggle of the modernizing Afghan rulers of the early twentieth century to assert their fragile authority over unruly tribesmen and oppositional clerics led Afghanistan's rulers into a familiar pact with leading Sufis.[106] In a region in which tribal loyalties to ancestral Sufi holy men were stronger than those to a distant king in Kabul, Afghanistan's centralizing rulers of the early 1900s found it politic to use Sufis as bridges to their unwilling subjects.[107] In 1919 this royal quest for power also involved the declaration of a holy war against a British Empire that, in the wake of the First World War, was too weakened to fully respond. When King Amanullah (r.1919–1929) publicly announced this unlikely *jihad* after a family power struggle that followed the assassination of his ruling father, he made sure he had the celebrated Naqshbandi master, Shah Agha (d.1925), standing by his side before then dispatching the Sufi and his brother Sher Agha to accompany his troops in battle.[108] In return for their support, the brothers received large land-grants on the outskirts of Kabul and honorific titles (such as Shams al-Masha'ikh, "Sun among Shaykhs"). When King Amanullah was toppled in a coup, his successor Nadir Shah (r.1929–1933) appointed Sher Agha as head of a new national committee of religious scholars and sent the third Sufi brother, Gul Agha, as ambassador to Egypt.[109] While Sufi influence was still high in the 1930s, the following decades saw a retraction of Sufi influence in Afghanistan. As in other regions, the last Afghan king Zahir Shah (r.1933–1973) preferred a secularizing modernism to alliances with living saints, while the intellectuals of the small Afghan middle class were coming under the influence of communist ideas from neighboring Soviet Central Asia and so regarded the Sufis as royal stooges. Even so, Sufism was still sufficiently embedded in the wider social order to make the reduction of Sufi influence an agenda for both religious and secular Afghan reformists.[110] Nonetheless, the mountainous countryside of Afghanistan preserved many aspects of the vernacularized regional forms of Sufi tradition that had by then disappeared under the modernizing or reforming pressures that had reshaped other Muslim countries in the twentieth century.[111] In the northern Afghan town of Tashkurgan (also known as Kholm), there survived vernacularized versions of tradition passed down by bilingual Persian/Uzbek pocket books

Figure 4.4   Afghan Allegiances: A Sufi Shrine-Residence in Kabul. (Image: Nile Green)

which connected carpenters, tanners and other craftsmen to the rituals and lineage of particular patron saints, with halva cooks being allied to Baba Farid of Multan.[112]

Expansion and Rejection: Postcolonial and Globalized Sufis, c.1950–2000

Sufis in the "old" Muslim World

Powered by new technologies of travel and printing, and confirmed in their positions of influence through shrewd alliances with ruling parties, in both colonial and non-colonial settings in many respects the nineteenth century saw the Sufis achieve the height of their social reach. Partly in reaction to the moneyed comfort and colonial compliance of the Sufi establishment and partly in response to the religious demands that came with exposure to new scientific ideas, the opening decades of the twentieth century saw the anti-Sufi reformists and Muslim modernists gain increasing influence. In the previous sections, we have seen how in certain regions by the early twentieth century Sufism was for the first time being suppressed in the service of nation-making. As we have already seen, in the Central Asian regions of the Soviet Union no less than in Republican Turkey, Sufism was suppressed in the name of a socialist or nationalist modernity. In other regions, particularly the Arab Middle East, modernists heightened their ideological attacks on Sufis as corruptors, collaborators or charlatans, while in institutional terms the nationalization policies of various postcolonial Arab states saw a further expansion of the long-term process of state regulation of Sufi brotherhoods.[113] In the new Saudi regime in Arabia, the teachings of the eighteenth century reformer Ibn 'Abd al-Wahhab were interpreted as wholly condemning the Sufis and installed as the ideology of the new state. We have already seen how the term "Sufism" itself was invented by European scholars in the colonial period and in their discussions came to the acquire meanings which in many cases were at odds with the Sufis' own understanding of their tradition. As Muslims in such late colonial environments as India and Egypt came to learn what European scholars had written about the Sufis, those who took the Europeans' understanding seriously were appalled by the excesses of the Sufis, while those who looked more skeptically at the European expertise were outraged at the misrepresentation of the spirit of Sufi teaching. Thus in late colonial India, in creating what was by any standards an inspirational body of poetry in Persian and Urdu, the reformist poet Sir Muhammad Iqbal (1877–1938) absorbed the colonial critique of modern day Sufis as lazy charlatans while accepting the same European scholars' praise of medieval Sufis as Islam's last true "mystics."[114] His ideas would become extremely influential in the attitudes towards Sufism of the postcolonial state of Pakistan which he helped establish. Similarly, in late colonial and postcolonial Egypt, the suggestion of European scholars that Sufism originated among external Christian and Hindu "influences," and was in any case an Islamic manifestation of a universal category of "mysticism," prompted Arab scholars to "re-Islamize" Sufism in response as a means of wresting back control of their own religious heritage.[115]

Like many other postcolonial attempts to re-appropriate a precolonial heritage, the project of re-Islamizing Sufism involved more a reinvention than a simple transmission of tradition. For before colonial scholars had suggested Hindu or even Buddhist sources for Sufi ideas, the notion of an "Islamic Sufism" (*al-tasawwuf al-islami*) was an unnecessary tautology. Moreover, in all corners of the Muslim world, the twentieth century witnessed an unprecedented pluralization of religious authority and doctrine through increasing access to education (whether secular or religious), new media technologies (whether printing or broadcasting) and new organizational forms (whether religious associations or political parties). The increasing range of Islams made available to believers served to relativize the Sufis' teachings and marginalize their brotherhoods in regions where they had long been dominant or major players. In short, by the mid-twentieth century, there were far more ways of being Muslim available. Faced with many more choices than following a Sufi master, millions of Muslims across the world elected to follow either one of the many new non-Sufi teachers or abandon external authority to follow their own conscience alone.

While the scale of Sufi influence undeniably declined, there remained many different forms in which the tradition of earlier centuries was passed on, albeit at times in distinctly modern forms. As we have seen earlier, there were reformist Sufis who adapted their teachings in response to their anti-Sufi critics. In situations where such critics had labeled many aspects of Sufi tradition nothing more than "superstition" (*khurafa*), Sufi reformers jettisoned many aspects of Sufi practice, particularly practices such as amulet-making or faith-healing for which the rise of modern medicine had anyway reduced demand. In more modernized and wealthy Muslim regions, Sufi activities were substantially truncated as a whole host of practices – from shrine veneration to miracle stories and talismanic objects – were discredited as the *disjecta membra* of modernity. Yet whatever the confident expectations of the secularization theories that shaped discussions of Sufism in the mid-twentieth century, modernization has not brought about a thoroughgoing disenchantment of Muslim religiosity. In various regions, particularly those in which Sufis managed to maintain their social status and institutional capital, Sufi tradition continued to be passed on, albeit under the increasing attacks of anti-Sufi reformers. Even in the most modernized regions of the world, the second half of the twentieth century saw Sufis respond to the transformations of self and society by creating new organizational formats or conceptual models by which to transmit their teachings. As the twentieth century drew to a close, there emerged new forms of Sufism in the countries of Europe and North America, which increasingly interacted and circulated with older Muslim regions.

Let us look at a few case studies of these different ways in which Sufism developed from the 1950s onwards. While in India and Pakistan, postcolonial governments weakened the old Sufi establishment by seizing control of many Sufi landholdings, tradition continued to be passed down in a far less truncated way than in the Middle East, where secular nationalism and religious reformism gained greater social ground.[116] Even so, in both India and Pakistan, Sufism was drawn into the postcolonial formation of new national identities. In India, certain forms of Sufism (particularly the musical performances and ecumenical shrines of the Chishti brotherhood) were promoted as tolerant forerunners of the multi-confessional secular Indian Republic, with their festivals receiving coverage on national television and their history being championed by university teachers. In Pakistan, the limited legitimacy of its postcolonial governments led a range of politicians to draw on the Sufis' prestige and connections in an echo of earlier colonial policies in the region. According to the varying ideologies of the political parties in question, Sufis were alternatively presented in Pakistan as missionary preachers of Islam or socialistic champions of the rural peasantry, with "research centers" or medical outlets being built as appendages to medieval shrines as the concrete expression of the new alliance of the Sufi and the President.[117] In the writings of the former Pakistani army officer and Sufi master, Captain Wahid Bakhsh Rabbani (d.1995), the memory of the medieval saints was turned even more explicitly towards national service. His Urdu work, *Pakistan ki 'Azim Ush-Shan Difai Quwwat* ("The Magnificent Power Potential of Pakistan"), presented a romanticized survey of the military and cultural history of Pakistan as a Muslim nation originally founded by Sufis and destined through the greatness of these saints and the soldiers they protected to be a beacon for the entire Muslim world.[118] As in Egypt, where we have seen European models of Sufism triggering a defensive "re-Islamization" of Sufi ideas, in Pakistan Rabbani similarly responded to European images of Sufism in his English work, *Islamic Sufism*. Here he argued against Orientalist notions of the external origins of Sufism to show the harmony of Sufi teachings with the Quran and Shari'a, while also drawing on an eccentric selection of French scientists and American New Age writers to prove the harmony of Sufism with science.[119] While in both India and Pakistan Sufis developed new formulations of doctrine in response to these larger postcolonial anxieties, the teachings and shrines of the region's Sufis nonetheless remain extremely important for many millions of Muslims (and indeed Hindus) to the present day. If the old practices of shared veneration of Sufi shrines has come under attack from Hindu no less than Muslim fundamentalists, hundreds of thousands of pilgrims from all religious backgrounds continue to make the pilgrimage each year to the medieval Indian shrine of Mu'in al-Din Chishti (d.1236).[120]

In Southeast Asia, parallel projects of modernizing nation-making had their impact on Sufism in new postcolonial states such as Indonesia and Malaysia. After achieving independence from the Dutch in 1949, between 1965 and 1998 Indonesia was pushed through an uncompromising "New Order" which saw the emergence of an educated modern population. Sufism moved in distinct directions during these years, whether moving into the new public sphere of Muslim political parties or withdrawing into the private sphere of the *kebatinan* or "esoterist" groups that promised their followers occult rather than political power.[121] Combined with the critiques of anti-Sufi reformists, such modernization rendered Sufism's old organizational format unappealing to the new generations of Indonesians, who came to regard the old brotherhoods as suspiciously secretive, anti-democratic and authoritarian.[122] In response, since the 1970s Indonesia's Sufi teachers have made radical breaks with their old institutions by creating new organizational formats to reach their modern educated compatriots, setting up seminars, workshops and retreats. By the 1990s, Sufi teachings were accessed through the Powerpoint presentations of suit-wearing Sufis who stressed the modernity of their teachings through such labels as "Neo-Sufi," "Practical Sufism," or "Tasawuf Positif." As a result, despite anti-Sufi polemics, increasing numbers of middle class and female Indonesians were won back to a form of Islam that promised an attractive combination of personal happiness and professional success. Such "lifestyle Sufism" also held the attraction of avoiding the stigma of political Islamism associated with Indonesia's other religious organizations.

Even in Central Asia, where as an "Islamic feudalism" Sufism had been brutally suppressed during seven decades of Soviet rule, the creation of new republics in the 1990s saw a massive revival of Sufi activity that was both state-sponsored and individual.[123] Since imperial Russian and then Soviet rule had brought about a decisive break with earlier tradition, what resurfaced in the 1990s was a curious hybrid of remembered rural folk traditions and nationalistic reinventions of patron saint cults.[124] This rupture with tradition had been reinforced by the Soviet replacement of Arabic script by Cyrillic and the promotion of Uzbek as a national language, which as in modern Turkey rendered earlier Sufi writings from the region in the Persian language and Arabic-script inaccessible except through the occasional translation. Since most of the old Sufi families had been persecuted and disinherited into obscurity, the new post-Soviet Sufi revivers were pious university professors such as the Uzbek writer Sadr al-Din Salim Bukhari, who under Soviet rule had established his career as an expert on the German poet Goethe.[125]

In Turkey, the period since the 1970s in particular saw a resurgence of the Naqshbandi brotherhood in Turkish life, not least under the institutional guise of socially conservative political parties.[126] As in other regions, the spiritual and intellectual if not the institutional traditions of the Sufis took on new guises in which, as in the Nurcu movement founded by the imprisoned Naqshbandi sympathizer Sa'id Nursi (1878–1960), Sufi nomenclature was avoided as a result of the stigmas it had gained under the critiques of secular nationalists and religious reformists.[127] In Turkey, Fethullah Gülen (1941-) managed a more open rapprochement with Sufism through preaching the importance of Sufi doctrines but not institutions.[128] Linked to pious industrialists rather than the imperial stipends and land grants of old, and founding schools in which a Sufi Islam was seen as being wholly compatible with a scientific education, the Gülen movement had by the 1990s outgrown its national origins and ventured into the religious markets opened in Central Asia by the collapse of the Soviet Union and its seventy year suppression of Sufi ways.[129] The success of his movement was viewed with ambivalence by Turkey's leaders and in 1998 Gülen emigrated to the United States, a decision that marked a new global moment in the expansion of his teachings. If, as in the Indonesian examples, the Gülen movement is in its concrete forms an entirely different entity to the brotherhoods and shrines of previous ages, in its appeal to a liberal and educated Muslim middle class, it represents a highly effective transmission of a truncated Sufi tradition to the present day.

In the Arab Middle East, the second half of the twentieth century saw Sufism in a perpetual dialectic with anti-Sufi reformists. Even so, for large numbers of followers, centuries of prestige enabled its preceptors to maintain their status as conduits of tradition.[130] Despite predictions during the heyday of Arab nationalism of the inevitable demise of Sufism in the Middle East, and the long reformist project of the individualization of religious authority, by the end of the twentieth century Middle Eastern Sufi masters still held sufficient esteem to attract followers from various backgrounds. In northern Syria, Sufi disciples range from university professors and wealthy industrialists to poor manual workers, whose shaykhs conduct them through grueling rites of passage that include handling live snakes, eating burning coals and piercing their bodies with skewers.[131] While in Egypt state regulation has sought to banish such dramatic practices from the saintly "birthday" festivals or *mawlids*, the Mubarak government still uses the festivals as platforms for political broadcasts and public orderliness, entering pacts with reformist Sufi leaders who own chemical factories and hold science degrees from communist Eastern Europe.[132] Albeit behind closed doors, ecstatic Sufi performances remain an important part of Egyptian Muslim life. As in the new brotherhood founded in 1952 after the Prophet Muhammad appeared in a dream to the civil servant Jabir Husyan Jazuli (1913–1992), there continue to emerge new organizations that now pass on tradition through cheap audio tapes, DVDs and home study materials designed to accompany the collective *dhikr* chanting sessions that first emerged over a thousand years earlier.[133]

Throughout the Middle East, Sufism has managed to maintain an appeal through recordings of its music, which despite involving a commodification of tradition has allowed the poetry of earlier centuries to reach young urban audiences, some of whom in turn take the step of formal initiation into a Sufi brotherhood.[134] Despite increasing government regulations, for many ordinary Egyptians the saintly *mawlid* festivals remain occasions of entertainment and emotional release. If the performances and fairgrounds that accompany such *mawlids* are not the mystical Islam imagined in many Western accounts of Sufism, then they are no less important an element of Sufism for all that. For many small town and rural Muslims in Egypt no less than Morocco, the shrines of the Sufi saints remain places of recreation and pilgrimage, where women take their relatives for picnics at the same time as buying affordable folk medicines and asking the saint for help with everyday struggles.[135] In a twist on the old alliances of state and Sufi, in the last decades of the twentieth century various Arab regimes supported Sufi groups as a counterweight to the modern Islamist organizations that opposed their rule, such as the Muslim Brotherhood. In some cases this has seen new vehicles of Sufi tradition emerge, which like other examples elsewhere play down the "Sufi" label to present themselves in more plainly Muslim or else modern guises. A Lebanese example is the *Jam'iyyat al-Mashari' al-Khayriyya al-Islamiyya* ("Society of Islamic Philanthropic Projects"), founded by the exiled Ethiopian Shaykh 'Abdullah al-Habashi, which has had considerable appeal among Lebanese Muslims tired with political Islam.[136] The stakes in such competition are now high and just as Sufi opposition to the Islamist Islamic Salvation Front in Algeria during the 1990s saw the slaughter of many Sufi Muslims and their followers, after fielding candidates for the 1992 national elections in Lebanon, the Society's vocal opposition to Islamist groups resulted in the assassination of its president.

Competition with Islamist organizations has also been a feature of Sufi history in postcolonial Africa. We have already seen prominent Sufis taking a leading role in political life in the years after independence in 1956 in Sudan. But since the 1970s the rise of such Islamist organizations as the Muslim Brotherhood and the National Islamic Front has marginalized Sudan's Sufis from public life. While Sudanese Islamists have attracted rich investments of oil money through the new global mechanisms of Islamic banking, the Sufis who had flourished under the Funj and British empires alike were left with the depleting resources of agricultural landholdings and economically marginal followers.[137] The picture looks very different in other regions of Africa. In West Africa, heirs to pre-existing Sufi brotherhoods have continued to flourish through making strategic alliances with modern political organizations. One example is the branch of the Tijani brotherhood led by Shaykh Ibrahim Niasse (1900–1975). He made canny alliances with many of the African and Arab independence leaders of the 1950s and 1960s, rose to become the Vice President of the Muslim World League and compiled his teachings in a book, *Kashif al-Ilbas* ('Removal of Confusion'), that in the second half of the twentieth century proved to be tremendously influential in West Africa.[138]

Elsewhere in the region, recent decades have seen the followers of the former colonial French prisoner Amadu Bamba keep pace with changes in West African society by appealing to a new following among rural migrants to the growing cities of Senegal.[139] Under his family successors, Amadu Bamba's Senegalese Mouride movement has also kept pace with developments in communication technology to maintain its followers' loyalty even in the extensive Senegalese trading diaspora that globalization has created in Europe and America.[140] While in Sudan, Sufis declined in relation to their Islamist rivals through comparative under-investment, in Senegal the Mouride brotherhood attracted expanding financial flows through the promotion of a pious business ethic that encouraged followers to see their international business travels as inseparable from their spiritual progress.[141] By the 1990s Sufism remained no less alive in neighboring Mali, through the rise of charismatic young Sufi leaders who, in such cities as Bamako and Ségou, were highly successful in promoting themselves among other urban young people.[142] In the case of Shaykh Soufi Bilal, this involved growing fashionable "rasta" dreadlocks, self-publishing booklets of his teachings and buying advertising airtime on local radio stations. As in other postcolonial environments, where modern citizens have been divorced from the literary traditions of their ancestors by colonial language policies, the writings of such Sufis as Soufi Bilal are in French rather than in the Arabic of the Saharan Sufis of former ages. But if this certainly involves a recasting of tradition, the pragmatic fact of the matter is that it is through French rather than Arabic that such Sufis are able to appeal to their mass urban audiences. As a kind of postcolonial vernacularization, such languages as French and English have followed where Persian and Turkish once led the way as new languages of Sufi Islam.

Sufism in the West

In the context of globalization, the rise of European languages as vehicles of Sufi expression can also be seen in the modern spread of Sufi brotherhoods into Europe and America. In moving to these new social contexts, at times Sufism was itself transformed by the demands of the different populations it addressed, some of whom had inclinations towards a universalistic "mysticism" but not towards Islam. As we have seen earlier, Sufis had already begun to move to Europe and America during the colonial period, whether through the North African travels of such Swiss esoterists as Frithjof

Schuon or the American itineraries of such Indian Sufis as 'Inayat Khan. This new diffusion increased in the more intensely globalized second half of the twentieth century.

Three general patterns can be observed among the increasing number of Sufi groups established in the West in the postcolonial period. The first pattern, comprising what we can designate as "community Sufis," involved the importation of Sufi groups as part of the larger establishment of immigrant communities. In such cases, the styles of Sufism varied in accordance with the regional, class and educational backgrounds of the migrant community in question and adapted as the religious preferences of those migrants themselves changed as a result of their experiences in their new homes. While the settings in which such community Sufis found themselves were new in themselves, as we have seen in earlier chapters, the pattern of Sufis migrating in the wake of wider population movements was much older. The second pattern, comprising what we can designate as "entrepreneurial Sufis," involved Sufis with no pre-existing immigrant host community who gathered followers who were either originally from different Muslim regions from themselves or else were new western converts to Islam. Again, while the setting was different, the pattern itself had various precedents, particularly in the mobile nineteenth century of the steamship and railway when we have seen similarly entrepreneurial Sufis emerging from Africa and Arabia who gathered followers from different ethnic groups in South and Southeast Asia. The third pattern, comprising what we can designate as "fusion Sufis," involved Sufis who were raised in Western countries of either Muslim or non-Muslim parentage and attracted followers who were similarly either converts or Western-born Muslims. Far more rooted in Euro-American ideas and expectations, these fusion Sufis were in many cases shaped by New Age or fashionable esoteric trends in the religious marketplace. While this final pattern certainly emerged out of colonial interchanges we have seen between European seekers and North African or occasionally Indian shaykhs in the early twentieth century, there were no substantive earlier precedents.[143] The following pages turn to examples of each of these three patterns in order to gain some sense of the variety of Sufi groups involved in this tripartite westward expansion.

Turning to the first pattern, we have already seen one of the most important examples of community Sufis in the case of the West African Mourides, whose itinerant trading has carried their practices into a Senegalese diaspora spread thinly through almost every European country. As Mourides spread first into France and then far beyond, the trade network that Amadu Bamba and family originally established with the French colonial economy has been continued into the postcolonial era by their Mouride followers who import their tradition along with their African handicrafts and reproduction watches by singing *dhikr* and fixing stickers of Amadu Bamba wherever they work.[144] In the case of South Asian community Sufis, Pakistani immigration to Britain has led to complex patterns of religious circulation as Sufi brotherhoods reared originally in the Asian homeland have taken on new forms overseas in Britain before being in turn exported back to Pakistan.[145] One example of this is the fellowship of Zindapir that emerged in the barren Himalayan foothills of Pakistani Kohat in the 1950s and gradually spread among British Pakistanis through the efforts of the former soldier and foundry worker Sufi Sahib in Birmingham. During the 1980s, what was originally a socially marginal fellowship in both Pakistan and England developed into a globalized Pakistani diaspora network through which flowed not only pilgrims and funding but ritual traditions, protective talismans and meditation practices. While constrained within a specifically Pakistani diaspora like other forms of community Sufism in the West, by offering a coherent mystical theology no less than exorcisms of demonic "genies" (*jinnis*), the Zindapir brotherhood appealed to the educated doctors no less than the unschooled housewives who at the end of the twentieth century comprised the global Pakistani community.

Similar forms of circulatory exchange can be seen among the community Sufism of Turkish immigrants in Germany, who in originating mainly in the Anatolian countryside maintained stronger bonds with Sufi tradition than more secularized urban Turks. One example is the fellowship of the Naqshbandi master Sulayman Hilmi Tunahan (d.1959) and his successor Kemal Kaçar (d.2000). Despite facing discrimination from both the Turkish and German governments, their brotherhood underwent a low-key but nonetheless rapid and simultaneous expansion in both countries due to the regular "migration and return" pattern that characterized Germany's guest worker immigration model, itself a mode of globalization.[146] Turning to the case of community Sufis in Italy, we find the act of migration reshaping the Sufi practices of Macedonian Roma members of the Khalwatiyya brotherhood who migrated to Italy in the 1990s. The Roma faced criticisms from Arab Muslims influenced by anti-Sufi Wahhabi Islam who were already resident in Italy that their "Gypsy" style of Sufism was not true Islam. As a result they abandoned certain practices such as kissing the hand of their shaykh.[147] In such cases, Europe itself becomes a place for the transformation as much as the transmission of Sufi tradition.

Turning to the second pattern among Sufis in the West, one of the most successful examples of an entrepreneurial Sufi is the charismatic Naqshbandi master, Shaykh Nazim al-Haqqani. Born on the island of Cyprus in 1922, Shaykh Nazim acquired his own Sufi training in Istanbul and Damascus after first studying chemical engineering.[148] The transnational character of his following was to some extent prompted by circumstances, in that at the height of Turkey's secular republicanism in the mid-1960s he appears to have been expelled from Turkey itself. While Shaykh Nazim was ultimately successful in building a following in Turkey as well as Syria and Egypt, he is most notable for his success in Europe and the United States. What is particularly striking about Shaykh Nazim is his ability to draw followers on a genuinely global level, not only from different countries but from different language and culture areas. In Europe, Shaykh Nazim has been particularly successful in attracting educated, middle class Germans, while in the United States he has largely attracted the Latinos and African-Americans who have in recent decades constituted the main American converts to Islam.[149] Unlike some of the "fusion Sufis" discussed below, Shaykh Nazim remained true to Naqshbandi tradition in upholding the importance of Shari'a in Sufi life. But he has been at the same time remarkably open to non-Muslims in accepting followers without their initial conversion to Islam. While his repeatedly unfulfilled predictions of the end of the world in 1996, 1997 and 1998 dented his credibility, his charismatic entrepreneurship saw him using a range of new media to attract followers. From allowing new disciples to take the traditional oath of allegiance through the Internet to flying around the world to give highly orchestrated *suhba* lessons and selling an array of mass-produced Sufi merchandise, Shaykh Nazim has cannily sought to reproduce tradition through the mechanisms of globalization. He has also proved to be a brilliant manager of his different audiences, which he achieves by adjusting the degree of male/female interaction, the strictness of dress codes and the avoidance (or promotion) of political causes according to which group of followers he addresses. Like other forms of globalized culture, Sufi tradition can alternatively be seen as having been diluted or democratized. What is clear, however, is the enhanced credibility of tradition in an age of inauthentic novelties.

Other entrepreneurial Sufi groups have limited their outreach to the West to particular regions, such as the Moroccan Boutchichi brotherhood. Under the aegis of Sidi Hamza Boutchichi (born 1922), the Boutchichi leaders have used business-style seminars to market their brotherhood as an authentic yet progressive alternative to political Islam.[150] Attracting not only French citizens of North African origin but also French spiritual seekers more generally, the brotherhood has managed to increase its profile through the cultural activities of high profile followers. These include the French public intellectual Faouzi Skali, who helped found the annual Fez Festival of Sacred Music, and the Congo-born French rap star Abd al-Malik, who through hip-hop and autobiography chronicled his journey to Sufism from the drugs and crime of the suburban *banlieues*.[151] During the 1980s there similarly developed in Germany domesticated offshoots of older Sufi brotherhoods founded by German converts with a good sense of the psychological demands of their fellow nationals.[152] One example is the bilingually-named Tariqat al-Safina or Schiffs-Weg ("Way of the Ship") established after the long Libyan residence of the German convert Bashir Ahmad Dultz (born 1935). After returning to Bonn in 1983, Dultz established several organizations devoted to inter-faith dialogue.[153] Along with such psychiatrically-inflected organizations as the Berlin-based Institüt für Sufi-Forschung (Institute for Sufi Research), such was the success of these German Sufi groups in attracting former followers of Hindu-derived new religious movements that the German tabloid newspaper *Bild* ran the headline, "Bhagwan ist out, Allah ist in."[154]

In the North American context, one of the most interesting entrepreneurial Sufis was Muhammad Raheem Bawa Muhaiyaddeen (d.1986).[155] After moving to the United States from his native Sri Lanka in 1971, Muhaiyaddeen attracted what was originally a white middle class fellowship to the rural retreat he established outside Philadelphia. He used the fashionable appeal of a vegetarian lifestyle, the recording of an album for Folkway Records and his own self-presentation as a "guru" who happened to be Muslim. His early English work, *Divine Luminous Wisdom That Dispels the Darkness*, published in the United States in 1972, brought together Islamic teachings with the Hindu-derived spirituality that was popular among the American counter-culture.[156] Yet even such globally-mobile entrepreneurial Sufism was subject to globalization and, as time passed, Philadelphia gained an immigrant Muslim population who encouraged Muhaiyaddeen to emphasize the more formally Islamic aspects of his teachings. In 1984, the converts from among his earlier American-born following joined with the immigrant Muslim newcomers to establish a mosque for the by-now considerable Muslim community of Philadelphia. Since the 1960s, scores of such entrepreneurial Sufis have acquired fellowships all over the United States. One recent survey described thirty-two significant Sufi organizations as active there, most of them led by immigrant Sufi leaders but some by converts who fit the pattern of the "fusion Sufis," to whom we will turn now.[157]

The final pattern of Sufi expansion into Europe and North America has centered on "fusion Sufis." These were typically raised in western countries (whether to Muslim or non-Muslim families) and attracted followers who were similarly either converts or Western-raised Muslims. In some cases, these fusion Sufi leaders were converts themselves. More influenced than any other Sufi movements by the post-1960s stress on "spirituality" and the "esoteric," several such fusion Sufis have gone so far as to entirely divorce Sufism from its Muslim framework while still looking backwards to draw on certain aspects of Sufi tradition.[158] While the community and entrepreneurial Sufis of the globalized era can by such means still claim a degree of continuity with tradition, de-Islamized fusion Sufism is clearly a newer response to the eclecticism of the global religious marketplace. The most fascinating early case study is Idries Shah (1924–1996), who was raised in England after being born to a Scottish mother and an Indian father of Afghan descent. After publishing an occultist manual on *Oriental Magic* in 1956 and a book of travels to Mecca in which his persona was very much that of the sardonic imperial Briton, in the early 1960s Shah became the secretary to Gerald Gardner, the impresario of neo-pagan witchcraft.[159] Then, as the hippy enthusiasm for Morocco and India shifted fusions towards eastern religions, Shah played on his family background to reinvent himself as the heir to an ancient lineage of Afghan aristocrats and Sufi masters that stretched into the ancient past of Persia. By "translating" digestible nuggets of doctrine from classical Sufi works into best-selling compendia, and attracting such avant-garde acolytes as the novelist Doris Lessing and the poet Robert Graves, Shah by the end of the 1960s acquired not only a wide following but also an institutional basis by way of his own publishing house and a charity he named the Institute for Cultural Research. While Shah was widely disparaged, he was, as a brilliant self-publicist, more responsible than anyone for the growth in Western awareness (if not always understanding) of Sufism. Building on the colonial routes to globalization, in the Anglosphere at least, Sufis with family origins in regions formerly under British rule were in many cases like Shah the ones who were able to establish networks in the West. This was particularly true of Sufis with links to the former colonial territories of India, whether Idries Shah or the descendants of 'Inayat Khan (1882–1927), whom we saw earlier in this chapter moving from India to Britain and then America. While as a migrant Sufi preacher to Western audiences 'Inayat Khan himself best echoes the careers of the entrepreneurial Sufis in the West, in the generations after his death his legacy was taken up in Australia by Sufis of the fusion kind. Of European rather than Asian descent, these Australian heirs to 'Inayat Khan by the 1990s had adapted the teachings of their Indian past master to fit the mores of their own society. They stressed informality, egalitarianism and feminism to such a degree that it caused tensions with the family descendants of 'Inayat Khan who also claimed to be his spiritual heirs.[160] In such ways, the fusion Sufism that emerged from the encounter of Sufism with the globalized religious marketplace of the late twentieth century tested the basic tenets of order and discipline that had for centuries served as the organizational basis of Sufi tradition.

Yet globalization offers no single trajectory of religious development. It has also brought new opportunities for the teachings of the Sufis to reach new audiences in new languages, whether through translations into Western languages of the teachings of such pillars of tradition as Rumi and Ibn al-'Arabi or through the writing of entirely new Sufi works in these lan-guages. All of the Sufi groups operating in the West have contributed to the development of a rich Sufi literature in European languages, helping raise English in particular to the language of global Islam. But it has been such fusion Sufis as Idries Shah and the Anglo-Californian Sufi, Llewellyn Vaugh-an-Lee (1953–), who have been most effective in entering the commercial publishing marketplace.[161] If such writings arguably exemplify the appropriation more than the continuation of tradition, then the development of tradition that we have seen over past centuries was also at times a process of appropriation, back-projection and even invention. However we evaluate them, the writings of such Western fusion Sufis are now important initial conduits for many global citizens seeking entry into the rich heritage of Sufism.

Summary

Amid the tumultuous collapse of Muslim power in the colonial era, from West Africa to Central Asia and India, many groups of Sufis found themselves on the front-line of European expansion. As such, they made use of the loyalties and logistics of the Sufi brotherhoods to construct forms of at times militant opposition to colonial conquest. However, more often than not, such Sufi resistance leaders tended to be "upstart" figures with little pre-existing authority. Attached to the state as they had been through their earlier negotiations with precolonial Muslim empires, in many regions members of the Sufi "establishment" were more willing to find means of accommodation with their new colonial rulers, even as some of the latter (French and Russians especially) viewed the Sufi brotherhoods with distrust. Thus, in many colonial settings no less than in such independent regions as Iran and the Ottoman Empire, Sufis were able to maintain and in some cases expand their ties so as to enter the twentieth century as among the few premodern Muslim institutions to survive colonization substantially intact. Yet whether with Muslim or European governments, such alliances with the ruling classes were ultimately counter-productive and from the late-nineteenth century the oppositional politics of Islamic reform rendered this Sufi establishment the natural target of critique. At the same time, the status of the Sufis became relativized by claims to religious authority being made by new organizations and individuals who rejected Sufi tradition and its templates of transmitted blessing and authority. Many of these new Muslim leaders emerged from such new middle-class professions as school teaching, journalism or medicine. This varied assortment of reformists and modernists rejected Sufism as the epitome of a degenerate traditionism that had allowed the Muslims to be colonized, so from the early 1900s placing Sufism under the most sustained and successful attack in its history.

Despite the expectations of scholars in the mid-twentieth century that Sufism would soon disappear beneath the wave of these more "modern" forms of Islam, through a series of adaptations to the new technologies and populations of the twentieth century, Sufism survived the onslaught of its critics, even if it lost vast numbers of followers in the process. In the globalized environments of the twenty-first century, what unites all of the Sufi movements now active in Europe and North America no less than in

Figure 4.5 Singing the Memory of the Saints: Qawwali Praise-Singers in India. (Image: Nile Green)

older Muslim regions, is their effective adaptation of new technologies and organizational formats to disseminate their message. In the towns of Morocco, Sufi masters often meet their disciples in venues that resemble business seminars more than the ceremonial gatherings of former times, while ritual gatherings of Sufi music and chanting are now more likely to be found in Los Angeles than in Shiraz. In an increasingly globalized environment, the idea of a dichotomy between a Sufism of the "Western" and "Islamic" worlds is less and less helpful. As the Naqshbandiyya-Haqqaniyya of the Cypriot Shaykh Nazim and the Gülen movement of the Turkish spiritual leader Fethullah Gülen operate as genuinely transnational ventures, there is every sign that Sufism will maintain a viable stake in the global religious market. If the effect of the anti-Sufi Muslim reform movements in the twentieth century meant that the heirs of Sufi tradition do not now always formally present themselves as "Sufis," this re-absorption of an unmarked Sufism into a larger conception of Islam in general marks in many respects a return to the older sense of Sufi tradition as inseparable from the Muslim faith.

For all the epistemic ruptures of modernity and the fashionable fusions of the global religious marketplace, in their emphasis on the authority of past masters and the teachings they have handed down through the ages, many of the Sufis in the world today constitute genuine bearers of the tradition that was created from the memory and legacy of the early Sufis of Baghdad. Other more "entrepreneurial" or "fusion" Sufis offer more clearly invented or appropriated forms of tradition, while still nonetheless drawing on the logic of tradition to connect themselves to the sayings and practices of the Sufi past masters. While there are undoubtedly more Islams now available for Muslims to choose from, and among them the old Sufi establishment only survives in much-diminished form, for many millions of Muslims the teachings of the Sufis continue to illuminate the road towards harmony with their divine maker. While the social contexts of Sufism have changed dramatically over the thousand-odd years of its history, as a tradition Sufism has been held together by the cords of texts and terminology, lineages and teachers, rituals and pledges, by which the living Sufis of each generation have pledged themselves to the re-enactment of morals, practices and beliefs they preserve as the secret doctrine of the Prophet. As a work of history pursuing only written signs and architectural traces, this book has undoubtedly missed much of the lived experience and felt ecstasy that for Sufis themselves has been the lifeblood of their tradition. Yet the words and places we have traced here were not only the cultural wherewithal that tied the Sufis to the world around them. They were also the tools of tradition that allowed them to transcend it. If we have not been able to follow them in these acts of transcendence, then this is because we have read their works concretely rather than contemplatively. In scanning so many texts of so many periods, we have risked missing the first act by which the Sufis set off on their ascensions: the contemplation of the b in the *bismillah* that is the opening word of the Quran. If for Sufis the dot beneath that letter was a pointer beyond history to the cosmic singularity in which all things begin and end, then what we have traced in these pages is the multifarious and all too human story of the Sufis in the world.

Notes

1. For the sake of clarity, I have used the more familiar modern names for these countries and other colonized regions discussed in this chapter.
2. C.W. Ernst, *Sufism* (Boston: Shambhala, 1997), pp.8–18.
3. F. Jahanpour, "Western Encounters with Persian Sufi Literature," in L. Lewisohn & D. Morgan (eds), *The Heritage of Sufism: Late Classical Persianate Sufism (1501–1750)*, vol. 3 (Oxford: Oneworld, 1999).
4. On the development of these pejoratives and stereotypes, see K.P. Ewing, *Arguing Sainthood: Modernity, Psychoanalysis and Islam* (Durham: Duke University Press, 1997), chapter 2, A. Knysh, "Sufism as an Explanatory Paradigm: The Issue of the Motivations of Sufi Movements in Russian and Western Historiography," *Die Welt des Islams* 42, 2 (2002), pp.139–173 and G.R. Trumbull, *An Empire of Facts: Colonial Power, Cultural*

Knowledge, and Islam in Algeria, 1870–1914 (Cambridge: Cambridge University Press, 2009), chapter 3.

5. For overviews, see de Jong & Radtke (1999) and E. Sirriyeh, *Sufis and Anti-Sufis: The Defence, Rethinking and Rejection of Sufism in the Modern World* (Richmond: Curzon Press, 1999).

6. R.S. O'Fahey, "'Small World': Neo-Sufi Interconnexions between the Maghrib, the Hijaz and Southeast Asia," in S.S. Reese (ed.), *The Transmission of Learning in Islamic Africa* (Leiden: Brill, 2004) and M.C. Ricklefs, "The Middle East Connection and Reform and Revival Movements among the *Putihan* in 19th-Century Java," in E. Tagliacozzo (ed.), *Southeast Asia and the Middle East: Islam, Movement, and the Longue Durée* (Singapore: NUS Press, 2009).

7. A.K. Bang, *Sufis and Scholars of the Sea: Family Networks in East Africa, 1860–1925* (London: RoutledgeCurzon, 2003); Reese (2008).

8. U. Sanyal, *Devotional Islam and Politics in British India: Ahmad Riza Khan Barelwi and his Movement, 1870–1920* (Delhi: Oxford University Press, 1996).

9. J.M. Abun-Nasr, *Muslim Communities of Grace: The Sufi Brotherhoods in Islamic Religious Life* (New York: Columbia University Press, 2007), chapter 8.

10. M. Gaborieau, "The 'Forgotten Obligation: A Reinterpretation of Sayyid Ahmad Barelwi's Jihad in the North-West-Frontier, 1826–1831," in J. Assayag (ed.), *The Resources of History: Tradition, Narration and Nation in South Asia* (Paris/Pondichéry: École Française d'Extrême Orient, 1999) and H.O. Pearson, *Islamic Reform and Revival in Nineteenth-Century India: The Tarīqah-i-Muhammadīyah* (Delhi: Yoda Press, 2008).

11. Pearson (2008), pp.38–40, 82–87.

12. Pearson (2008), p.82.

13. S.A. Kugle, "The Heart of Ritual is the Body: Anatomy of an Islamic Devotional Manual of the Nineteenth Century," *Journal of Ritual Studies* 17, 1 (2003), pp.42–60.

14. S.A.A. Rizvi, *Shah 'Abd al-'Aziz: Puritanism, Sectarian, Polemics and Jihad* (Canberra: Ma'rifat Publishing House, 1982).

15. B. Ingram, "Sufis, Scholars and Scapegoats: Rashid Ahmad Gangohi (d.1905) and the Deobandi Critique of Sufism," *Muslim World* 99 (2009), pp.478–501 and B.D. Metcalf, *Islamic Revival in British India: Deoband, 1860–1900* (Princeton: Princeton University Press, 1982).

16. A. Warren, *Waziristan, the Faqir of Ipi, and the Indian Army: the North West Frontier Revolt of 1936–37* (Oxford: Oxford University Press, 2000).

17. N.S. Green, "Breathing in India, c.1890," *Modern Asian Studies* 42, 2–3 (2008), pp.283–315.

18. On such Hindu patronage, see S. Gordon, "Maratha Patronage of Muslim Institutions in Burhanpur and Khandesh," in D. Gilmartin & B.B. Lawrence (eds), *Beyond Turk and Hindu: Rethinking Religious Identities in Islamicate South Asia* (Gainsville: University of Florida Press, 2000).

19. F. Robinson, "'Ulama, Sufis and Colonial Rule in North India and Indonesia," in Robinson, *The 'Ulama of Farangi Mahal and Islamic Culture in South Asia* (Delhi: Permanent Black, 2001), p.191.

20. S.F.D. Ansari, *Sufi Saints and State Power: The Pirs of Sind, 1843–1947* (Cambridge: Cambridge University Press, 1992) and D. Gilmartin, *Empire and Islam: Punjab and the Making of Pakistan* (Berkeley: University of California Press, 1988), chapter 2.

21. N.S. Green, *Islam and the Army in Colonial India: Sepoy Religion in the Service of Empire* (Cambridge: Cambridge University Press, 2009).

22. N.S. Green, *Indian Sufism since the Seventeenth Century: Saints, Books and Empires in the Muslim Deccan* (London: Routledge, 2006).

23. Cited in Green (2006), p.110.

24. U. Stark, *An Empire of Books: The Naval Kishore Press and the Diffusion of the Printed Word in Colonial India* (Delhi: Permanent Black, 2007).

25. C.W. Ernst, "Ideological and Technological Transformations of Contemporary Sufism," in M. Cooke & B.B. Lawrence (eds), *Muslim Networks: From Hajj to Hip-hop* (Chapel Hill: University of North Carolina Press, 2005), p.234.

26. On the rise of the doctrine, see A.F. Buehler, *Sufi Heirs of the Prophet: The Indian Naqshbandiyya and the Rise of the Mediating Sufi Shaykh* (Columbia: University of South Carolina Press, 1998), pp.134–138.

27. R.B. Qureshi, "'Muslim Devotional': Popular Religious Music and Muslim Identity under British, Indian and Pakistani Hegemony," *Asian Music*, 24, 1 (1992–1993).

28. D.A.S. Graham, "Spreading the Wisdom of Sufism: The Career of Pir-o-Murshid Inayat Khan in the West," in P.Z.I. Khan (ed.), *A Peal in Wine: Essays on the Life, Music, and Sufism of Hazrat Inayat Khan* (New Lebanon: Omega Publications, 2001).

29. N.S. Green, *Bombay Islam: The Religious Economy of the West Indian Ocean, 1840–1915* (New York: Cambridge University Press, 2011).

30. N.S. Green, "Islam for the Indentured Indian: A Muslim Missionary in Colonial South Africa," *Bulletin of the School of Oriental and African Studies* 71, 3 (2008), pp.529–553 and T. Tschacher, "From Local Practice to Transnational Network: Saints, Shrines and Sufis among Tamil Muslims in Singapore," *Asian Journal of Social Science* 34, 2 (2006), pp.225–242.

31. B.G. Martin, *Muslim Brotherhoods in Nineteenth-Century Africa* (Cambridge: Cambridge University Press, 1976), chapter 7.

32. On the rivalry, see S.S. Samatar, "Sheikh Uways Muhammad of Baraawe, 1847–1909: Mystic and Reformer in East Africa," in Samatar, *In the Shadows of Conquest: Islam in Colonial Northeast Africa* (Trenton: The Red Sea Press, 1992), pp.54–62.

33. B.G. Martin, "Muslim Politics and Resistance to Colonial Rule: Shaykh Uways b. Muhammad al-Barāwī and the Qādirīya Brotherhood in East Africa," *Journal of African History* 10, 3 (1969), pp.471–486. On more cooperative Sufis in German Africa, see A.H. Nimtz, *Islam and Politics in East Africa: The Sufi Order in Tanzania* (Minneapolis: University of Minnesota Press, 1980), chapter 8.

34. S.S. Samatar, *Oral Poetry and Somali Nationalism: The Case of Sayyid Mahammad Abdille Hasan* (Cambridge: Cambridge University Press, 1982).
35. S.S. Reese, *Renewers of the Age: Holy Men and Social Discourse in Colonial Benaadir* (Leiden: Brill, 2008), chapter 4.
36. F. de Jong, *Turuq and Turuq-Linked Institutions in Nineteenth Century Egypt* (Leiden: Brill, 1978), chapter 1.
37. F. de Jong, "The Sufi Orders in Egypt during the 'Urabi Insurrection and the British Occupation (1882–1914)," in de Jong, *Sufi Orders in Ottoman and Post-Ottoman Egypt and the Middle East* (Istanbul: Isis Press, 2000), p.147.
38. E.H. Waugh, *Visionaries of Silence: The Reformist Sufi Order of the Demirdashiya al-Khalwatiya in Cairo* (Cairo: American University in Cairo Press, 2008), chapter 4.
39. R.S. O'Fahey, "Sufism in Suspense: The Sudanese Mahdi and the Sufis," in F. de Jong & B. Radtke (eds), *Islamic Mysticism Contested. 13 Centuries of Controversies and Polemics* (Leiden: E.J. Brill, 1999) and J. Voll, "Mahdis, Walis and New Men in the Sudan," in N.R. Keddie (ed.), *Scholars, Saints and Sufis: Muslim Religious Institutions in the Middle East since 1500* (Berkeley: University of California Press, 1972).
40. M.S. Umar, "The Tijaniyya and British Colonial Authorities in Northern Nigeria," in J.-L. Triaud & D. Robinson (eds), *La Tijâniyya: Une confrérie musulmane à la conquête de l'Afrique* (Paris: Karthala, 2000), pp.330–331.
41. Umar (2000), pp.349–351.
42. R. Seeseman & B.F. Soares, "Being as Good Muslims as Frenchmen: On Marabouts, Colonial Modernity and the Islamic Sphere in French West Africa," *Journal of Religion in Africa* 39 (2009), pp.91–120.
43. Martin (1976), chapter 2.
44. 'Abd al-Qādir ibn Muhyī al-Din al-Ǧazā'irī, *Le Livre des Haltes: Kitab al-Mawaqif*, trans. M. Lagarde, 3 vols (Leiden: Brill, 2000).
45. David Commins, "'Abd al-Qādir al-Jazā'irī and Islamic Reform," *Muslim World* 78, 2 (1988), pp.121–131 and I. Weismann, "Between Sufi Reformism and Modernist Rationalism: A Reappraisal of the Origins of the Salafiyya from the Damascene Angle," *Die Welt des Islams* 41, 2 (2001a), pp.206–237.
46. S. Bazzaz, *Forgotten Saints: History, Power, and Politics in the Making of Modern Morocco* (Cambridge: Harvard University Press, 2010).
47. Bazzaz (2010), pp.93–94, 124.
48. Bazzaz (2010), pp.155–156.
49. J.A. Clancy-Smith, *Rebel and Saint: Muslim Notables, Populist Protest, Colonial Encounters* (Algeria and Tunisia, 1800-1904) (Berkeley: University of California Press, 1994), chapter 7.
50. Clancy-Smith (1994), pp.231–249.
51. M.J. Sedgwick, *Against the Modern World: Traditionalism and the Secret Intellectual History of the Twentieth Century* (Oxford: Oxford University Press, 2004), chapters 3& 4.
52. Sedgwick (2004), pp.61–62.

53. C.A. Babou, *Fighting the Greater Jihad: Amadu Bamba and the Founding of the Muridiyya of Senegal, 1853–1913* (Athens: Ohio University Press, 2007) and J. Glover, *Sufism and Jihad in Modern Senegal: The Murid Order* (Rochester: University of Rochester Press, 2007).

54. On the local colonial bureaucratic politics involved, see Babou (2007), pp.121–129.

55. Babou (2007), pp.136–139.

56. On the period of imprisonment, see Babou (2007), chapter 5 & 6. Cf. N.S. Green, "The Faqir and the Subalterns: Mapping the Holy Man in Colonial South Asia," *Journal of Asian History* 41, 1 (2007), pp.57–84.

57. J.F. Searing, *"God Alone is King": Islam and Emancipation in Senegal: The Wolof Kingdoms of Kajoor and Bawol, 1859–1914* (Oxford: James Currey, 2002), chapter 6. The role of peanut cultivation is played down in Babou (2007).

58. Searing (2002).

59. M. Gammer, "Shamil and the Muslim Powers: The Ottomans, the Qajars and Muhammad Ali of Egypt," in R. Motika & M. Orsinus (eds), *Caucasia between the Ottoman Empire and Iran, 1555–1914* (Wiesbaden: Ludwig Reichert, 2000).

60. M. Kemper, *Herrschaft, Recht und Islam in Daghestan: von den Khanaten und Gemeindebünden zum ğihād-Staat* (Wiesbaden: Reichert-Verlag, 2005), chapter 6 and A. Zelkina, *In Quest for God and Freedom: The Sufi Response to the Russian Advance in the North Caucasus* (London: Hurst & Co., 2000), chapter 18.

61. Kemper (2005), chapters 4–6 and Zelkina (2000), chapters 17–23.

62. R.D. Crews, *For Prophet and Tsar: Islam and Empire in Russia and Central Asia* (Cambridge: Harvard University Press, 2006) and Knysh (2002).

63. Crews (2006), pp.128–141.

64. A.J. Frank, *Muslim Religious Institutions in Imperial Russia: The Islamic World of Novouzensk District and the Kazakh Inner Horde, 1780–1910* (Leiden: Brill, 2001), pp.152–159.

65. M. Kemper, *Sufis und Gelehrte in Tatarien und Baschkirien: Der islamische Diskurs unter russischer Herrschaft* (Berlin: Klaus Schwarz, 1998), pp.43–50.

66. Kemper (1998), p.45. On Sufi Allahyar's works, see H.F. Hofman, *Turkish Literature: A Bio-Bibliographical Survey*, vol. 3, part 1 (Utrecht: University of Utrecht, 1969), pp.75–79.

67. A.J. Frank, "Islamic Shrine Catalogues and Communal Geography in the Volga-Ural Region: 1788–1917," *Journal of Islamic Studies* 7, 2 (1996), pp.265–286. Also Frank (2001), pp.98–106.

68. On the imperial "rediscovery" of Orthodox shrines and their histories, see M. Kozelsky, *Christianizing Crimea: Shaping Sacred Space in the Russian Empire and Beyond* (Northern Illinois University Press, 2009).

69. Kemper (1998), pp.368–369.

70. D. DeWeese, "The Politics of Sacred Lineages in 19th-Century Central Asia: Descent Groups Linked to Khwaja Ahmad Yasavi in Shrine Documents and

Genealogical Charters," *International Journal of Middle East Studies* 31, 4 (1999), pp.507–530.

71. J. Gross, "The *Waqf* of Khoja 'Ubayd Allah Ahrār in Nineteenth Century Central Asia: A Preliminary Study of the Tsarist Record," in E. Özdalga (ed.), *Naqshbandis in Western and Central Asia* (London: Curzon Press, 1999).

72. A. Bennigsen & S.E. Wimbush, *Mystics and Commissars: Sufism in the Soviet Union* (London: C. Hurst & Co, 1985).

73. A. Iloliev, *The Ismā'īlī-Sufi Sage of Pamir: Mubārak-i Wakhānī and the Esoteric Tradition of the Pamiri Muslims* (Amherst: Cambria Press, 2008), pp.89, 95–96.

74. Green (2011); M.F. Laffan, *Islamic Nationhood and Colonial Indonesia: The Umma below the Winds* (London: RoutledgeCurzon, 2003), O'Fahey (2004).

75. M. Sedgwick, *Saints and Sons: The Making and Remaking of the Rashīdi Ahmadi Sufi Order, 1799–2000* (Leiden: Brill, 2005).

76. M. Laffan, "The New Turn to Mecca: Snapshots of Arabic Printing and Sufi Networks in Late 19th Century Java," *Revue des mondes musulmans et de la Méditerranée* 124 (2008), pp.113–131.

77. B. Abu-Manneh, "The Naqshbandi-Mujaddidi and the Bektashi Orders in 1826," in Abu-Manneh, *Studies on Islam and the Ottoman Empire in the 19th century (1826–1876)* (Istanbul: Isis Press, 2001).

78. Abu-Manneh (2001), p.66.

79. A. Hourani, "Shaikh Khalid and the Naqshbandi Order," in. M. Stern, A. Hourani & V. Brown (eds), *Islamic Philosophy and the Classical Tradition* (Columbia: University of South Carolina Press, 1972).

80. Abu-Manneh (2001), p.69.

81. B. Abu-Manneh, "The Naqshbandiyya-Mujaddiyya in Istanbul in the Early Tanzimat Period," in Abu-Manneh (2001), pp.106–107.

82. I. Weismann, "Sufism and Law on the Eve of Reform: The Views of Ibn 'Abidin," in I. Weismann & F. Zachs (eds), *Ottoman Reform and Muslim Regeneration: Studies in Honour of Butrus Abu-Manneh* (London: I.B. Tauris, 2005).

83. T. Eich, *Abū'l-Hudā aṣ-Ṣayyādī: eine Studie zur Instrumentalisierung sufischer Netzwerke und genealogischer Kontroversen im spätosmanischen Reich* (Berlin: Klaus Schwarz, 2003).

84. Eich (2003), pp.53–69.

85. A. Ghazal, "Sufism, *Ijtihād* and Modernity: Yusuf al-Nabhānī in the Age of 'Abd al-Hamīd II,," *Archivum Ottomanicum* 19 (2001), pp.239–272; Weismann (2001a).

86. Ghazal (2001), pp.264–269.

87. I. Weismann, *Taste of Modernity: Sufism, Salafiyya, and Arabism in Late Ottoman Damascus* (Leiden: Brill, 2001b), chapter 7.

88. Sirriyeh (1999), chapter 4 and Weisman (2001b).

89. Quoted in A.H. Hourani, "Sufism and Modern Islam: Rashid Rida," in Hourani, *The Emergence of the Modern Middle East* (Berkeley: University of California Press, 1981), p.90.

90.   A. Azra, "The Transmission of *al-Manar*'s Reformism to the Malay-Indonesian World: The Cases of *al-Imam* and *al-Manir*," *Studia Islamika* 6, 3 (1999) pp.75–100.

91.   E. Daniel, "Theology and Mysticism in the Writings of Ziya Gökalp," *Muslim World* 67, 3 (1977), pp.175–184 and Sirriyeh (1999), pp.116–117.

92.   B. Silverstein, "Sufism and Governmentality in the Late Ottoman Empire," *Comparative Studies of South Asia, Africa and the Middle East* 29, 2 (2009), pp.171–185.

93.   H. Küçük, "Sufi Reactions against the Reforms after Turkey's National Struggle: How a Nightingale Turned into a Crow," in T. Atabaki (ed.), *The State and the Subaltern: Modernization, Society and the State in Turkey and Iran* (London: I.B. Tauris, 2007).

94.   R.W. Olson, "The International Sequels of the Shaikh Sa'id Rebellion," in M. Gaborieau, A. Popovic & T. Zarcone (eds), *Naqshbandîs: Cheminements et situation actuelle d'un ordre mystique musulman* (Istanbul: Isis Press, 1990).

95.   R. Gramlich, *Die schiitischen Derwischorden Persiens*, 3 vols (Wiesbaden: Kommissionsverlag Steiner, 1965–1981), vol. 1, pp.27–43 and L. Lewisohn, "An Introduction to the History of Modern Persian Sufism," *Bulletin of the School of Oriental and African Studies* 61 (1998), pp.437–464 and 62 (1999), pp.36–59.

96.   M. Miras, *La Méthode spirituelle d'un maître du soufisme iranien, Nur Ali-Shah* (Paris: Editions du Sirac, 1973), pp.319–331.

97.   R. Patai, *Jadīd al-Islām: The Jewish "New Muslims" of Meshhed* (Detroit: Wayne State University Press, 1997), chapter 3.

98.   H. Algar, *Religion and State in Iran, 1785–1906: The Role of the Ulama in the Qajar Period* (Berkeley: University of California Press, 1969), pp.105–106.

99.   Green (2011), chapter 4.

100. N.S. Green, "A Persian Sufi in British India: The Travels of Mirza Hasan Safi 'Ali Shah (1251/1835–1316/1899)," *Iran: Journal of Persian Studies* 42 (2004), pp.201–218.

101. N.S. Green, "Mirza Hasan Safi 'Ali Shah: A Persian Sufi in the Age of Printing," in L. Ridgeon (ed.), *Religion and Politics in Modern Iran* (London: I.B Tauris, 2005).

102. M. van den Bos, *Mystic Regimes: Sufism and the State in Iran, from the Late Qajar Era to the Islamic Republic* (Leiden: Brill, 2002), chapter 3.

103. Van den Bos (2002).

104. N.S. Green, "Defending the Sufis in Nineteenth Century Hyderabad," *Islamic Studies* 47, 3 (2009), pp.327–348.

105. N.S. Green, "Mystical Missionaries in Hyderabad State: Mu'in Allah Shah and his Sufi Reform Movement," *Indian Economic and Social History Review* 41, 2 (2005), pp.45–70.

106. D.B. Edwards, "The Political Lives of Afghan Saints: The Case of the Kabul Hazrats," in G.M. Smith & C.W. Ernst (eds), *Manifestations of Sainthood in Islam* (Istanbul: Isis Press, 1993).

107. S. Haroon, *Frontier of Faith: Islam in the Indo-Afghan Borderland* (New York: Columbia University Press, 2007), chapter 2.

108. Edwards (1993), p.172.
109. Edwards (1993), p.176.
110. A. Wieland-Karimi, *Islamische Mystik in Afghanistan: die strukturelle Einbindung der Sufik in die Gesellschaft* (Stuttgart: F. Steiner, 1998).
111. M.H. Sidky, "'Malang,' Sufis, and Mystics: An Ethnographic and Historical Study of Shamanism in Afghanistan," *Asian Folklore Studies*, 49, 2 (1990), pp.275–301 and B. Utas, "The Naqshbandiyya of Afghanistan on the Eve of the 1978 Coup d'état," in Özdalga (1999).
112. M. Centlivres-Demontin, "Un corpus de risâla du Turkestan afghan," in N. Grandin & M. Gaborieau (eds), *Madrasa: La transmission du savoir dans le monde musulman* (Paris: Éditions Arguments, 1997).
113. M. Gilsenan, "Trajectories of Contemporary Sufism," in E. Gellner (ed.), *Islamic Dilemmas: Reformers, Nationalists and Industrialization* (Berlin: Mouton, 1985) and F. de Jong, "Aspects of the Political Involvement of Sufi Orders in Twentieth-Century Egypt (1907–1970): An Exploratory Stock-Taking," in G.R. Warburg & U.M. Kupferschmidt (eds), *Islam, Nationalism, and Radicalism in Egypt and the Sudan* (New York: Praeger, 1983).
114. Ewing (1997), chapter 2 and A. Schimmel, *Gabriel's Wing: A Study into the Religious Ideas of Sir Muhammad Iqbal* (Leiden: E.J. Brill, 1963).
115. A. Christmann, "Reclaiming Mysticism: Anti-Orientalism and the Construction of 'Islamic Sufism' in Postcolonial Egypt," in N.S. Green & M. Searle-Chatterjee (eds), *Religion, Language and Power* (New York: Routledge, 2008).
116. C. Lindholm, "Prophets and *Pirs*: Charismatic Islam in the Middle East and South Asia," in P. Werbner & H. Basu (eds), *Embodying Charisma: Modernity, Locality and the Performance of Emotion in Sufi Cults* (London: Routledge, 1998).
117. K.P. Ewing, "The Politics of Sufism: Redefining the Saints of Pakistan," *Journal of Asian Studies* 42, 2 (1983), pp.251–265.
118. R. Rozehnal, *Islamic Sufism Unbound: Politics and Piety in Twenty-first Century Pakistan* (New York: Palgrave, 2007), pp.112–120.
119. Rozehnal (2007), pp.103–112.
120. On Hindu fundamentalist attacks on Sufi shrines, see Y.S. Sikand, "Another Ayodhya in the Making? The Baba Budhangiri Dargah Controversy in South India," *Journal of Muslim Minority Affairs* 20, 2 (2000), pp. 211–227.
121. M. van Bruinessen, "Saints, Politicians and Sufi Bureaucrats: Mysticism and Politics in Indonesia's New Order," in M. van Bruinessen & J. Day Howell (eds), *Sufism and the 'Modern' in Islam* (London: I.B. Tauris, 2007).
122. J. Day Howell, "Sufism and the Indonesian Islamic Revival," *Journal of Asian Studies* 60, 3 (2001), pp.701–729.
123. J. Gross, "The Polemic of 'Official' and 'Unofficial' Islam: Sufism in Soviet Central Asia," in de Jong & Radtke (1999)
124. M.E. Louw, *Everyday Islam in Post-Soviet Central Asia* (London: Routledge, 2007) and B.G. Privratsky, *Muslim Turkistan: Kazak Religion and Collective Memory* (London: Routledge, 2001).

125. V. Schubel, "Post-Soviet Hagiography and the Reconstruction of the Naqshbandi Tradition in Contemporary Uzbekistan," in Özdalga (1999), pp.77–79.

126. S. Mardin, "The Naqshibendi Order of Turkey", in M.E. Marty & R.S. Appleby (eds), *Fundamentalisms and the State: Remaking Polities, Economies, and Militance* (Chicago: University of Chicago Press, 1993) and M. Hakan Yavuz, *Islamic Political Identity in Turkey* (Oxford: Oxford University Press, 2003), chapters 6–8.

127. C.T. Nereid, *In the Light of Said Nursi: Turkish Nationalism and the Religious Alternative* (London: C. Hurst, 1998).

128. T. Michel, "Sufism and Modernity in the Thought of Fethullah Gülen," *Muslim World 95*, 3 (2005), pp.341–358.

129. B. Balci, *Missionnaires de l'Islam en Asie centrale: les écoles turques de Fethullah Gülen* (Paris: Maisonneuve et Larose, 2003).

130. V. Hoffman, *Sufism, Mystics, and Saints in Modern Egypt* (Columbia: South Carolina, University of South Carolina Press, 1995) and J. Johansen, *Sufism and Islamic Reform in Egypt: The Battle for Islamic Tradition* (Oxford: Oxford University Press, 1996).

131. M. Gilsenan, "Some Factors in the Decline of Sufi Orders in Modern Egypt," *Muslim World 57* (1967), pp.11–18 and P. Pinto, *Mystical Bodies: Ritual, Experience and the Embodiment of Sufism in Syria* (unpublished Ph.D. dissertation, Boston University, 2002).

132. S. Schielke, "On Snacks and Saints: When Discourses of Order and Rationality Enter the Egyptian Mawlid," *Archives de Sciences Sociales des Religions 135* (2006), pp.117–140.

133. K. Arai, "Combining Innovation and Emotion in the Modernization of Sufi Orders in Contemporary Egypt," *Middle East Critique 16*, 2 (2007), pp.155–169.

134. J. During, "Sufi Music and Rites in the Era of Mass Reproduction Techniques and Culture," in Özdalga (1999).

135. R. Chih, *Le soufisme au quotidien: confréries d'Egypte au XXe sièccle* (Arles: Actes Sud, 2000), pp.263–278 and H. Lang, *Der Heiligenkult in Marokko: Formen und Funktionen der Wallfahrten* (Passau: Passavia Universitätsverlag, 1992).

136. A.N. Hamzeh & R.H. Dekmejian, "A Sufi Response to Political Islamism: Al-Ahbash of Lebanon," *International Journal of Middle East Studies 28*, 2 (1996), pp.217–229.

137. M. Mahmoud, "Sufism and Islamism in the Sudan," in D. Westerlund & E.E. Rosander (eds), *African Islam and Islam in Africa: Encounters between Sufis and Islamists* (London: Hurst, 1997).

138. Z. Wright, "The *Kāshif al-Ilbās* of Shaykh Ibrāhīm Niasse: Analysis of the Text," *Islamic Africa 1*, 1 (2010), pp.109–123.

139. D.B. Cruise O'Brien, "Charisma Comes to Town: Mouride Urbanization, 1945–1986," in D.B. Cruise O'Brien & C. Coulon (eds), *Charisma and Brotherhood in African Islam* (Oxford: Clarendon Press, 1988).

140. J. Copans, "Mourides des champs, mourides des villes, mourides du téléphone portable et de l'internet: Les renouvellements de l'économie politique d'une confrérie," *Afrique contemporaine* 194 (2000), pp.24–33.

141. S. Bava, "De la '*baraka* aux affaires': ethos économico-religieux et trans-nationalité chez les migrants sénégalais mourides," *Revue européenne des migrations internationals* 19, 2 (2003), pp.1–13.

142. B.F. Soares, "Saint and Sufi in Contemporary Mali," in van Bruinessen & Howell (2007).

143. M. Sedgwick, "European Neo-Sufi Movements in the Inter-War Period," in N. Clayer & E. Germain (eds), *Islam in Inter-War Europe* (London: Hurst & Co., 2008).

144. V. Ebin, "Making Room versus Creating Space: The Construction of Spatial Categories by Itinerant Mouride Traders," in B.D. Metcalf (ed.), *Making Muslim Space in North America and Europe* (Berkeley: University of California Press, 1996).

145. P. Werbner, *Pilgrims of Love: The Anthropology of a Global Sufi Cult* (London: C. Hurst, 2003). Also R.A. Greaves, *Sufis of Britain: An Exploration of Muslim Identity* (Cardiff: Cardiff Academic Press, 2000).

146. G. Jonker, "The Evolution of the Naqshbandi-Mujaddidi: Sulaymançis in Germany," in J. Malik & J. Hinnells (eds), *Sufism in the West* (New York: Routledge, 2006).

147. F. Speziale, "Adapting Mystic Identity to Italian Mainstream Islam: The Case of a Muslim Rom Community in Florence," *Balkanologie* 9, 1–2 (2005), pp.195–211.

148. A. Böttcher, "Religious Authority in Transnational Sufi Networks: Shaykh Nazim al-Qabrusi al-Haqqani al-Naqshbandi," in G. Krämer & S. Schmidtke (eds), *Speaking for Islam: Religious Authorities in Muslim Societies* (Leiden: Brill, 2006), pp.244–249.

149. D.W. Damrel, "Aspects of the Naqshbandi-Haqqani Order in North America," in Malik & Hinnells (2006) and L. Schlessmann, *Sufismus in Deutschland: Deutsche auf dem Weg des mystischen Islam* (Cologne: Böhlau Verlag, 2003), chapter 4.

150. B. Godard & S. Taussig, *Les musulmans en France: courants, institutions, communautés* (Paris: Robert Laffont, 2007), pp.330–345.

151. Abd al Malik, *Qu'Allah bénisse la France* (Paris: Albin Michel, 2004).

152. L. Schloßmann, "Sufi-Gemeinschaften in Deutschland," *CIBEDO: Beiträge zum Gespräch zwischen Muslimen und Christen* 13, 1 (1999), pp.12–22.

153. Schloßmann (1999), p.20.

154. Schloßmann (1999), p.14.

155. G. Webb, "Third Wave Sufism in America and the Bawa Muhaiyaddeen Fellowship," in Malik & Hinnells (2006).

156. M.R. Bawa Muhaiyaddeen, *The Divine Luminous Wisdom That Dispels the Darkness* (Philadelphia: The Fellowship Press, 1972).

157. M. Hermansen, "Hybrid Identity Formations in Muslim America: The Case of American Sufi Movements," *The Muslim World* 90 (2000), pp.158–197.

158. P. Wilson, "The Strange Fate of Sufism in the New Age," in P.B Clarke (ed.), *New Trends and Developments in the World of Islam* (London: Luzac Oriental, 1998).
159. J. Moore, "Neo-Sufism: The Case of Idries Shah," *Religion Today* 3, 3 (1986), pp.4–8.
160. C.A. Genn, "The Development of a Modern Western Sufism," in van Bruinessen & Howell (2007).
161. M. Hermansen, "Literary Productions of Western Sufi Movements," in Malik & Hinnells (2006).

Glossary: A Sufi Lexicon of Arabic Terms

adab	"etiquette," the formal rules of the Sufi life
awliya	"Friends [of God]," the leading Sufi masters venerated as living or dead saints
baqa	"surviving," the experience of ultimate being after *fana* (*q.v.*)
baraka	"blessing, abundance," the sacred power of the saints
barzakh	"isthmus," the person or point of being in which the divine and human worlds join
batin	"esoteric," the hidden or invisible dimension of life
bay'a	"oath," a pledge of allegiance to a Sufi master
bid'a	"innovation," an action or doctrine with no sanction in the Prophetic Example or *sunna* (*q.v.*)
dhawq	"tasting," direct spiritual experience
dhikr	"remembrance [of God]," the ritual chanting of the Sufis
fana	"passing away," the experience of the dissolution of personal identity
faqir	"poor man," a mendicant, a Sufi

Sufism: A Global History, First Edition. Nile Green.
© 2012 Nile Green. Published 2012 by Blackwell Publishing Ltd.

Hadith	"reports," originally oral accounts of the sayings and deeds of Muhammad
hal (pl. *ahwal*)	"state, condition," a mystical experience
insan al-kamil	"perfect human," doctrine of the perfect saintly person who held complete knowledge of God
karama	"benevolent act," a miracle performed by a Sufi saint
khalifa	"successor, lieutenant," a deputy appointed by a Sufi master
khalwa	"seclusion," the practice of retreat from the world
khanaqah	residence of Sufis, a Sufi lodge (usually in Iran, Central Asia & India)
khirqa	"robe," a Sufi ritual cloak, often of distinctive color or design
kitab	"book," a text written in Arabic or other Islamic languages
madrasa	"place of study," a college for the study of the Islamic sciences
malfuzat	"speeches," a book of the spoken teachings of a Sufi master
maqam (pl. *maqamat*)	"place," a stage on the spiritual path towards God
mathnawi	"couplets," a poem in rhyming couplets, especially in Persian
murid	"aspirant," a Sufi disciple
murshid	"rightful guide," a Sufi master
nafs	lower soul
nur (pl. *anwar*)	"light," particularly the divine light of God
qalandar (Persian)	"clown, antinomian," a wandering Sufi vagabond
Quran	"that which was recited," the Muslim holy book revealed to the Prophet Muhammad
qutb	"axis," saint who serves as the axis of the entire cosmos atop of the hierarchy of *awliya* (*q.v.*)
ribat	fortified dwelling for warrior-ascetics or merchants in North Africa and Spain; later a term for a Sufi lodge

risala	short text or treatise
ruh	higher self or spirit
sama'	"listening," Sufi practice of listening to music or sung poetry
sayyid	blood descendant of the Prophet's family
shari'a	Islamic law, as formulated through interpretations of the Quran and Hadith (*q.v.*)
shath	"ecstatic utterances," the passionate or even heretical statements made during *hal* (*q.v.*)
shaykh	"elder," a title of respect for a Sufi master
silsila	"chain, line of succession," a Sufi lineage or royal dynasty
Sunna	"model," the body of traditions describing the life of Muhammad, the Prophetic Example
tabaqat	"classes, generations," the ranks among the spiritual elite or the generations of Sufis enumerated in biographical texts
tadhkira	"memory, remembrance," a biographical memoir or hagiography
tafsir	exegesis, a commentary on the Quran
tajdid	"renewal," the cyclical renewal of Islam each century and especially millennium
takiyya	"pillow, place of repose," a Sufi lodge
tariqa (pl. *turuq*)	"Path," the Sufi path, a Sufi brotherhood
tasawwuf	"To become a Sufi, to wear wool," Sufism
tawhid	"Unity," the doctrine of the indivisible oneness of God
'ulama	"learned ones," representatives of *Shari'a* and other normative traditions
'uqda	"allegiance," sworn bond between Sufi master and disciple
'urs	"wedding," saintly death anniversary celebrated as a wedding with God

wahdat al-wujud	"Unity of Being," doctrine elaborated by Ibn al-'Arabi (d.1240)
wali (pl. *awliya*)	"Friend of God," a Sufi saint
wilaya	"Friendship [with God]," the doctrine of sainthood
zahid (pl. *zuhhad*)	ascetics, practitioners of *zuhd* (*q.v.*)
zahir	"exoteric," the manifest or visible dimension of life
zawiyya	residence of Sufis, a Sufi lodge (usually in North and Saharan Africa)
ziyara	"visit," a pilgrimage to a Sufi shrine
zuhd	"asceticism," strict self-denial and discipline of the flesh

Further Reading

Early Sufi History

Julian Baldick, *Mystical Islam* (London: I.B. Tauris, 1989).
Ahmet Karamustafa, *Sufism: The Formative Period* (Berkeley: University of California Press, 2007).

Medieval & Early Modern Sufi History

Vincent Cornell, *Realm of the Saint: Power and Authority in Moroccan Mysticism* (Austin: University of Texas Press, 1999).
Carl W. Ernst, *Eternal Garden: Mysticism, History, and Politics at a South Asian Sufi Center* (Albany: State University of New York Press, 1992).

Modern Sufi History

Arthur F. Buehler, *Sufi Heirs of the Prophet: The Indian Naqshbandiyya and the Rise of the Mediating Sufi Shaykh* (Columbia: University of South Carolina Press, 1998).
Itzchak Weismann, *Taste of Modernity: Sufism, Salafiyya, and Arabism in Late Ottoman Damascus* (Leiden: E.J. Brill, 2001).

Contemporary Sufism

Martin van Bruinessen & Julia Day Howell (eds), *Sufism and the "Modern" in Islam* (London: I.B. Tauris, 2007).
Pnina Werbner & Helen Basu (eds), *Embodying Charisma: Modernity, Locality and the Performance of Emotion in Sufi Cults.* (London: Routledge, 1998).

Sufism: A Global History, First Edition. Nile Green.
© 2012 Nile Green. Published 2012 by Blackwell Publishing Ltd.

Sufis in the West

Jamal Malik & John Hinnells (eds), *Sufism in the West* (New York: Routledge, 2006).
Pnina Werbner, *Pilgrims of Love: The Anthropology of a Global Sufi Cult* (London: Hurst & Co., 2003).

The Sufi Brotherhoods

J.M. Abun-Nasr, *Muslim Communities of Grace: The Sufi Brotherhoods in Islamic Religious Life*. (New York: Columbia University Press, 2007).
Carl W. Ernst & Bruce B. Lawrence, *Sufi Martyrs of Love: The Chishti Order in South Asia and Beyond* (New York: Palgrave Macmillan, 2002).

Sufi Theology

William C. Chittick, *The Sufi Path of Knowledge* (Albany: State University of New York Press, 1989).
Henry Corbin, *Creative Imagination in the Sūfism of Ibn al-'Arabī* (Princeton: Princeton University Press, 1969).

Anti-Sufi Critiques

F. de Jong & Bernd Radtke (eds), *Islamic Mysticism Contested: 13 Centuries of Controversies and Polemics* (Leiden: E.J. Brill, 1998).
Elizabeth Sirriyeh, *Sufis and Anti-Sufis: The Defence, Rethinking and Rejection of Sufism in the Modern World* (Richmond: Curzon Press, 1999).

Sufi Poetry

Franklin D. Lewis, *Rumi: Past and Present, East and West* (Oxford: Oneworld, 2000).
Annemarie Schimmel, *As Through a Veil: Mystical Poetry in Islam* (New York: Columbia University Press, 1982).

Sufi Music and the Arts

Regula Burckhardt Qureshi, *Sufi Music of India and Pakistan* (Cambridge: Cambridge University Press, 1986).
Raymond Lifchez (ed.), *The Dervish Lodge: Architecture, Art, and Sufism in Ottoman Turkey* (Berkeley: University of California Press, 1992).

Index

Note: The prefix 'Al-' is ignored in alphabetical filing of entries. Listings are by first given name in text for Arabic names. Page references in italics are to illustrations. Page references in bold are to definitions.

Sufism: A Global History, First Edition. Nile Green.
© 2012 Nile Green. Published 2012 by Blackwell Publishing Ltd.

Index created by Meg Davies (Fellow of the Society of Indexers)